VALUING OLDER PE

A humanist approach to

Edited by Ricca Edmondson and
Hans-Joachim von Kondratowitz

This edition published in Great Britain in 2009 by

The Policy Press
University of Bristol
Fourth Floor
Beacon House
Queen's Road
Bristol BS8 1QU
UK

Tel +44 (0)117 331 4054
Fax +44 (0)117 331 4093
e-mail tpp-info@bristol.ac.uk
www.policypress.org.uk

North American office:
The Policy Press
c/o International Specialized Books Services (ISBS)
920 NE 58th Avenue, Suite 300
Portland, OR 97213-3786, USA
Tel +1 503 287 3093
Fax +1 503 280 8832
e-mail info@isbs.com

British Library Cataloguing in Publication Data
A catalogue record for this book is available from the British Library.

Library of Congress Cataloging-in-Publication Data
A catalog record for this book has been requested.

ISBN 978 1 84742 291 0 paperback
ISBN 978 1 84742 292 7 hardcover

Cover design by The Policy Press
Printed and bound in Great Britain by TJ International Ltd, Padstow.

Contents

Part Three: Ageing and wisdom? Conflicts and contested developments

Afterwords

List of tables and figures

Tables

Figures

Notes on contributors

Hans-Jürgen Andreß studied social sciences and research methods at the universities of Frankfurt/Main and Michigan (Ann Arbor). He gained his PhD at the University of Frankfurt/Main in 1983 and is currently Professor for Empirical Social and Economic Research at the University of Cologne, Germany. He has published in the field of labour markets, poverty research, social policy, and multivariate statistical methods.

Sue Baines is Reader in Social Policy at the Research Institute for Health and Social Change, Manchester Metropolitan University, UK. Her studies of marginal self-employment, rural small businesses and artistic livelihoods have been sponsored by the Economic and Social Research Council, the Joseph Rowntree Foundation and Arts Council England. She is currently interested in volunteering as well as notions of participation, interactivity and co-production in the research process.

Amanda Clarke is a senior lecturer in the Centre of Advanced Nursing Studies at the University of Aberdeen, UK. She has worked closely with older adults in clinical practice as a nurse and in health care research. Her main interests include developing innovative ways of working with older people as research participants, co-researchers and peer educators in research about pain and the end of life.

Peter G. Coleman has a joint professorial appointment in psychogerontology between the schools of psychology and medicine at the University of Southampton, UK. Besides working on the major psychopathologies of later life, he has contributed to the developmental psychology of ageing and is the author (with Ann O'Hanlon) of *Ageing and development: Theories and research*.

Adeline Cooney is a senior lecturer in the School of Nursing and Midwifery, National University of Ireland, Galway. She trained as a nurse and has a background in clinical nursing and nurse education. Her research focuses on older people and, in particular, on the quality of life of older people living in both community and long-stay care settings.

Svein Olav Daatland is a research professor and a social psychologist at Norwegian Social Research (NOVA), Oslo. He has been active in several Scandinavian and European comparative studies of ageing and later life. His publications include *Ageing and diversity* (with Simon Biggs) and *Aldring som provokasjon* (*Ageing as a provocation*), as well as work on age identifications, intergenerational solidarity and the family–welfare state balance.

Peter Derkx is Professor of Humanism and Worldviews at the University for Humanistics at Utrecht, the Netherlands. He chairs the research project Ageing Well: Wellbeing, Meaning and Human Dignity. His main fields of interest are the theory of humanism as a worldview, as well as science, technology and meanings of life. His publications include 'Substantial life extension and meanings of life', as well as other work taking a humanist view of genetic enhancement, ageing well and meaning frames.

Michele Dillon was educated at University College Dublin, and the University of California, Berkeley. She is currently Professor of Sociology at the University of New Hampshire, USA. Recent books include *In the course of a lifetime: Tracing religious belief, practice, and change* (with Paul Wink), and *Introduction to sociological theory: Theorists, concepts, and their applicability in the twenty-first century.* She is a former chair of the religion section of the American Sociological Association, and currently President of the Association for the Sociology of Religion.

Ricca Edmondson is a senior lecturer in the School of Political Science and Sociology at the National University of Ireland, Galway. After being educated at the Universities of Lancaster and Oxford, she carried out research at the Max Planck Institute for Human Development in Berlin before moving to Ireland. Her interests include ageing and the sociology of wisdom, ethnographic methods, intercultural understanding, rhetorical argumentation and the history of political thought. Her books and editions include work on rhetoric, argumentation and power, the sociology and culture of Ireland, health promotion and environmental argument. She co-organises the Research Network on Ageing in the European Sociological Association.

Eileen Fairhurst is Professor of Health and Ageing Policy at Manchester Metropolitan University, UK. She has published widely in the sociology of ageing, on topics such as qualitative methods, the body in mid-life, memories and life histories, social organisation of space in sheltered housing, assessments of time in the context of paid and unpaid work, and gender and changing identities of ageing. Her current research interests include policy ethnographies and cross-generational relationships.

Dina Frommert studied sociology, social psychology and media studies at the universities of Düsseldorf and Cape Town. Currently she works for the German Federal Pension Insurance as a specialist in empirical research and survey data, focusing on applied pension policy research.

Carmel Gallagher is a lecturer in sociology in the School of Social Sciences and Law, Dublin Institute of Technology. She obtained her PhD from the National University of Ireland, Galway in 2005 for a study now published as *The community life of older people in Ireland*, and continues to work and publish in this area.

Haim Hazan is a professor of social anthropology and sociology at Tel Aviv University. His areas of research include ageing, community, total institutions, globalisation, nationalism and anthropological theory. Among his books are: *The limbo people* (1980); *A paradoxical community* (1990); *Managing change in old age* (1992); *Old age: Constructions and deconstructions* (1994); *From first principles* (1996) and *Simulated dreams* (2000).

Thorsten Heien studied social sciences and economics at the universities of Osnabrueck and Bielefeld. He received his PhD in sociology from the University of Bielefeld. Currently working as senior consultant for TNS Infratest Social Research (Munich), he is mainly engaged in large-scale surveys dealing with social policy issues. He has also published on attitudinal research.

Dirk Hofäcker studied sociology and economics at the universities of Bielefeld and St Petersburg. From 2002 to 2006, he worked in the research project GlobaLife: Life Courses in the Globalization Process at Bamberg University. Currently he is a researcher at the Institute for Family Research at Bamberg University, Germany, and coordinates TransEurope, the international social science research network funded by the European Science Foundation. He specialises in comparative life course questions, welfare state and labour market research, attitudinal research and quantitative methods of social science data analysis.

Outi Jolanki is a researcher in the Department of Social Sciences and Philosophy, University of Jyväskylä, Finland, in a research project on combining work and assisting older relatives. She is also finalising her PhD thesis, on which she has published several articles, at the Tampere School of Public Health, University of Tampere. Her research interests include experiential and moral aspects as well as cultural representations of old age; also, health, identity and intergenerational relations, and qualitative methods.

Ronald J. Manheimer has served as founding director of the North Carolina Center for Creative Retirement at the University of North Carolina at Asheville, where he is also Research Associate Professor of Philosophy.

Kalyani K. Mehta is a professor in the Department of Social Work, National University of Singapore. She has published widely on topics within the field of social gerontology. As a nominated member of the Singapore Parliament, she advocates on policies and services for older people and has been invited regularly to give presentations at international and regional conferences.

Kathy Murphy is Professor and Head of the School of Nursing and Midwifery, National University of Ireland, Galway. Her clinical experience was in accident and emergency and older people's services. Her current research interest is older people and chronic disease management, and she has been a member of national research teams undertaking research on the quality of life of older people in Ireland.

James Nichol worked for many years in health promotion and health promotion management in Britain and New Zealand. While in New Zealand he managed an older people's mental health promotion project based in Auckland. Since returning to the UK and completing his doctorate, he has been involved in research for the University of the West of England, Bristol on older people's wellbeing, and on the role of complementary therapies within the National Health Service for the University of Bristol.

Hans-Joachim von Kondratowitz studied sociology, political science and history at the Free University of Berlin, at the University of Saarbrücken and at Washington University, St Louis. After working as assistant professor of sociology in Munich and as visiting professor for social gerontology at the University of Kassel, he is now a senior researcher at the German Centre of Gerontology in Berlin. He is also president of the social section (ESR) of IAGG-ER. His interests include international comparisons of long-term care arrangements, older people and family strategies in transnational migration, the development of welfare cultures, cultural definitions of ageing and community projects on ageing.

Lorna Warren is a lecturer in the Department of Sociological Studies at the University of Sheffield, UK. She has been involved in a number of studies looking at social care and older people, and is particularly interested in exploring new ways of working with older people in understanding their experiences of ageing and care.

Monika Wohlrab-Sahr is qualified in both sociology and protestant theology. She is Professor of Cultural Sociology at the University of Leipzig and has been a visiting scholar at the University of California, Berkeley, as well as a Fernand Braudel Fellow at the European University in Florence. She has published in the fields of the sociology of religion, the sociology of culture, biographical research and qualitative methodology.

Acknowledgements

For financial support in producing this book we should like to thank the Social Sciences Research Centre at the National University of Ireland, Galway; the German Centre of Gerontology (DZA) in Berlin; and the National Council for Ageing and Older People in Dublin.

The editors would like to dedicate this collection to Markus Woerner, Christopher Woerner, Tom and Abby Woerner-Powell and Ali Deniz Köcer.

Foreword

Judith Phillips

The study of ageing is continuing to increase rapidly across multiple disciplines. Consequently students, academics, professionals and policy makers need texts on the latest research, theory, policy and practice developments in the field. With new areas of interest in mid- and later life opening up, the series bridges the gaps in the literature as well as providing cutting-edge debate on new and traditional areas of ageing within a lifecourse perspective. Taking this approach, the Ageing and the Lifecourse series addresses 'ageing' (rather than gerontology or 'old age'), providing coverage of mid- as well as later life; it promotes a critical perspective and focuses on the social, rather than the medical, aspects of ageing.

Ricca Edmondson and Hans-Joachim von Kondratowitz together with the authors in this edited book address these issues in an original and refreshing way. *Valuing older people: A humanist approach to ageing* provides us with stimulating insights into the international debates, issues and challenges around the diversity of ageing, the norms and values practised by older people, their creativity and wisdom and the meaning they attach to life. The book addresses the centrality of the lifecourse, both in its importance of looking at and valuing people's lives and in its contribution to the study of critical gerontology.

The editors comment that concepts and languages concerning older people and ageing are in stark need of revision; this book does just that by providing new themes for exploration under a humanistic gerontology and by combining theoretical debate and empirical data with the voices of older people. The book is an original contribution, enhancing the limited material in humanistic gerontology, particularly outside North America. It will provide a good resource for undergraduates as well as postgraduates and, in particular, professionals working with older people.

Introduction

Ricca Edmondson and Hans-Joachim von Kondratowitz

Establishing a humanistic gerontology – challenges and opportunities

The meaning of 'humanistic gerontology'

Humanistic concerns build on a rich tradition that has developed through much of recorded history. This tradition was famously summarised in Cicero's quotation from Terence, intended to underline the fundamental connectedness of all human beings: 'I am a man, and nothing human is alien to me' (Cicero, 1991: I.30). In different guises, this tradition remained influential until well into the 20th century. The term 'humanist gerontology' was introduced to recent research by American scholars such as Moody and Manheimer. It stresses the fact that human activities (including gerontology itself) cannot be understood without taking seriously the different ideals, values, norms and goals that give actions their intelligibility and meaning. This brings to centre stage the practical knowledge that older people cannot be treated as alien by those who write about them. 'Valuing older people' demands comprehending them *as* people, not treating them as strangers whose predicaments are foreign to those of others. It requires gerontologists to work towards studies of ageing that incorporate this stance in a fundamental way.

A primary aim in this collection is therefore to explore a diversity of aspects of ageing while guided by the need to understand the people at the centre of enquiry, with their values and purposes. Contributions include longitudinal studies of the way in which people struggle to develop the meanings of their life courses and the resources they draw on; qualitative studies of ways in which individuals can be helped by cultural frameworks in different national settings to interpret their own ageing in constructive ways; and studies of social and institutional pressures and deficits which make this harder. Quantitative survey material is used to enhance conjectures about meanings that older people in varying circumstances attach to their relationships with their children, or about the willingness of others to allow for constructive public provision for older age. A study of older people in nursing homes is predicated on the question, could a person really pursue the aims and purposes of a normal human being in these circumstances? All this work focuses on human ideas and practices – and the limits they encounter. Humanistic enquiries interrogate the relations between human meanings and purposes and the circumstances – historical, political, economic – that enable or constrain them.

This book thus begins to make good a deficit in attention to norms and values pursued by older people, and to norms and values implicit in the circumstances affecting them. Responding to this neglect involves tensions: between accuracy and commitment, between engaged curiosity about the human condition and responding to the particularities of the people and predicaments that are the subjects of research. But the complexity and potential creativity of later life can be developed only within a vision of older people and ageing which stresses human beings' common participation in their own and others' developing life courses. Grasping the effects on ageing of its ethical and normative settings is a large part of developing this vision, whose aim is to reintegrate ageing as a central part of the human project.

This applies not only to social institutions and individuals in society, but also to the work of social and behavioural scientists themselves. The study of gerontology is affected by public attitudes to older people that are in many ways ambivalent, ranging between benevolence and resentment, often contradictory and confused. Concepts and languages concerning older people and ageing are thus in stark need of revision. They need to become more subtle and humane, situating older people as equals in a human predicament we share. Currently, outcomes for older people and attitudes towards them are at frequent risk of being undermined by both academic and social practices that stereotype, disregard or dismiss what goes on in later stages of the life course. We argue that a humanist approach is crucial if ageing – as is beginning to happen in contemporary societies – is to become less socially fixed and regulated. If ageing is to involve a process of continual negotiation about ways in which capacities and world views are bound together, this negotiation needs to be shaped by humanistic standards. It needs to be informed by an exploration of social norms and values affecting ageing and by a commitment to older people as co-equal members of society.

Contrasting discourses in gerontology

This is an ambitious project, still ongoing. What are its premises and central assumptions? First, the point of humanist gerontology is that in terms of theory, research and policy it centres on the human beings whose life courses are at issue. While other major issues are crucial to the exploration of older age – power, social structures and cultures, politics and the economy, physical and health-related questions – they need to be explored without losing sight of the human persons concerned. Second, we can see clear parallels between this and the intensive discussions about a 'critical gerontology' that occupied gerontology in the English-speaking world during the last two decades of the 20th century. Today, too, reflecting on how to devise a 'humanist gerontology' means becoming aware of deficiencies and shortcomings in the gerontological research agenda in general. Debates on these shortcomings have, time and again, highlighted the tendency for older people themselves to disappear from gerontology. Since the 'critical gerontology' debate identified particularly important issues in gerontology and made crucial calls to action, we shall reconstruct some of the arguments in connection with it. We shall then try to extend these arguments in terms of a 'humanist' gerontology.

To describe what constitutes the 'critical' in 'critical gerontology', we can turn to a valuable and condensed summary by Phillipson (1998):

> The critical elements in this gerontology centre around three main areas: first, from political economy, there is awareness of the structural pressures and constraints affecting older people, with divisions associated with class, gender and ethnicity being emphasized … Second, from both a humanistic as well as a biographically oriented gerontology, there is concern over the absence of meaning in the lives of older people, and the sense of doubt and uncertainty which is seen to pervade their daily routines and relationships … Third, from all three perspectives, comes a focus on the issue of empowerment, whether through the transformation of society … or the development of new rituals and symbols to facilitate changes through the life course. (Phillipson, 1998: 13-14)

These suggestions present the 'critical' dimension as comprehensive and multifaceted. We by no means reject this aspiration to diversity, nor the critical gerontologists' attention to political and economic forces to which older people, like others, are subject – and some forces oppress them with special vigour. But we claim that, at this juncture, moving forward the exploration of human ageing demands exploring humanistic concerns above all. Questions of meaning associated with the life course are not additions to gerontology, but should lie at its heart. Examining some current blockages in gerontological work will help to show why this is so.

To characterise the problem of meaning as the essential core of humanistically oriented gerontology is to open up the theme of norms and values: of what makes people's experiences into *life courses* rather than simple concatenations of events. It also allows us to unite features of gerontology that have been treated as alternative interests in sub-fields of the subject. This has produced a fragmentation in the study of ageing, highlighted by the fact that these dimensions currently reside in different lines of research and disciplinary backgrounds. Social historians such as Cole and Thane have vividly portrayed the ways in which expectations of ageing alter in different historical contexts; this makes clear that ageing cannot be regarded as an inevitable consequence of phenomena that are largely physical. They also stress ways in which expectations of ageing substantially affect the real, diverse opportunities and constraints that confront older people in different social and economic positions. Sociologists such as, for example, Katz (1996) or von Kondratowitz (1991) have reconstructed in detail the differentiated discourse formations dominating social and medical fields from the 18th century onwards. This process has seen the development of increasing bio-political regulation, whose impact is even more noteworthy at a time that also witnessed the increasing impact of anti-ageing movements. Gerontologists such as Walker, Phillipson and others have rightly underlined the substantial political and economic interests that lie behind the social structuration of contemporary ageing. All societies are marked by politico-economic forces of this kind; it would be entirely unrealistic to imagine human behaviour without them. Yet, in the gerontological literature, approaches tend to be too often *either* cultural-historical *or* politico-economic (see also Holstein and Minkler, 2007).

Furthermore, when psychologists such as Sternberg, Baltes or Staudinger have – importantly – explored gains in insight and wisdom associated with older age, these phenomena have scarcely been connected with the social, political, economic or cultural circumstances of older people. But such increments in capacity cannot be comprehended, still less explored adequately, within a single discipline. We argue that they must be investigated within a profoundly interdisciplinary framework. Finally, writers such as Tornstam have asserted that the insights developed by older people would more normally be associated with ageing were it not for the adverse conditions imposed by contemporary expectations of later life. (Insofar as it has confined itself to artificially decontextualised studies, gerontology itself has not been innocent of contributing to these conditions.) Tornstam's concept of 'gerotranscendence' is well known to researchers concerned with internal processes during the last phases of life, but this should not be a minority interest. The fact that it poses questions central to understanding the human condition should link it to the others mentioned here.

Concerns such as these reflect and continue approaches to ageing that have been significant since the times of antiquity – and not only on an individual level. As long ago as the times of the city-states of ancient Mesopotamia, there is evidence that in some quarters efforts were being made to conceptualise the life course; the same people were also enquiring why it is that some groups in society oppress others and about conditions for social justice (Denning-Bolle, 1992; cf Assmann, 1990). These impulses, of course, take very different forms in different societies. With the emergence of a public discourse on the constraints and potentials of ageing societies now in the public domain today, increasing numbers of questions and reservations are again being mooted in connection with values and norms embedded in the ageing phenomenon. These we begin to address in this volume, linking them in terms of an effort to foreground human beings and their life courses.

Yet why has there been resistance to this conception of gerontology as centred on the human person? From the beginning of the critical gerontology debate, Cole and Moody in particular commented critically on a specific transformation within gerontological reasoning. Ageing, they argued, was no longer viewed as an existential constellation in which a multiplicity of forms of life and subjective aspirations are centred. Instead, a concept of ageing that had been made manageable and researchable according to scientific standards and procedures had been adopted. This resulted in a reduction in relevant meaning domains, characterised for both authors by the term 'instrumental'. This associated current gerontology with the concept of 'instrumental reason' and its intellectual background in the Critical Theory of the Frankfurt School. Moody saw instrumental gerontology as too strongly linked with a view of the natural sciences as a source of tools with which to predict and control what human beings do. This is linked with a form of rationality that objectifies human experience, standing outside the process of ageing and seeking to control it through technological means. In Moody's view, the role played by values and norms is important here, not only as a driving force to stimulate the development of alternative models of ageing and to locate ageing within an emancipatory discourse, but also to help create and solidify 'an active societal and political movement' (Moody, 1988: 33).

Critical gerontologists did indeed intend to adopt a definite and deliberate normative outlook. They certainly defended the interests of older people, even if they sometimes neglected the theoretical implications of an increasingly social-scientific style in their work. And they found many reasons for dissatisfaction with gerontology as it was generally practised. Following this line we will turn to the challenge that a 'humanist gerontology' could pose to the gerontological enterprise, by inquiring further into the shortcomings of traditional gerontology identified by 'critical gerontologists'.

Deficiencies in current gerontology

If we look back at the history of gerontological reasoning, particularly in the light of the continued dominance of instrumentalism within it, it is remarkable that the need to reconsider values and norms in ageing as part of a humanistic agenda was already being articulated in the1970s and 1980s:

> Mainstream gerontology – with its highly technical and instrumental avowedly objective, value-neutral and specialized discourses – lacks an appropriate language for addressing basic moral and spiritual issues in our aging society. Researchers, teachers, students, professionals, patients, clients, administrators, and policymakers do not possess a ready way to speak to one another about fundamental questions of human existence. (Cole, 1992: XI)

This profound normative deficiency in gerontology can be traced back to wider societal developments. These include the century-long growth of a basically experimental concept of scientific endeavour, associated with a professionalisation centred around exclusive credentials, institutionalised intellectual work and the establishment of comprehensive rules in connection with this work. In particular, gerontology failed to maintain strong connections with fields of human thought where these criteria did not apply. Thus, even as a new and comparatively open enterprise, it soon became institutionally 'homogenised'. From the very start of the 20th century, amid debates on the normative foundations of medical and biological science and the influence of the social hygiene movement, the inherently multidisciplinary fundants of gerontology failed to compete with the influence of medical and biological discourses as they were conceived then.

Hence Cole is right to observe that, over time, the development of institutionalised science has contributed to eroding a 'common (if contested) language for discussing questions of meaning and value, justice, virtue, wisdom or the common good' (Cole, 1992: XI). Irrespective of the value of natural-scientific conventions in themselves, they have certainly been inappropriately applied. Indeed, we diagnosed this language problem in our argument at the beginning of this introduction. It produces a perspective in which older people are consistently viewed from the outside, as objects of need. In a slightly different context, Bytheway (2002: 73) argues that:

> No matter how often we might protest, much of our research is embedded within ageist assumptions about the societal implications of an ageing population. Even in the year 2002, it would be difficult to dispute Townsend's (1981) famous accusation of acquiescent functionalism.

This predicament is exacerbated by the influence of postmodern assumptions questioning the value of taking ethical problems seriously, by the increasing significance of diversity in life situations, by the diminishing roles of traditional bonds and by the intensifying impact of communication technology and media coverage on a global scale. Normative languages have been at least partially undermined; MacIntyre (1981) has pointed forcefully to the near-universal replacement of ethical by emotive terms. On the other hand, precisely in reaction to postmodern developments, these languages are becoming more urgently needed. The question of enduring moral obligations and the increasing potential of spiritual dimensions in everyday life – as well, Manheimer (2007) reminds us, as their communal dimensions – can be expected to gain a new relevance throughout human life courses. Deep-rooted social changes have repercussions for the positioning of life phases. These developments cannot leave normative contexts of ageing untouched and in the future they can be expected to provoke the mobilisation of new stocks of knowledge and debate.

But, if the ethical and political conundrums at the heart of studying human beings cannot be evaded, this poses a challenge to the human studies that is only starting to be confronted. Several chapters in this volume, for example, stress moral and political implications of the public discourses about ageing that older people are constrained to adopt. To explore the implications of moral languages further would require social scientists to refrain from bracketing out ethical enquiries by keeping their own real commitments largely off the printed page (Edmondson, 1984). Rather than 'quarantining' philosophical questions (Stempsey, 1999), they need to explore more openly what attitudes and discourses should be supported, and why. Thus Manheimer (1999), for instance, combines philosophy and narrative to explore insights gained from talking with older people. But this in turn demands a more radical and serious multidisciplinarity than is currently common in the field.

The special appeal of the 'humanities'

In this context it is high time to return to approaches to knowledge that have been neglected in the human sciences, or even rejected as of limited value for modern societies: the realm of the 'humanities'. Central to the humanities is precisely their concentration on questions concerning the human condition. This makes them of key interest to gerontology, as the field where life courses are studied. But the humanities too have internal problems today.

The criteria determining their contents and methods are themselves controversial, and are influenced by long-term cultural traditions in different societies. In terms of disciplines, the humanities are traditionally constituted by history, philosophy, literature, religious and cultural studies as well as those areas of the social sciences that concentrate on value-transfer and interpretation. The humanities ought also to embrace other sources of appreciating human experiences – for example, the arts, sources of surprising originality and experience that cannot be reduced to calculation. In Charles Frankel's words, as reported in the report of the Commission on the Humanities:

> The humanities are that form of knowledge in which the knower is revealed. All knowledge becomes a humanistic one when this effect takes place, when we are asked to contemplate not only a proposition but the proposer, when we hear the human voice behind what is said. (Commission on the Humanities, 1980: 2)

Concentrating on the humanities' impact on the design of a new gerontological perspective for research as well as policy could make this 'human voice' work for a future-oriented gerontological research. Exploring the arts would offer an experiential perspective, putting questions of value transmission and normative frameworks at the centre of attention for teachers, administrators, researchers and public policy. The challenge would be to make this compatible with the rigour that gerontology also requires.

Different approaches to the humanities and their role in knowledge and research need to be taken into account here. Particularly in American universities, the liberal arts, history and languages, sometimes also the social sciences, are interlinked. The situation in Europe is more diverse. The Renaissance *studia humanitatis* embraced grammar, rhetoric, logic, poetry, history and usually ethics (as well as arithmetic, geometry, music and astronomy); those who studied them termed themselves orators, disputants for what is good in human affairs (Baxandall, 1971: 1). Since the early 19th century, in central European countries the humanities have had long but diverse traditions of developing methodological, philosophical and scientific systematic discourses. The French tradition, for instance, perceives the *humanités*, in Marc Fumaroli's words, as 'la mémoire vivante du passé' (Fumaroli, 2000: 'the living memory of the past'; cf also Soll, 2003; Fumaroli, 2008). This approach is particularly critical of academic specialisation and its consequences. In the German-speaking countries, with their tradition of the *studium generale*, the concept of the *Geisteswissenschaften* (cf the work of Wilhelm Dilthey) led to complex debates in the 19th and early 20th centuries. Some writers nursed the (questionable) ambition that the humanities could become authoritative meaning providers for entire societies; this hope clearly faded during the 20th century. In the closing decades of the century, the idea of the humanities' 'societal inevitability' was widely discussed (by Odo Marquard among others). It was hoped that the humanities could protect cultural traditions in an era of fragmentation, compensating for perceived losses caused by historical change. This represented a relatively pragmatic turn, which freed the humanities from an overload of expectations obliging them to become sources of social meaning on their own. A cautious rapprochement seems to be developing today between these different positions. Yet, in different ways that need to be explored, each still conveys its own preoccupation with what it sees as central to the project of living a human life.

The ambivalences of 'traditional' gerontology

Despite or because of these developments in the study of the humanities, humanistic concerns did not, in practice, become central in gerontology. During the 1970s and 1980s, frustration was still felt about the intellectual standing of this new multidisciplinary discipline. On the one hand, it still needed to struggle to justify its existence and establish its legitimacy. On the other, disillusion arose from social gerontology's collection of more and more empirical material on ageing – without supplying any further intellectual direction for research. At the same time, practitioners in the field pointed to deficits in strategies concerning the dynamics of use. Both insisted that traditional gerontology should thoroughly examine its theoretical assumptions and reorient its research strategies.

This potential reassessment of gerontology was negotiated under the general heading of an essentially critical perspective. The general implications of defining a movement in science as 'critical' have been expressed by Phillipson and Walker (1987: 12):

> In any discipline, or sub-discipline, a mainstream or orthodoxy develops which is often conservative and rarely self-critical. There is a need, particularly in a relatively young field of study, for a constant reappraisal of concepts and ideas in order to prevent the orthodox approach becoming stultifying.

Here the development of a critical position is interpreted as a sign of progress in any discipline that wishes to avoid intellectual immobility and the petrification of its concepts. Critical contributors can have rejuvenating effects, provoking new patterns of perception and stimulating theoretical reasoning in the interests of new and surprising developments. In many ways this argument recalls the juxtaposition of 'normal' and 'revolutionary' science, as developed in the Kuhn and Lakatos/Musgrave debate. 'Critical' movements can be agents for revolutionising academic discourse.

'Critical' innovations also point to potential areas of gerontological research that are neglected, or unrecognized as important, in mainstream gerontology. In ageing studies, the critics' central emphasis was the elaboration of a political economy of ageing, reversing the previous overemphasis on psychological dimensions. They focused on structural determinants and distributional dynamics of the ageing process, opening gerontological analysis to the dimensions of the economy and of policy formation. Such a comprehensive theoretical framework for analysing the structural constraints of ageing was a highly promising and welcome new perspective.

But, in practice, addressing structural issues in such a decisive manner could easily go hand in hand with neglect or disregard of moral as well as symbolic and cultural dimensions of ageing. Several advocates of the political economy of ageing tried to correct this apparent deficiency, presenting different attempts to balance out this approach. One such attempt uses a straightforwardly eclectic compensation strategy. Adding on approaches such as ethnomethodology, cultural analysis, or biographical studies is taken without further reservation to be an adequate remedy (cf Estes, 1991, 1999). It is simply assumed that this covers the 'other side' of the political economy approach, directing attention to the differential cultural and moral aspects of ageing. A second approach (Minkler and Cole, 1991, 1999; Hendricks and Leedham, 1992), less naively, connects the political economy theme with studying the 'moral economy' of a society (Thompson, 1978), seeing this latter in terms of popular consensus about the legitimacy of resistance practices based on shared social norms. This was intended to integrate questions about the production of norms and values in relation to ageing into a political economy approach.

Finally, there is a third way (for example, Moody, 1988, 1989, 1993), in which an orientation towards a political economy of ageing is interpreted as itself a potentially valuable analytical schema. Here – again on a critical basis allied to the Frankfurt School – it was not only the 'instrumental orientation' of gerontology that was attacked, but also the inherent potential of this orientation to *deprive* the last stages of life of their peculiar meaning and experiential richness. Here the tradition of the humanities was brought up again. It was seen not only as an important source of inspiration, but also as a basis for developing and elaborating moral standards for ageing.

The culturisation of 'critical gerontology' and humanism's special approach

Since the 1980s and 1990s, the spectrum of possible approaches for shaping a 'critical gerontology' agenda has widened and become further differentiated. The growth of cultural discourse in the social sciences in general has consequences here. A variety of theoretical positions are now available to social gerontology, from Bourdieu's theoretical work and Foucault's micropolitical analyses to ethnologically inspired theories such as Clifford Geertz's theory of cultural forms. And with the further elaboration of post-colonial perspectives, as well as Eisenstadt's multiple modernities approach, changes focusing on the developing world will also influence international research on ageing. The increasing diversity of life situations in old age themselves will also augment the 'culturalisation' of gerontology. Moreover, the theoretical approaches used for cultural analyses of ageing already possess critical potential of their own. Under their influence the political economy of ageing has recently undergone a welcome resurgence in interest within the gerontological community (Walker, 2006).

The indebtedness of a 'humanist gerontology' to the discourse on critical gerontology is immediately apparent in Moody's 1993 paper, where the question heading his last paragraph – 'What may we hope?' – refers to Kant's three questions defining the philosophical enterprise. (The others are 'What can we know?' and 'How should we act?') Moody's answer is 'humanistic or cultural gerontology' (Moody, 1993: XXXii; cf Anderson, 2002). But cultural gerontology and humanist gerontology are not necessarily the same things. For a humanist gerontology, the standpoint of the person needs to be *central* if the rest is both to make sense and to avoid the objectifying effects already criticised here. As we have indicated, 'add ons' or 'patches' dealing with, say, culture or biography fail to transform approaches that are themselves fundamentally instrumental. To take a *perspective* focusing on human purposiveness and interconnectedness is itself to take a theoretical position (Edmondson, 1984). As the humanistic orators of the classical world and the Renaissance were aware, perspective rules what elements in a discursive field are treated as more important than others, what elements are perceived in the light of those significant items and what others may be obscured entirely. In addition, a humanistic approach demands the activation of certain key capacities. Some of these are highlighted in Martha Nussbaum's (1997) argument for what is essential to 'cultivating humanity'. They include, besides taking a critical approach to one's traditions and one's use of them, the (Ciceronian) stance of regarding oneself as a person bound to all other people by 'ties of recognition and concern' and, furthermore:

> ... the ability to think what it might be like to be in the shoes of a person different from oneself, to be an intelligent reader of that person's story, and to understand the emotions and wishes and desires that someone so placed might have. (Nussbaum, 1997: 10-11)

We see some of these capacities reflected as the writers in this collection confront questions raised by humanist approaches to the life course, showing how they can inform empirical as well as theoretical work. The book is structured into three sections. Contributors to the first section, while remaining aware of political and economic contexts and pressures, explore older people's internal lives, from different national and empirical perspectives. They deal with older people affected by the churches' neglect of their critical needs for meaning and purpose, in the UK; people's uses of values in making ageing a positive experience, in Singapore; or the role of values in the ways in which people in later life cope with challenges in creating meaning in their personal lives, in the US. The next chapter moves on to some older people's tentative explorations of religious ideas, in a setting defined by novel generational relations: the former East Germany. The section ends with a warning from an Israeli study that we should not impose our own hopes and expectations on people nearing the ends of their lives. This chapter not only struggles to formulate ways in which very frail older people might feel but also warns us that understanding them depends heavily on our own approaches and our investments in wanting to envisage them in a manner consonant with our own wishes.

The central section of the book thematises the study of gerontology itself, and its relations with other structural and philosophical issues. This section too begins with a chapter that makes us aware that there are different ways of regarding the phenomenon of ageing and that we need to be conscious of them. This introduces the subsequent articles, which confront issues crucial to understanding ageing in the contemporary world: intergenerational relations, public attitudes to pension provision and the quality of life in nursing homes. The section ends with a philosophical reflection on how we should react to the extension of lifetime itself: a question that goes to the heart of contemporary dilemmas in relation to ageing. (Humanism itself can be either religious or otherwise; the last mentioned chapter emanates from a humanist university that is explicitly non-religious.) The last section of this collection – directly or indirectly – develops notions of wisdom and insight that, as we have already argued, are central to the study of ageing. How can we trace the development of wisdom across diverse groups of older people with diverse experiences? What real obstacles are there to particular older people's construction of meaningful lives? What is going on when they feel they are ageing well?

Movements towards a 'humanist gerontology'

The lives of older people are heavily marked by changes and developments in values – their own values as well as those of other individuals, of groups such as the family, of larger-scale social institutions, and of cultures and societies in general. Public policy on older people is largely steered by evaluative decisions, overtly so or otherwise. And the quality of life enjoyed by older people is closely related both to their own values and to the impacts on them of social values.

Studying these values and their effects demands empirical accuracy and finesse; yet it also forces us to admit the inevitability of normative stances *towards* the people who are researched. Human subjects cannot be described in a way that is devoid of any attitude at all (Edmondson, 1984). In this volume Gallagher, for example, specifically defends the value of her subjects' insights. Hazan defends, not his subjects' values specifically, but their entitlement to be free of the weight of others' expectations. Such work is thus forced to be multidisciplinary, or to recognise its own multidisciplinary expectations. Edmondson acknowledges this by combining philosophical with ethnographic approaches in weighing and interpreting different conceptions of wisdom, as well as drawing on excerpts from a contemporary play to support some of her claims.

There is no single methodological recipe for these evaluative responses. 'The difference … is not in the method but in the objectives of knowledge' (Gadamer, 1960: xxix). Some commentators locate the key to engaged gerontology in treating older people as 'us' rather than 'them'. Close as this comes to Cicero's stress on the commonalities of humankind, it needs further elaboration rather than literal interpretation. Many of our contributors do treat those about whom they are writing as a separate group – rightly so. Dillon, for instance, is commenting on a longitudinal study of a number of Californians born in the 1920s. Patently, she does not belong to this group. But her enquiry is motivated by a respectful attempt to comprehend the views of those who do. At least part of its aim is also to understand the human condition better. Does older age necessarily involve existential crisis and declining self-confidence, for instance? How can we understand the role that religious and other forms of meaningful enquiry can play for people with different personalities? This signals a return to the 'big questions', but it does so in a fashion that does not impugn the accuracy of Dillon's material. Her selections and interpretations, inevitably, are engaged, but they are public and contestable. This is not an intrusion of subjectivity into gerontology that needs to be counteracted by an authorial statement of her position. It is an intrinsic effect of argument in public about human affairs.

In the past, disciplinary boundaries have been allowed to narrow the potential of gerontological enquiry by separating questions of ethical stances towards older people from the conduct of inquiry itself, attempting to treat them as purely technical issues. This we reject, hoping to reopen the discourse on ageing to a dimension of reflexivity that has become occluded or even lost. This collection combines work drawing on sociology, political theory, psychology and philosophy. We intend the power of these combined disciplines to help create a new language for appraising claims about issues such as 'the meaning of a life', which are of great importance to the public, but to which academic research has to date not contributed enough.

Humanist approaches of the text

We can effectively begin to emphasise our shared predicament with older people by directing attention to a common need: to endow the life course with meaning and purpose. Hence this volume's opening section focuses on ageing as a process of creating meaning, one carried out by older people but affecting those around them, and affected by the norms and values of societies in which they live. Since, as a matter of empirical fact, much creation of meaning is associated with religious traditions, many of these chapters enquire into the role of religion in older people's lives.

This section explores a variety of ways in which meaning-creation can be attempted or accomplished. It explores some of its diversity and its individuality, and the ways in which it is influenced – for good or ill – by social and material circumstances, and by questions of health. For the UK Peter Coleman underlines the fact that the organisations traditionally associated with co-creating meaning in the lives of older people, the churches, appear to be retreating from this task, leaving a certain amount of bleakness and resentment in their wake. He asks whether a humanistic welfare policy should directly thematise sources of meaning and social belonging, including religious ones. Coleman's empirical data concerns 'some of the most interesting cases to investigate': 'those persons who score in between' on scales of religiosity 'and thus tend not to be highlighted by the statistical analyses, for example people who retain loyalty to a religious faith but continue to question within it'. In contrast, Kalyani Mehta, who holds that 'the search for meaning and purpose in life' is 'a strong existential and emotional need' as people's life courses progress, investigates attitudes to ageing among different ethnic groups in Singapore. Using interviews with members of the majority Chinese (usually Buddhist) and the minority Malay (Muslim) and Indian (Hindu) communities, she shows how older people in these groups very actively, and rather differently, use religious and ethical beliefs in practices of meaning-creation with clear relationships to the society about them.

Interpreting data from the US, Michele Dillon offers evidence from a longitudinal study of 184 Californians, now in later life, who are responding with generosity and subtlety to the task of creating meaning in their lives. She objects to the 'long-standing tendency in social science to pathologise life transitions', offering us empirical evidence of people who explore the meaningfulness of their lives effectively but in strongly contrasting ways. Many of them show evidence of increasing commitment to a 'Golden Rule' ethic, suggesting that 'a more universalising world view' may indeed be 'distinctive of late adulthood'. Like Kalyani Mehta, she highlights the way in which older people, far from simply 'adopting' systems of beliefs, make creative use of them in a purposeful process of dealing with their own life courses. They do not all do this by recourse to religion, and the next contribution, by Monika Wohlrab-Sahr, explores intergenerational debates about religion and meaning within families in a society, the former German Democratic Republic, that has in the past explicitly discouraged religion as a world view. She stresses scepticism on the part of the older generation and tentative questioning by those who are younger. These current changes do not amount to a religious revival; rather, Wohlrab-Sahr sees them as an inchoate reawakening of religious perspectives that is experimental and syncretistic rather than traditional and church-bound. The process of comprehending one's own life is, though, not just individual and social: it depends too on one's physical circumstances. Nor can we demand that it necessarily produce results we see as harmonious and palatable. Lastly in this section, Haim Hazan uses Israeli research to explore possible ways of understanding those older people who, in periods of advanced old age that involve extreme physical fragility, inhabit a world – 'the fourth space' – whose meaning is almost opaque to us. Approaching this 'unfathomable realm' is a delicate enterprise, yet Haim Hazan seems able to make it understandable for us, even if not comfortable. It is the imaginative power of Hazan's writing, approaching 'the artistically metaphoric', which accounts for the extent to which he can 'articulate the literal, timelessly transcendental experience of existing in the inaudible fourth age'.

These contributions make clear that societal circumstances play significant roles in circumscribing or liberating older people's efforts to live meaningful lives. Hence, the second section of the book deals with the impact of social norms on older people's capacities to age in creative ways – for example by endorsing institutional and societal supports for later stages of the life course, or else by failing to do so. Hans-Joachim von Kondratowitz introduces this section by stressing that ideas and expectations about ageing in the contemporary world are inescapably marked by stronger normative undercurrents than ever. These undercurrents are the products of the distinct but highly ambivalent historical heritage of modernity. He discusses the historical adoption of ideas and practices relating to 'gerontocracy' and dissects claims about a traditional veneration of old age; then he traces the invention of the idea of 'generation'. His main aim is to reconstruct the different historical settings in which discrepancies between hidden normative impacts and an ensuing societal ambivalence took shape. This allows him to call for us to investigate new normative developments and the new visibility of societal ageing processes, heightened by the multiplication of intermediary institutions in modern welfare states. Illustrating his contentions with comparative material on ageing from German-speaking countries, von Kondratowitz shows how urgently these issues need to be taken into account in studies of ageing.

Subsequent contributions to this section therefore deal with different social norms and their impacts on ageing. Svein Olav Daatland examines evidence about European family norms and relationships from the OASIS study of European countries. He explores intergenerational relationships with an emphasis on how they are perceived by the *parental* generation. Family relations are, and always have been, complicated, ambivalent and mixed, but he finds evidence of new forms of what might be termed loving independence between family members. Independence and emotional concern, he speculates, might be less oppositional stances than commentators have assumed. Frommert, Hofaecker, Heien and

Andreß use recent Eurobarometer data to demonstrate that, despite heated debate on problems arising from the 'greying' of contemporary societies, public attitudes towards older people and their pension provisions are in many respects positive in Europe. Why, then, does this not translate into clearer policies? The most generally popular solution to the pensions crisis among the public is the one most feared and least favoured among policy makers. Thus the relationship between social norms and what actually impacts on older people's lives is complex: it may be mediated more sharply by institutional and power-related factors than attitudes to ageing *per se*. Here the contribution by Cooney and Murphy shows another and sometimes darker side of the picture. On the basis of interviews and focus groups, it examines life in a number of private and public nursing homes in Ireland. While some of these treat older people as adults in their own rights, in others residents live in permanent wards, getting up, eating and sleeping when instructed, even wearing clothes selected for them by staff. Although it was demonstrably important to residents to be able to exercise choice and independence in the details of their everyday lives, this possibility was sometimes drastically curtailed. What relations do these conditions have to contemporary norms and values? Potential evaluative confusion is also dissected in Peter Derkx's account of social debates about the meaning of older age. It might unreflectingly be assumed that extending the period of healthy ageing in human lives is a good thing – but, interrogating different approaches to the idea of life extension, Derkx illuminates the complexities of bioethical argument. This discussion, he observes, cannot be carried out without discussing ethics and values associated with ageing, nor without revisiting the ways in which we conceptualise what 'ageing itself, and being human', is all about. Derkx concludes that only a humanistic approach to older age will allow us to deal adequately with new forms of bioethical dilemma.

The third section of the book returns to the question of what is involved in conferring meaning on the process of ageing. In former times, the idea of a meaningful later life was popularly associated with the idea of wisdom. Becoming wiser, and allowing others to benefit by one's wisdom, was an aim to which older people could at least aspire. Ricca Edmondson opens this section with examples of forms of wisdom that have been popularly associated with ageing in western societies. She argues that it is misplaced to regard these as purely individual forms of life. As previous contributions to this collection have shown, the ways in which people shape the meanings they give to their own and others' experiences are connected heavily with their responses to their cultural circumstances and the ways in which these are shot through with specific norms and values. Interpreting both ethnographic and artistic evidence from the West of Ireland, Edmondson claims that wise interventions can be enabled or even constituted by social interaction.

Carmel Gallagher's contribution examines the lives of older people in two locations in Ireland, an area of North Dublin and a country village in Donegal. For Gallagher, the everyday activities of the older people she has studied are central to co-creating 'a more habitable social world'. She highlights daily practices that make up 'a form of generalised friendship' among older people: apparently insignificant interactions are in fact of high importance. Gallagher shows that older people in both the areas she studies play active and vital roles in the lives of their communities, supporting each other through practices that we might term wise. These are wise norms rather than beliefs *about* wisdom, to the extent that they are not consciously thematised as wise. James Nichol's chapter contrasts the notion of 'eldership' in New Zealand, which does thematise wisdom, with the expressed views of people who are entering on later life in the UK. Nichol used 'cooperative enquiry' to study 16 people, including himself, born between 1940 and 1956. But participants not only resisted the idea of eldership, they also moved away from the idea of 'age' itself. They preferred the idea of activities and views of life that they connected with being 'the best version' of the people who they are, rather than conforming to conventional standards of social behaviour. There is clearly much that these participants would like to pass on to others of what they have learned about life, but the language of wisdom does not come easily to them. Similarly, participants in a study by Lorna Warren and Amanda Clarke have insights and experiences they would like to convey, but it is not always easy for them to say what this means or in what terms they could communicate it. These authors draw on a series of biographical interviews with 23 older people, exploring 'the fit between discourses of active ageing in policy and older people's views of possibilities for being and acting'. They argue that, rather than simply promoting personal freedom predicated on 'relentless projects of self-reflection and improvement', 'active ageing' is often used by older people themselves in choosing to help *others*.

This section of the book thus points to a crisis in language about ageing, which either does not do what people would like it to do – or does much that they do not like. Outi Jolanki's research in Finland into the seemingly innocuous language of 'active ageing' reveals that it can carry ethical overtones with oppressive effects. It is a language that, to her respondents, seems to *oblige* them to be active and healthy if they are to be regarded as citizens in their own right. If they are not well and hence not active, they do not feel in a position to be treated as adults. The idea of adult independence seems linked to *control* in the eyes of these respondents; they are anxious, even desperate, to be seen to have retained it. The intendedly liberating effects of the idea of 'active ageing' can thus have the opposite results. The scientised interpretation of older age as fundamentally a health problem imposes on older people a way of thinking about their own social and moral status that does not begin to do justice to the lives they are actually living. They are forced to adopt personas stressing activity, because to do otherwise would make them feel morally at fault. Jolanki, in other words, explores the worlds of older people who are struggling valiantly to live engaged and meaningful lives, but dominant social discourses undermine this effort. Her respondents' attempts to use a 'wisdom' discourse are 'weak' in comparison with their anxiety to demonstrate how active they are. There is a dearth of accessible languages in whose terms they can communicate what they have learned in their long lives.

The chapters in the collection thus emphasise the complexity and creative potential of people in later stages of the life course; they highlight, too, some of the forces with which they must contend. They explore some of the ways in which older people can confront religion, spirituality and the attribution of meaning to their life courses in much more complex, critical and independent ways than is often expected. Our grasp of people's engagement in late-life processes of meaning-creation demands much more sophistication; we need to know more about people's uses and the impacts on them of social norms and beliefs, habits and languages. These questions are of the utmost importance for ageing societies and for ageing in society. They must be treated as a key subject of research as well as of public discourse. This claim is underlined by the two Afterwords to this book, by Eileen Fairhurst – who explores some ethical and political aspects of visual images of ageing – and Ron Manheimer. As the latter makes clear, contemporary challenges associated with ageing also offer much that is positive. When older people really explore their potential for contributing to the world, who knows what they might not achieve?

A humanist approach to ageing makes up a paradigm within which questions like these are central to understanding the life course. Humanist gerontology would therefore concentrate on the social complexity of the human condition: what matters to people as they age, what makes their lives meaningful, what sense can be given to human 'development' in a situation characterised by increasing heterogeneity in opportunities? This means adopting an approach that essentially acknowledges people's life courses as needing and creating meaning. In some sense, it takes account of the commonality among people, however difficult this commonality may be to describe, at the same time as accepting their enduring diversity. Humanist gerontology will create and establish an emancipatory, holistic discourse that both explores the processes of interpretation that make up sociality and aims at criticising the structures and oppressive practices that distort it. It is oriented towards what Moody (1988: 32–3) calls 'freedom beyond domination (autonomy, wisdom, transcendence)', challenging those aspects of the contemporary world that undermine human efforts (and needs) to imbue it with significance.

This approach also entails acknowledging and exploring the multidisciplinary roots of gerontology: not confining it within a rigidly defined set of methods, but seeking to understand how each can be expanded to become more adequate to explaining and illuminating what concerns human beings as they age. This does not delineate a single recipe or approach; we have already quoted Gadamer's dictum that it is the *interest* directing the methods that counts. Clearly, different individuals are comfortable with techniques in which they have become skilled, but humanist gerontologists can be expected to be tolerant of other methods of exploring human lifetimes and actively to seek to expand their methodological horizons. This means responding both more sensitively and more radically than is regularly done at present to the different elements within the subject. It is not enough merely to note that historically, culturally oriented versions of the subject exist, while exclusively exploring, say, only physical or survey-oriented data (or vice versa). Rather, it is important to disinter the bases of these approaches and the often-unacknowledged notions of the human being they incorporate; the point of this is to interrogate these notions and weigh both their compatibility and their acceptability.

Humanist gerontology thus also means understanding the theoretical aspects of the subject: seeking to practise philosophical and political discourse, for example, in a way that is aware of the theoretical decisions and implications of gerontological work. Which aims and needs on the parts of people as they age do we honour and explore, and which ones do we neglect or regret, and on what grounds? Humanistic gerontologists need to develop some capacity for theoretical debate – rather than, as sometimes occurs, adopting phrases such as 'empowerment' or 'autonomy' and using them unquestioningly or in reified ways. But this is theory oriented towards practice: not undertaken in isolation and for its own sake, but part of a way of interacting with older people and the ageing process itself. In this volume we hope to offer a forward-looking and stimulating perspective on this work.

References

Anderson, L. (ed) (2002) *Cultural gerontology*, Westport, CT: Greenwood Press.

Assmann, J.A. (1990) 'Weisheit, Schrift und Literatur im alten Aegypten', in A. Assmann (ed) *Weisheit*, Munich: Wilhelm Fink Verlag, pp 475-500.

Baxandall, M. (1971) *Giotto and the orators: Humanist observers of painting in Italy and the discovery of pictorial composition, 1350-1450*, Oxford: Oxford University Press.

Bytheway, B. (2002) 'Positioning gerontology in an ageist world', in L. Andersson (ed) *Cultural gerontology*, Westport, CT: Greenwood Press, pp 59-76.

Cicero, M.T. (1991) *On duties* (ed E.M. Atkins, trans M.T. Griffin), Cambridge: Cambridge University Press.

Cole, T. (1992) 'The humanities and aging', in T. Cole, D. van Tassel and R. Kastenbaum (eds) *Handbook of the humanities and ageing*, New York: Springer, pp XI-XXIV.

Commission on the Humanities (1980) *The humanities in American life, 1*, Berkeley, CA: University of California Press.

Denning-Bolle, S. (1992) *Wisdom in Akkadian literature: Expression, instruction, dialogue*, Leiden: Ex Oriente Lux.

Edmondson, R. (1984) *Rhetoric in sociology*, London: Macmillan.

Estes, C.L. (1991) 'The new political economy of aging', in M. Minkler and C.L. Estes (eds) *Critical perspectives on aging: The political and moral economy of growing old*, Amityville, NY: Baywood Press, pp 19-36.

Estes, C.L. (1999) 'The aging enterprise revisited', in M. Minkler and C.L. Estes (eds) *Critical gerontology: Perspectives from political and moral economy*, Amityville, NY: Baywood Press, pp 135-146.

Fumaroli, M. (2000) 'Histoire et mémoires', in: J.-C. Berchet and P. Berthier (eds) *Chateaubriand memorialiste. Colloque du cent cinquantenaire (1848-1998): Histoire des idées et critique littéraire*, Geneva: Droz, pp 38-49.

Fumaroli, M. (2008) 'Les humanités aujourd'hui', Une conférence du cycle: 'Quels humanismes pour quelle humanité aujourd'hui ?', 16 October, www.canalu.tv/producteurs/universite_de_tous_les_savoirs/dossier_programmes/les_conferences_de_l_annee_2008/quels_humanismes_pour_quelle_humanite_aujourd_hui/les_humanites_aujourd_hui_marc_fumaroli

Hendricks, J. and Leedham, C. (1992) 'Towards a political and moral economy of aging: an alternative perspective', *International Journal of Health Services*, vol 22, no 1, pp 125-37.

Holstein, M. and Minkler, M. (2007) 'Critical gerontology: reflections for the 21st century', in M. Bernard and T. Scharf (eds) *Critical perspectives on ageing societies*, Bristol: The Policy Press, pp 13-26.

Gadamer, H.-G. (1960) *Wahrheit und Methode*, Tübingen: Mohr-Siebeck.

Katz, S. (1996) *Disciplining old age: The formation of gerontological knowledge*, Charlotteville, VA/London: University Press of Virginia.

MacIntyre, A. (1981) *After virtue: A study in moral theory*, London: Duckworth.

Manheimer, R. (1999) *A map to the end of time: Wayfarings with friends and philosophers*, New York: W. W. Norton.

Manheimer, R. (2007) 'Becoming historical to oneself', *Journal of Aging Studies*, vol 22, no 2, pp 177-83.

Minkler, M. and Cole, T. (1991) 'Political and moral economy: not such strange bedfellows', in M. Minkler and C.L. Estes (eds) *Critical perspectives on aging: The political and moral economy of growing old*, Amityville, NY: Baywood, pp 37-49.

Minkler, M. and Cole, T. (1999) 'Political and moral economy: getting to know one another', in M. Minkler and C.L. Estes (eds) *Critical gerontology: Perspectives from political and moral economy*, Amityville, NY: Baywood, pp 37-49.

Moody, H. (1988) *Abundance of life: Human development policies for an aging society*, Columbia, OH: Columbia University Press.

Moody, H. (1989) 'Gerontology with a human face', in L.E. Thomas (ed) *Research on adulthood and aging: The human science approach*, New York: State University of New York Press, pp 227-39.

Moody, H. (1993) 'Overview: what is critical gerontology and why is it important?', in T.R. Cole, W.A. Achenbaum, P.L. Jakobi and R. Kastenbaum (eds) *Voices and visions of aging: Toward a critical gerontology*, New York: Springer, pp XV-XLI.

Nussbaum, M. (1997) *Cultivating humanity: A classical defense of reform in liberal education*, Cambridge, MA: Harvard University Press.

Phillipson, C, and Walker, A. (1987) 'Introduction: the case for critical gerontology', in S. di Gregorio (ed) *Social gerontology: New directions*, London: Croom Helm.

Phillipson, C. (1998) *Reconstructing old age: New agendas for social theory and social practice*, London: Sage.

Soll, J. (2003) 'Empirical history and the transformation of political criticism in France from Bodin to Bayle', *Journal of the History of Ideas*, vol 64, no 2, pp 297-316.

Stempsey, W. (1999) 'The Quarantine of philosophy in medical education: why teaching the humanities may not produce humane physicians', *Medicine, Health Care and Philosophy*, vol 2, nos 1-2, pp 3-9.

Thompson, E.P. (1978) *The poverty of theory and other essays*, London: Merlin Press.

Townsend, P. (1981) 'The structured dependency of the elderly: the creation of social policy in the twentieth century', *Ageing and Society*, vol 1, no 1, pp 5-28.

von Kondratowitz, H.-J. (1991) 'The medicalization of old age: continuity and change in Germany from the late eighteenth to the early twentieth century', in M. Pelling and R. Smith (eds) *Life, death and the elderly: Historical perspectives*, London: Routledge, pp 134-64.

Walker, A. (2006) 'Extending quality life: policy prescriptions from the Growing Older programme', *Journal of Social Policy*, vol 35, no 3, pp 437-54.

Part One

Religion, spirituality, cultural resources and creating meaning

Religious belonging and spiritual questioning: a Western European perspective on ageing and religion

Peter G. Coleman

Introduction: ageing, religion and tradition

Social change provides a double challenge to the ageing person. Older people are expected to give witness to what has been important in their lives and what is of lasting value. They need to do this also for maintaining their own sense of identity. At the same time their own adaptation to new times and customs requires that they acknowledge and accept inevitable change. To deny change is not an option, for life necessarily involves change. Balancing these two needs and requirements is no easy task, particularly in today's fast-altering society.

In traditional societies, value identification is closely associated with socialisation to the religious beliefs of the group's culture. Older members usually play a major role in this process, by articulating and giving witness to the value choices that they have made in the course of their lives, and to the religious underpinning of these values. Such witness helps reinforce younger people in the often hard, because self-denying, character of the choices that they need to make (Gutmann, 1997).

In modern and postmodern societies, however, such processes of value transmission and witness have become immeasurably more complicated, and both older and younger people have had to come to terms with a greater plurality of value choices in the often fast-changing societies in which they live – which contain people of various as well as no religious commitments. Not only does this greater flux appear to threaten any continuing role that older people might have in transmitting beliefs and values to the younger generation, it can also lead them to question their own faith as well as their value choices – at a time of life when renewal might seem implausible (Coleman and O'Hanlon, 2004).

Religious doubt is still often perceived as an abnormal state in later life. Faith, it might be thought, should grow stronger, not weaker, as death approaches. Indeed the empirical evidence suggests that the health benefits of religious belief and practice, from quicker recovery from physical and mental illness to lowered mortality rates, are at their strongest among older age groups (McFadden and Levin, 1996). There are a number of theoretical considerations that would explain these findings. Traditional religious cultures in particular ascribe important roles to older people and in this way also promote their mental health (Gutmann, 1997). Religious beliefs help to address issues surrounding limitation and finitude as well as questions of loss and suffering, which appear to figure more highly in people's consciousness as they age (Black and Rubinstein, 2004). Religion thus provides resources in responding to questions about survival in states of growing dependency and frailty. In facing the various crises of meaning that can beset older people, from the meaning of their individual lives to that of life in general, religion has been described as a potent friend of ageing (Coleman and O'Hanlon, 2004). Losing faith at the end of life might therefore seem particularly problematic. Religious beliefs not only help to address issues of bereavement and people's own impending mortality, but also provide resources to deal with survival in states of growing dependency and infirmity.

Despite these issues' close relationship to the well-being of older people, welfare policy on ageing has been reluctant to address them. They have been raised by some commentators, notably by the London-based Centre for Policy on Ageing in its report on religion and spirituality in later life (Howse, 1999). But, especially since faith-based terrorist attacks emerged as major threats to western societies, their liberal governments have become even more uncomfortable about any suggestion of intervention in the area of personal beliefs. Yet surely welfare policy should be concerned with promoting sources of meaning and belonging, even though that inevitably means involvement with religious organisations? Such concerns may appear unnecessary in a strongly religious society such as the US, where spiritual choices are readily available, but in the secular and welfare states of modern Europe where most religious organisations have been declining in numbers over the last half century, they are legitimate and challenging questions.[1]

It should be pointed out that the older person's traditional role as the custodian of faith and values does not exclude innovation. Older as well as younger people can be radical in the religious and spiritual arena (Coleman et al, 2006). Faithfulness to a tradition is compatible with and may also require readiness to accept new insights into that tradition's meaning. It is often older people who have the necessary maturity of mind to integrate the tension between tradition and change (Sinnott, 1998). But, where the religious changes are not of the older generation's making, and where education and consultation have been deficient as well (as can be argued has been the case in many changes in forms of Christian worship over the last half century, such as those in the Roman Catholic Church following the reforming Vatican Council of the 1960s), they are likely to lead to some degree of alienation of the religion's older membership.

Despite this, older people continue to search for forms of meaning in their lives and many still look to their religions of origin for inspiration. The Christian churches to which the majority of older people in England belong, or have belonged, stress in their doctrines that the discovery and practice of religious meaning are not entirely individual affairs but depend on the community that gives witness to a shared faith. This makes the churches' current neglect of older people all the more remarkable.

Decline of religious belonging

As Davie (2002) has argued, although many Europeans may think they are following a progressive post-Enlightenment trajectory in abandoning religion or at least loosening its prescriptive ties, they rather than the American population constitute the 'exceptional case'. Religious differences between European countries on the one hand and America on the other hand need to be understood in historical terms. In the first place most European countries have painful memories of religious persecution in which the state played a major role in enforcing the religious orthodoxy of the time, and looked with suspicion on any dissent and questioning of the teaching authority of the official church. Some states, such as England in the 16th century, experienced a succession of changing religious regimes to which conformity was required. Religious toleration was established only after a long period of struggle, and the relationship between the state and the dominant church (Anglicanism) has remained controversial. In many parts of Europe, persecution on religious and ethnic grounds has continued to haunt the continent until the present day. The US by contrast was itself established in large part by religious refugees from Europe and freedom of belief was built into the constitution from its beginning. Although the state has no role in promoting religion, America has remained a very religious nation.

However the historical memories of religious persecution do not in themselves explain the escalating changes of recent years. This is an area of some controversy. Some authors (eg Brown, 2001) argue that the roots of contemporary British secularism and its rejection of traditional Christian culture lay no further back than the 1960s. Others, more conscious of the hollowness of the Victorian Church, see a steady decline of genuine religious sentiment over a much longer time period. But the end product in either case is a greatly diminished church attendance. Total Sunday attendance in Great Britain has declined to 7.9% of adults for all denominations (England 7.4%, Wales 7.4%, Scotland 13.4%) (Brierly, 2003). Research over a 14-year period, which included detailed information from parents, partners and children across the UK, has demonstrated that parents are the most important influence on religiosity, but that in current circumstances institutional religion appears to have a 'half-life' of no more than one generation. According to Voas and Crockett (2005), two religious parents have a roughly 50–50 chance of passing on their beliefs; one religious parent does only half as well; two non-religious parents generally pass on their lack of faith.

The consequences for older people of the ebbing of traditional faith in younger generations deserve more attention than they have received. This oversight is perhaps at least partly because older people in general are perceived as being more religious than their younger counterparts. Certainly age differences in religious activity have been regularly found in the US over the last 50 years. Their consistency over time has led commentators to posit a developmental explanation, with the ageing process itself being conducive to spiritual reflection and belief (Moberg, 2001). The situation in the UK however is different. The Anglican

Church census data shows that the age break in under- and over-representation of age groups in attendance at Anglican Church services is steadily approaching the third age itself. Most evangelical concern within the Christian churches is understandably focused on younger people's reluctance to commit to church, but the data suggests that work with older people should also be given more consideration. As Merchant (2003) has pointed out, it will not be very long before the churches face the challenge of evangelising the newly retired 'baby boom' generation born after WWII, who in large part rejected religion when they were young but could be offered opportunities to re-engage (Merchant, 2003). Any justification for taking the older generation for granted will have disappeared.

Indeed superficial perceptions of substantial faith present among older generations may conceal a decline in the allegiance of recent and current cohorts. Our own analysis of data from the 25-year Southampton Ageing Project showed that, during the 1980s in particular, the sample displayed a significant distancing from religion (Coleman et al, 2004). Although religion continued to have considerable importance in the lives of up to half of our participants, approximately one quarter of the sample expressed a declining commitment to a religious faith and to church membership, and very few indicated a shift to religious allegiance. Our latest surveys in fact suggest that church membership among the older age groups is less than one third.

Although these studies have taken place in only one city in England, they do suggest – in the absence of any other more nationally representative evidence – that the national decline in church attendance and membership has already affected the older population. A contributing factor is likely to have been failure to transmit faith to the younger generation, and indeed an internal dialectic with their children's own views on religious faith was evident in participants' comments.

Rising interest in spirituality

It is important to point out that the Southampton Ageing Project, along with most research in Western Europe that has approached the subject of older people's belief, has investigated only religious allegiance, not the more general salience of spiritual questioning in people's lives. Studies of the British population over the last quarter century have demonstrated that most people continue to believe in God, surveys over the last years suggesting that around 70% of the population believe in God or some form of higher power. Admittedly this is one of the lowest proportions in the world. However Grace Davie (2002) has employed this and other evidence to suggest that the situation in the UK is one where many people of Christian origin want to 'believe without belonging'. Europeans, she argues, appear to want religious organisations to continue functioning, and to be able to make use of them at certain key points in life, especially for births, marriages and deaths. Davie employs the term 'vicarious' to refer to this different use of religion where 'significant numbers of Europeans are content to let both churches and churchgoers enact a memory on their behalf' (Davie, 2002: 19). This is a concept, Davie points out, that Americans with their different religious history find very difficult to understand. It should be pointed out that not all sociologists working in this field accept Davie's thesis of 'believing without belonging'. Voas and Crockett (2005), for example, argue that the evidence favours interpretation in terms of increasing disengagement from religion in Britain, with declining numbers of yearly baptisms and weddings taking place.

Nevertheless, alongside this decline, there is a growing phenomenon of 'spirituality shopping' where people consider a variety of religious traditions and take what suits them. Despite the undoubted benefits of the greater exercise of individual choice in spiritual matters, eclecticism comes at the expense of depth of understanding of a religious tradition's beliefs and practices. For example, belief in reincarnation has increased in Britain as people have become more acquainted with Hindu and Buddhist teaching. This does not mean that they have converted to a new faith. Heelas expresses the British situation in the following sociological terms:

> Rather than authority and legitimacy resting with established orders of knowledge, authority comes to rest with the person ... What the traditional used to demand has transformed into lifestyle options ... People no longer feel obliged to heed the boundaries of the religions ... Instead they are positively encouraged to exercise their 'autonomy' to draw on what has diffused through the culture (Heelas, 1998: 4–5)

However, the changes in religious and spiritual discourse in the UK and many other parts of Western Europe have tended to separate the old from the young. Getting the older generation to speak about spiritual beliefs outside of the context of specific religious beliefs is not easy, and the suggestion of distancing from religious allegiance more anxiety-provoking than releasing. They may be dissatisfied with religion but are not yet secure navigators on the sea of spirituality. As even Voas and Crockett (2005) admit, British older people still tend to see themselves as 'religious', whereas middle-aged people already prefer the term 'spiritual'.

Researchers need to remember that older people in Western Europe were brought up in a much more religious society than they now inhabit. In many erstwhile Catholic parts of the continent, such as the southern Netherlands and Belgium, the previously considerable authority and even the very presence of priests and nuns within local communities disappeared over a period of less than 20 years from the 1950s to the 1970s. In other Catholic countries, such as Ireland and Spain, the changes have been more recent. In Britain most people from Christian backgrounds, whether Catholic or Protestant, attended Sunday schools right up to the 1950s. This was an institution that according to Davies (2004) had an important influence on developing the self-restraint and orderliness of the British character for much of the last century. Certainly, older people were influenced by their religious upbringing to a much greater extent than is generally recognised, and tend to define themselves in relation to it, either as having been influenced by it positively or having been affected adversely.

Uncertain and unsupported belief

One of the limitations of analyses using indices of religiosity and spirituality is that the assumption tends to be made that being 'religious' or being 'spiritual' is a fixed and stable characteristic. But the process of becoming or remaining religious/spiritual is interesting in itself. Some of the most interesting cases to investigate are those people who score in between on both scales and thus tend not to be highlighted by the statistical analyses – for example, people who retain loyalty to a religious faith but continue to question within it.

Christianity, for example, has a complex theology that emerged only after much debate in the early centuries after Christ. So it is perhaps not surprising that even fundamental doctrines, as the full divinity and humanity of Christ and the concept of God as a Trinitarian community of three persons in one, continue to be revisited by people as they age. The difficult experiences associated with age also lead some to doubt God's providential care. However, what appears to me striking from our data is not the fact that such doubts are expressed but that they seem for the most part to remain within the individual person and are apparently not communicated to ministers or other church members.

From our studies we have found it important to recognise rising rates of uncertain, unsupported and troubled belief among the current generations of older people in Britain and the consequences of this for their mental health. In trying to explain our findings on declining church allegiance, we were struck by the specific examples of disappointment with religious ministry, particularly in situations of loss, and especially bereavement. For example, a widower commented on the shock he experienced after the funeral following the sudden death of his wife:

> After the funeral the parson just said, 'Cheerio, I'm off' and nobody even bothered whether I was all right or not.

He saw no point in continuing contact. His church had not delivered the expected spiritual benefit when he needed it, even though it was probably hard for him to articulate precisely what he had expected.

Another example was a woman who also said she had begun to lose faith when her husband died, but felt sad and nostalgic about it. She remembered how as a child she had gone to church three times a day on a Sunday, to morning and evening services, and to Sunday school as well in the afternoon. It had meant a lot of walking. She still felt shame about not attending church more as an adult:

> We all pray when we are in trouble; God must think they only come to me then!

Life had just been too busy. But her husband's death from cancer at the age of 63 led her into a prolonged period of depression and made her start questioning things that she had previously taken for granted, such as the truths of the Bible, especially its accounts of creation. She remembered once asking herself 'and who made God?' and being disturbed by her own question. Nevertheless she still argued about God with her son whom she described as a 'Darwinist'. What was striking about her and so many other people we interviewed was their lack of contact with members of their local church *despite* their history of belonging. Many raised the difficult theological problem of evil ('How could a good God allow…?'), apparently unsupported and in isolation.

We continued with a small but intensive study on the role of spiritual beliefs in cases of bereaved spouses (Coleman et al, 2002, 2007). We followed bereaved spouses from the first to the second anniversary of death and made use of a questionnaire developed at the Royal Free Hospital in London to assess strength of belief in a spiritual power operating in people's lives (King et al, 2001). We got to know our participants very well in the course of three interviews over the year of investigation and were able to tease out their religious history and something of the internal spiritual dialogue going on in their lives, as well as the support they had received since bereavement. The findings were striking. Depressive symptoms, as well as the absence of personal meaning, were concentrated in those of a weak to moderate faith in a transcendent power operating in their lives. For example a depressed widow described the pain of her gradual loss of belief:

> I hear the church bells ringing … and I think, if you don't go today you're never going to believe in any of it again, so you'd better go and see … I am hoping that He might give me some kind of a sign but I don't know what it is.

Those who had maintained a strong belief or who had adopted an atheistic belief system were much better protected.

From a cross-sectional comparison it is not possible to deduce the direction of causation. Depression could itself lead to loss of faith. But the longitudinal element in our case studies and the evidence from the retrospective spiritual histories that we collected suggests the opposite. A similar curvilinear relationship between strength of religious involvement and adjustment has been identified in studies of feelings of self-worth and death anxiety (Kalish and Reynolds, 1976; Krause, 1995; Wink and Scott, 2005).

In our work we have been impressed by the scant opportunity that our older participants have had for discussing issues of faith, belief and values. We decided to advertise our bereavement study in a magazine for older people and were astonished at the huge response we received. We obtained funding to investigate their views in greater detail. There is no doubt that many older people want to feel more able to express their views within their churches and other religious communities, and not always to be seen as dependent and in need of care. At the same time they need to feel part of the community and to know that they are genuinely wanted – for example to be missed and contacted if they are unable to attend a service. What this requires in terms of new forms of ministry to older people needs close consideration. The time when older people could be taken for granted in the religious and spiritual context has long passed (Coleman et al, 2006).

The implications of the turn to spirituality

What is required is closer engagement of older people in the new forms of spiritual discourse. If spirituality is essentially about the task of affirmation and integration of what is of ultimate meaning in life, older people in principle should have much to contribute from their life experience. But the problem is, as Sheldrake (2005) has pointed out, that spirituality is always grounded in its particular historical-cultural context, and the present culture is hostile to the idea of tradition and learning from the old:

> Western cultures currently appear to be becoming history-less and memory-less ... The past is what has happened rather than something that sustains our present and invites us to reflect on our future and on what to aspire to ... 'History' and 'tradition' are also perceived by some people as conservative forces from which we need to break free if we are to live a more mature and rational existence. The power of history-as-myth to sustain entrenched social, religious and political divisions tends to reinforce this negative view. (Sheldrake, 2005: 38)

The shift away from religious to spiritual discourse appears to face many older people with an awkward choice, whether to maintain loyalty to their own tradition or not. This is less a problem for younger people more ready to accept that spirituality matches better than any one religion onto a complex, pluralistic and fragmented world. Spiritual teachers reach out beyond their own traditions. Religious practices, like yoga and t'ai chi, have been taken up across their original borders. Although these points might seem to apply more to Eastern religions than, say, to Christianity, there has been a trend also for Christians to disseminate their teachings and practices more widely than before. There is less anxiety that such practices must occur within the discipline of a particular religious community or authority. New spiritual movements arise outside of institutionalised religious settings, responding to current issues of concern, as in the concerns for the environment and for women's rights that have produced creation-centred spirituality and feminist spiritualities. There is now even talk of workplace-based spirituality in response to the perceived growing pressures of modern office life.

Younger people in Europe no longer accept that their first choice of spiritual discipline should be the religion of their parents. Indeed, in many countries, they may receive only a rudimentary or no education at all in their parents' religion tradition. Older people may indeed feel that their witness to their own tradition is no longer relevant or appreciated. They are perceived as being ignorant of the wider picture.

At the same time many other features of contemporary spiritual movements are ones with which older people no less than younger people can identify. For example, older as much as younger people appreciate the growing emphasis on the interdependency of the human species with all that exists and the concept of the human person not as self-contained but as constituted by the relationships in which the person is engaged.

Older people can also draw on some of the new possibilities being offered by spiritual direction. For example, there has been a rediscovery of the transformative dimensions of sacred reading. Texts can have multiple meanings and the older person is also entitled to his or her interpretation, enlivened by life experience and present circumstances. Such meanings are no longer attributed to:

> … divine agency implanting more-than-literal meanings in the text but to the nature of texts themselves, which are always somewhat indeterminate, semantically autonomous in relation to the intention of the author, and thus always 'completed' by the interpretive activity of the reader. (Schneiders, 2005: 66)

It is important that older people are not neglected in these developments. Indeed the rediscovery of the value of sacred texts could be one of the main sources of re-evangelism of the coming older generations.

European variation

Europe is far from homogeneous in its present religious trajectories (Greeley, 2004). Generally speaking, religion is weak in North Western Europe (with the notable and perhaps temporary exception of Ireland), increasing in strength in Eastern Europe and remaining relatively strong in Southern Europe despite some decline. But even within these broad geographical regions there is considerable variation. For example, whereas in France, Britain and the Netherlands there has been a continuing falling away from church allegiance, the rates in Scandinavia, although even lower, have not fallen further. Nevertheless, it is clear that in most of North-Western Europe the traditional role of older people as guardians and transmitters of Christian religious doctrine and practice has almost vanished. In contrast, in the heartlands of the Roman Catholic Church, including Italy, Spain, and Poland, religion remains strongly associated with national and ethnic culture, and older people continue to fulfil, albeit in a diminished way, their traditional role as religious mentors to the younger generation.

In Eastern Europe the situation is different because of the relatively recent history of religious persecution by secular authority. Partly because of this persecution, older people's role in religious education has remained very important. We have conducted research on Russian Orthodox older people's faith histories in Moscow, examining the survival of religious life under the 70-year-long Soviet persecution. What is so apparent, besides the vicious record of destruction, murder and imprisonment, is the stubborn faith of Russian older people, particularly older women, who were less subject to surveillance and were more able to persist in religious practices that they had learned from their parents and grandparents – taking their children and grandchildren to church and giving them basic instruction, often protecting the adult men by keeping this secret from them. The present generation of older people who attend church in Russia did not do so when they were younger adults because it was not allowed, but they do have the memory of the example of their mothers and especially their grandmothers, and therefore they are able to continue where they left off (Coleman and Mills, 2004). As a result religious practice has survived relatively intact through more than 70 years of persecution and has grown strongly in the post-communist era.

Variation is also evident in Eastern Europe. For example, Bulgaria and Romania are neighbouring countries of similar socioeconomic status and orthodox tradition. But, whereas Christianity survived well the attacks of the post-WWII communist regime and remains strong today in Romania, the communist regime in Bulgaria seems to have been much more successful (even than the Soviets) in relegating religion to the status of a museum piece from which recovery is slow (Kanev, 2002). The historical and cultural bases of these differences deserve examination.

Faiths other than Christianity, especially Islam, have an increasing presence in Europe, largely as a result of immigration from former European colonies in Africa and Asia. It is interesting that, as part of the recent national programme of research on enhancing older people's quality of life funded by the UK Economic and Social Research Council (ESRC), some of the most striking illustrations for the benefits of religion are provided by older British people from religions other than Christianity, where identity and practice remain strong. Despite scoring low on other indices of quality of life, such as income, housing and environment, minority ethnic groups scored high on indices of community and belonging. An older Muslim, for example, might have been involved in the building of the mosque in his local community in earlier adulthood and in later life continued to have a meaningful role in opening and tending the mosque every day (Nazroo et al, 2004). Total Muslim religious participation is approaching Christian religious participation in France and Britain, despite the relative imbalance of numbers. But few studies have examined how older Muslims experience their religion and the inevitable tensions of living in a more secularised society than the society into which they were born.

Conclusion

It would seem unwise to make definite predictions about the future of religion in Europe. Just as earlier immigration has altered the Christian–Muslim balance in Europe, so the recent immigration from Eastern Europe and other parts of the world is changing the character of existing religious institutions. In Britain, attendance at Roman Catholic churches is exceeding that of the established Church of England for the first time since the Reformation. This is due to the influx of Catholic immigrants, especially from Poland and elsewhere, which is already setting major challenges to current provision of religious services, including a demand for a greater intensity of sacramental life (Von Hugel Institute, 2007). Thus this seems to be an example of a trend towards the reintegration of spirituality with religion.

Our approach in Southampton, similar to that of Pargament (1997) in the US, is to study faith in the midst of daily life, and particularly in times of crisis. For older people perhaps more than younger people, these crises often raise issues of the meaning of life to which religion traditionally has provided the most robust answers. To date few studies have been conducted in this field in Europe, but the evidence does support the benefits of strong belief – for example, in situations of bereavement and increased frailty (Walsh et al, 2002; Kirby et al, 2004).

The religious and spiritual context in Europe poses particular challenges of adaptation to the older generation who need to be consulted more by religious organisations about changes, for example, within forms of worship and pastoral care. Researchers need to address the influence not only of different forms and intensity of beliefs, but also of support for those beliefs within local communities and cultures. Religious/spiritual belief is not only an individual but also a shared matter, which is closely related to a sense of belonging and generally expressed within community.

Executing comparative research involves finding solutions to a number of methodological problems. For example it is necessary to be sensitive to differing standards and norms in the religious field. Some forms of religion (such as Catholic Christianity) may involve frequent attendance at relatively short services of worship; others involve particular attention to fasting and other penitential practices (for example, Islam or Orthodox Christianity). A recent Finnish study has demonstrated an effect of church attendance on 12-year survival rates in older women (Teinonen et al, 2005). However, the categories of attendance employed in this research were quite different from those in a typical US study, where approximately half of the older population attend religious services at least weekly. In fact only 1.1% of over 65s did so in the particular area of Finland studied. Prayer was a much more regular occurrence. Nevertheless, even though relatively infrequent by American standards, church attendance could be demonstrated to have an influence independent of health status.

Comparisons across countries and cultures should also help research on religion, spirituality, health and ageing to consider more complex comparisons than simply between the presence and absence of faith, and between different forms of religion. There are often substantial qualitative differences among members of the same religious body. Not all share the same degree of faith, or experience the same level of support, even though indices of religious attendance and practice may be fairly homogeneous. Studies of faith in action should include detailed attention to the precursors and consequences of moderate, uncertain and troubled faith, not only of strong belief and unbelief.

Note

[1] According to the *Daily Telegraph* (2 January 2009), a recent Saga survey of 15,500 respondents shows that a quarter of older people term themselves agnostic or atheist, and that the majority pray or worship less than they used to do. One in five said that their religious beliefs were weaker now than earlier in their adult lives; 14% said they now had more doubts about the existence of God.

Acknowledgements

The author acknowledges the support provided to the Southampton research programme by the Economic and Social Research Council (UK) and the Nuffield Foundation (London), and the contributions of various colleagues, particularly Dr Marie Mills and Revd Prebendary Peter Speck.

References

Black, H.K. and Rubinstein, R.L. (2004) 'Themes of suffering in later life', *Journal of Gerontology: Social Sciences*, vol 59B, no 1, pp 17-24.

Brierley, P. (2003) *UK church handbook of religious trends, 2003/2004*, no 4, London: Christian Research.

Brown, C.G. (2001) *The death of Christian Britain*, London: Routledge.

Coleman, P.G. and Mills, M. (2004) 'Memory and preservation of religious faith in an atheistic society: accounts of the practice of religion in the former Soviet Union', in A. Portelli (ed) *Proceedings of the International Oral History Association Conference*, Rome: University of Rome (no page numbers available).

Coleman, P.G. and O'Hanlon, A. (2004) *Ageing and development: Theories and research*, London: Hodder Arnold.

Coleman, P.G., Ivani-Chalian, C. and Robinson, M. (2004) 'Religious attitudes among British older people: stability and change in a 20 year longitudinal study', *Ageing and Society*, vol 24, no 2, pp 167-88.

Coleman, P.G., McKiernan, F., Mills, M. and Speck, P. (2002) 'Spiritual belief and quality of life: the experience of older bereaved spouses', *Quality in Ageing – Policy, Practice and Research*, vol 3, no 1, pp 20-6.

Coleman, P.G., Mills, M. and Speck, P. (2006) 'Ageing and belief – between tradition and change', in J.A. Vincent, C. Phillipson, C. and M. Downs (eds) *The futures of old age*, London: SAGE, pp 131-40.

Coleman, P.G., McKiernan, F., Mills, M. and Speck, P. (2007) 'In sure and uncertain faith: belief and coping with loss of spouse in later life', *Ageing and Society*, vol 27, no 6, pp 869-90.

Davie, G. (2002) *Europe: The exceptional case. Parameters of faith in the modern world*, London: Darton, Longman & Todd.

Davies, C. (2004) *The strange death of moral Britain*, New Brunswick, NJ: Transaction.

Greeley, A.M. (2004) *Religion in Europe at the end of the second millennium. A sociological profile*, New Brunswick, NJ: Transaction.

Gutmann, D.L. (1997) *The human elder in nature, culture and society*, Boulder, CO: Westview Press.

Heelas, P. (1998) *Religion, modernity and postmodernity*, Oxford: Blackwell.

Howse, K. (1999) *Religion and spirituality in later life: A review*, London: Centre for Policy on Ageing.

Kalish, R.A. and Reynolds, D.K. (1976) *Death and ethnicity: A psychocultural study*, Los Angeles, CA: University of Southern California Press.

Kanev, P. (2002) 'Religion in Bulgaria after 1989: historical and socio-cultural aspects', *South-East Europe Review*, vol 1, no 1, pp 75-96.

King, M., Speck, P. and Thomas, A. (2001) 'The Royal Free Interview for Spiritual and Religious Beliefs: development and validation of a self-report version', *Psychological Medicine*, vol 31, no 6, pp 1015-23.

Kirby, S.E., Coleman, P.G. and Daley, D. (2004) 'Spirituality and well-being in frail and non-frail older adults', *Journal of Gerontology: Psychological Sciences*, vol 59B, no 3, pp 123-9.

Krause, N. (1995) 'Religiosity and self-esteem among older adults', *Journal of Gerontology: Psychological Sciences*, vol 50B, no 5, pp 236-46.

McFadden, S.H. & Levin, J.S. (1996) 'Religion, emotions and health', in C. Magai and S.H. McFadden (eds) *Handbook of emotion, adult development and aging*, San Diego, CA: Academic Press, pp 349-365.

Merchant, R. (2003) *Pioneering the third age. The Church in an ageing population*, Carlisle: Paternoster Press.

Moberg, D.O. (2001) *Aging and spirituality. Spiritual dimensions of aging theory, research, practice and policy*, Binghamton, NY: The Haworth Press.

Nazroo, J., Bajekal, M., Blane, D. and Grewal, A. (2004) 'Ethnic inequalities', in A. Walker and C. Hennessy (eds) *Growing older. Quality of life in old age*, Maidenhead: Open University Press, pp 35-59.

Pargament, K.I. (1997) *The psychology of religion and coping: Theory, research, practice*, New York: Guilford Press.

Schneiders, S.M. (2005) 'Spirituality and scripture', in P. Sheldrake (ed) *The new SCM dictionary of Christian spirituality*, London: SCM Press, pp 62-7.

Sheldrake, P. (2005) 'Spirituality and history', in P. Sheldrake (ed) *The new SCM dictionary of Christian spirituality*, London: SCM Press, pp 38-43.

Sinnott, J.D. (1998) *The development of logic in adulthood: Postformal thought and its operations*, New York: Plenum Press.

Teinonen, T., Vahlberg, T., Isoaho, R. and Kivela, S.-L. (2005) 'Religious attendance and 12-year survival in older persons', *Age and Ageing*, vol 34, no 4, pp 406-9.

Voas, D. and Crockett, A. (2005) 'Religion in Britain: neither believing nor belonging', *Sociology*, vol 39, no 1, pp 11-28.

Von Hugel Institute (2007) *The ground of justice. A draft report of pastoral research enquiry into the needs of migrants in London's Catholic community.* Cambridge: Von Hugel Institute.

Walsh, K., King, M., Jones, L., Tookman, A. and Blizard, R. (2002) 'Spiritual beliefs may affect outcome of bereavement: prospective study', *British Medical Journal*, vol 324, no 7353, pp 1551-4.

Wink, P. and Scott, J. (2005) 'Does religiousness buffer against the fear of death and dying in late adulthood?', *Journal of Gerontology: Psychological Sciences*, vol 60B, no 4, pp 207-14.

TWO

Spirituality: a means for achieving integration in personal and community spheres in an ageing Singapore

Kalyani K. Mehta

Introduction

The search for meaning and purpose in life is far from a speciality of the young; it has been documented as a strong existential and emotional need for older people, especially those who are later in life, 75 years and older. It has been suggested that, within the realm of psychosocial adjustment of those aged 70-84 years, the integrative process plays a critical role. Thus Erikson (1963) postulated eight psychosocial stages of lifespan development, with a focus on the crisis of integrity versus despair at the final stage of life. Since then, many scholars have chosen phenomenological approaches, as well as the social constructionist perspective, to study the ageing process at the micro-level in order to deepen our understanding of the meaning of senescence. The phenomenon of the self (Kaufman, 1986; Sherman, 1991) has been examined in studies and the process of integrating the self in terms of time (past, present and future) as well as space (the various facets of oneself) have been explored. Reker and Wong (1988), Coleman (1990), Sherman (1991) and Tobin (1991) among other researchers have contributed substantially to our understanding of the inner processes that occur within individuals as we age.

Meaning and purpose are intertwined with issues related to spiritual matters and values, and the latter are connected to ethnic norms and beliefs. Hence, in a multicultural and multi-religious society such as Singapore, the journey to study these aspects of ageing inevitably leads one to examine the experiences of older people in the three major ethnic groups: the Chinese, Malay and Indian communities. What can this contrast tell us about different ways in which older people seek, and indeed create, meaning in their lives and those of others?

The Singapore context and this study

Singapore is a natural laboratory for researchers who wish to study cross-cultural and cross-religious social dynamics because it has a multicultural, multilingual and multi-religious population. According to the Census of Population 2000, the three major ethnic groups, the Chinese, Malay and Indian communities, comprised 76.8%, 13.9% and 7.9% of the total population respectively (Census of Population, 2001: 4). The religions that are practised correlate closely with ethnic distribution. The majority of Chinese are Buddhists, the majority of Indians are Hindus and almost all Malays are Muslims. Singapore is a fast-ageing society; it is projected that the proportion of people above 65 years will reach 13.1% in 2020 and 18.9% in 2050 (Interministerial Committee on the Ageing Population, 1999: 29).

The authors designed a micro-level qualitative study with a case study approach bearing in mind the age of the interviewees and the personal nature of topics covered.[1] The focus in this study was on older people living within the community rather than in institutions. Thus 64.5% of the respondents lived with family members, 5% lived with a relative, 17.5% lived with non-relatives and 9% lived alone. In terms of gender distribution, there were eight men and seven women from each ethnic group. As for religious affiliation, there were 15 Muslims, nine Christians, eight Chinese religionists (consisting of Buddhists, Taoists and Confucians), seven Hindus, four Sikhs and two in 'other faiths' (such as Jains). Twenty-six were married, 15 widowed, two divorced and two were single. Eighteen of them were between 70 and 74 years, 18 between 75 and 79 years, and nine between 80 and 84 years. Health status was measured by self-reporting using a global measure and by referring to any physical illnesses or disabilities. The majority (18) said that their health was fair, but seven stated 'very good', nine said 'good', eight said 'poor' and three said 'very poor'. Using a combined socioeconomic status (SES) measure (of present income, assets and type of dwelling), 16 were in the high income band, 15 in the middle band and 14 in the low band. Lastly, as far as educational attainment is concerned, six had no schooling at all, eight had gone only to religious schools (these were Muslims), 18 to primary school, 11 to secondary school and only two had attended post-secondary school.

This chapter focuses on the theme of spirituality as it weaves into the personal and community spheres of integration of Singaporean older people. Embedded within the mosaic of different paths of spirituality are the ethnic beliefs that pervade in a multicultural society such as Singapore. The processes of personal and community integration of older people are best understood when contextualised within the different ethnocultural systems.

Personal integration

Personal integration is treated here as the inner process of achieving harmony within oneself using links or connections such as the person's philosophy of life, value system and/or religious beliefs. We might expect it to have cognitive, emotional and existential aspects because the individual needs to find both meaning and self-worth at the final stage of life (Tornstram, 1997; Moberg, 2001). For the purposes of this study we understand personal integration to include coming to terms with past events, present circumstances and the reality of death in the imminent future. This understanding arises in part from the gerontological literature to which we have already referred, but in part it is a response to what respondents themselves take their preoccupations to mean. Yet within the three population groups there are distinct ethnic patterns, within which this overall tendency is interpreted differently.

The Chinese pragmatic pattern

The distinctive features of the Chinese pattern were its pragmatic, functionalist and moral aspects. Confucianist values and teachings deeply influenced the outlook of very old respondents in the study. Two main ideas that were repeated in many of the transcripts were that:

- The people interviewed wished to remain useful to their family and society until the very end.
- They hoped to be physically healthy till death and did not view poor health as an inevitable companion to old age.

A 'this-worldly' orientation, which meant that they placed little emphasis on the afterlife as an organising principle in old age, was found to be a salient thread throughout most of the Chinese interview transcripts. Statements such as 'I live one day at a time' reflected this orientation.

In the Chinese culture, cultural scripts regarding old age emphasised propriety of behaviour, especially in relation to interpersonal relationships. The Confucian concept of *li* (Tseng, 1973: 195), which refers to propriety or fitting conduct in the context of *ren* or 'human-heartedness',[2] was aimed at regulating ethical relations in society:

> At 70, one should be able to do anything at one's will without transgressing propriety.

Li is taken to have moral implications:

> In old age when one's powers are declining one must guard against avarice. (Lee, 1986: 89)

Two major cultural values that were commonly expressed by the Chinese respondents were: 'Harmony within oneself and with others' and 'Tolerance and moderation'. These were rooted in Confucianist and Taoist teachings. In Confucian philosophy, the 'Doctrine of the mean' endorsed moderation in behaviour and lifestyle. Our respondents expected tolerance and moderation in one's interpersonal relationships to lead to harmony:

> As long as you know how to discipline yourself and behave, you'll hardly have any conflicts with others. (Chinese respondent)

Moderation was also related to following the middle path:

> We don't go to extremes. Know what is right and what is wrong and don't go to extremes. [We have a] sense of conscience; whether we should do a thing or not. (Chinese respondent)

Were good values and ethical principles adequate for ensuring positive integration in old age? The following statement by a Chinese respondent threw light on this:

> But according to me, as long as one has principles in life, it's all right already. No need to have religion. (Chinese respondent)

In sum, the Chinese cultural script placed emphasis on leading a moral and harmonious life, practising tolerance and moderation, and remaining useful to society.

A cultural script of old age that had a moral but not religious emphasis and a concept of death and afterlife that lacked a soteriological goal (that is, it did not promise salvation) explained the practical and secular nature of personal strategies of integration. The majority of Chinese respondents were followers of Taoism or Buddhism.

Values operated as strong linkages across the personal domain, while religious beliefs played a minor role. The majority of the respondents underscored values such as diligence, self-reliance and perseverance in the face of adversity.

The Malay religious pattern

The central characteristics of the Malay integrative pattern were the religious focus and the attendant Islamic injunctions about interpersonal and social behaviour. The penetrating influence of the Quran was apparent in the lives of Malay older people, nearly all of whom were Muslims.

Almost all of the Malay respondents prayed five times a day and their daily routine was organised around this religious behaviour. Common activities in which they were engaged included attending Islamic religious classes and Quran recitals, and listening to religious talks on the radio. To quote a respondent:

> We have to be more religious because we are entering death [nearing death]. (Malay respondent)

Participation in religious activities, as contrasted to the secular activities of the Chinese, characterised Malay older people. Old age was interpreted within the Malay culture as a time to achieve atonement for past sins. An 'other-worldly' orientation and a concept of death and the afterlife that had a soteriological goal explained the religious emphasis in the Malay integrative pattern. The respondents assigned their hardships in old age to the will of Allah. The following quotation illustrates the importance of the afterlife:

> Our life on earth is only temporary; our life after death is permanent.
> (Malay respondent)

While good social behaviour is encouraged in all religions, in the Malay Muslim culture it is a clear injunction. According to the Malay respondents, the character of a Malay Muslim was judged by their behaviour, not only in religious but also in social respects.

The Malay culture stresses old age as a time to reflect on one's past life and achieve progress in religious knowledge. Religious activity was the primary focus of all but one Malay Muslim in the sample. This atypical Malay woman was an interesting contrast to the rest. She described her childhood as being different from those of other Malay children because, instead of living in a 'kampong' or Malay village, she had lived in the neighbourhood of European or Chinese families. This was because her father worked as a chauffeur and, in those days, the driver's family lived in the back portion of the employer's house. She did not attend religious school, as most Malay children did, because they lived too far away and therefore it was not feasible. Religion did not feature as an important facet of her adult life either, so in old age, although she espoused traditions of the Malay culture, religion had a relatively peripheral role in her life.

A significant aspect of Malay Muslim cultural expectations of older people was the behavioural dimension. This was a theme that emerged in all of the Malay transcripts and it was supported by the Malay literature available (Tham, 1979; Li, 1989). The following quotations from Malay respondents reflect the cultural definition of behaviour expected of older people.

> When you are old you have to change. You have to do good deeds as examples for the young people to follow. If not they will not respect you. When we are old, we do things the old people's way.

> The first action would be the way you [ie as an older person] talk. If an old man talks he should not hurt other people's feelings. Even if people were to do something wrong, he should call them, advise them, speak to them nicely. But don't hurt them ... He should not bother young ladies. That is the action of young boys.

What needs to be emphasised at this juncture is that the cultural prescription of religiosity among Malays had a social corollary that was equally important. The Malay concepts *ihsan* and *maruah* succinctly explain this. The former refers to the practice of sincere and benevolent conduct as specified in the Quran, and the latter refers to the avoidance of bad or evil acts that would lead to the loss of self-respect. To summarise, the Malay cultural script stressed adherence to the Islamic religion and placed high value on good, helpful behaviour in the daily context within family and community.

The Indian spiritual pattern

The major characteristics of the Indian pattern were its spiritual, individualistic and philosophical dimensions. Since the majority of the Indian respondents were either Hindus or Sikhs, their beliefs in the concepts of reincarnation and *karma* (the principle of cause and effect) coloured their interpretation of death and the afterlife. The centrality of the concept of *atman* (soul) as the immortal link between lifetimes as well as within a lifetime explained the spiritual focus.

In the Indian context, the four stages of the life cycle (*asramas*) according to Hindu philosophy had a salient bearing on the experience of old age.[3] In the fourth stage, old age, or *sanyasa,* there was a strong emphasis on spiritual pursuits and a gradual decrease of worldly involvement. Old age was defined as a time of *araam* (rest) and indulgence in the care to be provided by one's children and children-in-law (Vatuk, 1980: 126-48).

Interviewer:	Are you satisfied with your present circumstances?
Indian respondent:	Yes, I am. They [children] tell me to lead a life of *araam*. All my life I've worked very hard. Now I can get rest but I like to help people out. I get exercise and the other person is assisted.

This cultural formula was followed by most of the Indian older people interviewed, regardless of religious affiliation. Some older people, both male and female, who continued to perform their family roles – for example, taking care of grandchildren – combined religious prayers and these responsibilities.

The emphasis on the journey of the soul through births and rebirths until spiritual realisation takes place explained respondents' focus on their individual progress. Among Indians, in accordance with their goal of inner spiritual realisation and their belief in the law of karma, their journey in old age was an individual one. Although communal religious gatherings were attended, the emphasis seemed to be on a personal search for spiritual truths. This contrasted with the importance placed on social relationships, which had strong normative connotations for the Chinese community and religious connotations for the Malay community. To recapitulate, Indian cultural conventions stressed personal religiosity, the goal of spiritual realisation and withdrawal from worldly concerns.

An 'other-worldly' orientation, which stemmed from the concept of reincarnation and a cultural script that highlighted old age as a time for spiritual/religious pursuits, characterised the Indian pattern. The main linkages were religious beliefs and, to a lesser extent, values such as endurance, peace and the importance of the family.

The Indian transcripts had an abundant supply of literary quotations, proverbs, poems and common sayings ranging over a wide array of topics such as life, death, the purpose of human existence and truth – for example, 'Life is unreal, death is the only real truth.' Typically, the Indian respondents had a high tendency to philosophise. Many upheld the belief that it was the body that aged, but not the soul (Tilak, 1989). Since it was the salvation of the soul that was of ultimate importance, physical ageing was treated as inconsequential. An Indian respondent stated:

> Death is only the death of this body, this vehicle or boat. Not the soul because the soul is eternal. The *atman* [soul] is the only truth in this world … I don't worry about my health.

Other Indian respondents said:

> Age comes to the body, there is no difference to the soul.

> Only your good deeds will follow you after death, not your bungalow, car or money.

There prevailed a cultural emphasis on treating old age as the final opportunity to gain spiritual progress, since worldly or material responsibilities were now diminished.

The essence of Indian acceptance and understanding of death as a transition was captured by the following words uttered after a person had died:

> *Pura ho gaya* – meaning that 'He is complete'; that is, his soul has joined the supersoul.

In these terms, if a person has made sufficient spiritual progress in his human life he may be released from the cycle of birth and death, otherwise his soul will assume another form and return to earth. As we have seen, in the Malay and Indian cultures, religious preparation for the afterlife provided the spiritual dimension to personal integration before death.

Religious and spiritual beliefs, principles or concepts served an important function in linkages of the past, present and future for individuals. Major world religions contain notions of the afterlife, the preparation for which preoccupied human beings in old age, especially in advanced senescence. Religious beliefs thus differed from values in their integrative function in terms of their capacity to forge the subjective integrative process of the older person into his or her future temporal dimension.

Generally speaking, the Malay and Indian patterns had more similarities when contrasted with the Chinese pattern. In trying to understand the role of religion as a way of preserving the self in old age (Tobin, 1991: 119-35), the concepts of extrinsic and intrinsic religiousness are helpful (Thomas and Eisenhandler, 1994: 5). In the Chinese culture, although religion was considered important, its extrinsic function in people's lives explained its peripheral role in the integrative process as compared to the Malay and Indian cultures where religion had an intrinsic function (Mehta, 1997). It is worth noting here that, although the transcendental focus prevailed in the Malay and Indian patterns, the former was tailored along doctrinal lines while the latter was defined by broader philosophical and existential characteristics.

The three patterns described here emerged clearly from the interview material and were strongly supported by the focus group and secondary data. Confirming the predominance of these patterns was the fact that they persisted, with minor modifications, across gender as well as different economic, health and educational levels. A caveat to add is that, although these patterns apply to the Singaporean context, they might not apply to similar cultural or religious groups in other parts of the world. While some cultural characteristics have their echoes in communities scattered across the globe, the societal context in which they exist impacts on their manifestations. Cross-cultural research on similar ethnic communities in other nations would enlighten scholars on relevant similarities and differences in a variety of cultural settings.

Community integration

One of the major findings of the author's research was that, in Singapore, increasing age did *not* lead to the marginalisation of the oldest older people. A main contributory factor for this was the active web of ethnic community bonds to which the majority of this cohort of very old people was still connected. The ethnic construction of community ties was their way of dealing with the problem of diminishing social relationships.

Kin or relatives were subjectively perceived by the oldest of the older people to be the closest social circle, in terms of support, after the immediate family. There are several deep implications of this perception, especially in the area of long-term care. The negative attitude of the older Singapore population towards institutional care when they were frail, which has been documented in the past (Chen and Cheung, 1988; Mehta et al, 1995), stems largely from this perception. However, during in-depth interviews, some respondents remarked that, for the destitute, institutional care was necessary.

Why was the process of establishing and sustaining social links in the community significant from the point of view of the oldest older people? The following quotations from Chinese respondents offer insights:

When we mix around, our brains get polished.

If you are active, you feel happy, peaceful, not dull.

Socialising helps open–mindedness. (Mehta, 1994, pp 226)

Peers, especially relatives and friends, provided a positive social context in which the older person often constructed and reconstructed his or her life review process (Sherman, 1991). It was also conducive to sharing feelings about the person's present situation and future concerns, such as death and the afterlife. This process of reviewing the past and anticipating the future played a crucial part in the psychological integration of very old people. But, while researchers in the past have emphasised the life review, this study has shown that, for those at the very old phase, anticipation of the afterlife (for believers) was just as important. The appropriate social context was needed for such a psychological process to flourish, hence the importance of social integration.

There were differences as well as commonalities across the ethnic manifestations of community integration. These commonalities arose for two main reasons. First, all of the three ethnic cultures were Asian. Second, the external forces in the wider society tended to have a 'levelling' effect on the ethnic groups; this included, for example, the process of urbanisation.

Commonalities across ethnic lines

Some of the relevant commonalities can be summarised at this point. Kinship ties were perceived by the oldest respondents to be significant within the social network. Cross-cultural studies of the self have marked the greater importance of kin within Asian cultures as compared to western ones (Marsella et al, 1985). The majority of organisations that the oldest people had joined were ethnic based. This might, of course, reflect the particular cohort that was studied and might not be replicated in future cohorts. Friendship bonds were structured along *ethnic* and *gender* lines in most cases. My findings differ from Rosow's (1963) who found that, among American older people, the probability of their social integration was significantly affected by the availability of age peers of similar social status in the neighbourhood. In this study, it was the availability of people with similar ethnic background and gender that affected the respondents' social integration in their neighbourhoods. However, there were some inter-ethnic friendships, particularly within certain contexts, such as relationships formed during the Second World War, at the workplace and in poor neighbourhoods where the common bond of poverty overshadowed ethnic differences.

Assisting voluntarily in arrangements at funerals, and advising family members on religious rites and rituals were functions that older people were often involved in among all three ethnic groups. And a favourite venue that cut across ethnic boundaries was the 'void deck', that is the ground floor of government public housing flats (known as Housing and Development Board or HDB flats). Here was a neutral meeting place that was convenient, protected from rain and belonged to everyone (it was a public space). With tables and stools provided by the government, the venue was felt by older people to be a good way to achieve a change in environment from their homes.

Involvement in formal organisations, ethnic, religious or secular, was noted to be a function of earlier membership. It was apparent from the interview and focus group material that earlier involvement in organised community activities prompted older people to continue contributing as far as they could even in very old age. Another factor that facilitated frequent contact with organisations was whether or not the individuals lived sufficiently close to the buildings concerned.

The data revealed that there was a positive correlation between how long a person had lived in the neighbourhood and the extensiveness of his or her informal social networks. Frequent residential mobility, whether voluntary or involuntary, militated against the development of neighbourhood bonds. On the other hand, integration within one's ethnic group was less dependent on biographical or geographical variables. Common meeting grounds such as religious or sub-ethnic institutions, family occasions such as weddings and ethnic shopping areas like Little India all facilitated social contact.

Differences between ethnic groups

There were, of course, also a variety of different cultural practices among our respondents. First, they belonged to different ethnic organisations according to their ethnic identities. In addition, Chinese older people were particularly interested in health-related activities; therefore many of them were involved in *tai qi* and *qi gong* exercise groups. For male older people, meeting at 'coffee shops' with close friends and chatting for hours was a favourite pastime. For females, it was the 'wet market' where fresh vegetables and meat were sold, and the children's playgrounds where grandmothers brought their grandchildren for recreation.

Links with formal organisations such as senior citizens' clubs were more common among Chinese than among Indian and Malay communities. Factors such as language barriers, types of activities and timing of activities affected the participation of the minority ethnic groups. The replacement of 'village natural social support systems' by new social organisations was clearly seen in the Malay community. Our respondents were members of 'block associations', a 'dying aid society' and *senoman* (often known as 'kitty groups', where females meet monthly to make a collection and each time one member withdraws a fixed sum).

The communal activities of the Indian and Malay communities tended to have a stronger religious focus than those of the Chinese community. Religious activities included reciting religious verses, chanting religious songs (*satsang* for the Indian community), advising on preparations for religious festivals, volunteering to serve food to the community (*seva*) and listening to religious lectures.

For the Indian respondents, communal ties with relatives and friends in the homeland – that is, India, or Sri Lanka or Pakistan – were preserved with regular visits. Emotional and sentimental ties are reflected in words such as, 'I was born and brought up there'. Helping the poor and making pilgrimages to temples in India were other reasons for trips back home.

Conclusion: spirituality, religious involvement and personal meaning

This research in a multicultural and multi-religious society, Singapore, has illustrated the significance of spirituality and religious involvement for meaningful processes of personal and community integration for its inhabitants. But the authors' inter-ethnic comparisons have indicated that there were differences as well as similarities across ethnic groups in the way the spiritual 'thread' is woven into the lives of older people. Another important point that emerges from looking at the life stories is that earlier involvement in spiritual and/or religious pursuits is a frequent antecedent to late-life patterns.

Examining the patterns of community integration highlighted that, when the physical environment changes, community integrative processes and forms go through permutations; new forms emerge to fulfil the same human needs for social bonding and mutual help. Finally, auspicious occasions offer opportunities for older people to display and transmit their talents and cultural knowledge, thus enabling them to remain in the midst of their communities.

For frail and less mobile older people, options for socialisation and travelling to their place of worship as well as pilgrimages are very limited. They compensate to some extent by watching television shows and videos of these places. Frequent telephone conversations with their frail peers gave them some sense of company, albeit not as satisfying as meeting other people in person. Some respondents voiced their sense of helplessness as a result of ill health; however, they were thankful that voluntary welfare organisations were helping them to cope. When their life circumstances and material conditions seemed bleak, many older persons could look to the richness of their values and cultural norms for strength and courage.

Notes

[1] The researchers used a non-probability purposive sample since the research was intended to be illustrative and not representative, and each respondent was interviewed at least twice. A total of 105 interviews were conducted. Each interview was tape-recorded, with the respondent's consent, and transcribed

verbatim. Interviews that were conducted in a non-English language or dialect were translated and then transcribed into English.

[2] *Li* is based on Confucius' view that, though *ren* is the basic guide to human action, people also need 'more immediate and concrete guides' for everyday life; these can be found in rules of propriety governing customs and relationships 'established by human practice over the ages': 'the ceremonial or practical means by which the potential of humanity (*ren*) is realized' (Koller, 2007: 221).

[3] According to the Hindu scriptures, the life cycle is divided into four phases called *asramas*. These are *brahmacharya* (student), *garhastya* (householder), *vanaprasta* (late middle age withdrawal from worldly activities) and *sanyasa* (old age – the period of renunciation). For further reading see Unni and Paran (1988).

References

Census of Population (2001) *Release No 4*, Singapore: Department of Statistics.

Chen, A.J. and Cheung, P.L. (1988) *The elderly in Singapore. Singapore country report. Phase 3 ASEAN Population Project: Socio-economic consequences of the ageing of the Population*, Singapore: Ministry of Health.

Coleman, P. (1990) 'Adjustment in later life', in J. Bond and P. Coleman (eds) *Aging in society: An introduction to social gerontology*, London: SAGE, pp 89-122.

Erikson, E.H. (1963) *Childhood and society* (2nd edn), New York: W.W. Norton.

Inter-Ministerial Committee on the Ageing Population (1999) *Report of the Inter-Ministerial Committee on the Ageing Population*, Singapore: Ministry of Community Development.

Kaufman, S.R. (1986) *The ageless self: Sources of meaning in later life*, Madison, WI: University of Wisconsin Press.

Koller, J. (2007) *Asian philosophies*, Upper Saddle River, NJ: Pearson Prentice Hall.

Lee, S.M. (1986) *Spectrum of Chinese culture*, Petaling Jaya, Malaysia: Pelanduk.

Li, T. (1989) *Malays in Singapore: Culture, economy and ideology*, Singapore: Oxford University Press.

Marsella, A.J., Devos, G. and Hsu, F.L.K. (1985) *Culture and self: Culture and Asian perspectives*, New York: Tavistock.

Mehta, K.K. (1994) 'The dynamics of adjustment of the very old in Singapore', Unpublished Ph.D. thesis, Department of Social Work and Psychology, National University of Singapore.

Mehta, K. (1997) 'The impact of religious beliefs and practices on aging: a cross-cultural comparison', *Journal of Aging Studies*, vol 11, no 2, pp 101-14.

Mehta, K., Osman, M.M. and Lee, A.E.Y. (1995) 'Living arrangements of the elderly in Singapore: cultural norms in transition', *Journal of Cross-Cultural Gerontology*, vol 10, nos 1 and 2, pp 113-43.

Moberg, D.O. (2001) 'The reality and centrality of spirituality', in D.O. Moberg *Aging and spirituality: Spiritual dimensions of aging theory, research, practice and policy,* New York: Haworth Press, pp 3-20.

Reker, G.T. and Wong, P.T.P. (1988) 'Aging as an individual process: toward a theory of personal meaning', in J.E. Birren and V.L. Bengston (eds) *Emergent theories of aging,* New York: Springer, pp 214-43.

Rosow, I. (1963) 'Adjustment of the normal aged', in W.R. Tibbits and W. Donahue (eds) *Processes of aging,* vol 2, New York: Atherton, pp 195-222.

Sherman, E. (1991) *Reminiscence and the self in old age,* New York: Springer.

Tham, S.C. (1979) 'Social change and the Malay family', in C.Y. Kuo and A. Wong (eds) *The contemporary family in Singapore,* Singapore: Singapore University Press, pp 88-114).

Thomas, L.E. and Eisenhandler, S.A. (1994) *Aging and the religious dimension,* Westport, CT: Auburn House.

Tilak, S. (1989) *Religion and aging in the Indian tradition,* Albany, NY: State University of New York Press.

Tobin, S.S. (1991) *Personhood in advanced old age,* New York: Springer.

Tornstram, L. (1997) 'Gerotranscendence: the contemplative dimension of aging', *Journal of Aging Studies,* vol 11, no 2, pp 143-54.

Tseng, W.S. (1973) 'The concept of personality in Confucian thought', *Psychiatry,* vol 36, pp 191-202.

Unni, P.N. and Paran, T.P. (1988) *Understanding Hinduism,* Singapore: Stamford Press.

Vatuk, S. (1980) 'Withdrawl and disengagement as a cultural response to ageing in India', in C.L. Fry (ed) *Ageing in culture and society: Comparative viewpoints and strategies,* New York: Bergin.

THREE

Integrating the sacred in creative ageing

Michele Dillon

Seeking some insights into the ways Americans in later life currently make sense of their lives and the process of living them, this chapter reports on a longitudinal study of 184 Californians born in the 1920s whose participants are now enjoying a relatively comfortable older age. It argues that later life is not necessarily fraught with anxiety; neither is it necessarily religious. Nonetheless, the participants in the study do inhabit a social context whose values have been associated with religion, and the majority are still associated with religious practices and communities. Among these, it is possible broadly to distinguish people who actively grapple with meaning-related issues in their lives – the 'spiritual seekers' – from those whose involvement is more organisationally oriented. Confronting problematic experiences is, or has been, important for the former group in particular, but our evidence does not suggest that creatively constructing a meaningful life is associated with traumatic phases of the life course in particular. The hope of the chapter is to take us further into a set of diverse approaches to this meaning-creating process.

There is a long-standing tendency in social science to pathologise life transitions. This view sees changes in the life course as threatening to the self, placing the individual at risk and in need of some kind of expert intervention. It has been argued, for example, that middle age is a time of personal crisis (Levinson, 1978), that menopause shatters a woman's sense of femininity (Deutsch, 1945) and that the empty nest threatens the stability of marriage (Bart, 1971). All of these predictions, however, have been shown to be untrue (see Wink, 2007). Only a small percentage of individuals experience a midlife crisis (Wethington et al, 2004), menopausal symptoms do not tend to have a detrimental effect on women's well-being (Rossi, 2004) and, contrary to the empty nest hypothesis, marital satisfaction tends to improve rather than decline once parents no longer have to deal with the stress of having adolescent children at home (Helson and Wink, 1992).

The transition to old age has been similarly depicted as a time of crisis. Even Erik Erikson (1963), who assumed that the transitions to early and middle adulthood proceeded smoothly, took a different view of late adulthood. Indicative of the expectation of crisis that social scientists impute to late adulthood, it is the only phase in Erikson's developmental model that requires the individual to make an active effort to preserve psychological health and to ward off negative feelings that threaten to destabilise the person's sense of integrity and wholeness. For

Erikson, what differentiates old age from the identity tasks of early and middle adulthood is the threat posed by impending mortality and the finality of life. As a stage in the life course, late adulthood confronts the individual with a decline in social roles, the increased imminence of the approach of death and the dawning of the realisation that any regrets about lost opportunities, misdeeds and fractured relationships cannot be mitigated.

Erikson's view of older adulthood as a time of threat to the individual's self-integrity has been highly influential among gerontologists. The concept of 'life review', for example, the need for older-age individuals to review and make peace with their past in order that they can come to terms with the finality of life, was widely popularised by Robert Butler (1963), the first director of the US National Institute of Ageing. And, today, the idea that old age confronts the individual with psychological dangers is implicitly reflected in the widely used concept of 'successful ageing'. This phrasing suggests that some older-age individuals manage to age successfully while others do not. The fact that the term 'successful' has not been applied to any other stage of the life course is indicative of the assumption that old age brings with it special challenges not encountered in adolescence or in early and middle adulthood. These challenges threaten individuals with failure – the lack of success – unless they undertake some remedial work to attenuate the impending crisis.

It is not surprising that the received wisdom on ageing as a time of crisis promotes the idea that religion plays a central role in the process of successful ageing (Rowe and Kahn, 1998). If, indeed, late adulthood is a time of increased social isolation and threat, then it may well be that religion would provide an important source of personal meaning and social support for older-age individuals. Religious belief offers consolation and the hopes of redemption and of life after death. Additionally, church participation provides the individual with a community of like-minded individuals who can offer each other social and emotional support.

But does religion in fact promote successful ageing? Despite the intuitive sense that religion should make a difference, the evidence in support of a positive relation between religiousness and psychological health in late adulthood is mixed and far from overwhelming. On the one hand, meta-analytic reviews of the existing literature provide compelling evidence that religious individuals tend to stay healthier and to live longer than non-religious individuals (eg Koenig et al, 2001). And the evidence suggests that the effect of religiousness on health and mortality cannot simply be accounted for by the fact that religious individuals have better health-related habits – that they, for example, consume less alcohol, or smoke less, or engage less in other risky behaviours. On the other hand, although numerous studies find that religious individuals tend to be less depressed than non-religious individuals, the size of the statistical effect is small (McCullough and Smith, 2003). Similarly, the evidence suggesting that religiosity suppresses an individual's fear of death is tenuous at best (Fortner and Neimeyer, 1999). And, contrary to the view that old age ushers in an existential crisis, fear of death tends to decline rather than increase with age (see Tomer, 2000).

The mixed role of religion in buffering individuals in older adulthood might well stem from the possibility that old age may not be as threatening to the self as assumed by some scholars. An alternative perspective on older adulthood and life in the post-retirement period is offered by the British demographer Peter Laslett (1991). He noted that the accumulation of wealth and the increase in life expectancy throughout the industrialised world in the 20th century has resulted in a large number of individuals surviving into old age in relatively good health and with adequate disposable income. He argues that these 'third agers', far from being threatened by social disengagement and impending mortality, are in a unique position to enjoy the freedoms that come with the post-retirement years.

A growing body of research supports Laslett's conclusion that the transition into the post-retirement period, like any other expected life course change, does not necessarily result in depression, anomie and a decline in life satisfaction. To the contrary, in the US, for example, the majority of individuals in their late 60s and 70s appear to relish the freedom of the post-retirement period and lead active, purposeful lives travelling, volunteering and pursuing various hobbies and interests (eg Midanik et al, 1995; Weiss and Bass, 2002; James and Wink, 2007). We found a similar pattern in our longitudinal research with two cohorts of Californian men and women who were born in the 1920s. Over half of the study participants came from middle-class families and over a third from working-class families, and the participants themselves went on to attain higher levels of educational and occupational attainment than other Americans of their generation (Eichorn et al, 1981: 412). Though there continued to be socioeconomic variation among our study participants, their comparative socioeconomic advantage continued throughout their lives; in late adulthood, most of the participants were economically secure, in good health and enjoying highly satisfying lives.

Socio-demographic characteristics and living circumstances in late adulthood

This chapter uses longitudinal data from the renowned Berkeley Guidance and Oakland Growth studies established by researchers at the Institute of Human Development (IHD) at the University of California, Berkeley, in the 1920s. The participants were studied intensively in childhood and adolescence, using a range of standardised interview, observation and self-report methods until they graduated from high school (the older cohort was born in 1920-21 and the younger cohort was born in 1928-29). The participants were first interviewed in adulthood in 1958 (aged in their 30s) and were interviewed subsequently in 1970 (aged in their 40s), 1982 (aged in their 50s and early 60s) and 1997-2000 (aged in their late 60s and 70s). At each adulthood assessment, the participants were interviewed in depth about all major aspects of their lives and they also completed lengthy structured questionnaires. The study therefore has an enormous amount of data across multiple decades and encompassing a wide range of social and psychological topics. Today the IHD study is comprised of close to 200 women and men who have been intimately tracked through in-depth personal interviews across their entire lives, from early adolescence through late adulthood (age 70s). Our research using statistical, qualitative-thematic and individual case study data from the IHD study is published in Dillon and Wink (2007).

This chapter is based on results of our interviews with 184 individuals in late adulthood, one third of whom were born in the early 1920s (36%) and two thirds in the late 1920s (64%). At the time of our interviews (between 1997 and 2000), the older participants were approximately 77 years old (on average) and the younger participants were 69.[1] Born in Oakland or Berkeley, in late adulthood, most still resided in Northern (69%) or Southern (12%) California, or in a western or south-western state (12%).

As in the original sample, the social-class origins of the participants interviewed in late adulthood were relatively evenly distributed, with just over one third coming from upper-class professional or executive families (36%). Another one third were of middle-class origins (32%) and the remaining one third (31%) came from working-class backgrounds. Almost half (47%) were college graduates and, in social status, over half of the participants (or their spouses) were upper-middle-class professionals or executives, a fifth were lower middle class and another fifth were working class.

Though all of our study participants were over the traditional retirement age of 65, a quarter of them (26%), irrespective of cohort, were still working for pay, mostly part-time, and this was also true of a similar proportion of spouses (22%). Most of the participants were economically well off. Over two thirds (69%) had an annual household income of over $40,000, a figure that is substantially higher than that for same-age married households nationwide, with 17% reporting an income exceeding $100,000. Further indicative of the high level of economic security enjoyed by the sample as a whole despite their income variation, a remarkable 90% said that they were not financially constricted from doing any of the activities they wanted to do.[2]

The study participants' living circumstances in late adulthood were impressively good and conducive to positive everyday functioning. Very few had remained single (4%); most were still married (70%), some were divorced (9%) and quite a few were widowed (17%). Seventy-one per cent (85% of men and 55% of women) were living with their spouse or a partner, figures that parallel the census data for same-age Americans.[3] Among those who were married, a majority (55%) said they were exceptionally happy and that their marriage fulfilled most of their expectations, and a further third (33%) described their marriage as a good one. Men, irrespective of cohort, reported being more satisfied with marriage than women.[4] The modal number of children per participant was three and the modal number of grandchildren was five. Most of the study participants reported feeling close to their children and it was also apparent that they enjoyed their grandchildren's company and took pride in their activities and accomplishments.

Social scientists (eg Erikson, 1963; Bellah et al, 1991: 275-76) have long recognised the importance of purposefulness in everyday life, of living attentively in the present in order to maintain a personally meaningful and socially integrated life. The reduced number of social roles that older-age individuals confront during the post-retirement period, coupled with an increase in physical health challenges, gives added concern that late adulthood may be a time when individuals are more likely to withdraw from the hobbies and social activities that are critical to injecting meaning into life. Vital involvement in life, as so phrased by Erik Erikson (Erikson et al, 1986), is thus seen as a hallmark of positive ageing.[5]

Not surprisingly, given the constellation of positive economic and social circumstances shaping our study participants' lives in late adulthood, most of them were leading a fairly purposeful and active older adulthood.[6] Large majorities of men and women frequently read newspapers, magazines (92%) and books (66%). Many frequently engaged in some form of physical exercise such as walking, tennis, swimming or golf (55%), travelled (44%), informally visited with relatives (55%), friends and neighbours (44%), participated in community service (25%) and engaged in a range of personal hobbies (36%) including gardening, arts and crafts, and woodwork projects. A good few enrolled in adult education classes (21%), went to concerts, plays, museums, or lectures (21%), played a musical instrument (6%) or sang in a chorus (8%), and played competitive card and board games such as bridge or chess (17%), as well as playing solitary games and doing puzzles (19%).[7]

We also found that the process of life review, contrary to earlier assumptions (eg Butler, 1963; Erikson, 1963), is far from being an imperative of old age and is characteristic of only a minority of older adults (eg Coleman, 1986). Moreover, the vast majority of older-age individuals who do not review their lives do not appear to suffer any detrimental psychological consequences resulting from not doing so. Among our study participants, the majority (52%) did not engage in life review and yet at the same time were highly accepting of their past and were not in despair about the future.[8] This figure is too high to suggest that all of these individuals were in denial of their mortality or in despair as a result of not coming to terms with mortality. To the contrary, most of our study participants were very frank in expressing uncertainty about what would happen to them in the next five years, and did not hesitate in openly discussing the financial, funeral and other logistical arrangements they had made in anticipation of their own death.

Only 19% of the participants could be described as having successfully reviewed their lives. These people showed clear evidence of having used reminiscences about their past experiences to develop a new understanding of their sense of self. Our data indicated, moreover, that these individuals, mostly women, were introspective throughout adulthood, not just in old age, and were accustomed to psychologically working through personal adversity, having had conflicted family and personal life experiences earlier in adulthood (Wink and Schiff, 2002). Less than one third of the study participants were not accepting of their past. Even though some of these people had engaged in reminiscence, this psychological work did not help them come to terms with their lives. Taken as a whole, however, our data does not support the notion of late adulthood as a time of crisis nor the assumption that older adults need to make serious psychological adjustments in order to age successfully.

David Allen

David Allen is an excellent illustration of what might be considered 'purposeful' ageing. When we interviewed him at his sun-drenched home on the shore of Lake Tahoe in the summer of 1997, he was as articulate, insightful, optimistic and as energetic at age 76 as he had been during earlier interviews in his 30s, 40s and 50s. Retired from an economically successful career in which he combined high-school teaching and a mountain resort business, David continued to work part-time restoring and managing rental property. He was highly involved in local community politics and, as a committed member of the League to Save Lake Tahoe, was at the vanguard of a struggle to curb overdevelopment of the lakeshore. He was also active in the Sierra Club, a member of SIRs (Sons in Retirement), a retired men's group whose local chapter presented a monthly luncheon and speaker series. With no physical ailments or complaints, David continued to ski and hike, and he played in a weekly golf tournament with a group of mixed-age men with whom he also socialised. David and his wife made several trips to Europe, and he took much pleasure in the good relations he had with his adult children, despite earlier tensions with them surrounding his divorce from their mother in the early 1960s. He was especially generous to his grandchildren and, on the day of the interview, had just purchased a new computer for his college-bound granddaughter.

Although David was in excellent physical health and full of energy – he had played 27 holes of golf in the sweltering Nevada heat the day before our interview – he fully accepted his age: 'Well I look at [being older] as a part of the life process ... And I have no fear whatsoever of growing older and dying. I just hope that I don't deteriorate to a point where I'm a burden on myself or on anyone else.' David's contentment and high life satisfaction in late adulthood derived in large part from his pride in having raised five fine children, although, at the time of the interview, he was still grieving over the death from AIDS of his oldest son, Oliver.

David also took considerable pride in the impact he had had in shaping young lives as a history teacher. Several times during the interview he mentioned unexpected encounters with his past students and their comments, variously telling him, as one recently had, 'You know, you were one of the most important teachers in my life.' David clearly derived as much pleasure from the altruism of teaching as from the monetary rewards of a successful business career.

The vibrancy of David Allen's everyday life in his 70s is at odds with a view of late adulthood eloquently evoked in contemporary fictional literature (eg Roth, 2006). His ageing is devoid of the personal despair that is thought to accompany the onset of the realisation that one's mortality is no longer in the way-off remote future but is near. As was true for the majority of our study participants,

David's transition to late adulthood was characterised by continuity rather than change and without the tendency to dwell on past achievements, mistakes and lost opportunities. When asked whether he now reflected more about his life, David stated:

> I think occasionally I do, but it's kind of a rarity that I go back and try and dig [things] up ... I rarely reflect. I think I'm looking much more forward ... I just think you're a lot better off looking ahead and trying to plan for next year and plant a few fruit trees that 20 years from now will bear fruit.

What is also striking about David's energetic and purposeful life in late adulthood is that he was among the least religious of our study participants. Religion – whether church-based or reflecting newer forms of spiritual seeking – is, as is well documented, much more visible and vibrant in the US than in most Western European countries, with the exception of Ireland (eg Greeley, 2003). Close to two thirds of our study participants came from mainline Protestant families (eg Presbyterian, Methodist, Episcopalian), one tenth from non-mainline Protestant backgrounds (eg Mormon, Christian Science), less than a fifth came from Catholic families and fewer than one in ten came from non-religious families. In late adulthood (when they were in their late 60s and 70s), 24% of the participants were not church members and approximately another 15% did not actively identify with a denominational tradition. Thirty-four per cent were mainline and 9% were non-mainline Protestants, 16% were Catholic and 2% were Jewish.

Like the vast majority of our study participants, David Allen had been religiously involved as a youth. And, indeed, for a while in his 30s he took the lead in organising the building of a new Presbyterian church in the suburbs north of San Francisco. He wryly commented at the time (when interviewed in 1958) that, though he was active in building the church, he was not an active worshipper. Rather, he felt that religion was more of a 'wholesome social' than a spiritual experience. Church continued to be unimportant in David's life subsequently, though his religious background still informed his ethical views in late adulthood. He commented:

> I'm certainly an agnostic and probably an atheist at this point. But the religious principles that [I learned at Sunday school] still have a good deal of influence. And I think also the Boy Scout oath and all of those moral principles are still quite strong.

Nevertheless, David did not need church or spiritual engagement to anchor his life or enrich its meaning. In 1997, he summarised his view of religion, saying:

> I don't think religiously, but I might sometimes think of the Lake God as being angry today when the waters are rough or the Sun God as

particularly influential. But somehow I'm too much of an evolutionist to think of The God, whatever that is. And I think 'Is the Muslim God the same as the Christian God? The same as the Greek God?' Now I look at this a little bit and think we needed this [religion] in a primitive time but I don't think organised religion is any longer part of my thought processes.

Religiousness and spiritual seeking in ageing

Unlike David, however, many of our study participants maintained a relatively stable level of church-based religious involvement throughout their lives, notwithstanding evidence of a small intermittent decline in their levels of commitment during middle adulthood. And, coinciding with the cultural changes in the US in the late 1960s and 1970s, changes that saw a greatly expanded spiritual marketplace (Wuthnow, 1998; Roof, 1999), a minority of our study participants, then at midlife, showed clear evidence of an increase in a largely non-church-based spiritual seeking that continued through their late adulthood years.

We extensively investigated whether religiousness and spiritual seeking had an impact in shaping the everyday social and psychological functioning of our study participants in late adulthood. Our findings indicated that highly religious and/or highly spiritual individuals tended to be more involved than their non-religious and non-spiritual peers in social and community activities and everyday hobbies. We also found that church-centred religiousness, but not spiritual seeking, buffered against depression and the loss of life satisfaction during times of adversity, and against the fear of death. Spiritual seeking, on the other hand, was associated with engagement in life review. Overall, however, though statistically significant, these differential effects were small. Religiousness and spiritual seeking certainly mattered in many individuals' lives, but for many others in our study, like David Allen, a vitally involved older adulthood was not dependent on religious or spiritual engagement.

Integrating emotion and values in ageing

Independent of whether or not religiousness or spiritual seeking enhances everyday life in specific ways in late adulthood, it is nonetheless evident that these meaning systems contribute to the fabric and the texture and tone of how people age. Here, we highlight some of the key ways in which religiousness and spirituality penetrate and intertwine with the ageing process. We begin with spiritual seeking. Some of our spiritual seekers engaged primarily in Eastern meditation practices, others were committed to a nature-centred spirituality and still others found spiritual discipline and growth across a mix of church-centred and newer spiritual activities. But, though their specific practices varied, spiritual seekers in late adulthood were unified by an early church-based religious involvement, a trajectory of post-midlife spiritual growth and a personality style characterised by introspection. It is also interesting to note that our spiritual seekers tended to have experienced significant emotional turmoil, especially in their 30s. Spiritual seekers' personal crises developed in association with their experience of negative life events such as bereavement, family illness and divorce, and from conflicted family and other personal relationships. By contrast, church-centred religiousness in late adulthood was not related to antecedent negative life events. These findings underscore that spiritual – and religious – engagement does not occur in a vacuum. In addition to the maturational, life-course and cultural forces that shape individuals' spiritual and religious commitments, the person's socio-emotional context also matters. For spiritual women – and it was mostly women who were seekers – these experiences of turmoil were especially influential if they were accompanied by openness and introspection. Thus, in our study, spiritual growth was especially characteristic of women who had the psychological insight and strength to turn personal pain into a transformative spiritual experience.

The fact that spiritual development, and personal transformation in general (Stokes, 1990: 176), may be facilitated by the experience of personal trauma or hardship suggests a parallel between spiritual seeking and wisdom whose development, too, has been linked to the experience of stressful life events (eg Wink and Helson, 1997). In any case it was certainly true in our study that spiritual growth was aided by intense emotional pain and the ability to positively learn from and integrate that pain. Our data thus gives flesh to Schopenhauer's (1788-1860) insight:

> For man to acquire noble sentiments ... for the *better consciousness* to be active within him, pain, suffering and failure are as necessary to him as weighty ballast is to a ship, which attains no draught without it. (Safranski, 1990: 198, emphasis in original)

Or, in the more prosaic wisdom of the Chinese proverb, 'A smooth sea never made a skilful mariner.' Obviously, we are not implying that the church-based religiously involved individuals in our study were incapable of noble sentiment. Our findings suggested, rather, that there are different paths to religious engagement in old age. In the case of spiritual seekers, this process takes the form of a 'hero's journey' that involves active confrontation with one's inner 'demons' and that results in dramatic change (see Campbell, 1990). In contrast, for church-centred individuals, a sustained religious commitment is less reliant on open struggle with personal adversity and the experience of emotional turmoil and pain.

Kate Ward

Several aspects of Kate Ward's personality and life story illuminate the emotional pain, independence and insight that frequently accompany the development of spiritual growth. She also exemplifies the compatibility between church-based religiousness and engagement in spiritual seeking beyond church. Kate was one of the few women in our study who never married and who had no children. Born in 1929, the youngest of three siblings, she grew up in a high-status family in which intellectual and community activities were emphasised. Kate was a popular girl, vibrant and smart yet easy-going and with a good sense of humour; she was actively involved in sports and was a leader in classroom and school activities. Although her parents were not churchgoers, they sent Kate to the Episcopal Sunday school. In adolescence, Kate told her interviewer that she liked the way the pastor 'boils down the sermon so you can understand it' and, like many of her peers, she enjoyed the church's social activities. But, at 16, Kate had stopped attending church. She explained then:

> I've been pondering over what I believe this year and can't quite take the bible and the sermons. I'm not an atheist but I'm not a believer. I can't decide if I am religious. I believe in the spirit of religion but I can't believe in the detail.

Kate certainly had the introspection that characterised the spiritual seekers in our study. Talking about herself at age 16, she stated that, although she was a 'good sport' and adaptable and non-rebellious in social situations, 'In an argument, I'm apt to take a stand on the opposite side but I always know what I think. No one makes up my mind for me. I'm honest with myself.' Similarly, the psychologist who interviewed Kate at this time described her as 'honest [and] full of surprising insights about herself and others'.

After high school, Kate went to a prestigious college in the North East, majored in social science and began a career in public administration. But, in early adulthood (1958), she felt that her life was at a 'depressed impasse', she was not living up to her potential and she was grieving over the sudden death of the one man with whom she had had a meaningful relationship. She spoke of her longing to be married to a man who 'is strong, competent, and intellectually interesting; who would not only permit but who would expect me to be a person in my own right'. Kate went into psychotherapy in her early 30s for three years mostly 'as an existential thing' and also because she felt helpless and had suicidal thoughts. Psychotherapy, by her own account in 1970, did not make her lose her hang-ups, but it 'completely changed [her] whole life direction'; made her more aware of her strengths and weaknesses, and helped her 'find a way to grow and develop'.

Kate was working at an interdenominational, church-based teenage social action programme in Philadelphia and had chosen to live in the integrated inner-city neighbourhood in which she worked, though there was 'constant theft'. Her interest in social problems extended beyond the inner city to include a broader critique of how society in general was organised. Explicitly articulating the anti-institutionalism that national opinion polls were beginning to document in the late 1960s, she was especially critical of institutions – 'universities, churches, hospitals', stating, 'I think they're all bad, all need to be changed'. But, despite her constant readiness to engage in institutional critique, Kate was passionately involved in their everyday work. She continued, for example, to be an active member of the Episcopalian church – highlighting our study's general finding that religious involvement in early adulthood (age 30s, 1958), was a significant predictor of late adulthood spiritual seeking.

Kate was uncertain, however, whether she believed in God, though at the same time expressed awareness and appreciation of a divine presence:

> I don't know what to say – I think God is a wretched term – and I just don't know. I believe perhaps in something, some kind of power or force. I don't know whether it really exists or whether it's just, you know, I can rationalise it and say, 'Well man just needs to have that there – so that's why we have it'. But, in times of stress and trouble, it kind of makes sense. And it's helpful … It's very comforting to think that there's something else. I think religion, it doesn't matter what religion it is, gives depth and a way of life and meaning to life that life in and of itself simply does not have.

At midlife (age 49, 1970), Kate held out the possibility that she might still marry and have children, but she primarily talked about the future in terms of her commitment to self-growth:

> I would almost do anything to allow myself options to grow and to develop and to do different kinds of work and not to be into one thing … I don't ever want to get locked into one thing … I just really want to be able to have the opportunity to keep options open.

Twelve years later (1982), Kate was co-owner and manager of group houses for troubled teenagers. Her spare time was taken up with her spiritual development: 'Spiritual discovery and development and growth has been very influential in determining my sense of self,' she said and she talked at length about the many domains of her life in which she experienced personal growth and a coming to terms with who she was.

Although Kate already showed signs of spiritual seeking in adolescence and during her early adulthood existential crisis, she – like others in our study – experienced the most spiritual growth from her early 40s onward. On returning to California in the mid-1970s – right during the blossoming of the new religious consciousness (Glock and Bellah, 1976), Kate 'felt the spiritual nudging again'. She first got involved with a group of Catholic Charismatics until she found a progressive Episcopal church – 'So now that is where I am and that's my sort of home' – a spiritual home that also provided her with much social and emotional support. She was also a member at that time of a 'house church' comprised of 12 adults who met weekly for spiritual sharing and discussion.

Kate referred to the flowering of her long-term spiritual quest using language most usually associated with evangelical conversion (a vocabulary that was becoming increasingly accessible as a result of the evangelical resurgence in American society in the late 1970s/early 1980s). She explained: 'What happened was that, in quotes, I was "born again". I can't think of any better way to put it than that.' The catalyst for this experience was an episode of physical and emotional exhaustion brought on by intense work-related pressures. During this time Kate gradually realised that she needed to surrender to God rather than control everything herself. She explained:

> I've never been a true believer [in anything]. Let's put it that way. I've had a lot of interests and a lot of enthusiasm in everything I've done ... Unfortunately now I'm a true believer [laughs] ... It's a constant struggle. Constantly you're giving up. You have to, every day you have to give up. It's a real struggle. It's a constant giving up of yourself ... You cannot get away with being sloppy.

On retirement, spiritual seeking continued to be a dominant force in Kate's life. She was involved in a couple of different non-church-based women's spiritual groups and was also, as she said, feeding her soul through a lot of church activity: attending the Episcopal Church almost weekly and highly involved in the United Church of Christ – going to weekly services, participating in a morning spirituality discussion group and involved in the church's retreat planning committee. When asked about what kept her going in times of trouble, Kate referred to a practical attitude, 'It can't stay this bad all the time,' and her strong faith. She explained:

> I have a belief, a faith, I'm not quite sure what the correct word would be, in a universal spirit that's connected to human spirit. And that, if you just are plugged into that, you get renewed. And you receive guidance and you keep going.

One of the ways in which Kate was renewed by her belief in a universal spirit was through her extensive reading and meditating on the complex connections between nature, science and spirituality, and the search for a meaningful cosmic order.

Despite the centrality of religion in Kate's life, she was hesitant to describe herself as religious, preferring to say she was spiritual. Echoing remarks she had made 40 years earlier, she explained:

> The word religion is a really, really wretched term. And I look upon it really negatively now. It's a system of beliefs. And, even though I'm a churchgoer, I'm totally unorthodox in any Christian beliefs. I take the good things, you know. I don't believe in original sin or in any particular theology. But there are many good things to be exemplified and utilised in Christianity ... And I feel the same way about Buddhism. I think that there are many tenets of Buddhism that I find to be

really excellent dictums by which to live. And their whole concept of meaningfulness, I think is great. I think that that's a good way to be and to live and to strive for. But religions, per se, I think have given us as much trouble as they have given us good ... And so I make the distinction there. And I would say I am very much so a spiritual person. I think that that's something that's growing in me.

Thus, while Kate was critical of religion's association with violence and coercion, she, unlike a small number of participants in our study who were similarly critical of organised religion, spent much of her adult life nurturing a spirituality that derived from both church and non-church activities. Through her diverse religious and spiritual activities, Kate conveys how individuals can be highly active spiritual seekers as well as being highly committed, though selectively so, to institutionalised religion. The compatibility between religiousness and spiritual seeking shown in Kate's life thus illuminates Ann Patrick's (1999) evocative simile of religiousness and spirituality as two rivers with shared tributaries that can unite and flow together.

Life course change in the meanings of religiousness

Although, as noted, our study found much evidence of continuity in individuals' levels of church-centred religiousness across the life course, the personal meaning of religiousness can change for individuals as they age. Among American scholars of religion, James Fowler (1981), for example, argues that, as people age, their faith becomes less concretistic and more contemplative, personal yet universalising in scope, and accepting of the contradictions and paradoxes of everyday life. Fowler's view of age-related changes in religiousness reflects the ideas of a growing number of psychologists who argue for distinct stages of cognitive development in adulthood. Therefore, though the ability to understand the basic principles of scientific reasoning develops in late adolescence, post-Piagetian theorists argue that, as a result of the need to experience varied life experiences, it is not until middle adulthood that adults acquire the ability to truly embrace the paradoxical nature of the universe and the relativism and uncertainty of human knowledge.[9]

The idea of age-related changes in apprehending the complexities of life is quite compelling and, by extension, the idea too of age-related change in the personal meaning of religion. Fowler has been criticised, however, for not testing his model with longitudinal data and, especially, for not including data from older adults in the original study in which he outlined his thesis (McFadden, 1999). Another source of concern is that Fowler's definition of faith is so expansive that it incorporates both religious and non-religious attitudes in a way that makes it hard to empirically investigate his model.

The question of whether late adulthood religion takes on a distinctive character has also engaged Lars Tornstam (1999). He argues that the cumulative life experience of ageing pushes individuals toward a shift in meta-perspective, that is, in how they view the world. This process, Tornstam maintains, brings about less concern with materialism and rationality, and an increase in intergenerational spiritual connection, wisdom and meditation, changes that are indicated by a decrease in material interests, self-centredness and superfluous social interaction, a shift that he and others call 'gerotranscendence'. Empirical studies conducted in Sweden based on older-age individuals' retrospective accounts of ageing support Tornstam's thesis (1994, 1999) of a shift toward gerotranscendence. Retrospective self-report accounts among older Americans of changes in the content of their prayers are also suggestive of a shift towards less materialistic concerns (Ingersoll-Dayton et al, 2002; Eisenhandler, 2003).

Findings from the Ohio Longitudinal Study of Ageing Americans (Atchley, 1999), however, offer only partial support for the gerotranscendence thesis. Ohio respondents who attached importance to being religious were (in support of gerotranscendence) more likely to feel a greater connection with the universe and to take more enjoyment from their inner life. Contravening Tornstam's thesis, over three quarters of the OLSAA participants reported that material things meant more (not less) to them in old age, they were more likely to take themselves more (not less) seriously and to see less (not more) connection between themselves and past and future generations. In short, whether religion takes on a distinctive character or meaning in old age finds mixed support in the research to date.

We wondered whether the IHD longitudinal data might shed some light on this question of change in the character of religion. In view of current increased attentiveness to gerotranscendence as a characteristic of late adulthood religion, we used the participants' narratives on religion – their answers to open-ended questions about religious beliefs, attitudes and habits – to explore whether there was a discernible shift in the meaning of religion for them over time. We were interested in particular in whether there were differences in how the participants spoke of religion in late adulthood (when they were in their late 60s and mid-70s) compared to early adulthood (when they were in their 30s).

What did we find? Qualitative analyses of the themes that emerged in the participants' narratives suggested that, while there were definite continuities in how study members talked about religion across adulthood, it was apparent that some themes gained in prominence in late adulthood. For example, substantially more participants affirmed a Golden Rule philosophy during late adulthood (63%, 1997-2000) compared to when they were interviewed in early adulthood (29%, 1958), and its invocation did not vary by denomination, level of religiousness, gender, or social class.

The increased use of the Golden Rule in late adulthood, especially because it is based on data assessing the same individuals over time, may be seen as reflecting a developmental maturational increase in the interviewees' appreciation for the more universal principle summarised in the Golden Rule. Because the study participants came of age at a time in American society when the language and ethos of the Golden Rule was already prevalent (see, for example, Dillon and Wink, 2004), it is unlikely that their increased tendency to invoke it in late adulthood was a function of an increase in its cultural accessibility to this particular generation. Our finding of an increase in the participants' invocation of a Golden Rule ethic thus lends support to scholars who argue that a more universalising world view is distinctive of late adulthood (eg Fowler, 1981; Tornstam, 1999).

Commitment to the universality of the Golden Rule was expressed eloquently by Martha Wilson. Martha was a lifelong, highly committed Presbyterian who had taught Sunday school for many years and, in late adulthood, she was very active at a liberal Presbyterian church that was accepting of gay people and of women priests. Martha attended weekly services with her husband, was a member of the board and was involved in the church's outreach community work with senior citizens and homeless people. She also sang the Taize chant, what she described as 'a beautiful prayer for peace' at the Catholic Church, and prayed, she said, 'all the time'.

Martha was not one of the study participants who came to an appreciation of the Golden Rule with age; when interviewed in her 30s she cogently summarised her moral philosophy as 'Loving thy neighbour as thyself'. Yet at that time she also acknowledged that she often had prejudices towards some people on account of their beliefs. In late adulthood, however, there was a discernible shift in her attitude. Her explanation of the practical challenges mandated by the Golden Rule nicely captured the expansive world view associated with gerotranscendence, as well as suggesting that she herself had come to a deep acceptance of the beliefs of others. When asked to describe her beliefs and values, Martha elaborated:

> Well, I think that it really is true that you do have to love your neighbour. I do believe that God really did create us all equal, although we haven't figured out that quite yet. I believe that you really, really have to love one another. You don't have to like everybody, but you do if we're ever going to live in this world in peace, you have to love everybody. I think that people have got to quit worrying about sexual preference. I believe that God made us the way we are and if you're gay or lesbian, that's the way you were made unless you strayed off the track somewhere and you're a voyeur or whatever. I believe that you have to accept people, truly accept them. And as I said I don't think you have to like everybody. I don't think that's possible. But I do think you have to love everyone. And that includes the criminals and everybody. And no matter how hard that is. And there's lots of people who are not very lovable. (Age 77, 1998)

Martha's ethic of love extended to a pluralistic and individuated view of religion notwithstanding her own strong commitment to Christianity. She stated:

> I think you come to God in your own way. If I didn't believe that, I'd be very upset with my older child who's so involved with, it's not Hinduism, it's some Fetameditation but it certainly has its roots in

Hinduism. I believe that she sees God, or feels God in her life the way I feel the presence of God in mine. And no less. So I believe that you have to find the way that's right for you.

We also found that faith-related references and experiences certainly seemed to come more easily into our study participants' conversations about religion in late adulthood compared to early adulthood. The increased prominence of a vocabulary of faith in older adulthood – though not necessarily indicative of an increased religiousness – fits with Tornstam's idea that the ageing process makes people more detached from concrete material and personal ambitions, and more at ease with non-material matters and their place in the larger universe. This perspective was well captured by one highly successful, professional man in the study who went to the Congregational church twice a month. Among the principles he lived by in late adulthood, he said, were a greater awareness for beauty, nature and music, and a greater attentiveness to

> … religious feeling … A feeling of humbleness and being properly insignificant as a person. Because when you're young you're pretty much self-centred. You know everything is yours. And the whole world revolves around what you do. And as you get older you realise that you're not very much. You're just another little speck in the universe.

This contrasts with his perspective when interviewed in early adulthood. At that time, he was Presbyterian and, though he acknowledged his commitment to being a good citizen, he also spoke about how much he valued 'the idea that each man has the opportunity to achieve as much for himself as possible and to live his own life as an individual'. In fact, it was this view and his dislike of being tied down on Sundays that largely contributed to his sporadic church attendance back then.

Lillian Sinnott, for whom the social aspects of church were very important in adolescence and in early adulthood, continued to value the sociability of church throughout adulthood. In her late 60s, Lillian was attending Unitarian church services every week and singing in the choir. She was also on the church's board and the children's religion education committee. But now, rather than talking of church primarily in terms of how it provided her with 'an audience' (as in adolescence) or how it suited her particular social needs (she chose to get married in an Episcopalian church because it was the right size for the number of guests invited), she spoke of it in terms of greater communal mutuality:

> The church is my community, I think. That's why it's important to me more than anything religious. It's my community. It's a group of people that I like and enjoy being around because they're intelligent and we always have something to talk about.

Additionally, Lillian now expressed a more universal and awe-filled view of the sacred and related her values to a broad mix of sources including the Golden Rule, religious teachings, self-worth, nature and a universal spirituality. She believed, she said, in the

> … worth and dignity of all human beings. And the web of life on earth we live in. The ecology. All that … do the best you can. And without hurting other people. But also do what's best for yourself. Don't short-change yourself in order to be a martyr … My main values I guess are the values of the greatest teachers and philosophers through the times. The Golden Rule is a good one. And they all taught that. And I like the seven-fold path [towards] enlightenment. The Buddha. And I like the teachings of Jesus. I guess those are pretty much in my value system … I'm a very spiritual person. And I get it in different ways. When I'm singing some magnificent works I get tremendous spiritual uplift. And there are certain talks and certain things that uplift the spirit to do better things. To me spiritual is being the highest you can be in life I guess. I don't know how to describe it. It's personal … Nature to me is so magnificent. And how it keeps pushing through the cement and it's going to bloom. And it's going to come up and the birds keep coming back despite all the spray and everything. I don't know. And whatever makes this happen, I don't know what it is, some creative spirit, but I don't know how spirit can make something happen … But it's still magnificent.

Summary

In sum, our research using qualitative and statistical data from the IHD study indicated that the social and economic circumstances of our study participants in late adulthood were remarkably good. The majority of participants were financially secure, living with their spouse or partner, in good health and generally leading active lives. We looked too at the ways in which they were instilling purposefulness and meaning into these lives. Many of the participants were engaged in either church-centred religious practices or newer forms of spiritual seeking. As a general trend, we found that religious and/or spiritual individuals were more likely to be leading more active everyday lives in old age than their non-religious and non-spiritual peers. However, as the case of David Allen highlighted, it is possible to carve out an engaged and purposeful existence without concern for religion. Nonetheless, for many in the study, religiousness and spiritual seeking occupied a highly meaningful space and in varying ways propelled their integration of the ageing process. In this chapter we have tried to convey something of the variety and the depth of insight that life course construction can involve in later life.

Notes

[1] Because of the eight-year age difference between participants in the two original samples (GS and OGS), it was not surprising that, by late adulthood, the older OGS group had a higher mortality rate (40%) than the younger GS cohort (approximately 10%). Similarly, given gender differences in mortality, slightly more women (53%) than men (47%) were interviewed in late adulthood.

[2] Specifically, in late adulthood, 59% were upper middle class, 19% were lower middle class and 22% were working class. The figures for the IHD participants' college education and household income are substantially higher than for same-age Americans nationwide. Approximately 20% of Americans are college graduates and only 49% of same-age married households nationwide have an annual income over $40,000 (Smith, 2003: 3-4). Women reported lower household income than men ($F(1,147) = 7.74, p < .01$).

[3] IHD women were significantly more likely than men to live alone; χ^2 (1,182) = 8.78, $p < .01$. Among similar-age Americans nationwide, 7% of men and 53% of women live with their spouse (Smith, 2003: 3). There were no cohort differences among our study participants in regard to who tended to live alone ($\chi^2 = (1,175) = 1.85, ns$).

[4] This gender difference in marital satisfaction was statistically significant, $F(1,134) = 4.93, p < .05$.

[5] Several empirical essays in James and Wink (2007) highlight the importance of purposefulness to positive ageing across diverse samples.

[6] We investigated the purposefulness or vital involvement of the study participants in late adulthood using a self-report measure of involvement in everyday life tasks (Harlow and Cantor 1996). This scale assesses the frequency of an individual's participation across a range of 26 activities including reading magazines and newspapers, physical exercise, entertaining friends and family, helping neighbours, playing a musical instrument, painting, playing board games and travelling.

[7] These percentages are based on a sample size of 157, primarily using responses to self-report questionnaires. Of the 184 participants who were interviewed in late adulthood, 156 also provided self-report questionnaire data. On religiousness, spiritual seeking and other socio-demographic characteristics, the study participants for whom the authors have both interview and self-report data do not differ from those who were interviewed in-depth but who did not complete the self-report questionnaire.

[8] Engagement in life review was rated using a five-point scale assessing the degree to which the individual used reminiscences to reach a new level of

self-understanding. The ratings based on answers to interview questions about frequency of reminiscing and its use in self-exploration were done by two coders. The Kappa coefficient of reliability between the two raters was .59. In addition to the 52% who were rated low on life review and high on acceptance, 19% of the IHD sample were classified as high on both life review and acceptance, 14% fell into the high life review/low acceptance category and 15% were classified as low on life review and low on acceptance (see Wink and Schiff, 2002).

[9] These ideas are elaborated by Kohlberg (1981); Labouvie-Vief et al (1989); and Sinnott (1994).

Acknowledgement

I am very grateful to Ricca Edmondson and Hans-Joachim von Kondratowitz for the invitation to participate in the European Conference on Ageing held in Galway in 2006, and to Ricca Edmondson for her many insightful comments on an earlier draft of this chapter and the generosity of her work in bringing this volume to fruition.

References

Atchley, R. (1999) *Continuity and adaptation in ageing: Creating positive experiences*, Baltimore, MD: Johns Hopkins University Press.

Bart, P. (1971) 'Depression in middle-aged women', in V. Gornick and B.K. Moran (eds) *Women in sexist society*, New York: Basic Books, pp 99-117.

Bellah, R., Madsen, R., Sullivan, W., Swidler, A. and Tipton, S. (1991) *The good society*, New York: Knopf.

Butler, R. (1963) 'The life review: an interpretation of reminiscence in old age', *Psychiatry Journal for the Study of Interpersonal Processes*, vol 26, no 1, pp 65-76.

Campbell, J. (1990) *The hero with a thousand faces* (2nd edn), Princeton, NJ: Princeton University Press.

Coleman, P. (1986) *Ageing and reminiscence processes: Social and clinical implications*, Chichester: Wiley.

Deutsch, H. (1945) *The psychology of women*, vol 2, New York: Grune and Stratton.

Dillon, M. and Wink, P. (2004) 'Religion, cultural change, and generativity in American society', in E. de St Aubin and D.P. McAdams (eds) *The generative society*, Washington, DC: American Psychological Association Press, pp 153-74.

Dillon, M. and Wink, P. (2007) *In the course of a lifetime: Tracing religious belief, practice, and change*, Berkeley: University of California Press.

Eichorn, D., Mussen, P., Clausen, J., Haan, N. and Honzik, M. (1981) 'Overview', in D. Eichorn, J. Clausen, N. Haan, M. Honzik and P. Mussen (eds) *Present and past in middle age*, New York: Academic Press, pp 411-34.

Eisenhandler, S. (2003) *Keeping the faith in late life*, New York: Springer.

Erikson, E. (1963) *Childhood and society* (2nd edn), New York: Norton.

Erikson, E., Erikson, J. and Kivnick, H. (1986) *Vital involvement in old age*, New York: Norton.

Fortner, B.V. and Neimeyer, R. (1999) 'Death anxiety in older adults: a quantitative review', *Death Studies*, vol 23, no 5, pp 387-411.

Fowler, J. (1981) *Stages of faith*, New York: Harper & Row.

Glock, C. and Bellah, R. (eds) (1976) *The new religious consciousness*, Berkeley, CA: University of California Press.

Greeley, A. (2003) *Religion in Europe at the end of the second millennium*, New Brunswick, NJ: Transaction.

Harlow, R. and Cantor, N. (1996) 'Still participating after all these years: a study of life task participation in later life', *Journal of Personality and Social Psychology*, vol 7, no 6, pp 1235-49.

Helson, R. and Wink, P. (1992) 'Personality change in women from the early 40s to the early 50s', *Psychology and Ageing*, vol 7, no 1, pp 46-55.

Ingersoll-Dayton, B., Krause, N. and Morgan, D. (2002) 'Religious trajectories and transitions over the life course', *International Journal of Ageing and Human Development*, vol 55, no 1, pp 51-70.

James, J. and Wink, P. (2007) *The crown of life: dynamics of the early post-retirement period*, New York: Springer.

Koenig, H., McCullough, M. and Larson, D. (2001) *Handbook of religion and health*, New York: Oxford University Press.

Kohlberg, L. (1981) *Essays on moral development. Volume 1. The philosophy of moral development*, New York: Harper & Row.

Labouvie-Vief, G., De Voe, M. and Bulka, D. (1989) 'Speaking about feelings: conception of emotion across the life span', *Psychology and Ageing*, vol 4, no 4, pp 425-37.

Laslett, P. (1991) *A fresh map of life: The emergence of the third age*, Cambridge, MA: Harvard University Press.

Levinson, D. (1978) *The seasons of a man's life*, New York: Ballantine.

McCullough, M. and Smith, T. (2003) 'Religion and health: depressive symptoms and mortality as case studies', in M. Dillon (ed) *Handbook of the sociology of religion*, New York: Cambridge University Press, pp 190-204.

McFadden, S. (1999) 'Religion, personality, and ageing: a life span perspective', *Journal of Personality*, vol 67, no 6, pp 1081-104.

Midanik, L.T., Soghikian, K., Ransom, L. and Tekawa, I. (1995) 'The effect of retirement on mental health and health behaviors', *Journal of Gerontology: Social Sciences*, vol 50B, no 1, pp S59-61.

Patrick, A. (1999) 'Forum on American spirituality', *Religion and American Culture*, vol 9, no 2, pp 139-45.

Roof, W.C. (1999) *Spiritual marketplace: Baby boomers and the remaking of American religion*, Princeton, NJ: Princeton University Press.

Rossi, A. (2004) 'The menopausal transition and ageing processes', in O. Brim, C. Ryff and R. Kessler (eds) *How healthy are we? A National study of well-being at midlife*, Chicago: University of Chicago Press, p 153-201.

Roth, P. (2006) *Everyman*, Boston: Houghton Mifflin.

Rowe, J. and Kahn, R. (1998) *Successful ageing*, New York: Pantheon.

Safranski, R. (1990) *Schopenhauer and the wild years of philosophy*, Cambridge, MA: Harvard University Press.

Sinnott, J. (1994) 'Development and yearning: cognitive aspects of spiritual development', *Journal of Adult Development*, vol 1, no 2, pp 91-9.

Smith, D. (2003) *The older population in the United States: 2002* (Current Population Report P20-550), Washington, DC: US Census Bureau.

Stokes, K. (1990) 'Faith development in the adult life cycle', *Journal of Religious Gerontology*, vol 7, no 1, pp 167-84.

Tomer, A. (ed) (2000) *Death attitudes and the older adult*, Washington, DC: Taylor and Francis.

Tornstam, L. (1994) 'Gero-transcendence: a theoretical and empirical exploration', in E. Thomas and S. Eisenhandler (eds) *Ageing and the religious dimension*, Westport, CT: Auburn House, pp 203-25.

Tornstam, L. (1999) 'Late-life transcendence: a new developmental perspective on ageing', in L.E. Thomas and S. Eisenhandler (eds) *Religion, belief, and spirituality in late life*, New York: Springer, pp 178-202.

Weiss, R. and Bass, S. (eds) (2002) *Challenges of the third age: Meanings and purpose in later life*, New York: Oxford University Press.

Wethington, E., Kessler, R. and Pixley, J. (2004) 'Turning points in adulthood', in O. Brim, C. Ryff and R. Kessler (eds) *How healthy are we? A national study of well-being at midlife*, Chicago: University of Chicago Press, pp 586-613.

Wink, P. (2007) 'Everyday life in the third age', in J. James and P. Wink (eds) *The crown of life: Dynamics of the early post-retirement period*, New York: Springer, pp 243-61.

Wink, P. and Helson, R. (1997) 'Practical and transcendent wisdom: their nature and some longitudinal findings', *Journal of Adult Development*, vol 4, no 1, pp 1-15.

Wink, P. and Schiff, B. (2002) 'To review or not to review? The role of personality and life events in life review and adaptation to old age', in J. Webster and B. Haight (eds) *Critical advances in reminiscence work*, New York: Springer, pp 44-60.

Wuthnow, R. (1998) *After heaven: Spirituality in America since the 1950s*, Berkeley, CA: University of California Press.

FOUR

Atheist convictions, Christian beliefs or 'keeping things open'? Patterns of world views among three generations in East German families

Monika Wohlrab-Sahr

Introduction

In the past in Europe, as it is in the present in many parts of the world, attachment to religion has been part of the accepted image of older people. Religious ideas have been important vehicles for making sense of profound questions dealing with life and death, and their association with religiosity has had significant, if varied, effects on older people's relations with younger people and with society at large. What, then, are the ideas exchanged on these topics in societies where religion plays very little part? This chapter explores attitudes to death and the afterlife among three generations in East German families.

One of the most highly secularised parts of the world, East Germany is a region where Christian traditions have largely vanished and most people have grown up without a religious socialisation. Although the secularisation process was imposed mainly by the dominant political party, it succeeded in creating secular mindsets and atheist convictions throughout the population. People from different generations played different roles in this process. Some had to decide whether to give up or to maintain their religious affiliation, whereas others were fully socialised within the new a–religious framework. After the socialist regime ended, the conditions for adopting religious perspectives changed significantly. Today, the religious change that can be observed is not a simple religious revival; it is an inchoate reawakening of religious perspectives that is experimental and syncretistic rather than traditional and church–bound. Ideas about the afterlife are a significant part of this religious reawakening and these ideas are adopted mainly by younger generations. In some families, we observed a process of inverse socialisation, in which young people introduced new religious perspectives to their older family members.

Enforced secularisation in the German Democratic Republic

In East Germany, a virtually unique break with religious tradition took place during the time of the German Democratic Republic (GDR). In 1949, the founding year of the GDR, 91% of the population belonged to one of the two major Christian congregations; in 1989 only 29% did. Since then, church membership has dropped even further. Today, only 21% of the population in the new states of a unified Germany are members of the Protestant Church and only 4% are members of the Catholic Church (Pollack, 2000: 19).

In the West, the decline of traditional religiosity was a gradual process impelled by changing values and steadily dissolving ties with church institutions. In the GDR, the situation was more complex. Here, overlapping social, political and economic factors coincided to produce the lowest rates of church membership and individual religiosity in the world (Schmidt and Wohlrab-Sahr, 2003).

First, the churches had lost influence throughout Germany both before and during National Socialism. In some parts of what later became the GDR, historians have shown that the population was already detached from the Church before the national socialist regime (Nowak, 1996) and even earlier. Using church statistics from the Protestant part of Germany since 1850, Lucian Hölscher (2000: 7) has shown that an East–West divide in participation in church activities was already evident in 1910. At that time, the regions with low church participation were also the most highly industrialised. Secular movements were popular there, not only among the intellectual elite, but also among the members of the Social Democratic Party, which preached 'a synthesis of Marxism and Darwinism' (McLeod, 1992: 66; Kaiser, 2003: 120).[1] Thus, the historical setting in East Germany was one of coinciding secular influences, one deriving from movements based on the antagonism between science and religion. These influences prepared the soil in which the Socialist Union Party of Germany (SED) planted the seeds of their secularist ideas.

Second, from the formation of the GDR until the end of the 1960s, the massive decline of church membership and religiosity in East Germany can be attributed to state repression, ritual competition and a clash of world views. To compete with the Protestant ritual of Confirmation, the SED revived the *Jugendweihe*, a secular coming-of-age ceremony, which remained popular even after the breakdown of the regime. The introduction of this ceremony was a central element in the SED's struggle for the hearts and minds of the younger generation. Borrowed from older secularist traditions, it was introduced throughout the GDR as a substitute for Confirmation. Five years after its introduction in 1954-55, the *Jugendweihe* had become successfully established. In 1960, two thirds of juveniles[2] participated in it, some in addition to Confirmation and some as a substitute for it (Pollack, 1994: 414). At the outset, the *Jugendweihe* was used to repress traditional religiosity, and the ceremony itself carried strong elements of ideological doctrine and anti-church polemic. Eventually it became a socialist rite of passage that focused more on practical life guidance than on ideological issues (Liepold, 2000).

In addition to this competition in ritual terms, the SED constructed a clash of world views by promoting a scientific or 'scientific' ideology (*wissenschaftliche Weltanschauung)*, which was based on the competition between religion and science (Wohlrab-Sahr et al, 2008). This position – which was termed 'scientific atheism', with its attendant scientistic ideology – explicitly *competed* with a Christian world view and was also meant as a substitute for religion in every domain of life, including questions of life and death. The German word '*Weltanschauung*' hints at the all-encompassing scope ascribed to this world view, which opposes the idea of functional differentiation; that is, it rejects the idea that religion, science and politics could be considered autonomous spheres in society and, despite competition, could coexist and refer to different functional problems in society (see Luhmann, 1995).

Under the SED, scientific knowledge and scientistic ideology were disseminated simultaneously throughout East Germany. Institutions of adult education, such as the Urania,[3] were established in many cities. Observatories were built, which became very popular, and public schools taught astronomy as a basic subject. Of course these institutions were not *only* ideological; all did actually spread scientific knowledge to the general population. But they operated with the purpose of creating a scientistic *Weltanschauung* (Mader, 1959) that was an explicit substitute for religion and 'superstition'. These institutions were instruments in a general process of disenchantment, a process that did not simply occur but was initiated deliberately. Even if these instruments were more ideological or less ideological in different places and at different times during the GDR regime, the element of disenchantment remained central (Schmidt-Lux, 2008).

Third, the lack of confessional affiliation, which became the normal pattern during the first decades of the GDR, began to have a socialising effect in itself. Today, in West Germany, people without religious affiliation have usually *renounced* their church membership, whereas, in East Germany, the majority of those people have *never* been church members, implying a tradition of non-affiliation and a-religiosity.

Finally, in most European countries, beginning in the 1960s, there was a general change in social values accompanied by increasing secularisation. In the GDR, these developments had a specific dynamic. At the same time as political transformation was taking place, there was a *cultural transformation* – a transformation that has been described as the emergence of a 'worker society' (Kohli, 1994) with a predominant 'worker culture' (Engler, 1999). It focused on issues of immediate necessity and practicality that seemed not in accordance with spiritual matters. These overlapping social, political and economic factors created a religious and ideological field entirely different from that in West Germany.

Religious change and generational relations in the GDR and after the transformation of 1989

Different generations were affected differently by the ideological changes that occurred during the GDR period. Three ideal-typical generations and their historical experiences can be described now in order to make these intertwined social developments clearer.

The first ideal-typical generation consists of people born in the 1920s and 1930s. They experienced the war and took part in the foundational years of the GDR as older juveniles or young adults. This generation has been labelled the 'constituent generation'[4] of the GDR. Statistically, they have the strongest church ties of the three age groups in the study. But many had already severed these ties during the GDR period. For some, this decision was a response not only to their secularist environment, but also to their experiences during the war.

The second ideal-typical generation consists of children born to the first generation in the late 1940s and in the 1950s. They were fully socialised in the GDR, a society that many of them experienced virtually without alternative. Their church ties, religious affiliation and religious beliefs are especially weak. Some have not been baptised, and for most, the Socialist rite of *Jugendweihe* replaced confirmation.

The third ideal-typical generation consists of the grandchildren of the first generation. They were born in the 1970s and were adolescents during the transformation of 1989. For most of these, the fall of the Wall opened new horizons just as their own perspectives were widening in the transition to adulthood. This wider perspective extended to religion as well. The members of this generation are still predominantly secular, but they exhibit a rising interest in religious quests, though mostly outside a church setting.

After the political changes of 1989, many observers predicted a revitalisation of religion and religious life in the Federal Republic's new states, and especially they anticipated success for the missionary groups that came to East Germany after 1989. Although this prediction remains unfulfilled, the religious situation there has not remained static.

While the church affiliation and religiosity of the two older generations continues to decline, recent general social surveys indicate that the youngest generation is growing more open to religious issues; in particular, an increasing number believe in life after death. In 2001, for example, twice as many respondents between 18 and 29 years of age supported the belief in an afterlife than had done ten years before (ALLBUS, 2002). In 2001, one third – 33.6% – of these respondents subscribed to such a belief. Surprisingly, this percentage was even higher than among the oldest generation, their grandparents, many of whom had maintained their church ties.[5] Clearly the result is complex if we consider different indicators of religiosity among different age groups. The oldest age group showed the highest levels of church membership and of belief in God – traditional measures of religiosity – but the youngest age group showed the highest level (and the largest increase) of belief in an afterlife. (Paradoxically, for many, this belief did not also imply the belief in a personal God.) The results were similar for questions on the subjective relevance of magic, spiritualism and the occult.

Using these two variables as indicators of religiosity, the youngest age group would be the most religious in East Germany, even more religious than their grandparents. This finding contradicts the normal pattern; the younger people are, usually the less religious they are.

This contradiction casts an interesting light on generational relations and their effects on religiosity. The youngest age group seems to be bringing a new dynamic to the field of religiosity and world views, operating outside the traditional patterns of church-bound religiosity. In contrast, recent work by Smith and Denton (2005) finds that North American teenagers fit a rather conventional pattern: belief in a personal God who created the Earth and maintains general order in life.

The finding that the youngest age group is also the most religious can be interpreted within the Mannheimian framework of the sociology of generations (Mannheim, 1972). The youngest age group experienced political and ideological change during their formative years and may thus be enabled to develop new perspectives that confront the dominant materialism of older generations.

This chapter presents findings of a research project that was undertaken at the University of Leipzig between 2003 and 2006. The subject of the project was change in religiosity and world views among three East German generations during the GDR period and after 1989. We tried to understand how families related to the state-promoted renunciation of church membership and religious affiliation in the GDR, as well as to the attempt to substitute scientistic ideologies for religious beliefs. We explored how they actively participated in it, promoted, refused or resisted it, and how they dealt with these issues following the fall of Socialism in 1989.[6]

The project used several kinds of interviews and group discussions. In this chapter, I shall refer to the family interviews in which we asked representatives of three family generations to tell the story of their family. We complemented this narrative approach with questions about different periods during the GDR period and about the time of acute political change in 1989-90, as well as about developments in specific areas of society. At the end of each interview, we asked certain questions to stimulate discussion among the family members. One of these questions was 'What do you think will happen after death?' (see also Wohlrab-Sahr et al, 2005).

Approaching the transcendent: 'What do you think will happen after death?'

Religions as organisers of 'great transcendences'

Dealing with death – intellectually, symbolically and ritually – and answering questions about death are tasks that usually fall to religions and religious communities. Indeed, coping with the problem of death is one societal function that is, to a large degree, still left to religious communities, even if other institutions have also developed secular rituals. Beliefs in an afterlife as expressions of 'great transcendence' are usually considered a hard test for the distinction between religious and non-religious attitudes, but such beliefs are also well suited for exploring innovations in the field of religiosity and world views.

Thomas Luckmann, a sceptic regarding the general connection between modernisation and secularisation, who considers the secularisation thesis one of the myths of modern societies (Luckmann 1980), nevertheless observes a 'shrinking' of transcendence in the course of modernisation. Referring to Alfred Schütz's (1962a) three distinct levels of transcendence, Luckmann posits that people in modern societies are more likely to adhere to the idea of small and intermediate transcendences than to great transcendences (Luckmann, 1990).

As Schütz (1962b) explains in his sociology of knowledge, 'small transcendences' refer to the experience that there is something beyond the here and now of my existence; that there was something before me and there will be something after me; and that there is something beyond the immediate scope of my reach. Grasping such transcendences is certainly constitutive for human beings, implying the potential ability to reach and think beyond the here and now of immediate existence. But this ability also lays the groundwork for the *possibility*[7] of religiosity, inasmuch as human beings have imagination and are able to think beyond the ends of their own lives.

The term 'intermediate transcendences' refers to the boundaries of other people and to the possibility of taking their perspectives and sharing their experiences. Many types of sexual experience as well as collective experience in groups and in large social settings are examples of this kind of transcendence. An example of the latter is the 'collective effervescence' that may result from collective celebrations or assemblies, described by Emile Durkheim in his *Elementary Forms of Religious Life* (Durkheim, 2001).

The term 'great transcendence' refers to extraordinary experiences that lead people into different modes of being that are very different from their normal, everyday states of mind. An example is ecstatic experience, which is often, but not necessarily, connected to religion. But the term refers mainly to the experience of death, which during lifetime can only be imagined. Almost all religions have developed ideas and rich imageries related to the experience of death and to the other-worldly existence that is thought to follow death: ideas of modes of existence between life and death, ideas of resurrection and reincarnation, images of a voyage of the soul, among others. Usually, specific practices and prescriptions are related to these ideas: how and where to keep the dead body, how to bury or cremate it, which objects to place in the coffin and how to mourn for the person who has died. Different cultures of burial and remembrance have developed, and these have undergone significant changes in the course of modernisation.

Processes of secularisation, too, have had significant effects on ideas and practices related to death and burial. Two such effects include the decline in belief in resurrection and changes in burial practices. In the 19th and early 20th century in the Judeo-Christian culture, for example, cremation was a highly contested issue. Today, private and anonymous forms of burial are not unusual, signalling a significant change in the cultural pattern.

As the statistics on belief in life after death among the East German population indicate, perspectives on an afterlife are an especially promising indicator of changes in the field of world views and religiosity. It was for this reason that we included the question about what will happen after death in our interviews.

What do you think will happen after death?

The discussions from our family interviews produced three types of response to the question 'What do you think will happen after death?'.

First, early on in our analysis of the interviews, it became clear that, despite the general influence of the scientific-atheistic world view and of materialistic views of death, Christian notions had been preserved through the GDR period, especially among people in the oldest generation.

Second, we found people who held explicitly atheist positions approaching the question of death from a strictly materialist, scientific perspective, excluding any further reasoning. The people most likely to hold this view also came from the oldest generation.

Third, in addition to the Christian and the atheist perspectives, unspecific references to transcendence also crystallised around the death question. We labelled these positions 'agnostic spirituality'. Usually, the term *spirituality* refers to religious experience that the spiritual person clearly distinguishes from institutionalised forms of religiosity, or it refers to the spiritual person's inner experience, something to be distinguished from external forms of religious dogma, practice, and affiliation. Here we use the term *spirituality* in a way that seems more appropriate to the secular context of East Germany. It describes a person who entertains notions that are different from both materialist viewpoints and traditional religious beliefs. For the interviewees who expressed this position, the question of what happens after death was a highly relevant issue and they responded readily to the question. We consider this spirituality *agnostic*, however, because it lacks any kind of positive religious experience; these individuals had not tried to gain religious experience by way of collective or individual practice. They referred to transcendence in a way that used neither traditional religious concepts nor those of abstract philosophies. Rather, during the family interview, they developed notions of transcendence related to a variety of images and concepts that were syncretistic borrowings from a common store of old and new systems of interpretation: religion, magic, parapsychology, humanism, but also science and media, especially film. The thematic references were experimental in a sense, expressing a notion rather than a specific belief.

I shall now present examples of the three types of response to the question of what will happen after death so that we can explore the relationship to religion that these responses may be taken to express.

Christian semantics

First, note that very few of the interviewees explicitly referred to Christian dogmas and beliefs. Even in families who had remained committed church members throughout the GDR period, only a few interviewees, mainly female members of the oldest generation (60 to 80 years old), referred to the idea of resurrection. Those who did so presented their belief as givens, whereas the younger family members tended to be more cautious, referring to general philosophical ideas rather than to Christian dogmas. The following interview passage reveals variations on the afterlife theme within a Christian framework:

GM: What will happen after death?\ I: uhuh\ We will resurrect.

D: We don't know that {laughing}.

F: That's what we hope ... That's what we pray for, that's what we hope, that's what we have been told, and what has been promised to us, and //we have and uh\

GM: //The spirit //will go into heaven.

F: //hoping, hoping that it will come true, we're satisfied with that.

D: I always like to compare this with the cosmos.

GM: When the time has come, //God, our father, will come to take us.

D: //eternal and eternal and eternal. There must be an end to it somewhere.

GF: Yes.

F: Or//

D: //Or it's always, when we//

F: //One solar system, another solar system, and another solar system. But what's//behind? The question is always there.

D: //When we're dead, then, then, I always think, then we will discover all that, and everything will be clear somehow. (Family 4)[8]

Although this family is clearly communicating within a Christian framework, there are interesting differences in perspective among the generations. The grandmother expresses no doubt in referring to the Christian idea of resurrection and to the symbolism of the spirit going into heaven. The younger family members modify this position slightly and make some theological corrections. They refer to the notion of *hope* and to the certainty given by the Christian *tradition*, both of which become substitutes for what cannot be experienced.

The daughter does not use the word *heaven*; instead, she speaks about the 'cosmos', thereby introducing a link to both the natural sciences and to philosophy (here, the problem of infinity). Her perspective clearly differs from a materialistic one in which everything in life (and death) is a matter of subjective enlightenment. But, for her, Christian dogmas and beliefs are not self-evident – as they may be for someone who is part of an integrated Christian milieu – but must be linked to scientific questions and secular perceptions.

In other interviews, Christian families frequently spoke of 'hope' or of a 'secret' that could not, or should not, be revealed. Indeed, the metaphor of the *secret* almost operated as a ban on religious images and language. The abstract references to *hope* implied the notion of transcendence without referring to specific Christian semantics that could support this hope.

In discussions about death as a great transcendence – an event you cannot experience in lifetime and whose comprehension therefore needs support from sources other than direct experience – the language of Christian tradition was still available to members of the first generation. The younger generations tended to rely on semantics that symbolised the *unknowable* – the *secret* – rather than the certainty of belief. Or they used scientific reasoning or scientific knowledge to connect religious answers to general problems of rationality, the problem of infinity, for example.

In some interviews, the notion of hope shrank to merely *keeping the possibility* of life after death *open*. This perspective challenges not only a dogmatic Christian position, but a clear atheist position as well. The latter is apparent in the following family interview:

> GM: No, I don't believe that\Life after death ... for me that's my children, my grandchildren, and my great-grandchildren. That's the line where you transfer something, and I don't think that there is something else.
>
> M: She's more pragmatic. I keep it open.
>
> D: Yes, I would also keep it open. I don't want to tie myself down. (Family 2)

The remark that the question of life after death should be kept 'open' is paradoxical. Certainly a religious person would consider this position wholly inadequate. Indeed, the interviewees reduce the idea of *great transcendence*, which the grandmother of Family 4 described using Christian dogma (resurrection, soul), to a matter of personal perception and decision. They articulate their indecision between religion and atheism as if they would like to keep a door open, but are unable to walk through it.

Atheism

At the other end of the spectrum were people who – confronted with the question of what comes after death – explicitly adopted an atheist and materialist position and clearly rejected the idea of a life after death. Again, this position was most common among the oldest generation. A female doctor, born in 1935, for example, gave the following answer to the question of what will happen after death: 'Ashes – and nothing more. That's what scientists think.' Then she described what in the GDR was called 'scientific atheism', a mutually supportive combination of scientism and atheism, a perspective in which religion is merely an irrational remainder in a thoroughly secular and rational world.

A variant of such atheistic positions is the view that the dead body itself is only material. One interviewee, from the middle generation, quoted her father, saying: 'My father always said, "Don't put me in a cemetery when I'm dead. Throw me on the compost heap instead, then I'll still be useful for something"' (Family 2).

An older, unmarried couple, whose former spouses had already passed away, planned to leave their bodies to the anatomy institute after their deaths, so that they could be used for medical students' training. Afterwards, their bodies would be buried in an anonymous graveyard.[9] The couple's children and grandchildren disagreed with this plan because they wanted the graves to be a place of personal remembrance. Holding a different view from the grandparents, they claimed that the dead live on in the memories of surviving relatives as well as in the values imparted to them. Still, the grandparents insisted that death implied the end of the individual person and that no aspect of that person would live on after the person's death. Indeed, when the interviewer asked the question what will happen after death, at first, the grandfather did not even understand that this might imply the issue of an afterlife; he immediately responded on the practical level of dedicating the dead body to the anatomy institute (Family 5).

Certainly such materialist perspectives represent the polar opposite of Christian beliefs. The body has no special significance (in contrast to Christian or Muslim notions of corporeal resurrection), and the traditional culture of burial and commemoration – which requires a body – is unnecessary. This is a clearly immanent perspective, with no link to any kind of great transcendence.

In our interviews, scientific atheism in its purest form was most common among the oldest generation, people born in the 1920s and 1930s. But, even in families where the grandparents presented a clear-cut atheist position, the younger generations were able to introduce new perspectives. One example was the family of the medical doctor who stated that only ashes remain after death. In this excerpt, her daughter disagrees:

I:	What do you think will happen after death?
GM:	Ashes.
I:	Ashes.
GM:	And nothing else. That's what scientists think.

M: Well, it's different with me.

GM: Well, I only said what I think about it.

M: Well, it's//different with me, well I …

GM: //50 years of medicine.

M: Well, //we don't know.

GM: //I haven't seen anybody rising//from death.

M: //Well I have dealt intensely with all these stories about near-death-experience. Well these, uhm these tunnels and stuff like that, you know?

I: Yes

M: Well, I've been thinking about that intensely. This is because of that experience by the ocean. I think I was three years old. I was caught by a wave and I was actually gone. I had stopped breathing and I was just seeing colours. It was so beautiful. And then they carried me out, and my huge father pressed on my chest, it was so//terrible.

GM: //reanimated.

M: I was so mad that they got me back. \GM: {laughing}\ … I remember it very exactly, it was really, everything was floating, there were colours everywhere, it was really beautiful. And I read a few things about it, which had the same//descriptions.

GM: //Well, it's not always, in neuro//surgery I ..

M: //well OK, your brains can//fool you, but. …

GM: //I saw countless people dying. Many of them die with a smile on their face.\ I2: uhu\

M: Right …

GM: Well, and what do you [asking her granddaughter] think what will happen then? You don't know yet, do you?

D: No, I can't tell exactly, because … But now I'm going to study medicine and it may be that I will have the same opinion as Grandmother some day. But I can't tell now.

GM: Well, you will share my opinion in 50 years' time.

D: Well, I do think that there will be something … I do think that there will be something, I can't tell exactly what, and don't know exactly if I really believe in God. But in any case I do believe in some higher power, definitely. Because there are so many mysterious things, and, I don't know, I just want it to be, because you preserve something for yourself. And it's also important in our community,[10] it's just normal. But I can't tell exactly …

GM: Well there are mysterious things, but they are just not yet explained by science, like many things in science …

M: Well, it's good that one doesn't know everything, isn't it?
GM: Well, that's right. Yes.
             {Everyone laughs}(Family 9)

This case indicates the stability of scientific atheism from generation to generation, as well as the disposition for religious renewal in the younger generation. It also shows how difficult it is for such renewal to resist the dominant view of scientific atheism. The mother – referring to what she calls a near-death-experience – tries to 'keep a window open' for some transcendent perspective. But ultimately the grandmother's view dominates. There may be 'mysterious' things today, but some day science will be able to explain them; they are just 'not yet explained'. Although the transcript indicates differences in perspectives among the generations, both the mother and the daughter have difficulty maintaining their views in the face of the grandmother's scientistic perspective. At first, the daughter states a general religious perspective, but then she retreats. What she calls belief in 'some higher power', which she relates to 'mysterious' things happening, falls prey to the grandmother's analytic, scientistic view. The fragility of the daughter's position is visible in her words. She *wants* God to exist in order to 'preserve something' for herself. This example clearly illustrates how much the survival of this 'deviant' position (in the atheist framework) depends on a supporting social context in which the belief in God is *just normal*. Religiosity (like other world views) needs a communicative context (Knoblauch, 1997) to maintain its plausibility. When the daughter considers the context of the grandmother's professional life and the experiences associated with that context, she concedes that her perspective might change in the grandmother's direction. It is as if she accepts that it is *normal* for a scientist not to believe.

The final statement in this passage – 'Well, it's good that one doesn't know everything, isn't it?' – is a formula for compromise. Science may, in the future, be able to explain what is 'mysterious' today, but the perspective of not *wanting to know* everything still has some value. This is not an *argument against* an exclusively scientistic perspective; it is a plea to *stop arguing*.

Agnostic spirituality

A third perspective on death is what I refer to as 'agnostic spirituality'. Though labelled 'agnostic', this perspective is not completely void of content, and it feeds on various sources such as science, magic, science fiction, popular beliefs and elements of different religious traditions. On the one hand, these sources compensate for the absence of direct experience of what happens after death. On the other hand, they provide new semantics for expressing religiosity that are not considered passé, as some clichéd popular religious notions and certain theological interpretations are. And finally they generate – particularly by picking up on scientific theories as well as on science fiction – plausible scenarios that provide the *irrational* aspect of the notion of life after death with a new kind of *rationality*.

In many interviews, reports of near-death experiences – which clearly fascinate many people – and of other psychic experiences, served as a bridge to non-perceptible things. Notions of reincarnation can be found in predominantly atheistic cultures as well. As one man, born in 1959, said, referring to his own death: 'There's no *exotus* [sic],[11] the brain cannot simply shut down. I don't believe that … By then you wouldn't see anything any more, right?' When his wife explained, ironically, to the interviewer that her husband believed in some kind of reincarnation and thought that at some point he would return as a 'flower in the meadow', he insisted that he wanted to return as *another person*. Clearly, this family had discussed reincarnation before. But the scenario that the father developed was not an elaborate religious theory, rather a narrative that ameliorated the horror evoked by the thought of departing this world and of the end of the individual person (Family 23). For many interviewees, this notion of reincarnation, which has little to do with its Hindu origins, was much easier to accept than the Christian notion of resurrection.

Another young woman, born in 1974, made a similar, but more abstract, argument. She developed the idea that, though the body decayed, breaking down into many molecules, her consciousness – she used the word *soul* – would remain and would be placed in a different body some day. She said: 'What happens to my body is meaningless to me, because that goes back into circulation. But I think that at some point there will be a human being, who, who is me.' Her atheist mother, somewhat disturbed by this response, asked 'That's what you think?' This example illustrates how, in the transformation of religious world views, the generations often diverge, younger family members potentially inspiring older family members (Family 18).

The perspectives of these interviewees indicate the problem of individuality underlying a person's reasoning about death and the afterlife. Atheist positions may align well with the natural sciences, but they offer little help in the problem of personal finitude. These interviewees attempted to deal with this problem without using the resources of the Christian tradition.

Some interviewees relied on science-fiction-like notions to deal with the problem of personal finitude, distancing themselves from atheist ideas and Christian beliefs alike. Others used scientific theories. A Catholic family, for example, agreed after extensive debate that a 'bundle of energy' remains after death, a conclusion clearly relying on the law of the conservation of energy.

During the GDR period, this family had been strongly integrated into an educated, middle-class Catholic milieu. When asked what will happen after death, the family members expressed different ideas:

I:	What do you think will happen after death? (8)
	{Several people laughing}
F:	It doesn't look very promising.
	{Everybody laughing out loud}
S:	That's the question. (5)

D: Nothing. (2) …

I: Nothing? (2)

D: But a kind of nothing that is not scary. \I: uhu\ Well, I don't think that you get into some kind of garden or anything like that.\ /I: Uhu\ (5)

M: No, I wouldn't say 'nothing'. (2) But, as she said, not like a garden or a cloud, but (3) maybe some kind of, this sounds silly, but some kind of (2) power, or matter, or soul, (2) something that is being conserved, in some form …

D: Do you also believe this when you think about someone who has already died? Do you think that this person somewhere … (2)

M: Yes, that's what I believe.

D: Well, tell me! \F, M: {laughing}\

M: I, I believe that somehow, something like a soul or (3), well that's not matter, but somehow, something like a bundle of energy or something like that {laughing} somehow is conserved \{laughing}\

F: Like in *Matrix*.

M: Uh, exactly {laughing}. No matter where \{everybody laughing}\.

F: All that matters is to be a bundle of energy …

M: Now tell you! What do you think? …

F: {Laughing} (3) Well, I hope that one's belief is good for something inasmuch as there still will be something. But I don't know what. One might call it bundle of energy …

S: Do you think that the others still will be there somewhere? …

F: That's why the universe expands, to give space to all of us … You could build a theory on that. (Family 1)

When approaching the issue of afterlife, the family's first statements – by the father and by the daughter, respectively – are 'This doesn't look very promising' and 'Nothing'. As the conversation continues, the family members do not adhere to these sceptical, even negative, statements, but it becomes clear that they cannot relate to Christian doctrines and religious semantics either. Instead, they develop the abstract idea that there will be (and should be) something after death, which – if it existed – would be permanent. Moreover, earthly images may not grasp the meaning of this *something* after death. But no one refers to the Christian idea of resurrection or to any similar idea. The mother's response to the daughter's 'nothing' is striking. She supplies the scientific metaphor of the *conservation of matter*, illustrated by the phrase 'little bundles of energy', which might be conserved after death. The father then relates this idea to science fiction films (*Matrix*) as well as to physical theories ('That's why the universe expands … You could build a theory on that'). Though the family obviously makes fun of the metaphor, they do not completely reject it. At one point, the children offered alternative scenarios of the afterlife using biological metaphors instead of scientific ones, living on in a tree, for example. However, those scenarios were rejected as well; such ideas were considered too profane, products of wishful thinking.

In the end, the product of the family's debate is an open question that requires further reasoning. The scientist metaphors of 'conserving matter' and 'little bundles of energy' are substitutes for religious semantics, but ideas of transcendence and of eternity are still visible.

Conclusion

The interviews and statistical information presented here illustrate a profound secularisation as well as slight tendencies toward de-secularisation. The East German example clearly indicates that enforced secularisation in the GDR succeeded in forming secular and atheist perceptions of the world in a large part of the population. Though the Communist politics of the SED are gone today, clearly the effects of its anti-religious policies remain.

The research also indicates one path that de-secularisation may take in a highly secularised context: agnostic spirituality. Syncretistic and experimental, this religious world view is not tied to traditional stocks of religious knowledge. And its semantics, without the anchor of a traditional religious institution or other stable community organisation, remains chronically unstable. However, it does articulate a certain openness to religious questions, bringing something new into play that is different from the materialism of the GDR, at the same time as it uses this materialism as a starting point.

These ideas – as minority ideas – were expressed mainly by members of the youngest generation, whereas the older generations tended to express more clear-cut religious or atheistic positions. But we also saw evidence of inverse socialisation, in which older family members considered or adopted ideas introduced by their younger family members. What became evident in the research was that, even in a highly secularised country like East Germany, the question of death and afterlife could provoke intense debates among the family members, touching issues of individuality and community, remembrance and oblivion, transience and eternity. Different from the expectations of scientist atheism, religious questions have again become a legitimate subject of communication. But they have become a subject of experimental exploration rather than of firm belief.

Notes

[1] Organised atheist groups in the 19th and early 20th century were concentrated in the part of Germany that later became the GDR: Berlin, Eisenach, Leipzig, Weimar, Jena, Magdeburg and Gotha. In comparison, West German locations are rare: Trier, Frankfurt and Kassel (see Kaiser, 2003: 124).

[2] It is interesting, as far as the study of the life course is concerned, that there is no really natural term for *Jugendliche* in English. 'Young people' is too broad a term and 'adolescents' seems to have distracting connotations relating specifically to emotional development.

[3] The original Urania was established in Berlin in 1888; its purpose was to disseminate scientific knowledge to the general population. After World War II, a form of the Urania was founded in both German states. The Urania of the German Democratic Republic was founded in East Berlin in 1954. It aimed to programmatically educate all parts of the population, to whom it intended to offer the 'light of science'. This involved cooperation with scientists and employees from various universities and research institutes, which offered a large number of lectures and other events. It had branches in literally every town in East Germany. As stated in the founding documents of the Urania, the new organisation was intended to propagate the scientific world view and to attack 'superstition and traditional thinking', which included religion. As a mass institution, it was one of the main institutional actors to support the atheist politics of the state, although always in combination with the spread of science.

[4] People of this generation built up the new socialist state and took central political positions in the GDR, in which they remained for many years.

[5] The second highest number was a 26% positive response among the 75- to 89-year-old respondents (see ALLBUS, 2002: 117, V172; calculation by the author).

[6] In the project, 26 family interviews were conducted, with members of three generations (three to five people) participating in the interviews. In addition, 27 narrative interviews as well as seven group discussions among the youngest generation were conducted. My collaborators in this project were Uta Karstein, Thomas Schmidt-Lux and Mirko Punken; research students were Anja Frank, Christine Schaumburg and Jurit Kärtner.

[7] In my opinion, this does not imply the *necessity* of religiosity. Thinking beyond one's death may also lead to agnostic or atheist perspectives and to hedonistic rather than religious forms of life.

[8] Abbreviations and symbols used in the interview quotes are as follows: GM = Grandmother; GF = Grandfather; F = Father; M = Mother; D = Daughter; S = Son; I = Interviewer; // parallel speaking; \ interruption; want emphasized; [asking her granddaughter] comment; ... omission; {Laughing} non-verbal behaviour; (8) seconds pause.

[9] This may also be designed as a solution to the possible question: should whichever partner dies first be buried in a new grave or in the grave of their first spouse?

---

[10] She is referring to the Catholic members of the Sorb community, to which her father – divorced from her mother – belongs and with which she has been involved.

[11] This seems to be a combination of 'exodus' and 'exitus'.

References

ALLBUS (2002) ZA-No. 3700, Cologne, www.gesis.org/Datenservice/ALLBUS/Daten/all2002.htm

Durkheim, E. (2001) *The elementary forms of religious life*, Oxford: Oxford University Press.

Engler, W. (1999) *Die Ostdeutschen. Kunde von einem verlorenen Land*, Berlin: Aufbau.

Hölscher, L. (ed.) (2000) *Datenatlas zur religiösen Geographie im protestantischen Deutschland. Von der Mitte des 19. Jahrhunderts bis zum Zweiten Weltkrieg*, Berlin/New York: de Gruyter.

Kaiser, J.-C. (2003) 'Organisierter Atheismus im 19. Jahrhundert', in C. Gärtner, D. Pollack and M. Wohlrab-Sahr (eds) *Atheismus und religiöse Indifferenz*, Opladen: Leske & Budrich, pp 99-128.

Knoblauch, H. (1997) 'Die Sichtbarkeit der unsichtbaren Religion. Subjektivierung, Märkte und die religiöse Kommunikation', *Zeitschrift für Religionswissenschaft*, vol 5, no 2, pp 179-202.

Kohli, M. (1994) 'Die DDR als Arbeitsgesellschaft? Arbeit, Lebenslauf und soziale Differenzierung', in H. Kaelble, J. Kocka and H. Zwahr (eds) *Sozialgeschichte der DDR*, Stuttgart: Klett, pp 31-61.

Liepold, R. (2000) *Die Teilnahme an der Konfirmation bzw. Jugendweihe als Indikator für die Religiosität von Jugendlichen aus Vorpommern*, Frankfurt am Main: Peter Lang.

Luckmann, T. (1980) 'Säkularisierung – ein moderner Mythos', in T. Luckmann (ed) *Lebenswelt und Gesellschaft: Grundstrukturen und geschichtliche Wandlungen*, Paderborn: Schöningh, pp 161-72.

Luckmann, T. (1990): 'Shrinking transcendence, expanding religion?', *Sociological Analysis*, vol 51, no 2, pp 127-38.

Luhmann, N. (1995) *Social systems*, Stanford, CA: Stanford University Press.

Mader, O. (1959) *Methodischer Brief zum Lehrplan für das Fach Astronomie*, Berlin: Deutsches Pädagogisches Zentralinstitut.

Mannheim, K. (1972) 'The problem of generations', in P. Altbach and R. Laufer (eds) *The new pilgrims: Youth protest in transition*, New York: David McKay and Company, pp 101-38.

McLeod, H. (1992) 'Secular cities? Berlin, London and New York in the later nineteenth and early twentieth centuries', in S. Bruce (ed) *Religion and modernization: Sociologists and historians debate the secularization thesis*, Oxford: Oxford University Press, pp 59-89.

Nowak, K. (1996) 'Staat ohne Kirche? Überlegungen zur Entkirchlichung der evangelischen Bevölkerung im Staatsgebiet der DDR', in G. Kaiser and E. Frie (eds) *Christen, Staat und Gesellschaft in der DDR*, Frankfurt am Main: Wallstein, pp 23-43.

Pollack, D. (1994) *Kirche in der Organisationsgesellschaft. Zum Wandel der gesellschaftlichen Lage der evangelischen Kirchen in der DDR*, Stuttgart: Kohlhammer.

Pollack, D. (2000) 'Der Wandel der religiös-kirchlichen Lage in Ostdeutschland nach 1989. Ein Überblick', in D. Pollack and G. Pickel (eds) *Religiöser und kirchlicher Wandel in Ostdeutschland 1989-1999*, Opladen: Leske & Budrich, pp 18-47.

Schmidt, T. and Wohlrab-Sahr, M. (2003) 'Still the most areligious part of the world: developments in the religious field in Eastern Germany since 1990', *International Journal of Practical Theology*, vol 7, no 1, pp 86-100.

Schmidt-Lux, T. (2008) *Wissenschaft als Religion. Szientismus im ostdeutschen Säkularisierungsprozess*, Würzburg: Ergon.

Schütz, A. (1962a) 'On multiple realities', in A. Schütz *Collected papers I*, The Hague: Nijhoff, pp 207-59.

Schütz, A. (1962b) 'Symbol, reality and society', in A. Schütz *Collected papers I*, The Hague: Nijhoff, pp 287-356.

Smith, C. and Denton, M.L. (2005) *Soul searching: The religious and spiritual lives of American teenagers*, Oxford: Oxford University Press.

Wohlrab-Sahr, M., Karstein, U. and Schaumburg, C. (2005): '"Ich würd' mir das offenlassen": agnostische Spiritualität als Annäherung an die "große Transzendenz" eines Lebens nach dem Tode', *Zeitschrift für Religionswissenschaft*, vol 13, no 2, pp 153-73.

Wohlrab-Sahr, M., Schmidt-Lux, T. and Karstein, U. (2008) 'Secularization as conflict', *Social Compass*, vol 55, no 2, pp 127-39.

FIVE

Beyond dialogue: entering the fourth space in old age

Haim Hazan

Introduction: exiled lives

Conventional wisdom has it that the final words attributed to the famous and infamous emit an aura of immortality by transcending the circumstantial time and place of their utterance. Edward Said's last unfinished book, posthumously published in 2006, not only confers a sense of such ultimate truth, but also, in its contents and contentions, offers a powerful key with which to enter the unfathomable realm of what I shall call the a-temporal territory of the fourth space. The book, entitled *On late style: Music and literature against the grain*, follows Theodor Adorno's inquiry into Beethoven's late style of composition. In his wake Said develops a concept of timelessness detectable in the last works of great musicians and writers. Contrary to cultural expectations of congruity between life stages and styles of art prevailing along the penultimate phases of the life course, coined by Said 'timeliness', the final burst of artistic expression is irreconcilable, discordant, contentious and timeless. It is an a-historical moment, surpassing the annals of epochs and breaking down normative conventions to the extent that, in his words:

> ... the artist who is fully in command of his medium nevertheless abandons communication with the established social order of which he is a part and achieves a contradictory, alienated relationship with it. His late works constitute a form of exile. (Said, 2006: 5)

Such an exile of lateness, described by Cohen-Shalev (2002: 155) as 'disintegrated and incommunicable old age style ... as a sign of wisdom', is hence the inspiration for this exploration of the uniqueness of banished existence in the land of the fourth space. The author could initially take a glimpse into that domain, as in so many other cases in which anthropological substance is probed, through stumbling on a seemingly merely methodological hitch.

It should be noted that, for our intents and purposes, any student of human behaviour, especially of the treacherous turf of old age, even if not wearing the coat-of-arms of anthropology, is willingly, or reluctantly, an honorary member of that disciplinary clan of witch hunters, diviners of fuzzy concepts and foragers among the remains of the social in the age-old forest of the wild signposted by old age.

Towards a dialogical impasse

What should such a proverbial anthropologist, addressing a designated 'other', make of the following repartee?

| Anthropologist: | Would you tell me your life story? |
| Other: | I don't know. Everything that happened just happened in its own right. No connection whatsoever between this and that. |

This scene, taken from a study of the construction of time among the oldest older people, gives the impetus in what follows to consider some of the general, rather than the situational issues involved in the failure of the two speakers' sentences to correspond with each other in cultivating a common ground for the emergence of a translatable and comprehensible research field dealing with advanced old age.

The idea of an ethnographic field as the origin of anthropological wisdom is stipulated by the coexistence of self and other in a shared dialogical frontier of betweenness (Bakhtin, 1981; Tedlock, 1983), whose possible discursive permutations might engender four types of translation potentialities. The first is centred around self-knowledge and reflexivity as the major tool for interpreting and articulating reality. Sometimes called autoethnography, the pith of its credo is Judith Okley's equation stating that 'personality is theory' (Okley, 1992: 9). Here, otherness is contained within self-awareness and subjective consciousness. The second possibility is an ideal type of interaction based on dialogical equality, mutual understanding and balanced reciprocity, with no need for mediation or restitutive measures to dispel obfuscation and rectify inequities. Self and other are interchangeable and merge into one. This Simmelian dyadic model of a field, almost Buberian, even Levinasian in spirit, serves as a politically correct banner for setting ethical bounds to anthropological exploits.

The third type of field is the perpetrator of most anthropological ills – succumbing to the structural-cultural inequalities between anthropologist and native who are positioned as strangers to each other. The ethnographic arena, constructed by these tensions of power and knowledge, requires for its viability the presence and services of a third party of translators in the form of local informants, cultural and political agents, alongside academic professionals whose involvement in the field renders it triadic in form and disputatious by nature. The fourth field is one beyond translation and arguably beyond comprehension, since no dialogue between anthropologist and other could take place. In this fourth field, the other is presented as ultimately inaudible.

These four types of fields, characterised by self-reflection, direct negotiation, mediation and incommunicability, suggest four respective epistemological spaces for mapping out the contours of the anthropological enterprise of constructing the limits of what is knowable. Hence, the pivotal concern of our exploration here is to scrutinise such limits, as manifested in the exposure to the third and fourth spaces and related to the specific recognition of old age. To arrive at this destination some preliminary issues regarding the problematics of enabling cultural translation ought to be broached. The author would like to contend that any such act of transferring symbolic capital, particularly in the third space, spells appropriation and transmutation of the 'them' into the 'us' and vice versa. When this assumption of constructible reversibility is removed, translation and translators are no longer rendered operational and plausible. Thus, the cessation of the possibility of translation is also the termination of articulate interpretation. It subsequently heralds the disappearance of communication.

The patterns of translation failure that break down dialogical moments are manifold, varied and embrace a whole range of discrepancies of genres, contents and epistemes. But, for the purpose of pursuing our dialogical dilemma, it is sufficient to restrict the scope of the discussion to problems relevant to the case of communicating with older people. We begin with one speech incongruity that infuses the ensuing argument: the distinction between the metaphoric and the literal. In the wake of Lakoff and Johnson's seminal work on the predominant role of metaphor in constructing and construing experience (Lakoff and Johnson, 1980), and pursuant to the legacy of symbolic interactionism, awareness of the place of symbolic exchange in human interaction has been profusely advocated in sociological thinking. It has gained ground almost to the extent of reducing any perspective on communication to manifestations of that trope. Anthropology, however, has always been attentive to the presence of other meaning-forming representational devices such as metonymy, synecdoche and the literal. (In metonymy, a word or phrase is replaced by another that is associated with it, such as 'Paris' for 'the French government'; synecdoche revolves around using the part for the whole, as in 'the Crown' for 'the monarchy'.) Thus, while metaphoric language enables associative, open-minded and open-ended creativity and communicability, the use of metonymical signs is self-referring and bound to one autonomous closed domain of meaning. Literal language goes even further, inasmuch as it unequivocally denotes the positively natural and resists multivocal symbolism (Turner, 1991; Hockey and James, 1993; Hazan, 1996). The impregnability of the literal to the transcendental, the abstract and the metaphoric, aligns its referential scope to an unadulterated description of material, tangible objects such as body parts, bodily inputs and outputs, somatic conditions and their functions. It is inhospitable to any adumbration of embodiment of the type ascertained by the currently proliferating scholarship of the body cultural (Fraser and Greco, 2005).

Such discrepant modes of reference and understanding of the multifarious metaphoric versus the unilateral literal may be accountable for yet another breakdown in translation, one that reflects fundamental differences in existential conditions. When a category of population is subjected to severe measures in which social identity is stripped off through forfeiting civil rights and cultural standing to a sovereign power, its subsequent bare life (Agamben, 1995), or as Bauman (2004) dubs it 'wasted lives', is also robbed of any symbolic signification. Thus, the biopolitical discourse of sovereignty, by reducing dependent populations to their mere vulnerable corporeality, precludes them from entering that discourse itself and hence curtails communication and translation. In turn, resorting to bodily anchored literal language is thus a common form of self-expression among those whose symbolic world is shattered, struck off and dissipated. People who are sick and bedridden, labour migrants, inmates in total institutions, refugees, homeless people, slaves and politically dispossessed people are but a few examples of categories of people whose forced preoccupation with somatic needs and properties confines their construction of reality to templates of the here and now of an extreme experience of existence and survival. No self-indulgent teleological quest for meaning is available to them.

Denied spatio-temporal perspectives to facilitate the absorption, processing and communicating of such non-reflexive language, the anthropologist often resorts to morally superimposed judgements and ethical deliberations, as in the case of organ transplantation (Scheper-Hughes, 2000) or human suffering (Kleinman, 2006). It would seem inconceivable to the academic translator to uphold the disciplinary ethos of faithful representation and reporting by giving linguistic and conceptual credit to a native's account when it is bereft of moral accountability. Thus, such eventual lacunae are filled in with the anthropologist's own world view, thereby usurping the advocated other and treating him or her as a mere mirror reflecting the researcher's sentiments and imagery. This disregards the possibility of sheer literal description free of value orientations.

This leads us to a subsequent ramification of this schism in linguistic levels of expression: namely, it is possible that there exists no common experiential ground between researchee and researcher. Even though anthropologists are supposed to partly assume the social identity of the other, their cloak of professional training and competence is often too short to cover the whole gamut of quintessential emotions, sensuous responses and subtleties of consciousness. This experiential void may be responsible for formidable and formative misconceptions of the hidden, yet fundamental agendas underlying the imagined reality of the other. For example, the prevalent focus in anthropological discourse on the body as a contested site for cultural reflections and negotiation spells an attempt to create a levelling mechanism for defining a shared geography of symbolic interaction. However, unless fully converted to the spirit and soul of the bodily experience of the other, the anthropologist's dilemma of accounting for the unaccountable might result in a disjuncture between the ethnographer's text and the ethnographic context. An epistemological void might be created, marked by mutual lack of recognition. This is prominent, for instance, in the case of cross-generational gaps or cohort differences, sometimes described as cultural autism (Melucci, 1996), emanating from exceedingly discrepant self-perceptions of body and mind.

The author would like to suggest that such a void could emerge out of a certain cultural state that amasses all translation failures. Rare and improbable though it might seem, such totality of conditions for mistranslation that does not necessarily implicate silence might be found in some research situations where, in spite of a seeming flow of interaction, an explicit breach in mutual understanding unfolds. The case selected above for testifying to the possibility of interactional incommunicability draws, as already mentioned, on an attempted interviewing of very old people. First, however, we should sketch a brief conceptual framework expounding the relevance to our argument of the case of comprehending old age as a bridge between methodological concerns with dialogical impasses, which brings us to the confines of the fourth space in the fourth age.

From third to fourth age

The main academic preoccupation with the 'otherness' of older people has been placed on the well-acquainted safe turf of what is sometimes described as the third age, namely the folk age category populated by extended midlifers whose mental, social and physical functioning capabilities can be assessed and measured by the standards of the cultural texts written by middle age (Hazan and Raz, 1997) – advocating nebulous universals of supposed 'normal', 'successful' and 'optimal aging' epitomised in Ryff and Singer's (1998) modernity-geared integrative concept of 'positive health'. The spectre of research agendas viewing old age strictly within the visible and readable discourse of modern middle age, gerontophobic norms and values of integration, self-realisation, sense of coherence and personal development haunts gerontological thinking and practice, harnessing the 'undisciplined discipline' (Katz, 1996) to the grand midlife project of the managing and surveillance of old age. This is accomplished through designating third-age incumbents to problem areas strewn with ominous, less than allegedly normal yardsticks of performance, legitimate and acceptable only in 'the secret world of subcultural aging' (Blaikie, 2002) – and rendered conveniently invisible to the gaze of its manufacturers through the stratagem of consigning them to disenfranchised 'cultures of ageing' (Gilleard and Higgs, 2000).

This reservedly controlled incorporation of the highly blurred category of the third age into the social construction of the prescribed western life course (Hareven, 1995) spells a mode of negotiating the terms and limits of a worthy preferable life, rife with meaning-construing devices conferred by ethical cultural imageries of the good or the bad death (Lavi, 2005).

Knowledge of the third age, therefore, acquires the reflected qualities of self-knowledge germane to the structures of authorship and authority that encode the midlife cultural order. The crafting of this category thus serves as the periphery surrounding the centre of mainstream discourses, through drawing marginal borders exhibiting the brinkmanship of self-justification – and beyond which looms a twilight zone of another human existence, a buffer area separating the living from the dead, sometimes conceived of as a domain inhabited by the oldest older people, otherwise known as the fourth age – marked by an accelerated thrust of decline. It should be noted, however, that the age index setting within whose boundaries the fourth age could be recognised and classified is an offshoot of the current rectangulation of compressed morbidity: this narrows down the actual phase of a rapid final deterioration, decreasing even further the last short term of life. It would, therefore, be appropriate to regard the concept as a metaphor for Baudrillard's depiction of very old people as an 'asocial slice of life' composed of undecipherable residuals (Baudrillard, 1993: 163), those beyond culture with whom communication is by definition rendered implausible.

The symbolic onset of incommunicability is not distinctly benchmarked by age, infirmity or institutionalisation. Rather, it is gradually and subtly signalled through the continuous process of constructing ageing, highlighted by landmarks such as retirement, resignation to sociopsychological disengagement, the rise in structural dependency and the growing awareness of ageist exclusionary messages. The cumulative effect accrued throughout this experience of ageing is the harbinger of radical transformations in spatio-temporal orientations, shifting the linearly narrated plot of a meaning-driven life course to a lateral, present-bound world, governed by activities of daily risk management. So foreign to modern conceptions of the sense of worthy living are such changes that some scholars ponder the academic and professional faculties at our disposal to account for the arguably mysterious life of fourth agers. Thus Baltes and Smith (2003: 114), while vacillating between a population-based and a person-based definition of the nebulous category of the fourth age, submit that under any definition:

> … the fourth age threatens some of the most precious features of the human mind such as intentionality, personal identity and psychological control over one's future, as well as the chance to live and die with dignity.

Embedded in this existential wonderment is an uncertainty about some taken-for-granted tenets underlying the established discourse of interpreting ageing. It is, indeed, a poignant critique of the desire to contain old age within some known and tested scheme of cultural repertoire, be it Swidler's (1986) cultural tool kit or Boltanski and Thévenot (1999) 'regimes of justification' (discourses in which conventions for praising or blaming are defended and legitimised). Such repertoires ignore extra-cultural situations governed by drives, exigencies and considerations, implying a mode of rationality incongruous with familiar measures and criteria. These extra-cultural alternative determinants of choice, risk taking, decision making, prioritising means and goals and, ultimately, rethinking ethics in terms of mere existence might overturn our run-of-the-mill conceptions of humanity. If this is the case for the inexplicability of the experience of being in the fourth age, then its inaccessibility and unapproachability ought to be reflected in encumbered channels of communication with those supposed to occupy it. Hence, the lack of cultural codes for making sense of this singular phase of life is tantamount to the absence of a pragmatic language enabling shared and meaningful interaction and dialogue.

This fleeting transition from third to fourth age, while signifying a possible breach in comprehension and communication, is predominantly highlighted by escalating changes in the structural relationship between agencies, namely the scriptwriters and directors of culture and the actors assigned to perform their texts and instructions. It is evident that the roles of writers and performers are constantly interchangeable, but they tend to be socially transfixed as people grow older. Hence, the masquerade of ageing identity (Biggs, 2003) manifested in anti-ageing practices and surface emulation of middle age places third agers in a cultural state highly reminiscent of what Bhabha (1994) has termed 'the third space', the 'in-between-ness' embracing colonised and coloniser in a mutual mirroring act of enchantment and subjugation, mimicry and translation, reversibility and fluidity. This apparent breakdown of dichotomies engenders a discourse of hybridisation and ambivalence that seemingly dissolves categories of power and domination but, nevertheless, retains and maintains the politics of cultural dependency camouflaged as symbolic exchange. At the same time it reinforces the mastery of the coloniser as a producer of knowledge of otherness. This interface state of otherness, coupling incorporation and disengagement, visibility and invisibility, autonomy and servitude could be deflected in the cultural space of the third age. The analogy between the third world, which germinates the third space, and the concept of the third age was succinctly pointed out by Baudrillard in his *Symbolic Exchange and Death* (1993: 163). As he states:

> … a third of society is thus segregated and placed in a situation of economic parasitism. The lands conquered on this death march are socially barren. Recently colonized, old age in modern times burdens society with the same weight as colonized native populations used to. Retirement, or 'The Third Age' says precisely what it means, it is a sort of 'Third World'.

However, Baudrillard's unequivocal parallelism loses sight of the more refined, sophisticated, albeit somehow sinister, view of the interaction between the two protagonists in a colonising condition where boundaries are blurred, but domination prevails. The emphasis on the proliferation of translated texts and the emergence of a social class of translators attests to the constant delineation of transcultural contact zones (Pratt, 1992), interweaving the two entities to form a common language that facilitates the flow of communication. However, under the guise of such dialogical exchange, translators preserve, furnish and accentuate the divisions between the 'unhomely' (Bhabha, 1994) of the third space and their colonising agents or, in our terms, between midlifers, who still dwell on metaphor, and the literally excommunicated oldest older people.

This liminal geography of the third age stretches between the face-lifted edges of dreamed of middle age and the murky terrains of lived in and feared old age. The flamboyant mass-media marketplace of contemporary consumer society celebrates the illusion of the upfront availability of goods and services that can be appropriated, many of which are time-structuring devices such as middle-class, middle-age related images embodying old-age resistance. The fine balance between the two vectors drafting the contours of third age space could be easily tipped, rendering its cultural edifice precarious and untenable. The process of inevitable ageing constantly shakes the defences of this post-middle-age, pre-old-age bastion and eventually transforms its third-space cultivated ground into a fourth-space rough terrain – populated, among others, with fourth agers.

The fourth space is, indeed, an antithetical sequel to the qualities of the third space. Contrary to the reversal of fortunes between self and other, the quest for dialogue and translation, the subsequent emergence of hybrid entities, presumably generating a culturally prescribed sense of meaning in a postmodern era, life in the fourth space harbours neither reminiscing nor forgetting. It consists of untranslatable fragmented texts, pure extra-cultural categories of sheer existence, inarticulate voices, subverted engagements and, consequently, a sense of being in the world incomprehensible to the outside observer. Identifying the indications of the fourth space, therefore, cannot rest on culturally accessible prior knowledge of modes of existence that are unresponsive to familiar discourses. In order to circumvent this barrier, some other cusps of extreme existence should be drawn on for recognising this form of uncharted territory.

The fourth space in the fourth age

It is the ambivalent nature of the third age, a variety of the third space, that foreshadows its transmutation into a fourth age – a version of the fourth space. Dwelling on the leisure phase between mid and later life, it is in and of itself a sort of discontinuity, a rupture reducing living into objectified styles and goods that divorce the ageing self from its predestined place along a life course whose fuzziness (Blaikie, 1999) in the popular media belies both the rigidity of its political economy and the prevalence of cultural ageism. This disjuncture between sources of interpretive agency and the preconditions of structure is a step towards what Anderson (1972) identified as the deculturation of older people and Hazan (1980) depicted as a limbo state. A further step in this discursive process of dehumanisation may be detected in the conspiracy of silence surrounding concerns associated with ageing and particularly with deep old age. This is social denial of the type described as the 'elephant in the room' of whose presence everybody is aware, but which nobody would dare mention (Zerubavel, 2006). However, reminders of such 'cultural residuals' invariably become conspicuously and unavoidably evident and noted, while glossing devices of jest, mimicry, humour, deference and avoidance are no longer effective. Consequently, the refined gatekeepers of audibility and visibility who fail to ward off the transgression of the prohibited fourth space into the reservedly legitimate third space must be replaced by harsher safeguarding mechanisms of surveillance.

Such fortified walls are erected by designated heterotopic enclaves for sequestrated populations of others, symbolically circumscribed as antonymous to the principles of social ordering and classification (Foucault, 1986). The mortification of self in total institutions, as described by Goffman (1961), and the bare life of concentration camp prisoners as analysed by Agamben (1995), are but two attempts at framing the parameters of the fourth space. This is one in which communication with inmates is usually conducted through channels of authoritarian management and as a result of which subjectivity reversibility and negotiability are expunged.

Fourth space experience, however, is not necessarily or exclusively delimited by barriers of social and physical isolation. The spreading of the therapeutic discourse with its legions of professional custodians creates medical, judicial and media environments, where fourth-space, socially discarded categories are confessed and cleansed, to be reborn from victims of social castigation and exclusion into tokens of cultural sacrifice on the altar of collective guilt. Revealing the shameful secret of belonging to the fourth space exposes its already branded inhabitants to what Taussig (1999) calls an act of defacement, unmasking a publicly known secret of the most powerful kind of knowledge: that of knowing what not to know.

The controlled voyeurism of tourist or media visits to the outlandish realms of the fourth space (for example, curative, corrective, incarcerating and decimating facilities) is, indeed, a defacement of the modern ethos of the uniqueness and sacredness of the autonomy of human life.

The presence of the fourth space, therefore, is not only a testimony to and a consequence of the total power of the social sovereign. It also exposes a constitutive force engrossed in mapping out areas of legitimate, accessible and processable knowledge – as against forbidden, taboo zones inhabited by varieties of the grotesque, the freakish, the condemned, the living dead and the disenfranchised. The organised peepshows that allow glimpses of pedagogical morbid curiosity into the unknowable reaffirm the potency of fourth spaces – daringly or playfully – to temporarily rob unruly viewers of their humanity; and to restore and confirm the proscription of interaction, communication and exchange between the gaze of the observer and that of the observed. Under these structural circumstances, almost all the pitfalls of translatability function to impede any attempt at transferring knowledge of the fourth space to more familiar areas of cultural cognizance.

Notwithstanding the overlap between fourth space and fourth age, this model is evidently problematic, since no straightforward parallel could be drawn between the two concepts. Some useful cues, however, could be taken from the idea of the fourth space as a non-negotiable, non-dialogical intercourse, to develop a number of insights into the social construction of the practical discourse of the fourth age. This could be manifested in the academic endeavour to elicit knowledge of the narrated experience produced in the course of interviewing the oldest older people, who constitute the most likely candidates to join the ranks of the fourth space. If our assumption regarding the untranslatability of texts from the fourth space is valid, then the contrived communication fabricated by customary routines of research acts aimed at fourth agers should yield a split non-discursive set comprising two unrelated utterances. The one set of utterances would be a rendition of cultural schemas reflecting academic scripts of assumed development, anticipated identity constructions through life reviews and declared meaningful reckonings of achievements and failures: in sum, a fully fledged picture of third-age, double-sided concern with inclusion and exclusion. The other rendition would apparently consist of utterances ostensibly unrelated to interview conventions, resisting any superimposed textual organisation in a narrative form. Devoid of meaning-seeking cues and composed of irregular grammatical fashions, such fragmented texts offer rickety templates for decipherment or even interpretation. In the relative absence of dialogical transaction, no shared symbolic capital could be forged and each textual presentation would follow its own linguistic-cum-existential rules. Thus our analysis presages a research situation in which doubt could be cast on the adequacy of an academic and professionally available equipment to tackle the premise of intersubjective, negotiated order. As such, it could serve as a test case for validating the constructionist models so prevalent in the humanistic-liberal approach to the study of old age, seen as a desired integral phase in the life span.

The case in point, to be sketchily reported here, is an ethnographic reflection on a series of open-ended interviews in a course of a study on a representative sample of the Israeli Jewish oldest older people with an average age of 93. In spite of the multicultural and functionally variegated profile of the respondents, a number of all-embracing insights could be gained from scanning the research files. Life stories recounted reached early old age or late mid age and ended their narrated yarn around the seventh decade of life. Regardless of the interviewers' attempts to engage in sympathetic and fruitful conversations in order to elicit scholarly predicted, life-reckoning reminiscing, leading to morales and visions, actual reactions were unemotional, non-pedagogical and, in the main, impartial as to anticipated feelings, ethics and values. Instead, disinterested accounts were emitted, arranged and reluctantly presented as a haphazard due paid to power relations and to the few leftovers of perfunctory politeness still embodied in the interviewees.

The metamorphosis from expected narratives in pursuit of meaning and sense to accounts with no such personal accountability corresponded to a transformation from causal to circumstantial construction of reality, namely from intentionally oriented perspectives to assertions of existential, instrumental, ad-hoc management. The past was incorporated into the present, as long as its memory funds could be invested into the capital of daily-living-attainable resources. The same principle of sustaining the subsistence economy of the here and now was applied to mainstreaming human relations and sociations. Family members, although declared cherished and valued, were practically judged by the support, or otherwise, they lent. Other caregivers, such as hired help, neighbours and professionals, were placed on a higher pedestal than late, hence ineffective spouses; the presence of offspring in the respondent's world was related with equanimity, even including the occurrence of their death. The language mode befitting these seeming mutations in world view required an unequivocal code of expressing experience. Thus, the literal replaces the metaphorical, irony is shunned and sequentially structured sentences give way to non-linear, often disjointed, fractured grammatical formations.

The literally concrete materialisation of reality also shapes the management of the environmental boundaries within which physical mobility and bodily manoeuvering is confined. The emphasis on the body literal, while de-emphasising the body metaphorical, is submerged into the materiality of daily coping with existence, to introduce a cleavage between the redundant temporal and exigent spatial. The divorce between time robbed of its past and future, and space centred around its present-bound location, depletes memory of its constructive and constitutive reservoirs, thereby converting retentive faculties for imagined identity into a preservative economy consumed by the business of practising survival.

Since the respondents were administered cognitive tests to assess their mental competence, their textual testimonies reflect a non-pathological construal of reality. Hence, contrary to situationally anchored assumptions concerning the dynamics of interviewing (Randall et al, 2006), the ruptured and interrupted dialogues are situationally emergent products of a bifurcated construction of a cosmology whose forked branches describing life grow apart as very old people move deeper and further beyond the pale of the fourth space. Chasing them into that realm of existence poses a research challenge, which is invariably met by a subterfuge which grafts the two branches into one theory, remodelling the 'we' and the 'other' in a contrived, familiar, third-space discourse of care, concern and predetermined formats of encoding experience.

Concluding remarks : beyond dialogue

The omnipotence of memory as the axis around which experience revolves and reverberates is, indeed, the cultural editor compiling the joint writing of a common life script based on presuming an uninterrupted ageless self (Kaufman 1986), covered by a mask of ageing (Featherstone and Hepworth, 1991). This unquestioned conception emanates from what Hacking (1998: 198) termed 'the sciences of memory' where

> ... memory, already regarded as a criterion of personal identity, became a scientific key to the soul, so that by investigating memory (to find out its facts) one would conquer the spiritual domain of the soul and replace it by a surrogate, knowledge about memory. The facts that are discovered in this or that science of memory are surface knowledge; beneath them is the depth knowledge, that are facts about memory to be found out.

This academically formulated, given understanding of the role of memory in constructing identity is, therefore, the surface knowledge on which the illusion of the plausibility of translating and articulating the fourth space is erected.

Undoing these assumptions, however, could help remove the shadow of memory from the discourse of the other in general and that of the fourth age in particular. Debunked of building blocks of memory layered with meaning and ethics, the following non-dialogical exchange would make sense of acquiescing in the recognition of untranslatability, testing the limits of constructionist discourse:

> Question: Would you tell me your life-story?
> Answer: I don't know. Everything that happened just happened in its own right. No connection whatsoever between this and that.

By way of inconclusive closure, I wonder if this assertion of disharmony is a descendant testimony of Said's old-style lateness shared by high and low cultures, the boundaries between which, as Adorno suggested, dissolve in the throes of industrial, secular, mass society. Perhaps Said's fascination with celebrated genius obscured his vision from perceiving the oneness of final works of art and the work of the art of existence common to all exiled sojourners passing through the fourth space. Or is it the case that scholarship by its discursive nature is impotent to capture the sense of being in the fold of that form of life and do justice to its quiddity? Instead, paradoxically, only the artistically metaphoric could articulate the literal, timelessly transcendental experience of existing in the inaudible fourth age.

References

Agamben, G. (1995) *Homo sacer: Sovereign power and bare life*, Stanford, CA: Stanford University Press.

Anderson, B. (1972) 'The process of deculturation – its dynamics among United States aged', *Anthropological Quarterly*, vol 45, no 4, pp 209-16.

Bakhtin, M. (1981) *The dialogic imagination. Four essays*, Austin, TX: University of Texas Press.

Baltes, P.B. and Smith, J. (2003) 'New frontiers in the future of aging from successful aging of the young old to the dilemma of the fourth age', *Gerontology*, vol 49, no 2, pp 123-35.

Baudrillard, J. (1993) *Symbolic exchange and death*, London: Sage Publications.

Bauman, Z. (2004) *Wasted lives*, Cambridge: Polity Press.

Bhabha, H.K. (1994) *The location of culture*, London: Routledge.

Biggs, S. (2003) 'Negotiating aging identity: surface, depth and masquerade', in S. Biggs, A. Lowenstein and J. Hendricks (eds) *The need for theory: Critical approaches to social gerontology*, Amityville, NY: Baywood Publishing Company, pp 145-62.

Blaikie, A. (1999) *Aging and popular culture*, Cambridge: Cambridge University Press.

Blaikie, A. (2002) 'The secret world of subcultural aging: what unites and what divides?', in L. Anderson (ed) *Cultural ferontology*, Westport, CT: Auburn House, pp 95–110.

Boltanski, L. and Thévenot, L. (1999) 'The sociology of critical capacity', *European Journal of Social Theory*, vol 2, no 3, pp 359–77.

Cohen-Shalev, A. (2002) *Both worlds at once: Art in old age*, Lanham, MD: University Press of America.

Featherstone, M. and Hepworth, M. (1991) 'The mask of aging and the postmodern lifecourse', in M. Featherstone, M. Hepworth and B. Turner (eds) *The body: Social processes and cultural theory*, London: Sage Publications, pp 371–89.

Foucault, M. (1986) 'Of other spaces', *Diacritics*, vol 16, no 1, pp 22–7.

Fraser, M. and Greco, M. (2005) 'Introduction', in M. Fraser and M. Greco (eds) *The body: A reader*, London: Routledge, pp 1–42.

Gilleard, C. and Higgs, P. (2000) *Cultures of ageing. Self citizen and the body*, Harlow: Prentice Hall.

Goffman, E. (1961) *Asylums*, New York: Doubleday Anchor.

Hacking, I. (1998) *Rewriting the soul: Multiple personality and the science of memory*, Princeton, NJ: Princeton University Press.

Hareven, T.K. (1995) 'Changing images of aging and the social construction of the life course', in M. Featherstone and A. Wernick (eds) *Images of aging: Cultural representations of later life*, London: Routledge, pp 119–34.

Hazan, H. (1980) *The limbo people: A study of the constitution of the time universe among the aged*, London: Routledge and Kegan Paul.

Hazan, H. (1996) *From first principles: An experiment in aging*, Westport, CT: Bergin and Garvey.

Hazan, H. and Raz, A.E. (1997) 'The authorized self: how middle age defines old age in the postmodern', *Semiotica*, vol 113, no 3/4, pp 257–76.

Hockey, J. and James, A. (1991) *Growing up and growing old: Ageing and dependency in the life course*, London: Sage Publications.

Katz, S. (1996) *Disciplining old age: The formation of gerontological knowledge*, Charlottesville, VA and London: University Press of Virginia.

Kaufman, S. (1986) *The ageless self: Sources of meaning in later life*, Madison: University of Wisconsin Press.

Kleinman, A. (2006) *What really matters: Living a moral life amidst uncertainty and danger*, New York: Oxford University Press.

Lakoff, G. and Johnson, M. (1980) *Metaphors we live by*, Chicago: The University of Chicago Press.

Lavi, S.J. (2005) *The modern art of dying: A history of euthanasia in the United States*, Princeton, NJ: Princeton University Press.

Melucci, A. (1996) *The playing self: Person and meaning in the planetary society*, Cambridge: Cambridge University Press.

Okley, J. (1992) 'Anthropology and autobiography: participatory experiences and embodied knowledge', in J. Okley and H. Callaway (eds) *Anthropology and autobiography*, London: Routledge, pp 1–28.

Pratt, M. (1992) *Imperial eyes: Travel writing and transculturation*, London: Routledge.

Randall, W.L., Prior, S.M. and Skarborn, M. (2006) 'How listeners shape what tellers tell: patterns of interaction in lifestory interviews and their impact on reminiscences by elderly interviewees', *Journal of Aging Studies*, vol 20, no 4, pp 381-96.

Ryff, C. and Singer, B. (1998) 'Psychological well-being: meaning, measurement and implication for psychotherapy research', *Psychotherapy and Psychosomatics*, vol 65, no 1, pp 14-23.

Said, E.W. (2006) *On late style: Music and literature against the grain*, New York: Pantheon Books.

Scheper-Hughes, N. (2000) 'The global traffic in organs', *Current Anthropology*, vol 41, no 2, pp 191-224.

Swidler, A. (1986) 'Culture in action: symbols and strategies', *American Sociological Review*, vol 51, no 2, pp 273-86.

Taussig, M. (1999) *Defacement: Public secrecy and the labor of the negative*, Stanford, CA: Stanford University Press.

Tedlock, D. (1983) *The spoken word and the work of interpretation*, Philadelphia, PA: University of Pennsylvania Press.

Turner, T. (1991) 'We are parrots "twins are birds": play of tropes as operational structure', in J. Fernandez (ed) *Beyond metaphor: The theory of tropes in anthropology*, Stanford, CA: Stanford University Press, pp 121-58.

Zerubavel, E. (2006) *The elephant in the room: Silence and denial in everyday life*, New York: Oxford University Press.

Part Two

Norms, values and gerontology

SIX

The long road to a moralisation of old age

Hans-Joachim von Kondratowitz

Perspectives for analysing normative frameworks of old age

Ideas and expectations about ageing in the contemporary world are today inextricably marked by strong normative undercurrents. These undercurrents are the products of a distinct but highly ambivalent historical heritage of modernity – one with which both gerontology itself and the institutional network of the modern welfare state are currently finding it difficult to deal convincingly. To explore this claim in more detail and to describe the dimensions of this ambivalence, this chapter's main aim is to reconstruct the different historical settings in which the discrepancy between this hidden normative impact and the resulting societal ambivalence took shape. The historical material to be utilised for this demonstration is taken from a European background, predominantly from German-speaking countries, and consists of a wide diversity of written and printed documents as well as interpretations of results from broader research in social and cultural history.

The empirical basis for this reconstruction is provided by three different sources of printed material:

- a comparison of articles concerned with ageing and life cycles in widely distributed and popular general encyclopedias from the early 18th century to the beginning of the 20th century;
- a comparison of entries on this subject matter in specialised medical encyclopedias from the 18th century to the beginning of the 20th century (von Kondratowitz, 1991);
- an evaluation of written material dealing with questions of societal ageing and its consequences – the material was produced by a wide range of experts and administrative personnel involved in social and medical reform in Germany from the end of the 18th century to present times (see von Kondratowitz, 1991, 2000a, 2000b).

Hence the content of this analysis will first of all be limited in scope to this specific background. Also in this chapter, the main emphasis will relate to adult and older life stages, which would in principle make it essential to complement this study by a thorough analysis of the other phases of life and their dynamics. But, despite these apparent limitations, it is nevertheless this chapter's intention to offer incentives for a line of research that would compare similarities and differences among the results presented here with sources and material from other European and non-European regions and countries, as well as their respective historical and cultural heritages.

In order fully to comprehend the implications of this line of analysis we should point to important results of historical discourse analysis for the particular situation in Germany (see Göckenjan, 2000). These research results have shown convincingly that in the Middle Ages as well as into early modern society it is not possible to speak of a coherent and comprehensive pattern of norms concerning and regulating old age for the whole society. Instead, Göckenjan has documented various and rather multifaceted ways of approaching old age in the life worlds of different social classes and professions, of the genders, and of different marginalised social groups within the population; this rules out any generalising homogeneity in approaching old age. Thus in early modernity there was a clear discrepancy between, on the one hand, visualising old age in personal encounters and going some way towards comprehending difficulties in the way of enjoying acceptable life circumstances and, on the other hand, the societal response that involved developing a perspective for dealing with and regulating relations concerning old age.

Then, from the late 17th century on, as the process of differentiation began to develop within modern society, the picture begins to change in the German-speaking regions. The gradual emergence of institutional settings for poor and older people, the establishment of a modern welfare state with its networks and regulatory legal devices influencing and channelling social articulations in daily life, all these developments resulted, among other social processes, in the invention of a fairly homogeneous normative framework for the life stage of older age. The accompanying discourse on old age is therefore characterised by Göckenjan as a discourse identified by increasing generalisation (Göckenjan, 2000: chapter 1). Such a discourse did not thematise diversity and the differentiated character of life forms and social milieus, but instead stressed commonalities between different forms of existence in old age. Moreover, there is embedded in this discourse a pressure towards taking the moral side of older people, defending them against societal hardships and unfavourable societal and sociopolitical developments. It is particularly this moralisation of old age that has found its climax in contemporary society. Such a moralisation certainly stands in clear and marked contrast to standards of treatment and conceptions of old age in the Middle Ages and in early modern society.

Unquestionably, this result, with its claim that 'old age' is a genuinely modern category, is surprising and unusual in several respects. First of all, it helps to dissolve a formerly clear 'camp building' among researchers on the historical legacy of old age, mainly between adherents of modernisation theory and its fervent critics.

But, moreover, such a perspective also offers the opportunity to question if not to deconstruct certain myths about old age. It contradicts long-familiar 'knowledge' that has been and still is quite widespread in the public domain as well as in more academic discourses. Such knowledge has often been associated with the idea of a supposedly 'golden' era for older people in ancient society and pre-industrial times. According to modernisation theory, the hidden theoretical basis of modern gerontology, this era was characterised by the still unchallenged status of older workers in rural and urban employment, by a well accepted position of older people inside the family, by a still strong and powerful role of older people in society and by the still influential role of transmitting oral traditions, storytelling and processing everyday experiences for social use. Modernisation theorists have claimed, in contrast, that in modern society all these characteristics of a traditional society for old age are replaced by a highly jeopardised and marginalised position for older people.

Social and cultural historical research has successfully directed much effort to refuting the claims of modernisation theory for the position of old age (see Ehmer, 1990; Conrad, 1994; Johnson and Thane, 1998). But regarding old age as a generalising concept produced by modernity can also challenge those gerontologists who prefer to view old age as a universal attribute of human life in all societal environments. Several scholars, such as Lawrence Stone (1981) and George Minois (1989), have insisted on the continuous presence of old age as an important social category in society. They have tried to reconstruct concepts of old age from times of antiquity onwards, certainly not denying considerable changes over time, but insisting on the basically universal character of old age distinguishable as an essential final stage of human life – in other words, as a set of elementary life experiences. Such a viewpoint, often intensified by reflections of a philosophical-anthropological quality, is not without persuasive power. Several recent historical contributions, critical of a culturalist, diversity-oriented line of research, have resubscribed to such a view. Indeed, at least in current historical work, there seems to be a new disenchantment with such a culturalist perspective. We can witness a re-emerging interest in universality and continuity within the ageing experience (see, for example, most of the contributions in Thane, 2005).

From the viewpoint of an orientation to continuity, some indicators that seem to show that old age was, in pre-modern times, already to a considerable degree normatively shaped, have been identified. For wealthy groups as well as rural landowners it is possible to trace the institutionalisation of different heritage arrangements and transfer regulations between generations. Also, beginning in the early 16th century, we can find the first visual representations of the life cycle in the form of the 'stairs of life'; these seem to depict a powerful normative framework towards old age. Equally, the influential claim that there was a universally continuous tradition of venerating older people, the 'honouring' of old age, has remained a central point of reference for the idea of the omnipresent concept of old age over time. But, here again, cultural and social historical research has been able to demonstrate that in the German-speaking countries of Austria and

Germany the distribution of such heritage arrangements was limited in scope to certain socioeconomic groups and cannot be generalised as a common feature, not even for pre-modern times. On the other hand, it must be conceded that the form of such arrangements has served as a model to be further elaborated and differentiated in legal terms within modern society. But this legal form reached its widest presence precisely in the 19th and early 20th centuries and not in early modernity – see, for example, work by Stefanova and Zeitlhofer for Bohemia and Langer-Ostravsky and Chvojka for Upper Austria in Ehmer and Gutschner (2000); also Mitterauer and Sieder (1991) and Sieder (1987).

Much the same applies to the visual 'life stair' model: it actually tends to depict gender and authority conceptions in pre-modern society as embedded in religious thought and tradition. It was never meant to reflect the reality of normative grading over adult life and old age. However, over time, such visual images seem to have acquired an immediate attractiveness and this material later gained a broad spatial distribution in Europe. Alhough these visual representations were already available and in use for several centuries, Ehmer (1996) has shown that they found their widest spread just as modern society penetrated into the early 20th century. They were used at that time especially often as wall decoration in rural dwellings and in small communities structured around rural and craft-based households. Originally, one important reason for the attractiveness of the 'life stairs' model seems to have derived from its resemblance to the sequence of seasons over the year, which later lent it an immediate plausibility in the rural environment.

Based on these observations it is already possible to offer a preliminary perspective by looking at the discourses presented here. It is remarkable that certain stocks of knowledge seem already to have been historically available in pre-modern times and early modern society. But their normative potential could not then flourish to its fullest extent. Indeed the main reason for this essential limitation seems to derive from the fact that these different arrangements, models and conceptions lack adequate generalising grounds for a broader social resonance, for conceiving of different and separate groups as exposed to comparable circumstances in the conduct of life. Thus since the 18th century we can witness in modern society the continuous, but transformed, adapted or further-developed presence and implantation of pre-modern normative features concerning old age. But in modern society this traditional heritage stands in competition and contrast to newly elaborated mechanisms for regulating and controlling older people, which are characteristic of this new societal environment and which expose their own normative power and moral stance. Retirement and its moral economy seems to be the most influential feature here, but other sociopolitical measures in health insurance, unemployment benefits, social assistance regulations and care arrangements have played equally important roles. All the richness of the historical examples presented here demonstrate that the interpretation of findings from the history of old age makes it necessary to follow multifaceted and ambivalent lines in reading and empirically re-evaluating such material.

Revering older people: misperceptions and ambivalences

The foregoing remarks are especially appropriate with regard to the well-known myth of a supposedly universal veneration of older people, with its strong normative implications. Examining the veneration of old age means at the same time studying the social processes bound up with the concept of the patriarchal family, of which this normative pattern is an essential part. Another dimension of veneration concerns the societal reputation of older people and the ways in which this reputation is acted out and institutionally secured. Both aspects were commented on, in an instructive and typically ambivalent manner, in the entry in Zedler's (1732) encyclopedia under 'old man'. This entry first follows the tradition of writers and philosophers from antiquity onwards in characterising older men as rather farcical creatures with strange behaviour patterns. Then it is confirmed, almost like an implicit apology, that: 'after all … old age has been held in honour and dignity and has been valued in all countries and at all times.' And, additionally, popular proverbs are quoted, such as 'the oldest, the best', 'old wine, healthy wine', 'old man, good advice' (Zedler, 1732:Vol 10, 1556-7). These are clearly intended to support the claim that old age is inseparably connected to the world of experience. An entry in another encyclopedia confirms this in a different way: 'In rights old age also has certain privileges, since older people of the same rank and standing take precedence among each other according to their ages' (Jablonski, 1721: 31). Additionally in the Zedler entry a typical description can be found of a flexible juridical concept of old age, as was common in early modern society; it required the further decision of a personage such as a judge to make a decision about, say, accepting guardianship. 'The *senes* do not have really determined years. Instead it depends on the good will of a judge whether he considers someone an "aged person"' (Zedler, 1732:Vol 10, 1553).

On the basis of such sources from early modern society, some German historians have arrived at far-reaching conclusions. They have tried to identify for this time-span in Germany a phase of societal disdain of old age (1350-1648/80), ending with the Thirty Years War and its disastrous cultural impact on everyday life, then followed (1648–1800) by a comprehensive phase of societal veneration for the aged (see Borscheid, 1987). The practice of making such condensed and generalised observations for such long time periods has been criticised by other researchers (Göckenjan, 2000; von Kondratowitz, 2000b: chapter 2). But, regardless of such attempts to group quite diverse and ambivalent social facts into changes *á la longue durée*, the topic of veneration of old age has continued to occupy an important place in academic endeavour as well as in practical negotiations of everyday behaviour until present times.

At the current juncture it is possible to observe a process of increasing 'scientisation' of this problem of veneration in which scholars turn to new fields of knowledge in order to make further contentions. Claims for a supposedly universal veneration for older people have often been legitimised by referring to mounting anthropological evidence on the strong position of older people in agrarian societies. But the oft-quoted work by Leo Simmons (1945) and other anthropologists was in fact quite cautious in asserting such unlimited universality. To the contrary, he directed attention to the considerable degree of variation in such normative arrangements. Moreover, anthropological research has always pointed to the fact of elder abuse and even gerontocide as an expression of conflict in tribal networks and household economies of non-industrial societies.

But, while research results from historical demography and family research have continuously emphasised questioning the idealisation of any veneration of old age, this myth has stubbornly survived in everyday life, regardless of such academic interventions. But it somewhat changed its function, taking the line of an implicit moralisation. However, at the present stage, 'veneration of old age' has lost the purpose of pure legitimation characterising different life worlds in pre-modern society. Now, in modernity, 'veneration' has turned at best into a rather private and casual gesture of politeness, an action according respect to an individual, or possibly pretending to take this attitude for strategic reasons in order to secure private advantages. This privatisation of normative conditions has led at the same time to a development in the normative setting of veneration: a gradually diminishing importance in official negotiations on a societal level, but a continuous impact of argumentation referring to the veneration of old age in personal and immediate relations. Thus, as early as the first half of the 20th century, in Germany, a long-term dissolution of this normative framework for venerating old age could be witnessed, coexisting with the use of normative expectations in everyday life.

We can demonstrate to which confusing confrontations this coexistence of diverging norms and values could lead by turning to the extreme example of the National Socialist era in Germany. This period of German history exhibits probably the last example of a definite policy of deliberately arguing in terms of the veneration of old age and using this to legitimate special sociopolitical measures for older people. The intensified establishment of homes for older people in Germany during the 1930s was justified and officially 'sold' by using the propaganda slogan of an 'Ehrendienst der Nation für seine älteren Volksgenossen' ('honourable acknowledgement of the elderly comrades of the nation'). This slogan (Wenzel, 1934; Mailänder, 1940) was widely distributed and replicated in the country (von Kondratowitz, 2000a). On an even larger scale, the rhetoric of venerating old age was used to establish a highly ambitious project of national socialist social policy, the 'Versorgungswerk des Deutschen Volkes', a newly designed plan to develop an insurance for old age, in particular for invalid workers of higher age groups (Teppe, 1977; Recker, 1985, von Kondratowitz, 2000a).

In both projects, using the argument of venerating old age always had an exclusive dimension insofar as the benefits of these sociopolitical measures were to be bestowed only on those older people who were considered 'valuable' members of German society. In other words, the Jewish community and people who were looked on as members of the political opposition would not be eligible as beneficiaries of this policy. It is striking that this policy of accentuating the discourse of veneration for old age was used from 1933 until approximately 1940. Then another group increasingly came under strong pressure: people with impairments, disabled people and psychiatric patients of the larger institutions, among them many older people. The consequence of beginning systematically to exterminate the members of these groups in special programmes started to develop around 1940. One incident reported in the files surrounding Action T4, as this euthanasia programme was unofficially called, gives a vivid example of how, even for the immediate officials engaged in this policy, the two directions in the rhetoric of veneration collided. One of the first institutions in which the gassing of the victims of these programmes was used experimentally was Castle Grafeneck in Württemberg. A first step in preparing such killings was collecting patients and inmates from smaller institutions to be bussed to the central extermination institution. The organiser of this process was the administrative official for medical affairs in Stuttgart, Dr Sprauer. But in August 1940 his efforts were met with resistance by the head of a smaller institution in Fussbach. This official was then asked to present himself in Stuttgart and to justify his obstructiveness. From his own report: 'Dr. Sprauer pointed also to the fact that I am a member of the SS and should understand this action. I answered Dr. Sprauer that, precisely because I am an SS-man, I am obliged to take up a negative attitude. What is happening is in blatant opposition to what has been preached by the highest party officials, that one ought to honour old age' (quoted in Klee, 1983: 238). As was to be expected, he was unsuccessful in his opposition.

Another way of exploring the veneration idea is to focus on the topic of gerontocracy and its historical features. The concept of 'gerontocracy', understood as government by the older men of high status in a given traditional and patriarchally organised society, is another example of how traditional constructions around old age have not only been interpreted as universal characteristics. Moreover, dealing with gerontocracy has also served as a kind of projection mechanism for controversial exchanges about political power-sharing that have been growing increasingly prominent in modern society. By using this term, a clear reference is made to the times of antiquity, a time period and an intellectual heritage that has had an extraordinarily high status in terms of orientation and commitment for the administrative elites and the educated classes of early modernity.

In antiquity the term 'gerontocracy' was first of all designed to indicate simply 'government by the elders', then later in the Roman empire to characterise the members of the 'senate'. Its central competence in decision making was to negotiate state politics between the Emperor and the representatives of the public. In order to legitimate this construction, often the justification of gerontocracy in Plato's *Nomoi* was positively interpreted. It was often complemented by considering the 'council of the elders' in Homer's *Iliad* as another famous example of a gerontocratic power structure. Besides these references discussion of the gerontocratic model has been centred, in early modernity as well as in the 19th century, instead around the Greek city-state of Sparta – and this not only in Germany (see Manso, 1805; Lachmann, 1836; Treiber, 1871; for France see, for example, Jannet, 1876, Bazin, 1884). Zedler's encyclopedia of 1732 had explained the position of the *gerontes* thus:

> … they were certain aldermen or elders, according to Lycurgo, on his account wise men, the Aeropagites, in Lacedaemon. Their number was 26, or according to other writers 32, and they could not be accepted into this position before the age of 60 … They possessed just as much power and freedom as the kings, and could never be removed, unless they had been accused of certain crimes. (Zedler, 1732, Vol 10: 1163-4)

Acclamation instead of election, non-removability, chronological age limits – these are identifying characteristics of the understanding of gerontocracy in early modern society. And it is remarkable that a fairly considerable number of influential jurists and philosophers were highly fascinated by the model of gerontocracy, particularly in its Spartan version, reaching from Thomas More, Grotius, Althusius and Helvetius to Jean-Jacques Rousseau. However, as the differentiating process of modern society took shape, this myth of a blissful political rule by elders and its connected figure, a universal veneration of the elders, began to seem questionable. In addition, the newly established discipline of archeological science shed preliminary doubts on whether or not chronological age was really used as a criterion for gerontocratic rule. In contrast, it was emphasised that in antiquity the term *gerontes* has had a different meaning than one would have expected. It meant a respected position in society regardless of chronological markers, rather than referring to men passing a certain age limit and acquiring additional entitlements (Brandes in Ersch and Gruber, 1819: 160ff). Also, inquiring historically about the examples of gerontocratic rules in Greece beyond Sparta (for example, in Crete, Elis or Ephesus) confirms that these power structures have always been challenged by other groups and factions in the constituencies of the time.

Moreover, to assume that gerontocratic rule would have been a characteristic of the Middle Ages and early modernity in general would be a misperception. Indeed, historical research has demonstrated that probably only the authority of the Doges in the coastal Mediterranean city republics of Venice or Genoa could be characterised as 'gerontocratic' (see, for example, Finlay, 1978). But, more importantly, as a model, any gerontocratic rule with its patriarchal foundation stood in clear antagonism to the idea of a liberal democracy and its rules of public government and electoral procedures. On the other hand, modern society often enough shows persistent 'pockets' of somewhat gerontocratic and male-dominated, power-elite structures in the economy, in culture as well as in politics. To this extent, the question of existing gerontocracies now requires a different framing in order to research the reproduction and persistence of gender-based elites in a democratic society and the role age plays in these processes.

Creating 'generation' as a new paradigm of normative discourse

Another important feature of an increasing generalisation of old age, with an implicitly dominant normative agenda, consists in the invention of the category of 'generation' in modernity. 'Generation' as a term for a specific type of social relationship was created in a complicated process in early modernity and as a motor for modern society. The following remarks are limited to this time-span because of restrictions of space. It is characterised by a highly significant ambivalence between biologically based criteria of naturalness and at the same time a meaning touching on a specific quality of social relations. The 'natural' perspective is apparent in the choice of wording: 'generation' meant the formation and production of an organism, especially of a human being, and was then generalised to refer to all humankind. The Zedler encyclopedia of 1732 reads: '*generatio*: the production or procreation of human mankind'. Further comments widen this view: 'with the word *generatio* originally nothing else is meant than intercourse itself, but some embrace not only conception, the maintaining and shaping of the child in the womb as well as the birth itself, but include also nourishing after birth' (Zedler, 1732: Vol 11, 848-9). With the passing of time this line could be transformed into a genealogical perspective, as a sequence of generations within lineages summing up the reproduction of the human species. Accordingly the *generationes* in Zedler are mostly associated with ancestors from a special part of society, the nobility and administrative officials. Here it was already possible to find the instrument of family trees and genealogical tables, which had themselves their precursors in biblical models – for example, the Tree of Jesse.

Another tradition of using the term 'generation' in early modernity is represented by attempts to subdivide a century into a sequence of, usually, three generations. The number of years differed from 28.98 years per generation, noted in 1775 by the demographer Süssmilch, to 33.3 years in other publications. In everyday life such classifications must have had some immediate attraction as simple modes of ordering human expectations. Even today the 25-year marker for determining the span of a generation is still used, although such a form of calculation comes originally from the realm of early modern society.

For modern society the genealogical dimension of the concept of generation has expanded to other social groups and professional settings and to this extent has been potentially generalised. But, with its foundation in ageing, mortality and reproduction, the term 'generation' developed into a socially meaningful category that tended to mirror and to guarantee the progress of history by following the lineages that organised the genealogy as a sequence. Hence the concept of generation represents a complex interplay of 'nature' and 'culture', because 'generation' marks the threshold between procreation and tradition, between descent and memory, between parentage and heritage (see Weigel, 2003).

Thus, in order to experience the newly attained richness of the concept of generation for modernity, it is first appropriate to look particularly for processes of *transfers* – transfers of properties, qualities, knowledge, resources and inheritances in a material as well as in an immaterial sense. The use of the term 'generation' as a metaphor for historical progress in the 19th century, later favoured enthusiastically by Auguste Comte, had in the times of the Enlightenment already centred around the transfer of knowledge. This was conceived in terms of promoting and developing means of broad and systematic education, organised as a chain of passing on experiences in a continuous fashion. Prepared by such French encyclopedists as Condorcet, Kant had expressed this idea in 1780 by pointing out 'that if we see one generation as transmitting their experiences and knowledge to the following one, which again adds something new for the succeeding one, an understanding of the appropriate form of education can arise' (Kant, 1968: 446). Friedrich Schleiermacher and also Johann Friedrich Herbart later extended this perspective in the Berlin lectures of 1826 to reach the concept of *Generationswechsel* (succession of generations). This was intended to legitimise the establishment of pedagogy in university and other institutions of higher learning in order to guarantee such a process of transmitting and forming *Bildung* (education) (Schleiermacher, 1826: 13, 114; see also Gadamer, 1965: chapter I1b).

While this idea of forming an educational system implied rather indirect and long-term normative effects and expectations for members of the older generation, the concept of generation had another even more important connotation. Pierre Nora has connected the invention of 'generation' in its most radical version directly to the French revolution with its modelling of a 'new mankind' and with its characteristic pattern of being hostile to the past and advocating rupture with tradition. In this sense the category of generation is for him 'the daughter of democracy and of the acceleration of history' (Nora, 1992: 940). It took effect in the revolutionary pamphlets in which the principles of inheritance, with its privileges based in genealogical lineages, were questioned. In contrast, these publications advocated a new generational law based on human rights, with the expectation of counteracting the power relations of the *ancien régime*. This strong normative dimension of 'generation' was also experienced in Germany and became apparent as a sudden awareness of witnessing essential historical changes in the aftermath of the revolution. After the fall of Napoleon, in a letter to a friend, the publisher Perthes observed that, in former times, diversity in political and cultural orientation was separated by centuries, but 'our time has united the completely irreconcilable in three generations now living at the same time; the extraordinary differences between the years 1750, 1789 and 1815 lack all transitions and do not appear as a one after another, but as a side by side in people living now, depending whether they are grandfathers, fathers or grandsons' (quoted in Koselleck, 1979: 367). However, in contrast to France, the generational élan in Germany for a democratic change was not successful for a considerable time.

The professionalisation of normative codes

In the late 18th and early 19th centuries, one can see first indications of trying to measure and determine old age in a more professional and systematic – that is to say, scientific – way. These signs came mostly from *medicine*, which was beginning to be interested in old age and therefore going back to the traditions and experiences of antiquity (Schäfer, 2004; von Kondratowitz, 2008). Nevertheless, it is not yet possible to speak about a common and full gerontological agenda in research. Knowledge about the health and well-being of older people was discussed on the level of different medical specialities, of pathology, of internal medicine, of psychiatry and of forensic medicine in order to work out procedures and indicators for determining the age of individuals (von Kondratowitz 1991). Out of these specialisations and their experiences with older patients a first discourse on developing a concept of illnesses of, and in, old age was elaborated in the early 19th century, under the term *Greisenkrankheiten* (Canstatt, 1839; Geist, 1860; Mettenheimer, 1863). Undoubtedly these scientists were influenced by the empirical medical approaches that were in use in France and Britain. Here notably the work of Charcot in the Salpêtriére, who himself had critically discussed the research perspective of Canstatt (Charcot, 1868: 5-6), provided an example of this new experimentally oriented research perspective in ageing research. But a comprehensive gerontological research agenda was a result of the 1920s and was, instead, an initiative by developmental psychology in Germany and Austria (for example, in the work of Karl and Charlotte Bühler).

If the influence of gerontology within the welfare state environment is to be taken as a central point of reference, the *formation of gerontological knowledge* must be examined as a distinctly historical process of developing and structuring the central components of this knowledge; in Stephen Katz's (1996) terms, the 'disciplining of old age'. At this *longue durée* level, everyday conceptions are shaped by *historical processes of expert dominance and administrative regulation* in the process of determining and shaping the 'risk of old age' in modern society. Thus we should follow the same line of questioning as in the other parts of this chapter: identifying the process of an increasing generalisation of normative standards for old age by, at the same time, pointing to the coexistence of habits, values, attitudes and arguments that had their origin in pre-modern times but are now given a new societal frame.

Table 6.1 tries to show how these typologies of old age or types of social construction were organised, processed and negotiated at societal level in Germany and how they changed over time, up to the early 1990s. Indeed they can be regarded as *social representations of old age* in their own right. As far as the differences in content between developmental stages are concerned, the explanatory remarks in the middle section of the table (under the heading of 'dichotomously organised social constructions') make some reference to the formation of age categorisations and their variability – they are to be found in

Table 6.1: Social representations of old age in modernity: distributional dynamic and presence of agents in socialisation

Dichotomisations of old age (social representations)	Essential content of dichotomously organised social constructions	Dominance of dichotomous models over time
1. High in age vs Worn out age (*Hohes Alter vs Abgelebtes Alter*)	Discourse of 'veneration' as reflection of an age-related power structure – gradual disappearance of 'vital force' over the lifetime	18th century to first half of 20th century
2. Still hale and hearty age vs Infirm/ decrepit age (*Rüstiges Alter vs Gebrechliches Alter*)	Remaining ability to show cooperative societal achievements – body images accentuate signs of weakening capabilities (using the metaphor of fragile bones)	Turn of 19th/20th century to mid-century
3. Normal age vs Pathological age (*Normales Alter vs Pathologisches Alter*)	'Majority' definitions of social adequacy of old age – 'minority' definitions of old age as 'unproductive' (Quetelet) or as a social burden	Late 19th century into the 1950s
4. Age in need vs Frail older age (*Bedürftiges Alter vs Hinfälliges Alter*)	Old age as increasingly exposing material and emotional needs – old age as dominated by the need to take care (using the metaphor of the fall syndrome)	Late 1940s to early 1970s
5. Active age vs Age in need of care (*Aktives Alter vs Pflegebedürftiges Alter*)	Construction of old age as participating in offers of local social policy and as increasing competence – health-impaired older people as potential clients of the service sector	In the 1970s
6. Young old vs Old old (*Junge Alte vs Alte Alte*)	Adopting the Anglo-American distinction between two different need constellations	In the 1980s
7. Third age vs Fourth age (*Drittes Lebensalter vs Viertes Lebensalter*)	Adopting the Anglo-American/French distinction between two complex and highly differentiated life situations in old age (explicitly 'value neutral')	In the late 1980s and early 1990s
8. Autonomous age vs Dependent age (*Autonomes Alter vs Abhängiges Alter*)	Emphasis on the degree of freedom to organise life in old age as a self-determined process – emphasis on the increasing need to negotiate service packages according to the relative status of health	In the early 1990s

much greater detail in the publications mentioned above (for these details see von Kondratowitz, 2002: 127-31).

The following remarks focus not so much on the content of the two opposing representations as on shifts in weighing them over historical time. Table 6.1 shows a clear dividing line between – to use Anthony Glascock's and Susan Feinman's terminology (Glascock and Feinman 1986) – 'intact age' as opposed to 'decrepit' or 'infirm age'. In its various representations, this dichotomisation table emphasises the presence or absence of *orientation* toward *societal achievement* in the course of the phase of life termed 'old age', while the associated need constellations (as representations of the developing and expanding welfare state) figure as the central elements in ascribing *societal inclusion* or *exclusion*.

While the empirical material offered by various studies demonstrates this impressive type of long-term continuity, there is also considerable change over time, and the closer one comes to the present, the *shorter* becomes the *span of time* involved. More and more emphasis is placed on the 'healthy' side, bringing an imbalance into the weighting of the two representations and putting more pressure on the 'decrepit' side – with a tendency almost to eliminate this less comforting part of old age. A process of *societal acceleration* is also apparent. Together with the extension of the healthy side and the contraction of the infirm side, models and concepts succeed each other at an *ever faster pace*, sometimes in competition and with more and more overlap as we approach the present day. German old-age policy design and implementation at the local authority level has been more than ever characterised by competition and interaction between the differing concepts of old age implemented at the central and local welfare state levels (see von Kondratowitz, 2000b).

The emphasis in Germany has for a long time been clearly on the healthy aspect of age, particularly before the unification process began. Only in the last 15 years has the topic of care of older people gained in importance because of the increasing impact of the demographic discourse. But, even the concepts for long-term care – with their explicit concentration on rehabilitation and prevention – appear to differentiate 'infirm age', but are in fact intensively committed to the vision of prolonged activity patterns even under less favourable bodily conditions. 'Intact age' now begins to extend even into the highest age groups, for which the discourse of medical science used to apply the term 'incurable' and which is now endowed with the new connotation of the 'chronic condition', with its perspective of lifelong development of illnesses.

Outlook

As much as Table 6.1 offers incentives for connecting present developments to long-term historical changes, it is nevertheless obvious that it is a result of processes that are already themselves becoming historical. The table mirrors a certain historical phase in German ageing policy and gerontological expertise before unification, and is therefore only valid for the sociopolitical and cultural background of the former West Germany. Hence, exploring and evaluating former East German normative frameworks for old age would be particularly important and it would be instructive to observe whether or not and in which form they have survived unification. The East's policy for older people followed a very strong veneration rhetoric – for example, in calling older workers in retirement 'work veterans', thus associating the arena of work with a battleground to be conquered. This also reflects traditions of the historical worker movements (see von Kondratowitz, 1988). Today the emergence of new normative frameworks such as 'successful ageing' and an increasing weight of 'active ageing' brings new questions to be set in comparison to these long-term changes. It would also be important to re-read the entire material presented here from a gendered perspective. But probably the most challenging task is to relate these historical observations to recent analyses on the bio-politics of ageing in postmodern societies (see Katz, 2008). The intensification and further differentiation of the anti-ageing movement and its strategies will give the subject of the normative implications of ageing policies a fundamentally new direction.

References

Bazin, H. (1884) *De lycurgo*, Paris: These.

Borscheid, P. (1987) *Geschichte des Alters*, Münster: Coppenrath.

Canstatt, C. (1839) *Die Krankheiten des hohen Alters und ihre Heilung*, Erlangen: Enke.

Charcot, J.M. (1868) *Lecons cliniques sur les maladies des vieillards et les maladies chroniques*, Paris: A.Delahaye.

Conrad, C. (1994) *Vom Greis zum Rentner. Der Strukturwandel des Alters in Deutschland zwischen 1830 und 1930*, Göttingen: Vandenhoeck & Ruprecht.

Ehmer, J. (1990) *Sozialgeschichte des Alters*, Frankfurt: Suhrkamp.

Ehmer, J. (1996) 'The 'life stairs': ageing, generational relations and small commodity production', in T. Hareven (ed) *Ageing and intergenerational relations over the life course: A historical and cross-cultural perspective*, Berlin/New York: Walter de Gruyter, pp 53-74.

Ehmer, J. and Gutschner, P. (eds) (2000) *Das Alter im Spiel der Generationen*, Wien/Köln/Weimar: Böhlau.

Ersch, J.S. and Gruber, J.G. (1819) *Allgemeine Encyclopädie der Wissenschaften und Künste*, Leipzig: Brockhaus.

Finlay, R. (1978) 'The Venetian Republic as a gerontocracy: age and politics in the Renaissance', *Journal of Medieval and Renaissance Studies*, vol 8, no 2, pp 157-78.

Gadamer, H.-G. (1965) *Wahrheit und Methode. Grundzüge einer philosophischen Hermeneutik*, Tübingen: J.C.B. Mohr/Paul Siebeck.

Geist, L. (1860) *Klinik der Greisenkrankheiten*, Erlangen: Enke.

Glascock, A.P. and Feinman, S.L. (1986) 'Treatment of the aged in nonindustrial societies', in C. Fry and J. Keith (eds) *New methods for old age research*, South Hadley: Bergin & Garvey, pp 281-96.

Göckenjan, G. (2000) *Das Alter würdigen. Altersbilder und Bedeutungswandel des Alters*, Frankfurt: Suhrkamp.

Jablonski, J.T. (1721) *Allgemeines Lexikon der Künste und Wissenschaften*, Leipzig: Fritsch.

Jannet, C.(1876) *Les institutions sociales et le droit civil a Sparte*, Paris: E. Plon, Nourrit et Cie.

Johnson, P. and Thane, P. (1998) *Old age from antiquity to post-modernity*, New York: Routledge.

Kant, I. (1968) 'Über Pädagogik', in F.T.Rink (ed) *Kants Werke-Akademie-Ausgabe*, Berlin: Akademie-Verlag.

Katz, S. (1996) *Disciplining old age: The formation of gerontological knowledge.* Charlotteville, VA/London: University Press of Virginia.

Katz, S. (2008) 'A new biopolitics of age: enhancement, performance, function', paper for the conference '(Re)constructing the ageing body: western medical cultures and gender 1600-2000', 26-28 September, Johann Gutenberg University, Mainz.

Klee, E. (1983) *Euthanasie im NS-Staat*, Frankfurt: Fischer.

Koselleck, R. (1979) *Vergangene Zukunft. Zur Semantik geschichtlicher Zeiten*, Frankfurt: Suhrkamp.

Lachmann, K.H. (1836) *Die spartanische Staatsverfassung in ihrer Entwicklung und ihrem Verfall*, Breslau: Grass, Barth & Comp.

Mailänder, K. (1940) 'Wohn - und Altersheime', *Blätter der Wohlfahrtspflege in Württemberg*, vol 93, no 7, pp 69-70.

Manso, J.C.F. (1805) *Sparta. Ein Versuch zur Aufklärung der Geschichte und Verfassung dieses Staates*, Leipzig: Dyck.

Mettenheimer, C. (1863) *Nosologische und anatomische Beiträge zu der Lehre von den Greisenkrankheiten*, Leipzig: Teubner.

Minois, G. (1989) *History of old age: From antiquity to the renaissance.* Chicago: The University of Chicago Press.

Mitterauer, M. and Sieder, R. (1991) *Vom Patriarchat zur Partnerschaft. Zum Strukturwandel der Familie*, München: C.H.Beck.

Nora, P. (1992) 'La génération', in P. Nora (ed) *Les lieux de mémoire, Vol III Les France (1. conflits et partages)*, Paris: Edition Gallimard, pp 931-71.

Recker, M.L. (1985) *Nationalsozialistische Sozialpolitik im Zweiten Weltkrieg*, München: Oldenbourg.

Schäfer, D. (2004), *Alter und Krankheit in der Frühen Neuzeit. Der ärztliche Blick auf die letzte Lebensphase*, Frankfurt/New York: Campus.

Schleiermacher, F. (1826) 'Grundzüge der Erziehungskunst', in F. Schleiermacher *Texte zur Pädagogik*, Frankfurt: Suhrkamp.

Sieder, R. (1987) *Sozialgeschichte der Familie*, Frankfurt: Suhrkamp.

Simmons, L.W. (1945) *The role of the aged in primitive society*, New Haven, CT: Yale University Press.

Stone, L. (1981) 'Old age', in L. Stone *The past and the present*, London: Routledge & Kegan Paul, pp 232-41.

Teppe, K. (1977) 'Zur Sozialpolitik der Dritten Reiches am Beispiel der Sozialversicherung', *Archiv für Sozialgeschichte*, vol 17, pp 195-250.

Thane, P. (ed) (2005) *The long history of old age*, London: Thames & Hudson.

Treiber, C. (1871) *Forschungen zur spartanischen Verfassungsgeschichte*, Berlin: C.F. Müller.

von Kondratowitz, H.-J. (1988) 'Zumindest organisatorisch erfasst ... Die Älteren in der DDR zwischen Veteranenpathos und Geborgenheitsbeschwörung', in G.J. Glaessner (ed) *Die DDR in der Ära Honecker. Politik-Kultur-Gesellschaft*, Opladen: Westdeutscher Verlag, pp 514-28.

von Kondratowitz, H.-J. (1991) 'The medicalization of old age: continuity and change in Germany from the late eighteenth to the early twentieth century', in M. Pelling and R.M. Smith (eds) *Life, death and the elderly: Historical perspectives*, London: Routledge, pp 134-64.

von Kondratowitz, H.-J. (2000a) 'Alter und Krankheit. Die Dynamik der Diskurse und der Wandel ihrer historischen Aushandlungsformen', in J. Ehmer and P. Gutschner (eds) *Das Alter im Spiel der Generationen*, Wien/Köln/Weimar: Böhlau, pp 109-155.

von Kondratowitz, H.-J. (2000b) *Konjunkturen des Alters. Die Ausdifferenzierung der Konstruktion des 'höheren Lebensalterrs' zu einem sozialpolitischen Problem.* Regensburg: Transfer Verlag.

von Kondratowitz, H.-J. (2002), 'Konjunkturen-Ambivalenzen-Kontingenzen: Diskursanalytische Erbschaften einer historisch-soziologischen Betrachtung des Alter(n)s', in U. Dallinger and K.R. Schroeter (eds) *Theoretische Beiträge zur Altersnsoziologie*, Opladen: Leske & Budrich, pp 113-37.

von Kondratowitz, H.-J. (2008) 'Alter, Gesundheit und Krankheit aus historischer Perspektive', in A. Kuhlmey and D. Schaeffer (eds) *Alter, Gesundheit und Krankheit*, Bern: Verlag Hans Huber, pp 64-81.

Weigel, S. (2003) 'Generation, Genealogie, Geschlecht. Zur Geschichte des Generationenkonzepts und seiner wissenschaftlichen Konzeptualisierung seit Ende des 18. Jahrhunderts', in L. Musner and G. Wunberg (eds) *Kulturwissenschaften. Forschung-Praxis-Positionen*, Freiburg: Rombach, pp 177-208.

Wenzel, Dr (1934) 'Altershilfe- ein Ehrendienst der Nation', *Freie Wohlfahrtspflege*, vol 8, no 4, pp 431-5.

Zedler, J.H. (ed) (1732) *Großes Vollständiges Universal-Lexikon aller Wissenschaften und Künste*, Halle/Leipzig: Verlag Zedler (Waisenhausdruck).

SEVEN

How to balance generations: solidarity dilemmas in a European perspective

Svein Olav Daatland

Contrasting expectations

Intergenerational family relationships are situated in a field of contrasting expectations, with dilemmas and ambivalences that need to be negotiated. Duty and need, self-interest and altruism, affection and conflict are among the motivations that pull and push in different directions. People's beliefs and values, their feelings about what should happen as well as their anticipations of what can be expected to happen, clearly play a part in sustaining the shapes these relationships take. Research into these matters, though, has tended to concentrate on the younger generation. This chapter takes a complementary perspective, that of the older generation, and suggests that parental norms and motivations may be just as influential in intergenerational relationships and exchanges as those of their adult children. The older, parental perspective is often neglected and yet the mutual expectations of the generations define each other. A new generation, when it is added, might push the older generation not only into grandparenthood, but also into the category of old age, which would transform an otherwise delightful event into something of a mixed blessing. The assumed dependency of old age might in earlier times, and in some cultures even today, have been a respected and attractive status to which people gladly adapted. Not so often now, when independence and autonomy seem to be regarded as ideal across the life course, with the possible exception of the very latest part of the fourth age.

This chapter starts out from the observation that modern older people tend to want to remain independent as long as they possibly can and they seem in particular to be reluctant to depend on their children. Older parents are often afraid to burden their children, they are hesitant to ask them for help and they tend to be net providers of support to their children most of their lives, if resources allow them. The general hypothesis put forward here is that older parents are balancing between obligating and de-obligating their children. Comparative data suggests that filial independence and a set of priorities operating *down* the generations are comparatively stronger in northern Europe – parents seeing themselves as obliged to care for their children more than they expect care. In contrast, filial obligations and priorities that operate *up* the generations – so that parents expect, and are expected to, receive support – are comparatively stronger in the south. The chapter thus aims to discuss the context and character of intergenerational solidarity, and in so doing to add to the understanding of how ageing and older age is perceived in modern Europe.

Knowledge about norms and ideals is important because they are guides for behaviour, and help us understand how people will behave. Equally important is information about the context where these ideals are played out and contrasted. Balancing between generations is a universal exercise, but it is played out in a great diversity of local forms, which makes it hard to separate what is specific to a certain time or place from what is more generally true. We therefore need comparative studies, across time and place, in order to understand better how generations make out and what the implications are for the quality of life of both older and younger generations. Population ageing, as well as radical changes in gender roles and family forms in late modernity throughout Europe, make it urgent to explore the implication of these changes. Meso-level social contexts such as the family often mediate between macro-level social change and individuals.

This chaper therefore explores intergenerational solidarity from both the parent and adult child perspective, and it does so by comparing countries that represent quite different family cultures. While norms and values are often explored via qualitative methods in order to understand their inner dynamics, this chapter adopts a quantitative approach and observes the ideals so to speak from a larger distance, but with a larger number of informants and thus possibly with added external validity. The two approaches may thus complement each other.

Intergenerational solidarity

Population ageing is a challenge to intergenerational solidarity, both privately within families and publicly in society. Concerns are raised about family as well as societal solidarity. In the larger societal context, this is a question of willingness to contribute to the common good via taxes and to support a redistribution of resources to benefit those in need. Within the microcosm of the family, which is the theme for this chapter, the responsibility for intergenerational solidarity is usually attributed to the younger generation. Will adult children be willing and able to support their older parents? There are two elements here. The first concerns motivation to support older parents, the second relates to the ability to do so.

As far as *motivations* are concerned – should we fear a change in the mental climate of families and societies? Will family norms lose their power? Will people grow more self-contained? Are families becoming less inclusive? These questions are far from new. On the contrary, they have followed us through time and, although their particular form may have varied, popular beliefs are basically the same: things were better in the past. Ethel Shanas (1960) wrote in her introduction to an article about family responsibility, nearly 50 years ago:

> There is a widely-held popular belief that affectional and other ties between older people and their families are weaker now than they were at the turn of the century or at other times in the past. (Shanas, 1960: 408)

The same phrase goes for today as well – and the same answer. To quote Shanas again: 'Empirical evidence … indicates that family ties between older people and their children are still strong and still functioning' (Shanas, 1960: 408).

A substantial body of literature currently concludes that filial responsibility is still considerable and that neither the welfare state nor an expanding individualism has corrupted it (eg Arber and Attias-Donfut, 2000; Bengtson and Lowenstein, 2003). Adult children may, however, have enjoyed the opportunities presented by the welfare state and may have found easier ways of carrying out their responsibilities when parents have access to services. Family care, while still dominant even in modern welfare states, is *less* dominant where professional long-term care is more easily available, as it is for example in Scandinavia (eg Walker, 1993; Daatland and Lowenstein, 2005).

There is perhaps more reason to be concerned about younger generations' *ability* to support older parents, first of all because of changes in the demographic balance. To put it directly: will family burdens come to outbalance family resources? Other concerns over capacities for support refer to competing obligations. For instance, it may have become more difficult to combine work and family commitments, first of all because women (daughters) have increasingly joined the (paid) labour market. Although I would acknowledge this as a problem, perhaps even a growing one, I do not want to exaggerate it. In fact, although these and other 'sandwich positions' are rather frequent, they are usually of short duration and in most cases are not very intense (Evandrou et al, 2002; Grundy and Henretta, 2006; Künemund, 2006). Besides, formal services have developed further during recent decades and in some countries they offer real alternatives to family care, in others at least a certain amount of respite and support to family carers.

Naturally, changes in the numerical balance between older and younger populations can add responsibilities to the younger. On the other hand, the older generation may represent resources, not only burdens. Older people pay taxes just like other citizens, many are active as volunteers and older parents are net providers of support to their children most of their lives, often to the age of 80 and even beyond if resources (such as pensions) allow. Moreover, living standards have increased in most of Europe, and this should have made both the younger and the older generations better able to cater for themselves and still retain some surplus with which to benefit others – as long as no change in outlook has intervened to make them more self-centred. Thus, however important it is to study intergenerational exchange from the standpoint of the younger generation looking up the generations, the complementary nature of the relationship makes it necessary to examine the opposite perspective too, that of the older generation looking down.

Balancing values

The change in balance between older and younger generations, and expanding female participation in the labour market, may have made the conflicting obligations within the family more apparent, but they are far from new. Intergenerational relationships are in their nature ambivalent and characterised by mixed feelings and conflicting motivations (Lüscher and Pillemer, 1998; Connidis and McMullin, 2002). Balancing between personal and family interests and between the interests of older and younger generations is a universal exercise, but it takes different forms in different times and contexts. Family obligations have always represented some constraints on individual freedom, but in Europe more so under the collectivist southern culture than under the more individualist northern ones (Reher, 1998). North-western European families have a tradition of allowing room for individual adaptation and of giving priority to the nuclear unit when 'starting' (as the saying goes) a family (Finch, 1989; Finch and Mason, 1993).

We should therefore study intergenerational relationships in context and do so from the perspectives of both parents and children. As far as caring for older parents is concerned, most studies have focused on adult children's reasons for giving or not giving support. We know far less about parental motives for accepting or not accepting such help. It takes two to tango and, if family care changes, the explanation may lie also in the older end of the relationship, among emerging cohorts of older people who to an increasing extent may perceive welfare state services as a right and an opportunity, rather than as a stigma and a second choice. Older parents, while often treated as passive recipients of help, are active players in the game. Here the roles played over time by their values and expectations cannot be ignored. In their younger years they balanced values by raising children to be both obligated and independent, and they may continue to balance these values as older parents.

The fact that older parents are often afraid to burden their children, and may be reluctant to ask them for help, was in fact reported as early as the 1950s, but thereafter it was seemingly buried under the widespread assumption that family care is the universally preferred choice. For example, Ethel Shanas, in the article already quoted from 1960, found that older parents were less likely than their adult children to expect that an adult daughter should take a widowed mother into her household. Attitudes to co-residence were (and are) quite negative, and even more negative among older parents than among adult children. These findings support the intimacy-at-a-distance ideal suggested by Rosenmayr and Köckeis in 1963. So also do later findings by McAuley and Blieszner (1985) from the US. They found that older people preferred ageing in place, but that they would rather receive formal care than family care in order to achieve this, although some mix of formal and informal care was their favourite choice. They also found that a majority of older parents would prefer to move to a nursing home than move in with a child if they could no longer live independently. Women were found to be more inclined towards formal care than men and the older to be more receptive to formal care than the younger. Similar findings are reported by Brody et al (1983, 1984) for the US, and by Daatland (1990) and Wielink et al (1997) for Europe.

Generally speaking, it is interesting that adult children tend to express a greater degree of filial obligations than what is actually expected from the parental side. The main story emerging from these findings is that older people want to remain independent as long as they possibly can and that they are often reluctant to be dependent on others – including their own children. What older parents do want from children is mainly social and emotional support, and companionship.

These observations are culturally biased, since they refer to the modern and western world, where individualism is highly valued. Different priorities might be discovered in other, more collectivist cultures, for instance in Asia and Africa. Old-age dependency may be less feared, even expected, in these areas, and the older generation may be accorded higher priority. There is as yet little research in these matters in developing countries, and the scant findings are mixed, partly pointing towards family collectivism, but partly also towards a growing preference for independence between generations, including separate households if and when possible (Bhat and Dhruvarajan, 2001; Aboderin, 2004). We know more about inter-country variation in Europe, between what Reher (1998) describes as the more individualist northern family and the more collectivist southern family. The remainder of this chapter will explore this variation using empirical data, contrasting Norway and Spain as representatives of each of these 'cultures'.

Hypotheses, data, and measurements

The hypotheses

The empirical section here focuses on intergenerational norms and values, in particular as they are perceived by the (older) parent generation. Thus we are not analysing what people are in fact doing, but what they see as the right thing to do. My general hypothesis contends that older parents' attitudes to family care are often ambivalent, balancing between expectations *from* children (filial responsibility) and a parental concern *for* children's autonomy and welfare (filial independence). I expect the former to be (comparatively) stronger in the more collectivist southern family and the latter to be (comparatively) stronger in the more individualist northern family. As will become clearer as this chapter progresses, interrogating anticipations like these will not only allow us to excavate some (partial) responses to them; it will also provoke new questions about norms and values active in the ways people negotiate their own and their families' life courses.

To state the starting-point here more bluntly, I assume that Spanish parents will expect more help from their children than Norwegian parents, while Norwegian parents will tend to de-obligate their children and be inclined to prefer services over family care. This is not to say that I expect a familistic response in Spain and a non-familistic response in Norway. Both responses may be family-motivated but, if so, they will be in different directions – towards filial obligations in Spain and towards filial independence in Norway. Put more directly, the expectations on children should then *increase* with needs and age (as a proxy for needs) in Spain, but *decrease* with needs and age in Norway. Both reactions may thus be family motivated, but the southern reaction is assumed to give priority to the older generation while the northern one is assumed to give priority to the younger.

Another deduction from the general hypothesis is that if – as common expectations and some of the literature would contend - women (mothers) are more family oriented than men (fathers) in both countries, they should 'gravitate' towards the dominant pattern in each country, that is towards filial responsibility in the south and towards filial independence in the north.

A final hypothesis, also linked to widespread social-scientific expectations, is that higher education should encourage an individualist orientation and reduce the power of more traditional (collectivist) norms. Support for filial obligation norms should then decrease with education in both countries, while the support for filial independence should increase.

These hypotheses can be summarised as follows:

1 Filial responsibility norms are expected to be stronger, and more unconditional, in the southern context (Spain) than in the northern one (Norway), while the opposite is expected to be the case for filial independence, as indicated by a parental preference for services over family care.
2 Filial responsibility expectations are assumed to increase with needs (age and disability) in Spain and to decrease with needs (age and disability) in Norway.
3 Women are assumed to be more family oriented than men in both countries, and thus to expect *more* filial responsibility in Spain and *less* filial responsibility in Norway.
4 Filial responsibility is expected to decrease with education, while filial independence is expected to increase – in both countries.

Data and measurements

The data used here is drawn from the OASIS study,[1] which was carried out in Norway, England, Germany, Spain and Israel in 2000-03. In each of the five countries, approximately 1,200 persons aged 25 and over, living at home in large cities (100,000+), were interviewed using a standard questionnaire. To enable more detailed analyses of older people's circumstances, those aged 75 and over were oversampled, to represent about one third of the sample. This chapter concentrates on Norway and Spain as two contrasting cases. They are contrasts both as far as family cultures and as far as welfare state regimes are concerned. It is difficult to disentangle the two dimensions because they are integrated in developmental terms; that is, certain family cultures tend to encourage certain welfare state models and vice versa.

To recapitulate, we are concentrating now on attitudes to filial responsibility and filial independence as perceived by older parents. *Filial responsibility* norms refer to expectations of adult children to provide support for ageing parents, and is measured here in terms of (degrees of) agreement or disagreement with a four-item scale developed by Lee, Peek and Coward (1998). The exact wording of items and questions is given in the notes to Table 7.1 later in this chapter.

Support for *filial independence* is taken to be indicated by a tendency to de-obligate children, in the sense of voicing a preference for other care providers (such as services). The preferences are measured in two domains, (1) as the *preferred care provider* (family, services, others) if one should be in need of long-term care in old age, and (2) as the *preferred housing arrangement* (institutional care or moving in with a child) if one could no longer manage by oneself in old age. A preference for the service option is taken as a reluctance to obligate children (who are the dominant family carers, together with spouses). This is possibly a debatable operationalisation, because the people who are surveyed may choose services on their own merits, in particular if they are perceived as reaching a high standard. People may also be hesitant to ask their children for help out of a concern for personal independence rather than out of concern for one's children. These and other controversial issues will be adressed in the discussion below.

Descriptive findings: what do people say?

Descriptive findings are presented for the total sample aged 25 and over. The variation with age, and more specifically how older parents respond, will be addressed in the analysis section.

Table 7.1A shows that both countries have substantial majorities in support of filial responsibility norms in the sense that they are in agreement with at least one of the four items of the filial obligation scale. The norms do, however, stand somewhat more strongly in Spain (82% in agreement) than in Norway (76%).

The two more prescriptive normative statements – (1) adult children should live close to their parents and (2) parents are entitled to returns (that is, the idea of reciprocal rights) – attract considerably more support in Spain (55-57%) than in Norway (29-38%). The two remaining possibilities – (3) should be able to depend on and (4) should be willing to sacrifice – are more general and open for negotiations about where and how they should be enacted. These more general norms stand equally strongly in the two countries, indeed across all five countries of the study (Table 7.1A).

The personal preferences for care provider lean strongly towards the services option in the Norwegian case and towards family care in Spain (Table 7.1B). Three out of four Norwegians say they would prefer professional services, while two out of three Spaniards would prefer family help. The other three countries occupy intermediate positions.

Table 7.1: (A) per cent in support for filial responsibility norms, (B) preference for care provider and (C) preference for housing arrangement, by country, age 25+

	Norway	England	Germany	Spain	Israel
(n)	(1,203)	(1,200)	(1,197)	(1,208)	(1,297)
A: Support for filial norms					
Prescriptive norms					
Item 1. Should live close	29	31	40	57	55
Item 2. Should reciprocate	38	48	26	55	64
Open norms					
Item 3. Able to depend on	58	41	55	60	51
Item 4. Willing to sacrifice	41	47	36	44	37
Agreement with at least one item	76	75	66	82	84
B: Preference for care provider					
Services	77	45	48	31	60
Family	18	51	45	68	21
Others	5	4	7	2	19
C: Preference for housing arrangement					
Institutional care	77	62	61	44	74
Living with a child	23	38	39	56	26

A: Filial obligation scale items: (1) adult children should live close to their older parents so that they can help them if needed, (2) parents are entitled to some return for the sacrifices they have made for their children, (3) older people should be able to depend on their adult children to help them do the things they need to do, (4) adult children should be willing to sacrifice some of the things they want for their own children in order to support their ageing parents. Response scale from 1: strongly disagree through disagree, neither-nor, agree and 5: strongly agree. Adapted from Lee et al (1998) by Daatland and Herlofson (2003).

B: Preference for care provider: suppose you should come to need long-term help on a regular basis with household chores like cleaning, washing clothes, etc, from whom would you prefer such help? From family, from organised services, or from others?

C: Preference for housing arrangement: If you could no longer live by yourself in older years, and had to choose between living with a child or in residential or institutional care, what would you prefer? With a child, in residential care, don't know? (Only parents).

The same contrast is seen in the preference for housing arrangement, for cases in which one can no longer manage by oneself in old age (Table 7.1C). Three out of four Norwegians (among the parents only) would then move to an institution, while a (more moderate) majority of Spanish parents (56%) would like to move in with a child.

The patterns observed here are in support of the general hypotheses. Filial responsibility norms are stronger and more unconditional in the south, while filial independence is comparatively stronger in the north, as indicated by a preference for services instead of obligating children or other family members. The trends are hardly surprising and might be interpreted simply as a response to differences of opportunity – that is, differences in the availability and standard of services in the respective countries. But, if this were the whole story, it would not be able to explain any within-country variation in norms and values according to gender, age, dependency and education, to which we will now turn.

Analytical findings: expectations from children and for them

The extent to which filial norms and preferences for care are differentially related to gender, age and needs in the two countries as suggested by the hypotheses can be tested in multiple regression analyses. Do Spanish parents expect *more* help from children than Norwegian parents, and *more* so the older they are and the more help they need? In contrast, do Norwegian parents value filial independence and therefore expect *less* help from children, and *less* so the older they are and the more help they need? Support for filial responsibility norms should in that case *increase* with age and dependency in Spain and *decrease* with age and dependency in Norway, and vice versa for filial independence. I also suggested that women would be more family oriented than men and therefore lean towards the dominant pattern in each country – i.e. towards filial obligations in Spain and towards filial independence in Norway. Finally, I expected the higher educated to be less inclined to support filial obligations in both countries.

Filial responsibility

A multiple linear regression of support for filial responsibility norms on age, gender, risk of dependency, education and family status gives considerable, but not unconditional support to the hypotheses I suggested. Support for filial responsibility norms does indeed decrease with age in Norway, but does not increase with age in Spain as was expected. A risk of dependency does, however, increase filial expectations in this country, but not so in Norway (Table 7.2). I take this as support for hypotheses 1 and 2, but not for all their details and not unconditionally so. Conditional support may also be counted for the impact of gender, as women tend to expect less filial responsibility than men in Norway, while there is no gender difference in Spain (Table 7.2), and therefore only partial support for hypothesis 3.

Having children (being a parent) reduces the support for filial obligation norms in both countries, indicating that parents are often ambivalent and try to balance between expectations from children and a parental concern for them. Parents possibly expect less from their children than the children themselves find reasonable to offer. Whether or not respondents' parents are still alive does not, however, impact on filial norms in any direction, while education contributes to fewer expectations from children in both countries, as was expected under hypothesis 4.

Table 7.2: Multiple linear regression of support for filial responsibility norms[a] in Norway and Spain, age 25+

	Norway	Spain
Age (1-7 = high)	−.121*	−.014
Gender (0,1 = women)	−.165***	−.003
Dependency (0,1 = at risk)[b]	.007	.098**
Have children (0,1 = yes)	−.117***	−.106**
Have parents (0,1 = yes)	.049	.000
Education (1–3 = high)	−.076*	−.140***
R^2	.073***	.033***
(n)	(1,103)	(1,110)

Notes: [a] Mean score on an additive scale for all four items. * p<.05, ** p<.01, *** p<.001
[b] Scoring among the lower sixth percentiles on the Short Form 12 Scale.

Figure 7.1 presents a case that is selected in a way that should be able to highlight the country contrasts and clarify under what conditions the hypotheses are valid or not. The case therefore includes only *mothers*, who are assumed to be the most family oriented, and support for *prescriptive filial norms* (items 1 and 2), where country differences are most evident (see Table 7.1). This case indeed gives more unambiguous support to the hypotheses. Support for (prescriptive) filial responsibility now not only *decreases* with age in Norway (for mothers), but also *increases* with age in Spain. Only the first of these criteria was met under the general condition (see Table 7.2).

Figure 7.1. Support for prescriptive filial norms[a] among mothers in Spain (n = 526) and Norway (n = 520), by age

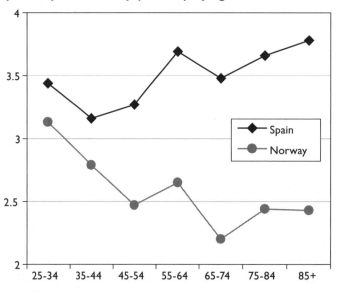

Note: [a] Mean score for items 1 and 2 of the filial obligation scale – see details in notes to Table 7.1A.

Filial independence

Preference for services over family care and for institutional care over living with a child are taken as indicators of filial independence and are analysed in logistic regressions as the dependent variable in these cases are dichotomous. Age is here treated as a categorical variable because preferences need not be linearly related to age. The youngest people (age 25-44) are used as the reference for the middle-aged people (45-64) and the older people (65+) in the analyses.

The findings are also here only partly in line with expectations. The preference for services (over family care) and for institutions (over moving in with a child) does indeed increase with age and risk of dependency in Norway, but does not decrease with age in Spain as was expected. There is a tendency in that direction in Spain only for the housing option, but this tendency does not reach significance (Table 7.3).

Table 7.3: Logistic regression of preference for services (over family care) and institutional care (over living with a child) by country, age 25+

	Preference for services		Preference for institutional care[a]	
	Norway	Spain	Norway	Spain
Age 45–64	1.765**	1.386	2.453***	1.352
Age 65+	4.568***	1.051	2.598***	0.669
Gender (1 = women)	1.646**	0.954	1.500**	1.344*
Dependency (1 = at risk)	1.388	0.910	1.777	1.188
Have children (1 = yes)	0.991	0.785		not relevant
Education (1-3 = high)	1.452**	1.086	0.836	1.336*
Constant	0.534	0.456	2.018	0.476*
Nagelkerke R^2	0.086	0.011	0.092	0.049**
(n)	(1,095)	(1,068)	(934)	(810)

[a]*Parents only.*

Norwegian women are less likely to prefer family care than Norwegian men (Table 7.3), just as they were less likely to expect filial responsibility (Table 7.2). This finding is in support with hypothesis 3, but the opposite does not hold in the Spanish case.

Parents 'gravitate' towards a preference for family care in Spain (but not significantly so), while Norwegian parents do not differ from the childless in these attitudes, possibly because mothers are reluctant to obligate their children while fathers are not. And, finally, education and a risk of dependency have impacts in the expected direction, but not consistently so and in all details (Table 7.3).

The contrast between the two countries is also here illustrated for a more 'clean case', namely for mothers only and their preference for institutional care. The countries indeed accommodate to the expected patterns under these circumstances in that Norwegian mothers prefer institutional care over obligating their children and increasingly so the older they are. The opposite is the case for Spanish mothers (Figure 7.2). While, in Norway, more than 90% of mothers aged 75 and over prefer institutional care, this is the case for only around 20% in Spain.

Figure 7.2: Per cent in preference for nursing home over living with a child among mothers in Spain (*n* = 413) and Norway (*n* = 449), by age

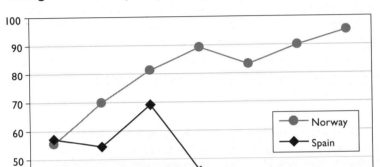

Interestingly, the younger cohorts of the two countries tend to agree in norms and preferences, while the older tend to hold different opinions and more so the older they are (Figures 7.1 and 7.2). The older cohorts have different orientations in the two countries, while the younger cohorts of both countries are closer to the northern average scores, indicating that southern populations might come to converge towards the northern position over time. An alternative explanation is that the younger respondents might have been rather uninterested in these questions, finding them irrelevant, and they might therefore have adopted a middle-ground response.

Discussion: expectations, explanations and more questions

The findings support Reher's (1998) idea about a north–south divide in Europe as far as family values are concerned. They are also in line with the 'intergenerational ambivalence' perspective (Lüscher and Pillemer, 1998; Connidis & McMullin, 2002) in that both parents and children are balancing obligations and independence, but in different equilibria in a northern (Norway) and southern (Spain) context.

Filial responsibility norms are stronger and more unconditional in Spain, while filial independence is comparatively stronger in Norway. Expectations of children *decrease* with needs and age in Norway, possibly in response to a parental concern for their children, while filial expectations tend to *increase* with parents' needs in Spain. It is important to keep in mind that both responses may be family motivated, but the southern approach gives priority to the older generation while the northern gives priority to the younger.

The findings also indicate how family care is constructed from both sides of the relationships. Older people often have strong opinions about who should take what kind of responsibility for them. In Norway they are strongly inclined towards professional services over family help if they need long-term personal care, while older people in Spain are nearly as strongly inclined towards family care. These attitudes will most likely have an impact on the actual care mix, but the precise details of the attitude–intention–behaviour nexus cannot be analysed here and need to be explored in future comparative studies.

The findings give only partial support for the hypotheses from which I started, which need to be refined in order to test under what circumstances they are valid or otherwise. Equally important is to explore the motivations and mechanisms that may have produced the patterns observed. Are they better explained by culture or by structure? To ask this more precisely, are the observed differences in filial responsibility norms and care preferences better explained by different family traditions (culture) or by different welfare state arrangements (opportunity)? This particular study does not allow us to disentangle the two dimensions, but earlier studies in Norway have found a change in preference from family care to services in response to service expansion between 1970 and the late 1980s (Daatland, 1990).

Attitudes are probably influenced both by culture and opportunity, and we need to separate the two more clearly in future studies – for example, by following developments in attitudes over time in response to policy changes. Triangulation with qualitative data on the motivations behind stated preferences might also help us to better understand the mechanisms. Important questions arise here. For example, is the preference for professional services in the Norwegian case actually most strongly motivated by parental concern for their children (that is, not being a burden on them), as this article has sometimes suggested? Or is it equally or even more strongly driven by a concern for oneself – demanding one's rights vis-à-vis the welfare state?

Valuable information may also come to light if more countries are compared. Preliminary findings by Jackson et al (2008) indicate that the US population is even more strongly in support of filial obligations and family care than are the Spanish, and more so among black Americans than among white. This within-country variation points towards cultural influence, but the generally high priority given to family care is probably (also) a response to low availability of decent standard services.

There is a need also for conceptual clarification. Are filial responsibility and filial independence two ends of the same scale or are they different dimensions where one may be 'both' or 'either'? Correlations between the two – that is, between filial responsibility on the one side and preferences for services/institutions on the other – are fairly low ($r = 0,2$) and this suggests that they are in fact different dimensions. This is a case in which large-scale data can alert us to ways in which our everyday thought about people's conduct is too crude. We need to discover much more about what responsibility and independence really mean in people's lives, in what they expect of others and from themselves. There are also loose ends on the explanatory side, which point to large gaps in our understanding of life-course related behaviour that need to be filled in. Why *should* filial responsibility norms be more unconditional in the south and/or when welfare state services are low? Why should mothers and fathers, sons and daughters respond differently?

And, finally, policy implications need to be studied in order to evaluate what is a sustainable balance between the family and the welfare state, and between older and younger generations in ageing societies. Democracies need policies that are responsive to the preferences of their citizens. These preferences are diverse just as populations are diverse. But the general trend emerging from this study is towards a mixed model of care; however a mix in which governments, whether or not in the shape of welfare states, take comparatively more responsibility than they do in today's often family- (and female-) dominated care systems.

Note

[1] The OASIS project (old age and autonomy – the role of service systems and intergenerational family solidarity) was funded within the fifth framework programme of the European Community, contract number QLK6-CT-1999–02182.

References

Aboderin, I. (2004) 'Decline in material family support for older people in urban Ghana, Africa: understanding processes and causes of change', *Journal of Gerontology, Social Sciences*, 59B, vol 3, no 3, pp S128-37.

Arber, S. and Attias-Donfut, C. (eds)(2000) *The myth of generational conflict: Family and state in ageing societies*, London: Routledge.

Bengtson, V. and Lowenstein, A. (eds)(2003) *Global aging and challenges to families*, New York: Aldine de Gruyter.

Bhat, A.K. and Dhruvarajan, R. (2001) 'Ageing in India: drifting intergenerational relations, challenges and options', *Ageing and Society*, vol 21, no 5, pp 621-40.

Brody, E.M., Johnson, P.T. and Fulcomer, M.C. (1984) 'What should adult children do for elderly parents? Opinions and preferences of three generations of women', *Journal of Gerontology*, vol 39, no 6, pp 736-46.

Brody, E.M., Johnson, P.T., Fulcomer, M.C. and Lang, A.M. (1983) 'Women's changing roles and help to elderly parents: attitudes of three generations of women', *Journal of Gerontology*, vol 38, no 5, pp 597-607.

Connidis, I. and McMullin, J.A. (2002) 'Sociological ambivalence and family ties: a critical perspective', *Journal of Marriage and the Family*, vol 64, no 2, pp 558-67.

Daatland, S.O. (1990) 'What are families for? On family solidarity and preferences for help', *Ageing and Society*, vol 10, no 1, pp 1-15.

Daatland, S.O. and Herlofson, K. (2003) '"Lost solidarity" or "changed solidarity"? A comparative European view on normative family solidarity', *Ageing and Society*, vol 23, no 5, pp 537–60.

Daatland, S.O. and Lowenstein, A. (2005) 'Intergenerational solidarity and the family–wefare state balance', *European Journal of Ageing*, vol 2, no 3, pp 174-82.

Evandrou, M., Glaser, K. and Henz, U. (2002) 'Multiple role occupancy in midlife: balancing work and family life in Britain', *The Gerontologist*, vol 42, no 6, pp 781-9.

Finch, J. (1989) *Family obligations and social change*, Cambridge: Polity Press.

Finch, J. and Mason, J. (1993) *Negotiating family responsibilities*, London: Tavistock/ Routledge.

Grundy, E. and Henretta, J. (2006) 'Between elderly parents and adult children: a new look at the intergenerational care provided by the "sandwich generation"', *Ageing & Society*, vol 26, no 5, pp 707-22.

Jackson, J., Antonucci, T.C., Brown, E.E., Daatland, S.O. and Sellers, B. (2008) 'Race and ethnic influences on normative beliefs and attitudes toward provision of family care', in A. Booth, A.C. Crouter, S.M. Bianchi and J.A. Seltzer (eds) *Intergenerational caregiving*, Washington DC: Urban Institute Press, pp 317-31.

Künemund, H. (2006). 'Changing welfare states and the "sandwich generation": increasing burden for the next generation?', *International Journal of Ageing and Later Life*, vol 1, no 2, pp 11-30.

Lee, G.R., Peek, C.W. and Coward, R.T. (1998) 'Race differences in filial responsibility expectations among older parents.' *Journal of Marriage and the Family*, vol 60, no 2, pp 404-12.

Lüscher, K. and Pillemer, K. (1998) 'Intergenerational ambivalence: a new approach to the study of parent–child relations in later life', *Journal of Marriage and the Family*, vol 60, no 2, pp 413-25.

McAuley, W.J. and Blieszner, R. (1985) 'Selection of long-term care arrangements by older community residents', *The Gerontologist*, vol 25, no 2, pp 188-93.

Reher, D.S. (1998) 'Family ties in Western Europe: persistent contrasts', *Population and Development Review*, vol 24, no 2, pp 203-34.

Rosenmayr, L. and Köckeis, E. (1963) 'Propositions for a sociological theory of ageing and the family', *UNESCO International Social Science Journal*, vol 15, no 3, pp 410-26.

Shanas, E. (1960) 'Family responsibility and the health of older people', *Journal of Gerontology*, vol 15, no 4, pp 408-11.

Walker, A. (1993) *Age and attitudes*, Brussels: European Commission.

Wielink, G., Huijsman, R. and McDonnel, J. (1997) 'Preferences for care: a study of the elders living independently in the Netherlands', *Research on Aging*, vol 19, no 2, pp 174-98.

EIGHT

Pension systems and the challenge of population ageing: what does the public think?

Dina Frommert, Dirk Hofäcker, Thorsten Heien and Hans-Jürgen Andreß

Introduction

Over the coming decades, population ageing is set to affect all European countries, probably resulting in a doubling of the ratio of pensioners to the working population within the next 50 years. At the same time, many European countries have until very recently experienced a significant decline in the employment participation of their older workforce, indicating a general trend towards 'early retirement'. The combined effect of both trends sets serious pressures on contemporary pension systems, since relatively fewer people will be paying taxes and social contributions just as the share of people receiving pensions rises.

European policy makers, scientists and other opinion leaders are currently discussing a variety of solutions to these common challenges. However, no political solution can be expected to succeed without considerable public support. Here we analyse most recent Eurobarometer data from 2001 and 2004 to explore the opinions of people in 15 countries of the European Union (EU-15) on alternative reforms mooted for the twofold problem of population ageing and early retirement. Additionally, we need to know how public support for reform proposals is determined. What are the – partly institutionalised – values and norms shaping Europeans' attitudes to pension policies? We shall start by examining suggestions outlined in the literature, then, using the most recent European survey data, test to see which accounts seem justified.

Population ageing and the 'double crisis' of pension systems

Demographic ageing

Nearly every European country is faced with the prospect of a population growing older, and eventually smaller. This development is due to both a decrease in fertility since the 1960s and a significant fall in mortality. In 2001, women in the EU-15 had, on average, 1.47 children (compared to 2.61 in 1960), whereas the average needed to replace the current population is 2.1 (European Commission, 2004a;

Fahey and Spéder, 2004). While fertility rates seem to have reached their lowest point in 1999, due to better socioeconomic and environmental conditions and improved medical treatment, life expectancy is still increasing in Europe (over the last 50 years by about 10 years in total).[1]

As a consequence, the ratio of those of retirement age (65+) to the working-age population (15-64) – the so-called old-age dependency ratio – will probably double within the next 50 years.[2] In the year 2000, people over 65 amounted to about one quarter of the working-age population; by 2050 it will be more than 50%, varying between 40% for Denmark and 68% for Spain (see Figure 8.1).

Figure 8.1: Old-age dependency ratio 2000 and 2050 (%)

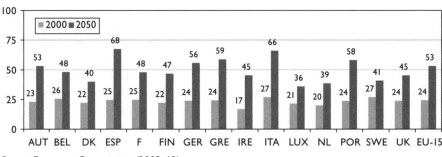

Source: European Commission (2003: 13)

The increasing old-age dependency ratio produces a major financial challenge for pension systems and this development may place an unsustainable financial burden on the active population, while at the same time adversely affecting Europe's economic growth.

Labour market crisis

The future sustainability of pension systems in Europe is not, however, endangered by demographic ageing alone. Driven by rising unemployment figures and the need for industrial restructuring and rationalisation in the 1980s and 1990s, most western industrialised countries have experienced augmented withdrawal of older workers from the labour market (Blöndal and Scarpetta, 1998; Blossfeld et al, 2006). As a result, the employment rates of older people (aged 55-64) in the EU-15 plummeted to as low as 36% in the late 1990s, although differences between countries are significant – ranging from 22% in Belgium to 63% in Sweden (European Commission, 2004b). This trend towards early retirement tends to intensify the disproportional relation between social security contributors and recipients. It artificially creates a reservoir of inactive pre-pensioners who receive early retirement or other welfare benefits while at the same time reducing the number of employed contributors to the national social security or tax systems.

As a reaction to these trends, many national governments have started to implement different policy measures to counteract the early retirement trend (Ebbinghaus, 2003; OECD, 2005). But, despite signs of a reversal of early retirement since the mid-1990s, the actual withdrawal age of older workers still remains below formal retirement standards, thereby sustaining the financial pressure on contemporary pension systems.

Possible policy solutions

In most public pension systems there are two basic possibilities for reform concerning challenges like these. The first involves paying less to everyone entitled to benefits and the second centres on increasing the amount of money to be spent. The second strategy can imply either increasing taxes and contributions, or increasing the number of contributors. Some of the policy options concern parametric reforms within a pension system – *internal* solutions; others – *external* solutions – concern other policy areas but have (side)effects that increase the available pension budget. Both types of options are featured in at least one recent Eurobarometer study.

Three internal policy reform items were included in the Eurobarometer studies in 2001 and 2004. While one option aims at raising the available pension budget by increasing contributions or taxes, a second option suggests lowering pension levels. Raising the (legal) retirement age is a third alternative, entailing that people work and contribute longer before claiming pension benefits. Simultaneously the number of eligible pensioners will decrease as people enter retirement later. In recent years, this measure was increasingly popular among pension policy experts, since the actual retirement age and the legal retirement age were sometimes up to four years apart. As these three policy options entail very different effects on national income distributions, we should find different policy preferences both between and within European countries.[3]

In the Eurobarometer survey in 2001, a number of additional items on external solutions such as government spending or the privatisation of pensions as well as labour market and family-oriented reforms were included. These proposals are discussed later in the article in connection with actual recent reform measures.[4]

Public attitudes: their role and determination

When dealing with the consequences of population ageing for pension systems in Europe, we might ask: do public attitudes really matter? Bearing in mind concerns about the nature and significance of public attitudes measured in surveys, especially in cross-national context (Brooks and Manza, 2006), we agree with Kohl that:

> … large-scale reform, especially in the field of pensions, will only be successful in the long run if it is in accordance with the basic value

orientations and beliefs of the citizens, or to put it in sociological terms: the public acceptance of a reform is a precondition of its long-term sustainability. (Kohl, 2003b: 3)

But public attitudes may not be uniform. They may vary with regard to both nation-specific and individual characteristics, so it is time to examine in more detail what makes them up. How does the literature try to explain what people's norms and values are, and to what extent do these explanations correspond with empirical evidence?

Individual-level explanations

Self-interest

A first individual-level explanation focuses on egoistic self-interest, hypothesising that individuals will evaluate positively those aspects of the welfare state from which they gain personally and will disapprove of the reverse. The literature usually concentrates on three types of interests.

First, *consumers* of services and transfers relying on the welfare state for material support will show a much higher degree of support than those who consume less (Cnaan et al, 1993). Thus older people may oppose pension cuts in favour of raising the retirement age, or increasing taxes or social contributions, as well as financial cuts in other policy areas. People without work may favour cutting unemployment and be hostile to increasing numbers of migrants – possible labour market competitors. Women especially may favour initiatives improving the compatibility of family and work.

Second, those contributing to the welfare state as *taxpayers* (and contributors to social insurance systems) may be likely to oppose attempts to increase taxes or social contributions or to cut spending in other policy areas to make more money available for pensions. Instead, they may favour pension cuts (Sihvo and Uusitalo, 1995).

Third, some people have interests in the welfare state as its *producers*. Those employed in the public sector seem more likely to be favourable towards the welfare state than others, because their employment, but also their careers, working conditions and economic rewards depend on the welfare state's prosperity (Forma, 1997; Pöntinen & Uusitalo, 1988). Public sector employees may thus favour financial cuts in other policy areas and oppose activities to privatise old-age security, for instance via financial tax incentives.

Differential socialisation

Another explanation assumes that individual socialisation processes will lead to different attitudes towards the welfare state. According to Inglehart (1977), younger age cohorts should be characterised by 'post-materialistic' values – endorsing values such as solidarity and community inherent in public pension systems. Since Inglehart's hypothesis dates back to the 1970s and post-materialism should have penetrated across age groups, we might now expect to observe this pattern of attitudes not only for younger people but also for those who are middle aged.

Similarly, a rich literature exists on different socialisation patterns for men and women. According to Svallfors (1997: 290), the specific experiences of women may make them more inclined to embrace a 'rationality of caring' in which concern, consideration and devotion to others are more prominent. The institutionalisation of caring services brings into the public realm what was previously a private matter, thus transforming a 'moral economy of domesticity' into support for state welfare. On this account, women should prefer reform proposals similar to those favoured by younger age cohorts.

Finally, employment in the public sector is connected with specific socialisation experiences, too. Various authors argue that working conditions in the public sector 'may create bonds of sympathy and solidarity with fellow public-sector employees and their clients, patients, and other welfare dependants' (Svallfors, 1995: 55). Public sector employees may thus also oppose proposals strengthening private pension schemes.

Aggregate-level explanations

It would be implausible to expect attitudes to pension reform to differ with regard only to *characteristics of individuals within a country*. They may also display systematic variations with regard to respondents' *national contexts*.

For example, individuals grow up in different *types* of welfares states, which may be expected to create specific *welfare cultures*, leading respondents to favour specific reform solutions and disapprove of others. In addition to this cultural argument, we might assume that respondents' opinions might be influenced by the *availability of reform options* in the respective national context. Thus, opinions on resolving the pension crisis by reducing unemployment may depend on the local degree and urgency of unemployment.

Furthermore, individuals may show more favourable attitudes towards reform solutions they already have *practical (and positive) experience* with. For instance, individuals living in countries where private pension schemes are already significant may be less reluctant to increase pension privatisation than those in more publicly oriented pension systems.

The following offers a rough classification of different national contexts based on general welfare state characteristics. This will allow us to develop hypotheses on country-specific support for the different reform opportunities surveyed in the Eurobarometer surveys, and thus to come closer to envisaging the evaluative terrain relevant to European pension reform.

General welfare state characteristics

Comparative welfare research has shown that European welfare states can be grouped into four different 'welfare regimes' (Esping-Andersen, 1990, 1999; Ferrera, 1996) characterised by specific ideas about the responsibility of the state, the family and the market in securing individual welfare (Gundelach, 1994; Svallfors, 1997; Andreß and Heien, 2001; Heien, 2002). Examining these, we can see that they lay out specific types of ethical and political landscape, with distinct sets of expectations regarding the provision of welfare.

- *Social-democratic* countries – most typically those of Scandinavia (here: Sweden, Denmark and Finland) – are characterised by a strong welfare state providing general and universal protection against a large variety of individual and labour market risks. Social policy aims to emancipate individuals from market dependence and to achieve a high level of social equality, especially gender equality. As comparatively high tax rates form the basis of this generous welfare system, Scandinavian countries tend to follow a labour market policy aimed at near-full employment for both sexes across the life course.
- The *liberal* regime, represented by the Anglo-Saxon countries (here: the United Kingdom and Ireland), constitutes a reverse 'mirror image' of the social-democratic type. Here the market plays the central role in distributing resources. Welfare benefits are usually means-tested and only ensure against 'negative risks' such as poverty. Individuals are required to maintain a decent standard of living through their own employment and additional private insurance.
- The *conservative* regime comprises most continental European welfare states (here: Austria, Belgium, France, Germany, Luxembourg and the Netherlands). Benefits are not as residual as in liberal countries but are bound to previous work performance, so that the extent of protection often depends on one's (former) labour market position. Welfare responsibility is shared between the family and the state, with the latter interfering only if the former fails to ensure security (the so-called 'subsidiarity principle'). Many welfare transfers are aimed at male household heads, while women's welfare is derived from their husbands' rights.
- A number of social scientists have suggested that Southern European countries (here: Greece, Italy, Spain and Portugal) should be considered a separate welfare regime type (Ferrera, 1996). Though they share some characteristics with conservative regimes (such as benefits' dependence on contributions and the derived welfare entitlements of women), their provision of welfare is lower, less universal and fragmented across regions and groups of recipients. Family ties in these countries are strong; the traditional breadwinner family is considered an 'explicit partner' of the rudimentary welfare state (Saraceno, 1994). Notably, pension policies occupy a prominent position: more than three quarters of social expenditure is invested into pension-related issues. Those entitled to full

benefits receive some of the most generous wage-replacement rates in Europe (Blöndal and Scarpetta, 1998).

Adjusting pension system parameters to demographic and labour market change

European welfare states have adjusted their pension systems very differently to the growing imbalance between contributors and recipients. But some parametric reforms were introduced in virtually every European country in the last decade (see European Commission, 2006; Vidlund, 2006). Most European countries currently have a formal retirement age of 65 years for men, with the exception of Ireland (66 years for the contributory pension) and Norway (67 years). However, *actual* retirement ages often lie below the *official* retirement age, a pattern most pronounced for continental and Southern European countries and least distinct in Sweden, Denmark and Norway (Blossfeld et al., 2006). Many policies to counteract this trend have focused on restricting opportunities for early retirement. Attempts to *raise the retirement age* itself have remained modest, often focusing on adjusting women's retirement ages to the men's. In addition, many European countries have implemented *reductions in pension benefits* by increasing the number of contribution years for full pension receipt, changing the benefit calculation formula or dispensing the indexing of pensions. In contrast, only for France, the OECD reports the use of an *increase in contributions* as the key strategy in averting pension crisis (see OECD, 2005; Zaidi, 2006).

Pension privatisation

While debate about pension privatisation is increasingly dominating public discourse, there remains large cross-national variation in Europe regarding the actual existence and extent of non-public pension components (European Commission 2006, 2005).

Private pension pillars play the most substantial role in *liberal* countries where public pension systems offer only basic material security, and private and occupational pension pillars make up a decent proportion of retirement income. *Social-democratic* countries were initially dominated by large public 'people's' pensions, but Denmark and Sweden have recently moved to 'mixed systems' with quasi-mandatory occupational pillars and a rising level of private pensions. In *conservative* countries, Belgium and the Netherlands stand out as countries where occupational and private pensions account for up to one third of old-age income. Such schemes are less important in other *conservative* countries as well as in *Southern Europe* where public pensions are still dominant.[5]

Increasing employment levels

Significant cross-country differences also exist regarding the extent to which European countries have been (and still are) affected by (structural) unemployment.

The unemployment problem appears to be most serious in *Southern Europe* (except Portugal) where unemployment, despite significant decreases in the late 1990s, still reaches about 10% and specifically long-term unemployment is prevalent. Unemployment in *conservative* countries has varied between 2.8% (the Netherlands) and 9.7% (France) but also tends to be long-term. These patterns apparently confirm the common view of conservative and Southern European countries as having 'insider-outsider' labour markets with structural unemployment and specific permanently excluded groups. Unemployment in *social-democratic* countries also rose in the early 1990s, but recently declined, and is currently at 5% in Denmark and Sweden, and around 9% in Finland. The fact that only 20-25% of it constitutes long-term unemployment points to the effectiveness of Scandinavian full-employment policies. Similar figures can be observed in the *liberal* countries of Great Britain and Ireland where the very high unemployment rates of the early 1990s steadily declined to 3-5% and – owing to flexible labour markets – long-term unemployment has to date been only moderate.

Fostering Migration may be another effective means of increasing pension contributors – though it may occasionally be confronted by nationalist objections that obstruct it.

Family measures

Measures to strengthen the family and the employment of women provide other final options to resolve the pension crisis. Comparative research has shown that, at present, European countries differ significantly with regards to the support for female employment and families in general (Gornick et al, 1997; Hofäcker, 2004, 2006). *Social-democratic* countries comprehensively foster the reconciliation of family and working life, displaying high and continuous female labour-force participation over the last three decades. Female employment rates in *liberal* countries have risen to similar levels, due less to public family support (which is rudimentary) than to a combination of financial necessity, the availability of flexible working hours and reconciliation measures provided through the private market. In many *conservative* countries, governments have supported families with comprehensive monetary transfers, but have invested little in work–family reconciliation policies. Thus, mothers often interrupt their careers at childbirth and later return only to part-time work. *France* stands out from this pattern with large public engagement in childcare and higher full-time employment of women. *Southern European* countries provide only very low public support to families with children, suggesting a 'male breadwinner' model.

External solutions and country-specific patterns of support: hypotheses

Table 8.1 summarises the results from the institutional comparisons and its implications for determining attitudes to pension reforms.

Table 8.1: Welfare regimes and institutional characteristics

	General welfare characteristics	Pension Privatisation	Unemployment	Policies to support families and reconcile family and work
Social-democratic	State-dominated, full-employment policy, gender equality	Moderate-high	Low, short-term	High female employment, comprehensive family support
Liberal	Market-oriented, low state benefits, high importance of private insurance	High	Moderate-low, short-term	High female employment, low family support
Conservative	Subsidiarity principle, moderate insurance, employment-based	Moderate-low	Moderate, structural	Moderate female employment (part-time), moderate family support
Southern European	Rudimentary and fragmented welfare state, family as main 'welfare partner'	Low	High and structural	Low female employment, low family support

What does this encourage us to expect different publics to feel about particular proposed pension reforms? First, we can assume that changes directly affecting pension parameters (*internal solutions*) may be met with some scepticism. Pension systems and related eligibility criteria are increasingly seen as historically acquired 'social rights' (OECD, 2005). *External solutions*, involving policy adjustments in other areas, may thus be preferred. Those in countries where retirement ages are already high (Ireland, Norway) may oppose further *raising of the retirement age*. Faced with future pension insecurity, individuals may favour adapting existing models through *increasing pension contributions* over the loss in value of public pensions implied by *reducing pension benefits*. We might expect this difference to be highest in countries where public pensions provide only a basic minimum (liberal countries) and in countries where cuts in pension benefits have already occurred (mostly conservative and Southern European countries).

Likewise, *cuts in other social policy areas* in favour of the pension system may be opposed in the residual welfare systems of liberal and Southern European countries. Respondents in social-democratic countries may also oppose this option, due to a generally generous welfare state culture. In contrast, *enlarging the financial basis* of public pensions could be equally supported in all of the four regime types.

Regarding the *privatisation of the pension systems*, we assume that respondents in liberal countries will show the most favourable attitudes, in line with the liberal welfare ideal of minimal state intervention. Citizens of social-democratic countries have recently had similar experiences but, as the basic concept of a strong welfare state may be offended by further privatisation, we should expect lower support levels in these countries. In conservative and Southern European countries where such measures are less common, we should expect more reluctance about pension privatisation.

Due to the fact that almost every European country endured high unemployment in the 1980s and 1990s, we assume that plans to *reduce unemployment* would receive high support in virtually every European country. However, support may be highest in Scandinavian countries where full employment is an explicit political aim and in countries where unemployment is a structural problem (conservative and Southern European countries). In contrast, in liberal countries where unemployment is often only temporary and the welfare ideology generally supports minimal state intervention, these measures may be favoured less. In contrast, we expect *migration measures* to be less popular in all regime types, except for smaller countries such as the Scandinavian ones where there is less local unemployment.

Finally, measures aimed at *strengthening the family* may be most welcome in conservative and Southern European countries where female employment and fertility rates are low. At the same time, family support measures are compatible with the general 'welfare partnership' between state and family in these countries. In social-democratic countries, family policies may receive less support, due to already wide implementation of these measures. In liberal countries, support will probably be lowest, since explicit family policies at least partly contradict the idea of low state interference in the private realm.

The Eurobarometer data

In the early 1970s the European Commission introduced the 'Eurobarometer' survey series to monitor citizens' social and political attitudes. The survey has since been carried out regularly in all member states at least twice a year. Topics range from attitudes towards European unification to diverse areas relevant to national and European public policy, with a regular sample size of 1,000 respondents per country (European Commission, 2009[6]).

Here we shall concentrate on data from 2001 (Eurobarometer 56.1; see Gesis, 2009[7]), since all the policy options discussed above were included in this survey. Internal reform options were also included in the 2004 questionnaire (Eurobarometer 62.1; see Gesis, 2009[8]), but comparisons over time are hindered by changes in the relevant questions' form and phrasing (see Table 8.2). Hence we shall compare only the rank order of the three policy options in these two surveys.

Table 8.2: Exact wording of 'internal solutions' items in 2001 and 2004

| Term used in the paper | 2001 | | 2004 | |
	Question	Exact wording	Question	Exact wording
Raise contributions	Q67.1[1]	Current pension levels should be maintained even if this means raising taxes or contributions	QB18A, QB18B[2]	(2) Maintain the retirement age and increase your social security contributions [paid by the workers]
Lower pension levels	Q67.2[1]	Contribution rates should not be raised even if this means lower pension levels		(3) Maintain the current retirement age and accept that you [one] will receive less
Raise age	Q67.3[1]	The age of retirement should be raised so that people work longer and therefore spend less time in retirement		(1) Work and contribute for longer

Note: [1]support and rejection, four options; [2]preference.

Source: Eurobarometer 56.1 (2001) and 62.1 (2004)

Results

Perception of the problem

Looking first at whether people in Europe perceive lower birth rates and increasing life expectancy as a problem at all, demographic ageing was described as a 'major problem' by more than 60% of the respondents (EU–15 average) in 2001 (see Figure 8.2).[9] This was especially the case in Southern Europe (Greece: 86%; Italy: 66%; Spain: 63%; Portugal: 62%) as well as in France (67%) and in Germany (65%). Only in Ireland (32%), the United Kingdom (UK) (46%) and Luxembourg (47%) less than 50% chose this answer.

In 2004 over 70% (EU–15 average) of respondents were not confident concerning the future of pensions (see Figure 8.3);[10] this is mostly due to high percentages of scepticism in the large EU countries (UK, France: 84%; Germany: 82%). With Portugal (75%), there is just one other country above the EU–15 average. Conversely, in Ireland (42%), Finland (43%) and Denmark (47%) under 50% of respondents were sceptical about future pensions.

Figure 8.2: Perception of demographic ageing as a 'major problem', 2001 (%)

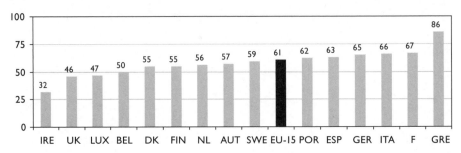

Source: Eurobarometer 56.1 (authors' calculations)

Figure 8.3: Confidence in the future of pensions 2004 ('rather not/not at all confident')(%)

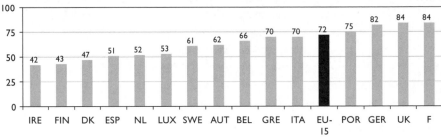

Source: Eurobarometer 62.1 (authors' calculations)

The results for the UK and Spain seem to be contradictory given the short time between the two surveys. Although the British did not assess demographic ageing as a (major) problem in 2001 (46%) they were not confident concerning the future of pensions in 2004 (84%). Conversely, the Spanish perceived demographic ageing as a (major) problem (63%) but were relatively confident concerning the future of pensions (51%).

Internal solutions

The rank order of the internal solutions remains remarkably similar over the EU-15 countries (Table 8.3). In virtually every country (except Greece with 57%) the support for 'raise contributions' is 60% or more, ranging from around 60% to about 80%, and is far higher than for the other two policy options. In most countries the second ranking option is to 'lower pension levels' and the option 'raise the retirement age' is the one least supported in all countries except the Netherlands, the UK and Ireland. In Ireland the option of raising the retirement age even tops lowering pension levels by ten percentage points. This is surprising as the employment rates of people aged 55-64, and the retirement age in Ireland, are already above the EU average (European Commission, 2006: 191). The unique economic boom in Ireland might have made it easier for people aged 50 and older to remain in employment and the option might thus seem less 'threatening'.

As far as the ranking of the policy options is regarded, virtually no systematic differences can be detected between different welfare state regimes. Only for actual percentages supporting 'raising contributions' do slight differences show. Whereas social-democratic and liberal countries show percentages above the EU-15 average, the Southern European ones (except Spain) generally fall below it, while the conservative ones (except the Netherlands) group closely around the mean. No similar pattern appears for the two other policy options (Table 8.3). The slight differences in overall support might be linked to nation-specific institutional characteristics. For example, contribution rates in Italy and Portugal are among the highest in the EU-15, which might explain the comparatively low support for higher contributions. In contrast, in the Netherlands and Ireland – and to some extent the UK – contribution rates are very low, a fact probably encouraging a more positive response to the item (ISG, 2006: 14).

Table 8.3: (Strong) support and ranking of internal solutions, 2001

Welfare regime/country		Raise contributions		Lower pension levels		Raise age	
		%[1]	Rank	%[1]	Rank	%[1]	Rank
Conservative	Austria	68 (28)	1 (1)	31 (11)	2 (2)	25 (7)	3 (3)
	Belgium	65 (28)	1 (1)	33 (10)	2 (2)	21 (7)	3 (3)
	France	69 (33)	1 (1)	37 (13)	2 (2)	25 (8)	3 (3)
	Germany	64 (22)	1 (1)	34 (8)	2 (2)	18 (4)	3 (3)
	Luxembourg	63 (32)	1 (1)	32 (16)	2 (2)	17 (6)	3 (3)
	Netherlands	78 (46)	1 (1)	22 (7)	3 (2)	24 (5)	2 (3)
Social-democratic	Denmark	86 (57)	1 (1)	31 (12)	2 (2)	28 (9)	3 (3)
	Finland	80 (40)	1 (1)	32 (9)	2 (2)	25 (6)	3 (3)
	Sweden	73 (42)	1 (1)	29 (8)	2 (2)	12 (4)	3 (3)
Southern European	Greece	57 (33)	1 (1)	35 (13)	2 (2)	13 (5)	3 (3)
	Italy	61 (22)	1 (1)	31 (7)	2 (3)	28 (8)	3 (2)
	Portugal	62 (14)	1 (1)	39 (11)	2 (2)	28 (8)	3 (3)
	Spain	72 (33)	1 (1)	27 (8)	2 (2)	20 (5)	3 (3)
Liberal	Ireland	76 (41)	1 (1)	31 (12)	3 (3)	41 (20)	2 (2)
	UK	78 (40)	1 (1)	22 (8)	3 (2)	24 (8)	2 (3)
	EU-15	69 (30)	1 (1)	31 (9)	2 (2)	23 (6)	3 (3)

Note: 1 'Strongly agree' or 'slightly agree' (only 'strongly agree').

Source: Eurobarometer 56.1 (2001) (authors' calculations)

Even though the range of percentages is broader if only the 'strongly agree' options are examined (Table 8.3, numbers in brackets), the pattern of support is mostly similar. Overall, it is remarkable how stable both the support for higher contributions and the rank order are.

Furthermore, the results scarcely vary with sociodemographic variables such as gender, education or occupation. Only for age groups are differences observed, with the favoured item 'raising contributions': the older the respondents, the more likely they are to agree. As this is the option that least affects pensioners and people close to retirement, it is in line with the theoretical assumptions we outlined.

Given the stability of the rank order over countries and sociodemographic groups, the time dimension is an interesting complement. From Table 8.4 it springs to mind immediately that the option most favoured by the respondents in 2004 remains 'raising contributions'. However, the second place is now most often taken by 'raising retirement age', which was *least* favoured three years earlier. It is unclear if the reason for this change in attitude is linked to reforms lowering pension levels before 2004, or if it is due to increased media activity and advertising by governments. It could also be a methodological artefact due to the new phrasing of the items. However, higher contributions do not only receive the highest support. The preference for this policy option seems to be stable over countries,

Table 8.4: Preference ranking of internal solutions, 2004

Welfare regime/country		Raise contributions		Raise age		Lower pension levels		Undecided
		%	Rank	%	Rank	%	Rank	%
Conservative	Austria	22	1	11	3	14	2	53
	Belgium	33	1	22	2	15	3	30
	France	32	1	24	2	10	3	33
	Germany	18	1	18	1	18	1	47
	Luxembourg	39	1	17	2	17	2	28
	Netherlands	42	1	17	3	22	2	18
Social-	Denmark	45	1	24	2	15	3	17
democratic	Finland	46	1	24	2	11	3	19
	Sweden	38	1	22	2	15	3	25
Southern	Greece	39	1	7	3	8	2	46
European	Italy	29	1	15	2	9	3	47
	Portugal	16	1	13	2	4	3	66
	Spain	25	1	15	2	9	3	50
Liberal	Ireland	51	1	20	2	14	3	15
	UK	35	1	15	2	9	3	41
	EU-15	31	1	18	2	13	3	38

Source: Eurobarometer 62.1 (2004) (authors' calculations).

sociodemographic groups and time. This is especially noteworthy because this option is still frequently believed to be the one least acceptable to the public.

The percentage of people who did not decide for any of the policy options supplied is surprisingly high. The numbers of people who stated (spontaneously) 'none of these', 'a combination' or 'don't know' range from 13% in the UK to 63% in Portugal ('undecided' in Table 8.4). This might be attributable to lack of opinion, lack of information, or an inability to decide for one single option only. It also depends methodologically on how the items are presented. The 2001 phrasing proved more effective in getting people to actually make a statement with the maximum percentage of 'don't know' answers ranging from 16% to 25%, all of these in Ireland.

External solutions

Tables 8.5 and 8.6 give an overview of European citizens' agreement (answers 'agree' and 'strongly agree') with several external reform options that go beyond adjusting pension parameters. They show that almost all external solutions are supported in a comparable fashion by at least two thirds of European citizens. The only exceptions are the suggestions of increasing pension contributions by *immigration* (supported by a majority of respondents in Scandinavia only) or by *family support* (where agreement varies strongly and falls below 50% in the Netherlands, Denmark and the United Kingdom). Generally, support for external reform alternatives tends to exceed that of reforms within the existing pension system, though there appear to be cross-country differences that point to some 'regime-specific self-interest'. The tendency to prefer external above internal reforms is most distinct in conservative and Southern European countries, notably those countries where public pensions still make up the lion's share of old-age income. Citizens of these nations may hence be more inclined to advocate adjustments in other policy areas than to allow changes or cutbacks in their well-established and financially dominant public pension systems. In liberal and social-democratic countries, support for increasing pension contributions is quite strong compared to external solutions, while other internal reform options appear to be equally unpopular in all countries. Also, cutting existing pension benefits occupies the very last rank in liberal countries, where pension replacement rates are lowest (Blöndal and Scarpetta, 1999: 62).

As the overall level of support varies only marginally across countries, the bracketed values in Tables 8.5 and 8.6 display the percentage of *strong* support. Although, from this perspective, cross-national differences become more visible, results still remain hard to interpret, as variations in cultural response behaviour appear to influence the results. In some countries (for example, Greece) respondents obviously display a tendency to show high levels of support to *all* policy options, while in other countries (for example, Portugal) they tend to use more moderate answer categories. The right columns of Tables 8.5 and 8.6 hence compare the rank order of the different policy alternatives only within the respective national context.[11] This perspective reveals some systematic regime patterns, which appear to be in line with our theoretical expectations.

This is especially true with regard to attitudes towards *pension privatisation*. As expected, pension privatisation ranks among the most preferred alternatives in the liberal countries where private pension systems are already significant. Privatisation measures are equally approved in Denmark, where the role of private and occupational pensions has continuously expanded since the 1970s. However, individuals in other social-democratic welfare states, especially those in Sweden, turn out to be more reserved about this policy option. Similarly moderate support can be observed in conservative countries, where pension privatisation proposals occupy a middle ranking. In Southern European countries, where pension privatisation is least advanced, these reform options constantly receive the lowest support.

Table 8.5: Support and relative ranking of external solutions (directly pensions related), 2001

Welfare regime/country		Change financing of pension systems				Pension privatisation			
		Cut spending		Pension reserve fund		Tax incentives		Allow private saving	
		%[1]	Rank[2]	%[1]	Rank[2]	%[1]	Rank[2]	%[1]	Rank[2]
Conservative	Austria	69 (45)	(3)	80 (51)	(1)	78 (42)	(4)	75 (39)	(5)
	Belgium	78 (40)	(3)	89 (51)	(1)	79 (36)	(4)	80 (34)	(5)
	France	86 (56)	(3)	91 (60)	(1)	72 (37)	(6)	80 (39)	(4)
	Germany	80 (37)	(6)	88 (44)	(2)	83 (40)	(4)	77 (35)	(7)
	Luxembourg	77 (44)	(3)	90 (56)	(1)	76 (39)	(5)	82 (42)	(4)
	Netherlands	69 (33)	(6)	80 (47)	(2)	78 (34)	(5)	75 (35)	(4)
Social-democratic	Denmark	72 (39)	(6)	76 (41)	(5)	87 (60)	(2)	89 (65)	(1)
	Finland	66 (28)	(6)	83 (38)	(2)	72 (25)	(7)	79 (31)	(4)
	Sweden	66 (31)	(8)	87 (55)	(3)	71 (32)	(6)	65 (32)	(7)
Southern European	Greece	90 (64)	(5)	95 (76)	(3)	70 (39)	(7)	83 (50)	(6)
	Italy	82 (41)	(3)	88 (42)	(2)	70 (23)	(7)	79 (29)	(6)
	Portugal	90 (39)	(1)	91 (31)	(3)	76 (20)	(6)	81 (19)	(7)
	Spain	77 (42)	(5)	86 (50)	(3)	67 (27)	(7)	64 (26)	(8)
Liberal	Ireland	71 (39)	(6)	88 (56)	(1)	86 (56)	(1)	80 (49)	(5)
	UK	59 (26)	(6)	84 (49)	(1)	82 (48)	(2)	89 (48)	(2)
	EU-15	77 (40)	(4)	87 (49)	(2)	76 (36)	(5)	78 (36)	(5)

Note: [1] 'Strongly agree' or 'slightly agree', in brackets: strongly agree only.
[2] ranking refers to 'strongly agree' only.

Source: Eurbarometer 56.1 (2001)

Table 8.6: Support and relative ranking of external solutions (other policy areas), 2001

Welfare regime/country		Labour-market based reforms				Family policy-based reforms			
		Fight unemployment		Immigration		Female employment		Family support	
		%[1]	Rank[2]	%[1]	Rank[2]	%[1]	Rank[2]	%[1]	Rank[2]
Conserva-tive	Austria	83 (49)	(2)	35 (10)	(8)	78 (38)	(6)	70 (33)	(7)
	Belgium	84 (44)	(2)	23 (8)	(8)	81 (33)	(6)	56 (22)	(7)
	France	88 (58)	(2)	29 (10)	(8)	81 (38)	(5)	66 (32)	(7)
	Germany	91 (60)	(1)	39 (11)	(8)	86 (41)	(3)	76 (38)	(5)
	Luxembourg	84 (47)	(2)	40 (15)	(8)	77 (37)	(6)	60 (28)	(7)
	Netherlands	82 (49)	(1)	40 (19)	(7)	75 (42)	(3)	34 (10)	(8)
Social-democratic	Denmark	87 (53)	(3)	62 (31)	(7)	81 (49)	(7)	33 (12)	(8)
	Finland	91 (56)	(1)	56 (22)	(8)	69 (33)	(3)	74 (30)	(5)
	Sweden	89 (63)	(1)	71 (43)	(4)	67 (60)	(2)	88 (38)	(5)
Southern European	Greece	93 (71)	(4)	50 (29)	(8)	94 (79)	(2)	96 (80)	(1)
	Italy	82 (44)	(1)	31 (8)	(8)	80 (35)	(4)	75 (34)	(5)
	Portugal	90 (34)	(2)	48 (14)	(8)	89 (31)	(3)	87 (31)	(3)
	Spain	86 (50)	(3)	49 (18)	(6)	89 (51)	(2)	88 (54)	(1)
Liberal	Ireland	86 (54)	(3)	45 (20)	(8)	82 (53)	(4)	63 (34)	(7)
	UK	83 (46)	(4)	26 (7)	(8)	77 (39)	(5)	35 (11)	(7)
	EU-15	87 (52)	(1)	37 (13)	(8)	83 (41)	(3)	67 (33)	(7)

Note: [1] 'Strongly agree' or 'slightly agree', in brackets: strongly agree only.
[2] Ranking refers to 'strongly agree' only.

Source: Eurobarometer 56.1 (2001)

Regarding measures aimed at *enlarging the financial basis* of pension systems, setting up a pension reserve fund receives, as expected, broad support and ranks among the three most favoured alternatives in almost every European country (except Denmark). The picture is far less clear for the idea of *cutting benefits in other areas.* In both liberal and social–democratic countries this policy option is comparatively unpopular, though possibly for different reasons. While, in social–democratic countries, cutting benefits may be at odds with the idea of a strong welfare state, people in the residual welfare context of liberal countries may see less opportunity for cutting already low state benefits. Results for Southern European and conservative countries are varied: in most, cutting spending is among the most favoured reform options but, in Spain, Greece, the Netherlands and Germany, it is less popular.

As expected, measures to *reduce unemployment* rank among the most popular in almost every European country. Especially in Germany and Finland they constitute by far the most preferred suggestion. Surprisingly, this idea occupies only fourth rank in Greece and Spain despite significant proportions of (structural) unemployment. However, differences between the 'top four' policy options are small (see Tables 8.5 and 8.6) and the results should not be over-interpreted.

In contrast, support for measures to *strengthen the family* show some regime-specific variations, with highest levels in Southern Europe. Here, respondents support both reform options almost equally, possibly due to the fact that general family support as well as work–family reconciliation measures are still weakly developed in these countries. Other respondents differentiate more distinctly. In social-democratic countries, measures to support mothers' employment are greatly approved, while general family support is favoured less. A reason for this may be that 'supporting families that want to have more children' is viewed as more conservative than measures to strengthen women's dual roles as both employees and caregivers. In conservative and liberal regimes, support for family-oriented measures is among the less preferred alternatives. At least for conservative countries, where fertility rates are low and female employment is at best moderate, this result is slightly surprising.

Turning from cross-national variations to *attitudinal differences at the inter-individual level*, our analyses reveal only minor variations in attitudes between different groups of individuals (results not shown here). The effects suggest that *self-interest* may have a certain influence on attitudes towards pension reform. Women tend to show a higher level of support for measures aiming to reconcile family and work. Respondents older than age 65 unsurprisingly advocate pension reforms more intensively than younger respondents, as they are more directly affected. Finally, those with lower education appear to oppose the migration proposal most strongly, possibly because they are more vulnerable to competition from foreign workers. On the other hand, the relatively low acceptance by older respondents of measures to foster women's employment may point to the importance of generation-specific *socialisation* experiences when evaluating different pension reform strategies.

European values and pension reform

What (political) conclusions can be drawn from these results?

First of all, our results suggest that in terms of public opinion there are much wider opportunities for pension reform in European countries than is frequently assumed. European citizens recognise the seriousness of demographic ageing as a political issue; their lack of confidence in existing pension systems suggests that they also see the need for reform.

Second, our results show that Europeans are ready to accept a wide spectrum of possible reform approaches. Only measures increasing migration or retrenching current pension rights – material (benefits) as well as temporal (retirement age) – are commonly rejected. Then, again, Europeans seem willing to increase their own contributions if pension benefits could be stabilised, a result clearly challenging the common view that raising pension contributions would be unacceptable to taxpayers. Furthermore, European citizens are ready to support a large variety of additional measures to avoid a future pension crisis, ranging from enlarging the financial basis involved to reforms based on labour market and family policy.

Third, support patterns for reforms to avert the pension crisis appear to be surprisingly homogeneous both between and within European countries. Similarities in attitudes across welfare-state regimes, countries, sociodemographic groups and time are fairly remarkable. Even across social and political classes, attitudinal differences remain very moderate and marked 'societal barriers' are not in evidence. This broad societal consensus may in practice make reform strategies easier.

Finally, our results indicate that, despite the consensus we have described, there are some solutions whose levels of support are more variable. This is especially true for suggestions tackling wider normative questions. The accord we have uncovered does not entail thoroughgoing normative homogeneity! National welfare cultures and the institutions to which people are accustomed doubtless do affect support for different roles of state and market, both in welfare provision (pension privatisation) and in the division of labour between the sexes (family policy options). Local policy makers will need to give careful consideration to the political climate in their own countries when drafting detailed measures.

Final decisions and their political implementation rest with policy makers. However, European citizens seem prepared to accompany them much further in the search for sustainable solutions to the upcoming pension challenge than is often assumed.

Notes

[1] In 2001, the life expectancy in the EU-15 was 81.6 years for women and 75.5 years for men (European Commission, 2004a).

[2] Note that there are other types of dependency ratio that might move in different directions, such as the one for children, but these cannot be considered here.

[3] The three different policy options can also be discussed in terms of intergenerational justice (see, for example, Kohl, 2003b: 4). However, pinpointing their effect is often not easy, as people might be affected at present or in the future or both.

[4] Another possibility for averting a future pension crisis would be to reverse the current early retirement trend. Though the Eurobarometer 2001 study contained questions regarding this measure, they were not asked referring to pension-related reforms. We therefore do not include them here (though see Kohl, 2003a, 2003b).

[5] Only in Spain, the national government has introduced favourable tax incentives for private savings, which have subsequently grown in importance (Bernardi and Garrido, 2006: 123).

[6] http://ec.europa.eu/public_opinion/index_en.htm

[7] http://zacat.gesis.org/webview/index.jsp

[8] http://zacat.gesis.org/webview/index.jsp

[9] 6 Although demographic ageing was not directly linked to pension systems, the question was asked in this connection. Alternatives were 'minor problem' (EU-15: 22%) and 'no problem at all' (8%); 9% of respondents gave no answer.

[10] 7 The answers 'rather not confident' (EU-15: 39%) and 'not at all confident' (34%) were grouped together. Alternative answers were 'very confident' (3%) and 'no problem at all' (21%); 4% of respondents gave no answer.

[11] 8 Kohl used a similar strategy to analyse other pension-related attitudes in the Eurobarometer study (Kohl, 2003a: 4).

References

Andreß, H.-J. and Heien, T. (2001) 'Four worlds of welfare state attitudes? A comparison of Germany, Norway, and the United States', *European Sociological Review*, vol 17, no 4, pp 337-56.

Bernardi, F. and Garrido, L. (2006) 'Men's late careers and career exits', in H.-P. Blossfeld, S. Buchholz and D. Hofäcker (eds) *Globalization, Uncertainty and Late Careers in Society*, London: Routledge, pp 119-39.

Blöndal, S. and Scarpetta, S. (1999) *The retirement decision in OECD countries*, OECD working paper no 202, Paris: OECD.

Blossfeld, H.-P., Buchholz, S. and Hofäcker, D. (eds) (2006) *Globalization, uncertainty and late careers in society*, London: Routledge.

Brooks, C. and Manza, J. (2006) 'Social policy responsiveness in developed democracies', *American Sociological Review*, vol 7, no 3, pp 474-94.

Cnaan, R.A., Hasenfeld, Y., Cnaan, A. and Rafferty, J. (1993) 'Cross-cultural comparison of attitudes toward welfare state programs: path analysis with log-linear models', *Social Indicators Research*, vol 29, no 2, pp 123-52.

Ebbinghaus, B. (2003) 'Exit from externalization: reversing early retirement in Europe, the USA and Japan', paper presented at 4th International Research Conference on Social Security, 'Social security in a long life society', Antwerp, Belgium, 5-7 May.

Esping-Andersen, G. (1990) *The three worlds of welfare capitalism*, Cambridge: Polity Press.

Esping-Andersen, G. (1999) *Social foundations of postindustrial economies*, Oxford: Oxford University Press.

European Commission (2003) *Adequate and sustainable pensions*, joint report by the Commission and the Council, Brussels: European Commission.

European Commission (2004a) *The social situation in the European Union 2004,* joint report by the Commission, the Directorate-General for Employment, Social Affairs and Equal Opportunities and Eurostat, Brussels: European Commission.

European Commission (2004b) *Increasing the employment of older workers and delaying the exit from the labour market,* communication from the Commission to the Council, the European Parliament, the European Economic and Social Committee and the Committee of the Regions, Com (2004) 146 final, Brussels: European Commission.

European Commission (2005) *Privately managed pension provisions,* Report by the Social Protection Committee, Brussels: European Commission.

European Commission (2006) *Adequate and sustainable pensions,* Brussels: European Commission.

Fahey, T. and Spéder, Z. (2004) *Fertility and family issues in an enlarged Europe,* Dublin: European Foundation for the Improvement of Living and Working Conditions.

Ferrera, M. (1996) 'The "southern model" of welfare in social Europe', *Journal of European Social Policy,* vol 6, no 1, pp 17-37.

Forma, P. (1997) 'The rational legitimacy of the welfare state: popular support for ten income transfer schemes in Finland', *Policy & Politics,* vol 25, no 3, pp 235-49.

Gornick, J.C., Meyers, M.K. and Ross, K.E. (1997) 'Supporting the employment of mothers: policy variation across fourteen welfare states', *Journal of European Social Policy,* vol 7, no 1, pp 45-70.

Gundelach, P. (1994) 'National value differences: modernization or institutionalization', *International Journal of Comparative Sociology,* vol 35, no 12, pp 37-58.

Heien, T. (2002) *Wohlfahrtsansprüche der Bürger und sozialpolitische Realität in Europa,* Berlin: Logos.

Hofäcker, D. (2004) 'Typen europäischer Familienpolitik –Vehikel oder Hemmnis für das Adult Worker Model?', in S. Leitner, I. Ostner and M. Schratzenstaller (eds) *Wohlfahrtsstaat und Geschlechterverhältnis im Umbruch. Was kommt nach dem Ernährermodell? Jahrbuch für Europa- und Nordamerika-Studien 2003,* Opladen: Leske & Budrich, pp 257-84.

Hofäcker, D. (2006) 'Women's employment in times of globalization: a comparative overview', in H.-P. Blossfeld and H. Hofmeister (eds): *Globalization, uncertainty and women's careers. An international comparison,* Cheltenham/Northampton, MA: Edward Elgar, pp 32-58.

Inglehart, R. (1977) *The silent revolution: Changing values and political styles among western publics,* Princeton, NJ: Princeton University Press.

ISG (Indicators Sub-Group of the Social Protection Committee) (2006) *Current and prospective theoretical replacement rates: Report on work in progress,* Brussels: European Commission.

Kohl, J. (2003a) 'Breite Zustimmung für Beibehaltung des Rentenniveaus auch bei steigenden Beiträgen. Einstellungen zur Alterssicherung im europäischen Vergleich', *Informationsdienst Soziale Indikatoren* (ISI), vol 15, no 29, pp 1-6.

Kohl, J. (2003b) 'Citizens' opinions on the transition from work to retirement', paper presented at the 4th International Research Conference on Social Security of the International Social Security Association (ISSA), 'Social security in a long life society', Antwerp, Belgium, 5-7 May.

Pöntinen, S. and Uusitalo, H. (1988) 'Stability and change in the public support for the welfare state: Finland 1975-1985', *International Journal of Sociology and Social Policy*, vol 8, no 1, pp 1-25.

Saraceno, C. (1994) 'The ambivalent familialism of the Italian welfare state', *Social Politics*, vol 1, no 1, pp 60-82.

Sihvo, T. and Uusitalo, H. (1995) 'Economic crises and support for the welfare state in Finland 1975-1993', *Acta Sociologica*, vol 38, no 3, pp 251-62.

Svallfors, S. (1995) 'The end of class politics? Structural cleavages and attitudes to Swedish welfare policies', *Acta Sociologica*, vol 38, no 1, pp 53-74.

Svallfors, S. (1997) 'Worlds of welfare and attitudes to redistribution: a comparison of eight western nations', *European Sociological Review*, vol 13, no 3, pp 283-304.

Vidlund, M. (2006) *Old-age pension reforms in the EU-15 countries at a time of retrenchment*, Eläketurvakeskus: Finnish Centre for Pensions Working Papers.

Zaidi, A. (2006) *Pension policy in EU25 and its possible impact on elderly poverty*. Vienna: Policy Brief of the European Centre for Social Welfare Policy and Research.

NINE

Ethos of care and environment in long-stay care settings: impacts on residents' lives

Adeline Cooney and Kathy Murphy

Introduction

In Ireland around 4.6% of older people currently live in residential care (Department of Health and Children, 2006) in either public or private facilities. Older people living in residential care cannot always exercise the 'consumer sovereignty' that is attributed to purchasers of market services, and the power relationship between the providers of care and residents is an unequal one. People living in residential care might be afraid to criticise the services provided to them, concerned lest such action might have negative repercussions. In addition, many residents might have little or no support outside the residential care setting and therefore have no alternative but to accept the treatment given to them. There has also been international disquiet about the standards of care within some residential care facilities (OECD, 2005). Is there in fact reason for anxiety whether people living in residential homes in Ireland are – within reasonable limits – able to pursue their lives as they would wish? This chapter reports residents' and staff's perceptions of quality-of-life issues in residential care. In particular, it enquires about the influence of ethos of care and physical environment on the continuity of daily life. We felt that we could contribute most effectively to debate here by concentrating on issues that could be regarded as relatively immune from dispute. We focused, then, on what we could discover about practical arrangements for offering care to residents and on the constraints and opportunities their physical settings provided. These did, however, prove to have far-reaching implications about the kinds of lives our respondents enjoyed.

The study: life in residential homes

The findings reported in this chapter are part of a larger study of residents' and staff's perceptions of quality-of-life issues in residential care settings (Murphy et al, 2006). The study used mixed methods, incorporating both qualitative and quantitative elements: focus groups, a quantitative survey of residential facilities and qualitative interviews with residents and staff. The findings reported here arise from the qualitative interviews with 101 residents and 48 staff.

In Ireland, residential care settings divide into five types: health board geriatric homes or hospitals, health board welfare homes, health board district/community hospitals, voluntary geriatric homes/hospitals and private nursing homes. We conducted interviews in 12 study sites, chosen through purposive sampling to reflect the range of residential provision in Ireland. The sample of residents was comprised of residents who were newly admitted, residents who had lived in the facility for longer than three months and residents who had some cognitive impairment but were able to understand questions and respond. Both male and female residents were included. All categories of staff were included: registered nurses, directors of nursing, health care assistants, cooks, cleaning staff, physiotherapists and occupational therapists. The aim was to gather as wide a range of perspectives as possible in the interviews, which lasted between 15 and 45 minutes.[1]

Questions and interpretations

In their conversations with our interviewers, residents described their day-to-day experiences from the time they woke up until the time they went to sleep. They also spoke about their capacity to make choices in the residential facilities where they lived and the extent to which they were included in decisions about their care. They spoke too about the attitudes they felt were taken by staff to caring. Staff members, for their part, also described the ethos of care in the facilities they worked in and identified factors that impacted on day-to-day care.

Promoting autonomy

Many participants identified what we interpreted as autonomy or personal independence as important for their quality of life. Autonomy in the sense we gave to it included the capacity to make choices and to be included in decision making. Participants wanted their opinions to be sought. This included apparently small questions such as what clothes a resident might wear on a particular day. Some participants found these choices were not offered to them:

> ... there is one nurse and she has a positive craze for this cardigan and I hate it but she insists on my wearing it. (Resident, private)

Yet both residents and staff participants in our study emphasised the importance of having choice within the day. Participants saw it as important to have choice about the time residents were woken, had breakfast, went back to bed and had meals, and also in what they did during the day. Care was demonstrably more routinised in some study sites than others, and this had an important effect on residents' ability to make choices in their daily lives. In the more flexible regimes, residents had more choice and they reported that this made life better for them.

Some participants felt that they could shape their days as they wished and these people reported that they felt at 'home' in residential care and that they were able to continue to live their lives as normal.

> I don't go to bed until around 10, I can go to bed any time that I like but after 10 suits me, I come in and look at my own television. (Resident, private)

Others however had their day prescribed for them. Some resident participants reported being awoken around 6 am to have breakfast and were clear that this would not be their own choice:

> ... you're told to get up at 7 and I think that is too early. (Resident, private)

It appeared from these residents' accounts that breakfast was traditionally given by the night staff. The early start was to ensure that this task was completed prior to the day staff arriving on duty – for a reason, therefore, focusing on the organisation of employees rather than on the comfort or independent choices of residents.

> ... you have breakfast at 6.30 because the night staff have to do it and they have 40-something people to deal with. (Resident, private)

Returning to bed in the early afternoon was also an experience of some residents, sometimes as early as 2.30 or 3 pm. While this was described as a choice by some people because they tended to get tired, for most it happened because residents were 'put' back to bed before the number of staff on duty decreased. Staff reported that the duty rota meant that fewer staff were available in the evening and therefore residents had to go back to bed early; there would not be enough staff in the evening to undertake the task of assisting them. Some participants felt they had little option but to fit into the prevailing routine and do what they were told.

Some residents identified choice about times of eating as important. Meals for most facilities were set at fixed times and often the day was shaped around these. In a few facilities, however, mealtimes were staggered to give residents some choice of eating time. Resident participants highlighted this as something that they greatly appreciated and that contributed positively to their quality of life.

While lack of choice around the day was evident in both private and public facilities, it was more prevalent in public ones. Study participants sometimes linked this to the lack of space and poor physical environments these facilities enjoyed. Choice was more difficult to operationalise when residents were in eight-bedded wards, or did not have their own room or private space:[2]

> ... you can't [give a choice], you have to have everybody up by a
> certain time because if you don't then the dinner is there and then
> you can't be coming into, we do not have the staffing levels to do
> that. (Nurse, private)

The physical environment was identified as important to quality of life by a number of participants. Residents found life in a communal ward difficult, and highlighted issues of privacy or lack of choice in listening to the television or radio. Poor physical facilities, particularly the lack of sitting areas, meant that some residents, mainly in public facilities, spent substantial time each day by their bedside.

> As you can see around it's a very open ward area, it's a very small space
> in terms of the environment, there is nothing of the notion of privacy,
> there's nothing of the notion really of a sense of choice either and that
> worries me a lot. (Nurse, public)

Some staff and resident participants also raised numbers of bathrooms and toilets as a concern. When the ratio of bathrooms to residents was low, residents were often bathed or showered in rotation, resulting in them only having the opportunity of being bathed or showered every few weeks:

> I love my bath, I look forward to it, it's once a fortnight but I think
> we should have it weekly. (Resident, public)

Another issue raised was that some bathrooms and toilets were too small. This was a problem because hoists could not be used in these small spaces. In one facility the toilets were so small that it was difficult for a staff member to enter with a resident to give help when required. Staff participants were extremely concerned about health and safety issues for residents and staff. It was evident that the physical environment and choice mattered to staff as well as to residents for quality of life.

Promoting and maintaining independence

The ethos of care environments also shaped the extent to which promoting and maintaining independence was embedded into the care of residents. Many participants expressed the desire to maintain or improve their current level of independence. This involved doing what you could do for yourself, participating in exercise classes if possible, keeping mobile and trying to maintain physical abilities. Some facilities ensured that residents were given every opportunity to do as much as possible for themselves and they focused care on supporting residents in this respect. The role of physiotherapists and occupational therapists was very important in this context as they worked with residents to regain and retain their capacities.

> They let me try and help myself as much as I can you know. (Resident, public)

In other facilities resident participants reported that there was a lack of therapeutic services, that they were rushed and that staff did things for them that in principle they could do themselves. Some residents felt they were not making the progress they could have achieved if the necessary services and support had been available to them.

> I did get a lot of physiotherapy [in an acute hospital], I got it for an hour a day but when I went to long-stay care, no physiotherapy. That's not right ... I was beginning to pick up and it would have made a lot of difference. (Resident, private)

Ethos of care

Staff participants were asked to describe the focus of care in the places where they worked. Some, when describing what was important to a resident's quality of life, stressed the need for care to be individualised. Many described care within the facility in which they themselves worked as individualised and tailored to the residents' needs. In these facilities care was structured around residents' needs and many residents could dictate their own patterns of care for the day. While staffing constraints were an issue for many of these facilities, care was organised in a way that attempted to give residents maximum flexibility. For management, this meant that off-duty rotas for all staff had to be organised in a fashion that facilitated resident choice. Therefore, the practice of rostering most nursing staff in the morning, leaving a minimum of nursing staff for the evening was discarded. New staff rotas were implemented to enable residents to get up and go back to bed at the times they desired.

In some facilities, both public and private, resident and staff participants commented on the caring ethos and how this shaped the way life was lived within the facility.

> We are trying to look at people as individuals, the respect and dignity and sense of humour, that's so important because people do not want to be a number in a bed. (Director of Nursing, private)

In some cases this ethos was based on resident inclusion in decision making, maximising resident capacity, facilitating choice and keeping residents involved. The manager's role in shaping this ethos was commented on by both staff and residents. One manager described the difficult and challenging road of implementing a new ethos of care and the time, commitment and support needed to see it through. Another manager described how the ethos pervaded all aspects of management of the facility. She described how this ethos involved caring for staff, and investing in training and induction so that the best level of care possible could be delivered for residents.

In other facilities the ethos of care was described as routinised. Here, care was perceived as focusing mostly on tasks. Residents' choices and individual preferences were subsumed into the routine of the day.

> I would feel it's very task orientated, you know, that the routine, ritualistic, we are doing this and that. (Nurse, public)

Residents perceived each day as the same and the days as boring; they did not feel they were treated as individuals but as one of a number:

> You're woken up quite early in the morning … So you're woken at 6 and breakfast isn't until 10 past 8, it's a long day, the nurses change at 6 o'clock and it wakes you up. So is there a routine here? There is yeah, OK. And is every day the same then? Every day is the same, absolutely the same … the day is very long, yeah, boring. (Resident, public)

Some staff were concerned that the social and emotional needs of residents were not being met in this 'ritualistic' system In some of these facilities, it was evident that there was a real desire to change care practices but that many constraining factors had held back the pace of change. In these facilities staff expressed the need for change in the routine of care and their frustration that little progress had been made. In other facilities, the focus on routine had become so embedded that staff were unable to see how it could change. They explained that current staffing levels and resources made change impossible. A few staff participants questioned the commitment to change of some other staff members, and suggested that a few were not in fact motivated to care for older people. In sum, then, facilities' ethos of care certainly seemed to shape residents' experiences. In particular, we might surmise that it seemed to dictate the extent to which they were able to maintain a sense of self in the places in which they were living.

Sense of self

Participants maintained their senses of self by various means. Some personalised their private space or room by putting personal possessions on show. However, opportunities for participants to stamp their own personalities on their environments varied across sites. Participants who had rooms of their own had an opportunity to create personal spaces. Some of these participants had put up pictures or brought a favourite piece of furniture with them. They also organised their rooms to make them more comfortable — for example, by positioning a chair near the window for the light or having a wardrobe specially built to house all their belongings. These participants tended to be the happiest and considered the residential care setting a 'home from home':

… I am very happy, like at home. That is my room, and this is my own furniture, and this all, yes, this was from my home when I sold, and this table is my one, small one. (Resident, private)

Int: And this is your own … duvet …?

Ah yes, my friend gave it to me, she moved house and she gave me that, and I love, I love my room and she gave me pictures … that one up there, I think that's the best.

Int: You've managed to make it homely in here!

Oh I do yes, I do yes, yes. (Resident, public)

It was evident from these participants' accounts that having an opportunity to organise their space helped them to feel at home. In contrast, others consciously brought very little with them. They saw little need: 'Everything you'd need is here.' Their rooms were less 'personal' and more functional:

> … there's very little I brought in from home, what would you want anything in here, I mean what would you want anything? … I gave all them things, I didn't have anything really, because I gave them all to the grandchildren, my own grandchildren at home, you know. (Resident, public)

These participants had clearly made a decision that this was now home, but not their preferred home. Others however were not at this point. They frequently spoke about 'going home' and may have seen their stay as short-term, and for this reason felt it was not worthwhile to personalise their rooms. In contrast to participants who 'organised' their spaces, these participants had not fully settled. Their 'home' remained their old home:

Int: Did you want to bring in any of your belongings with you,
             I see you've your own rug and things like that …

No, my own clothes of course, I hope to go home actually, my daughter is coming … and I'm going to go home for a couple of weeks, like to the house and I'll take back [some things] … I've never been home since I left.

Int: So you still have your house …

Oh yeah ... I wish there wasn't sometimes you know.

Int: Why is that?

[Pause] Because it makes me remember too much having this and I
feel that I could go home. (Resident, private)

In contrast to residents who had their own rooms, participants living in large
open-plan wards were very restricted in what they could bring with them. These
big open-plan wards were a feature of public rather than private facilities. Typically,
participants' space consisted of a small locker and a single wardrobe. Despite
space restrictions, many participants had a few personal items on display, usually
photographs or ornaments. Some participants, however, would have chosen to
bring other items with them if there had been sufficient room.

Although I have a computer of my own, I haven't got it here because
I can't you know, that is the difficulty with me here. (Resident,
public)

Photographs were greatly treasured by participants. They loved to talk around their
photographs, speaking at length about the people or events depicted. Photographs
provided connections to participants' past life, prompted memories and seemed to
help them maintain their sense of identity and uniqueness. Participants also used
photographs to illustrate their stories, referring interviewers to photographs so
they could see what they looked like when their hair was brown or know what
their sons or daughters looked like. Photographs had a particular significance
for participants living in multi-bed, open-plan wards. In sites where routine
dominated, participants seemed to view photographs of themselves as representing
their 'true' selves.

I'm there in a photograph where I'm lovely in it.

Int: Well I'll have to have a look at that ...

You can see it there ... I'd lovely black hair. (Resident, public)

There appeared to be two contrasting perspectives on the importance of having
'your belongings' around you. Some participants found it a comfort; their
possessions evoked happy memories and helped them feel at home. Others
appeared not to want such reminders.

Personal appearance and grooming

For women participants, how they presented themselves to the world appeared to be closely linked to their self-expression and positive self-esteem. This did not appear to be as great an issue for men. Female participants liked to wear their own clothes and tended to have strong opinions as to what they wanted to wear. They also enjoyed having their hair or nails done. The hairdresser's visit was a big event, creating a buzz of conversation about appointment times, hair colour and so on. In contrast, male participants rarely mentioned clothes or their personal appearance. In the majority of study sites, residents had their own clothes. (Only one man reported wearing the facility's clothes.) A female resident said:

> Oh yeah the hairdresser comes in, hairdresser comes in whenever I want you know, get a perm whenever I want it, it would want to be done again, I like a good shape on my hair, that's the way I like it. (Resident, public)

Opportunities to have a wash differed across sites. In private nursing homes, participants usually had a room with an en-suite. Consequently, they could have a bath or shower when they liked if they were able to wash independently, or when staff were available if they needed help. In contrast, the lack of bathrooms in public facilities meant that participants living there frequently were on a 'rota' for a bath, as we have already noted. Many participants in public facilities expressed a desire for more frequent baths.

> I love my bath.

> Int: You love your bath?

> Yes, I love my bath, yes, look forward to it.

> Int: Is that once a day, or once a week?

> Fortnight, but I think we could have it weekly.

> Int: That would be your preference?

> Yes, weekly. (Resident, public)

One issue that was raised by some residents was who assisted them with washing. Some female participants were shocked when a male carer helped them with washing or other intimate care. It would appear that, on occasions, women's preference for a same-sex carer could not be accommodated. The female participants who described this experience were clearly upset by it but 'got on with it':

> ... when I came in here, the second day ... I was in me room ... and this young fella was standing in the corner and, and eh, and the nurse came in and she says take off your [clothes], she says you have a shower today ... I said I'm not taking off my clothes, he has to leave, she said, you don't have to bother about him, she says you have got to take off your clothes and get washed, get your shower, so I done it and I threw all the clothes up in the corner. (Resident, private)

However, most participants volunteered the view that how kind and caring someone was meant more to them than gender. None of the men interviewed raised a similar concern.

Individuality

The extent to which residential care facilities met or responded to participants' individual preferences and needs varied greatly. At one end of the spectrum, participants were able to live their lives as normal and did not feel constrained by rules or regulations. They could 'be themselves' and felt they had the freedom to come and go as they pleased:

> ... meal times are fixed, but otherwise I'm a free agent and that appeals to me like ... there's a sense of freedom or something, there's no rules, like you get your meals and that sort of stuff, but I can go out for a walk, I mean you can come and go. (Resident, private)

At the other end of the spectrum, the routine dominated to such an extent that participants felt they had little autonomy. They felt they had to 'fit' their lives around the routine and obey the 'rules'. What the rules were was not always clear, but participants reported mirroring what the other residents did. They described their lives as monotonous and unchanging. One participant likened it to 'living in a prison', another to 'being in school':

> Ah sure, you'd have to get out, you couldn't be stuck in here the whole time.

> Int: Why?

> Oh God you wouldn't, never stick it, you might as well be in Mountjoy [an Irish prison] ... you're confined ... That's why I call it, I mean, you're confined here. (Resident, public)

> ... it's just that it's like a school, it's very, how shall I say, regimented you know, you do a thing now if it's handy for the hospital to do but if you want a cup of tea you couldn't get it ... in a democracy you have to do the best for everyone you know. (Resident, public)

Participants coped with this in different ways. The majority spoke about 'putting up with it' or 'getting on with it'. A few actively rebelled and did what they wanted irrespective of the consequences. Others worried about being viewed as a troublemaker or getting on the 'wrong side' of the staff.

A major difference between facilities seemed to us to centre on whether residents felt empowered or powerless in the system. Some facilities empowered participants by making them feel 'in charge', while others made participants feel powerless and vulnerable. The ability to make participants feel empowered was one that we saw as related to how well staff knew residents as individuals and showed interest in them as people. Some participants reported that staff spent time getting to know them and were willing to meet their individual needs. This was more evident in the smaller facilities than the larger, older ones:

> ... they understand a lot about me ... And then as we grew, as [the Director] and I grew together she understood me ... There are things that you don't do, naturally, and there are things that you can, she's very broadminded. So it took a while to settle in but it was a matter of getting used to ... It was a matter of getting used to know, them to know me. (Resident, private)

> Int: Do you feel that they know you, your likes and your dislikes, the staff here, would they know you well?

> I don't know about well but they know your dislikes and you're individual, they might, I mean they generally know that so and so doesn't like too much cream, they know generally but you'd have to remind them. (Resident, private)

Staff attitudes to residents therefore had wide-ranging implications for residents' well-being. Viewing residents as 'patients', for example, may result in a focus on physical rather than emotional care. Similarly, viewing the residential care setting as corresponding to a 'hospital' rather than a residents' home has the potential to place emphasis on nurse-centred care as opposed to person-centred care. This may be the legacy of some staff's experience of working in a general hospital.

Privacy

The degree of privacy enjoyed by participants largely depended on whether they had rooms of their own or not. Participants who lived in large open-plan wards in public facilities experienced the greatest lack of privacy. Many reported that it was a struggle to have any kind of private life. The curtains around their beds were the only means they had of shutting out the rest of the ward. However, curtains provided visual privacy only and many commented that, even when curtains were closed, 'Everybody knows what's going on':

> You only have a curtain separating you [sometimes] … [I]t usually doesn't matter that much but there are private things that you need to talk about, no matter how poor you are you need to get these things sorted out. (Resident, public)

Reality for residents living in these facilities is that their world shrinks to the space around their bed. All activities, eating, sleeping and socialising, are carried out in or beside their bed against the backdrop of a large, noisy ward. Residents who were fit and active had the option of taking a walk outdoors or going 'down town'. Those who were physically dependent had little option but to 'put up with it':

> I was in a ward with a number of other men you know, but I wanted to be on me own.

Int: What was hard about living with a group of people?

> Ah just fellows there all the time. Somebody might want to sing.

Int: So having your own room gives you a bit of peace?

> Oh absolutely yes … I hate to be with somebody who is rabbiting on all the time. (Resident, public) (This resident now has a room of his own.)

Many participants longed for a private room but believed that there was little 'hope' of getting one. Residents who lived in two- or three-bedded rooms had fewer issues. They tended to be positive about sharing and liked the company. Many of the private study sites had a few two- or three-bedded wards. In these facilities participants who shared usually had opted to share rather than have a room of their own. In other words, it was their choice, unlike the cases of participants in large open-plan wards who had no other option.

Participants who had a room of their own had a degree of privacy and control not open to residents living in multiple-occupancy rooms. Simply having a room gave them choices. They could choose to join other residents or had the option of retreating to their room if they wanted to be alone. Having a door literally meant that they could shut out the rest of the world if that was what they chose. A room of their own also freed them from the worry of disturbing others. They could choose to look at television or turn up their radio if they wished:

> I've a very nice little room, comfortable bed … I have privacy if I wanted to go down and sit there or go down and listen to the radio or lie on the bed or whatever I like. And then if I want to mix with some of the other people I can come up and mix with them. (Resident, public)

Privacy is often assumed to be about physical privacy only. However, in this study, participants gave equal weighting to social, psychological and physical privacy.

> I always had me own room till I came here. There's nowhere to get away on your own. (Resident, public)

The lack of 'peace and quiet' and having nowhere private to talk to their visitors was problematic for residents living in multiple-occupancy wards.

Self-respect

Acknowledging residents' value was key to their self-respect. When staff drew on residents' expertise or life experience in some way – for example, asking them to help out or sit on a committee – this gave the message that they still had something to offer:

> I'm now on the committee [responsible for setting up the garden] … I'm more on the administration end, I did a lot of gardening before I came and I won prizes … That's why I do that here and once they got it going here I'm helping them, so they're still getting it going. (Resident, public)

Recognition of achievement was also important to residents. Acknowledgement could be either formal or informal, for instance including a piece in the hospital newsletter or simply thanking or praising them for their help:

> I like to get out there and do a bit of gardening, and when I'm doing my garden I sit down on a little stool, cos I'm not, well I am mobile all right, but em, my feet, like you know, at my age, 80 I feel a bit of a cripple [laugh] … I love flowers and, when I do my garden, everybody tells me its looks lovely. (Resident, public)

Some facilities made it possible for participants to help with the running of the facility in some way – for example, helping with the garden or setting up the altar in the chapel. Participants derived great satisfaction from this. Some facilities deliberately involved residents in the running of the facility; it was part of their approach to care. Others, however, did not seem to see this as important. However, it was important to residents. It was noticeable that participants living in facilities where no formal opportunities to help were provided, 'created' ways to help where they could. This might be assisting a roommate who was more disabled than they were, or fetching and carrying for someone in a wheelchair. In interviews these participants proudly described how they 'helped out'.

Visiting study sites revealed distinct differences in attitudes to the contribution and achievements of residents. Some facilities made great efforts to acknowledge residents' accomplishments. Staff had put their artwork on display or had put up photographs of residents when on trips or at parties. Indeed, some residents in the photographs had since died but there was a sense that they were remembered and the other residents still talked about them. These facilities managed to generate an atmosphere that the older people living there were important, mattered and were respected. Other facilities, while bright and cheerful, had bare walls or hung up formal pictures instead of contemporaneous records of residents' lives or achievements. There was a feeling of a hotel rather than a home, a sense that residents were transitory. The essential difference was that some facilities managed to make residents feel valued and this was linked to a sense of feeling comfortable and at home.

Conclusion: environment and ethos

Residents' accounts suggest that one of the most significant factors to impact on their continuity and quality of life is the environment and ethos of care. The ethos dictates the general approach to care, staff attitudes, care priorities and resident autonomy. It therefore has a tangible impact on residents' quality of life. In some facilities residents felt empowered, whereas in others they appeared powerless and constrained. Our findings suggest that most residents are able to maintain a sense of self in residential care facilities. The ease with which they can achieve this varied across sites, however, with residents living in old, large public facilities having the greatest difficulty.

We identified a number of enabling or inhibiting factors. Chief among these was whether residents had rooms of their own or a choice to share if that was their preference. A private room was the norm within the private sector but rare within the public sector. Residents with rooms of their own had greater privacy, more scope to live their lives as they liked and opportunities to adapt their environments to suit themselves. In contrast, residents living in open-plan wards had little privacy and limited opportunity to do as they pleased.

The key difference between facilities was thus the extent to which residents were empowered or disempowered. Residents who felt empowered perceived that they could shape their days and had the potential to make choices. Residents who felt disempowered felt constrained by the 'rules' and by routine. They perceived themselves as 'one of a number' rather than as individuals and this impacted negatively on their sense of self and personal identity. The current trend in gerontological nursing is a move to a more person-centred service. A person-centred service should be based on consultation, autonomy, choice, individual care and resident involvement in decision making (Davies et al, 1999; Clark et al, 2003; McCormack, 2003). If residential services are to become more person-centred, it is important that these concepts drive the philosophy that facilities exemplify. Steps need therefore to be taken to embed these concepts into the way in which care is delivered.

The findings of the research reported in this chapter suggest, however, that a move to person-centred care will require a fundamental shift in the way in which services are managed and delivered. The international literature suggests that the nurse manager in a residential facility is key to making this shift; many studies have found that this individual has a powerful role in shaping the philosophy of the facility or unit and in leading change (Kitson, 1991; Wright and McCormack, 2001; Redfern et al, 2002). Management training and continuing education for staff needs therefore to focus on creating an ethos of care that enables and empowers older people and preserves residents' senses of self. Older people in residential care are more than just patients; they are individuals who deserve to live their lives with dignity and respect. Residential care settings are not places to die, they are places in which to live, and live well. The impetus is now on regulators, policy makers and practitioners to ensure that residents in these facilities are guaranteed the best quality of life possible.

Notes

[1] Prior to interviews, written consent was gathered from all participants and ethical clearance was given by the University Research Ethics Committee. An interview schedule was used to guide interviews, but was used flexibly. Interviews were transcribed verbatim and the constant comparative technique was used to analyse this data (Strauss and Corbin, 1998). Thus, a process of continuous comparison enabled the collapse of category domains and the identification of overarching themes.

[2] We do not have figures indicating exactly how many people currently live in an open-ward setting, but can attempt a rough estimation. If we take it that there are four million people in the republic of Ireland, with 11% aged over 65, this gives 440,000 older people; of these, 4.6% live in residential care. This gives around 20,240; of these, 40% are in public care. This calculation yields an approximate figure of 8,000 people still living in open wards.

References

Clarke, A., Hanson, E. and Ross, H. (2003) 'Seeing the person behind the patient: enhancing the care of older people using a biographical approach', *Journal of Clinical Nursing*, vol 12, no 5, pp 697-706.

Davies, S., Laker, S. and Ellis, L. (1999) *Dignity on the ward: Promoting excellence in care. Good practice in acute hospital care for older people*, London: Help the Aged.

Department of Health and Children (2006) *Long-stay activity statistics 2006*, Dublin: Department of Health and Children, www.dohc.ie/publications/pdf/long_stay_2006.pdf?direct=1

Kitson, A. (1991) *Therapeutic nursing and the hospitalised elderly*, London: Scutari Press.

McCormack, B. (2003) 'A conceptual framework for person-centred practice with older people', *International Journal of Nursing Practice*, vol 9, no 3, pp 202-9.

Murphy, K., O'Shea, E., Cooney, A., Shiel, A. and Hodkins, M. (2006) *Improving quality of life for older people in long-stay care settings in Ireland*, Dublin: National Council on Ageing and Older People.

OECD (Organisation for Economic Co-operation and Development) (2005) 'Ensuring quality long-term care for older people', *Policy Brief*, www.oecd.org/publications/policybriefs

Redfern, S., Hannan, S., Norman, I., Martin, F. (2002) 'Work satisfaction, stress, quality of care and morale of older people in a nursing home', *Health and Social Care in the Community*, vol 10, no 6: 512-17.

Strauss, A. and Corbin, J. (1998) *Basics of qualitative research – grounded theory procedures and techniques*, Newbury Park, CA: Sage Publications.

Wright, J. and McCormack, B. (2001) 'Practice development: individualised care', *Nursing Standard*, vol 15, no 36, pp 7-42.

TEN

Engineering substantially prolonged human lifespans: biotechnological enhancement and ethics

Peter Derkx

Introduction

Substantial extension of the human lifespan has recently become a subject of lively debate. One reason for this is the completion in 2001 of the Human Genome Project and the experimental avenues for biogerontological research it has opened. Another is recent theoretical progress in biogerontology. In the 1990s more and more biogerontologists began to agree on the evolutionary cause of senescence: it results from a trade-off between the investment of resources in reproduction on the one hand and in maintenance and repair of the body on the other. This represents a powerful simplification of the theoretical underpinnings of biogerontological research, necessary to make anti-ageing technology a plausible idea (Hayflick, 1994; Holliday, 1995, 2006; Austad, 1997; Kirkwood, 2005).

But the character of modern culture is at least as important an explanation of the current debate on life-extension intervention. Three existential factors playing a role here are fear of death (fear of no longer existing), fear of the suffering involved in the process of dying, and the sometimes obsessive desire to preserve good health in order to pursue life projects and goals (Turner, 2004). The historical background of this motivational pattern is

> ... the decline since the Renaissance of faith in supernatural salvation from death; concern with the worth of individual identity and experience shifted from an otherworldly realm to the 'here and now', with intensification of earthly expectations. (Gruman, quoted in Post, 2004a: 82)

A specific occasion for strong interest in 'anti-ageing medicine' is the ageism many people seem to encounter in conventional medicine:

> Anti-aging practitioners largely rebel against the age norms accepted by more mainstream medicine. In other words, for these practitioners, there is no 'normal' that should be accepted for a man of 72 years

when, instead, we can *target* his care toward the 'norms' of a 30 year old man. (Mykytyn, 2006: 282, emphasis in original)

Interest in substantial life extension is large, therefore, and in a volume on ageing and values such a project might easily be assumed to be worthy of support: if later life is good, more of it would be better.

But would this really be a good thing? Experience with other revolutionary technologies is that, once they exist, they can no longer be stopped. Too much has been invested in them: once research has produced an effective technology catering to all-too-human desires, there is seldom a return path. We had better investigate the ethical aspects of considerable human lifespan extension now, before this extension has become genuinely practicable, or before large sums of money have been spent on it. We shall see, first, that these apparently technical, biomedical questions cannot be discussed without considering ethics and values, and, second, that this investigation inevitably demands that we try to conceptualise something of what ageing itself and being human is about.

Substantial extension of human lifespan: what are we talking about?

Before embarking on an ethical discussion it has to be clear what we mean by 'substantial extension of human lifespan'. We can distinguish between four possible outcomes of a biotechnological enhancement of the human lifespan. Varying on work by Harry Moody (1995), Eric Juengst and others (Juengst et al, 2003: 24-8), we can term these extended morbidity, compressed morbidity, decelerated senescence and arrested senescence.

Extended morbidity means that the average human life becomes longer because the period of (co)morbidity at the end is lengthened. Through good hygiene, nutrition, education, housing, medical care, welfare arrangements and social services, older people with one or more chronic diseases stay alive longer. This means that average life expectancy increases, but this need not be an increase in human flourishing and cause for joy. Extended or prolonged morbidity does not entail an increase in maximum human life expectancy. A typical time structure for a human life with extended morbidity could be: growing up from 0 to 20, adult health span 20 to 55, period of growing morbidity up to 95 as the average age at death and with an unchanged maximum of around 120. Extended morbidity is a scenario some scientists (Baltes, 2003: 17) fear as the most likely one, with Alzheimer's disease as one of the main threats.[1] Since nobody wishes it to become reality, we shall not discuss the ethical desirability of this type of life extension here.

Compressed morbidity is a scenario in which the onset of serious age-associated maladies is delayed as long as possible and thus these are compressed into a shorter period. The maximum human lifespan of around 120 is accepted as fixed. The focus of compressed morbidity is that the average human health span is extended to a much longer period from 20 up to 'the ideal average life span, approximately

85 years' (Fries, 1980: 130) followed by a relatively short period of decline before death, a period of one or two years at the most.

The feasibility of compressing morbidity for the life stage between 55 and 85 was first argued for by James Fries in 1980 and it has been embraced by many – for example, the biogerontologist Robert Arking (2004: 179). Not long ago three officials of the World Health Organization (WHO) wrote that Fries's tenets and vision 'now lie at the heart of today's approach to NCDs [noncommunicable diseases], ageing and health with its focus on the life course, health promotion, and "active ageing" [use it or lose it]' (Kalache et al, 2002: 243). Because its original assumption is that the maximum human lifespan is biologically predetermined at around 120 and that death at an average age of 85 is 'natural' and even 'ideal', compression of morbidity is not a form of substantial life extension. It must be noted, however, that many gerontologists hold that compression of morbidity is actually impossible. They think it highly unlikely that we will be able to increase health span without simultaneously increasing lifespan and the period of morbidity at the end.[2] Compression of morbidity then turns out to be practically the same as delayed or decelerated senescence.

Decelerated senescence is an outcome in which processes of biological ageing are slowed, resulting in higher average life expectancy and probably higher maximum life expectancy. Decelerated senescence means that the period of good health in a human life is extended (as in the scenario of compressed morbidity), but the period of morbidity remains the same or is lengthened as well (as in extended morbidity). The average pattern of a human life in this case could be: growing up 0-20, adult health span 20-90 and period of decline after that with death at an age of 112. Maximum life expectancy at birth might be 140 years.

Richard Miller is a respected biogerontologist who considers that such a retarded or decelerated senescence is the most likely development:

> Nature can slow down aging, and so, it turns out, can we. There are so far two approaches that work for sure: diminished total caloric intake and changes in genes that regulate the rate of early-life growth. (Miller, 2004: 233)

A recent and clear manifestation of the idea of decelerated senescence can be found in an article by Jay Olshansky and others, including Miller (Olshansky et al, 2006). They can be regarded as representatives of a growing chorus of scientists terming themselves 'moderate', 'modest' and 'realistic'. They firmly believe that an investment now of three billion US dollars annually will make it possible to decelerate ageing and the onset of ageing-related diseases and disorders among the baby boom cohorts by seven years:

> People who reach the age of 50 in the future would have the health profile and disease risk of today's 43-year-old; those aged 60 would resemble current 53-year-olds, and so on. Equally important, once

achieved, this seven-year delay would yield equal health and longevity benefits for all subsequent generations, much the same way children born in most nations today benefit from the discovery and development of immunizations. (Olshansky et al, 2006: 32)

Arrested senescence refers to relatively complete control of the biological processes of senescence. In this scenario, ageing in the sense of senescence or physical and mental deterioration does not occur any more, or the human organism is cared for very well (maintenance) and what senescence occurs is periodically repaired by a rejuvenation cure. For decades or centuries the chance to die does not increase with age any more, but stays rather constant. People still die, but they no longer die from the slow accumulation of damage and chronic deterioration. Instead they die from accident, murder or war. In this scenario people can become very old. Average life expectancies of 150, 500 or even 5,000 years are thought to be possible.

Discussing the engineering of arrested senescence may evoke images of quackery, pseudoscience or science fiction. But a number of important organisations that promote anti-ageing and eventually arrested senescence exist: the American Academy of Anti-Aging Medicine (A4M), the Gerontology Research Group, the Longevity Meme, the Immortality Institute, the Maximum Life Foundation, the Life Extension Foundation and the World Transhumanist Association. Influential individuals promoting arrested senescence include Deepak Chopra, Ronald Klatz, Michael Brickey, Jean Carper, Gary Null, Walter Pierpaoli, Johannes Huber, Joao Pedro de Magalhaes, Max More, Nick Bostrom, James Hughes, Robert A. Freitas, Jr and Ray Kurzweil.

One of the strongest defenders of the scientific credibility of Strategies for Engineering Negligible Senescence (SENS) is the English biogerontologist Aubrey de Grey. He not only vehemently argues that humanity needs to set aside massive sums of money for a war on ageing, he also has embarked, together with relevant specialists, on detailing biotechnological measures we could use to beat the 'seven deadly things'[3] that accumulate with age as side-effects of metabolism (de Grey et al, 2002; de Grey, 2003, 2005). He expects that, between 2025 and 2040, we will be able to fix these problems (to a large extent through genetic interventions and stem cell therapies) and that, around 2050, 'robust human rejuvenation' will be generally accessible. He realises that the first fixes will be imperfect, but they will give us time to develop better repair methods. According to de Grey, cancer is the hardest problem to solve, but he thinks it possible. Highly respected biogerontologists have attacked de Grey's ideas forcefully (Warner et al, 2005; Estep et al, 2006). It is important to note, however, that differences of opinion are mainly political, ethical and related to funding and estimates about the speed of future developments, and not about the possibility of substantial life-extension in itself.

We should note that the (US) President's Council on Bioethics has taken 'the possibility of extended youth and substantially prolonged lives' very seriously. In its 2003 report *Beyond therapy* (President's Council on Bioethics, 2003: 159-204) the Council *warns against* substantial life extension as a threat to the meaning of human lives.

Life extension and ethics

To offer some insight into the ethical aspect of life extension, I shall try to summarise the major ethical arguments for and against effective substantial extension of human lifespan, though intricate examination of each will not be possible. By substantial extension I mean decelerated senescence and arrested senescence as outlined above. Decelerated senescence is much more probable as the scenario for decades to come, but arrested senescence is certainly interesting and cannot be completely ruled out for the long run. From an ethical point of view, arrested senescence is significant. It forces us to think in new ways about what we consider most important in our lives and societies. This is significant even if arrested senescence itself turns out to be impossible.

Interpreting and adding to the framework by Stephen Post (2004b), I have organised the arguments in the following categories: autonomy, beneficence (including non-maleficence), distributive justice and meaning of life.

Autonomy

It is true that the principle or value of autonomy does not figure prominently in the ethical debate about life extension. Moreover, it is possible to regard autonomy or freedom not as an overriding principle but as one of the good things we value – discussing it under the category of beneficence. However, various kinds of consent and refusal are crucial in traditional biomedical ethics (Beauchamp and Childress, 2001), so it would seem anomalous not to approach it explicitly; besides, 'autonomy' is often referred to as a fundamental value in liberal democracies.

First of all, substantial extension of lifespan in the sense of decelerated or arrested ageing at this moment is (still) very much a *collective* matter. Decisions to try to extend human life substantially remain for the time being political or corporate decisions, for instance about priorities in medical research. Thus, taking autonomy seriously comes down to taking liberal democracy and citizenship seriously. Of course, there is debate about the best way to shape democracy in a highly multicultural, globalised and technological era (Benhabib, 1996; Habermas, 1998; Carens, 2000; Korten, 2000; Marres, 2005). The democracy debate is not uniquely concerned with matters of lifespan extension, but is highly relevant for how political decisions on life extension can best be made. How will it be possible, for example, to prevent social wrongs and injustice and at the same time respect individual reproductive liberty? Will future wealthy parents have the right to give their children genetically engineered substantially extended life expectancies that will be inheritable? Should the state be allowed to intervene in reproductive decisions in order to prevent injustice (Holm, 2004)?

Decisions about priorities in medical and biotechnological research will have impacts on future generations. Inevitably we must act paternalistically towards future generations; we cannot consult them. We can only try to judge imaginatively what will be good for them and not harm their interests. In some cases we can take precautionary measures, making it easier for people coming after us to reverse our decisions. This implies that we should be cautious with lifespan extension involving germline, hereditary genetic engineering. We must be conscientious in our judgements about what is good for future people. Perhaps engineering substantial life extension gives people a real choice they lack now; perhaps this is no problem at all, because people with extended lifespans could always decide for themselves and opt for suicide (Horrobin, 2005: 19). But would it not be problematic to create a society in which more and more people required this extraordinary exit strategy?

Beneficence

If society opts to allow itself and individuals the opportunity to make autonomous decisions about life extension, why should they choose or not choose much longer lives? An important aspect of the answer concerns the positive or negative effects that may reasonably be expected of the decision. Beneficence concerns the moral duty to contribute to the experience of things human beings value, including the duty to prevent harm – that is, the experience of things we value negatively. Now, what this means depends on what we ultimately value positively and negatively. Ultimate positive values that are often mentioned are preservation of (the quality of) life; enjoyment, pleasure, happiness, fulfilment or welfare; human company, friendship or community; self-respect and being respected by others; achievement despite obstacles; self-realisation or authenticity; creation and contemplation of beautiful things; knowledge; freedom, autonomy, independence or power; a healthy mind in a healthy body. Things that are valued negatively are the lack or loss of these things and pain and suffering.

The preservation and continuation of life is often mentioned first, but on closer inspection it is not life itself we ultimately want, but a certain quality of life characterised by a healthy body and an active mind endowed with memory and not overcome with pain (Brandt, 1959: 342; see also Horrobin, 2006). Christine Overall holds that the main argument in favour of life extension is not that life in itself is valuable, but 'that a longer life is the prerequisite for almost everything else that one might want' (Overall, 2004: 287). Because of the many possible things people might judge to be ultimate values, and because in a democracy we want to let people decide for themselves about this as much as possible, Overall's argument looks strong, because it is so general. But much longer life comes at a cost. Jeanne Calment, who died when she was 122, stood at the graves of her husband, all her friends, her only daughter and even the grave of her only grandchild (Baars, 2006: 199). The vulnerability of human beings is not simply physical. It also has a crucial social dimension. Living very long might be attractive only if the people around you also live as long. Moreover, life extension also comes at a cost literally. Money spent on research into fundamental processes of biological ageing cannot be spent on asthma research or on education or art subsidies. And a society with a growing number of older and really old people will need much reorganisation. Costs and benefits (negative and positive effects) of life extension and longevity must be weighed against each other. Because it is not life in itself that we want, there might be things that are more important than longer life.

The quasi-neutral aspect of longevity – everybody can decide for themselves what to do with a longer life – makes it fit nicely into a liberal democracy and an individualistic society. But longer lives can also cause problems for what we think valuable. During the last decade we have seen many discussions about the 'greying' of society and the problems this will cause. This chapter can only deal with examples chosen to illustrate the nature and variety of problems involved.

The danger of an overpopulated world and the problems it entails has often been offered as an objection to substantial life extension. Population growth or reduction is not just the result of the death rate; the birth rate is at least as important a factor (Dykstra, 2002: 8). In general, birth rates tend to fall as life expectancy increases. Reproductive decision making governing fertility and parental investment might be driven by a human psychology designed by natural selection to maximise material wealth, not just the largest number of surviving and reproducing children (Borgerhoff Mulder, 1998; see also Hrdy, 1999). Many other, highly unpredictable factors are in play. To mention just one:

> ... human vulnerability [might increase] due to new infectious diseases or antibiotic resistant strains of bacteria ... Disease may well continue to be an effective leveller, improving its technology as we improve ours. (Harris, 2003: 75)

However, if substantial life extension is achieved and the death rate drops dramatically, would the decline in birth rate keep pace? Or would governments have to resort to drastic measures, prohibiting either life extension or children? It seems at first a decisive argument when de Grey or de Magalhaes writes that it is morally unacceptable to let old people die in order to solve problems of an overpopulated world. However, is it really obvious that extending the lives of people who already exist is always better than opting for children? Even recognising the fact that people who do not yet exist cannot suffer, a society with children might still be better than one without, for people who do exist.

Another social problem is presented as a beneficence argument in favour of accepting substantial life extension. Stephen Post argues from his expert knowledge of Alzheimer's and the pain, suffering and lack of community, self-respect and independence that go with this disease. He writes:

> The stark reality of our already aging societies is that ... [m]any will experience chronic illness for which old age is the dominant risk factor,

ranging from Alzheimer's and Parkinson's to osteoporosis and vascular disease ... The solution to this problematic of age-related disease may rest with advances in the basic science of aging that would achieve even greater prolongevity in a manner that avoids the massive debilitation that currently plagues us. (Post, 2004b: 537)

Because we *might* be able to prevent the strong negative value of age-related chronic diseases by anti-ageing interventions, *must* we develop these? They will deliver extended life expectancy, but according to Post this is a necessary price to pay for success in the fight against horrible suffering (if it is a price). Rudi Westendorp, a Dutch biomedical gerontologist, takes a similar view, but warns that effective therapies for the age-related diseases we know now will extend average life expectancy and this will unmask new diseases related to newly possible longer lives. Therapies will be needed for diseases we now know little about (Köhler, 2004) – and so on. Post's argument turns out to be not so self-evidently in favour of anti-ageing interventions. His solution is not definitive; hard choices will be needed.

Although new technological possibilities, expensive drugs and new conditions such as obesity will also be very important factors contributing to an expected rise in medical expenditure, 'an increase in life-expectancy that is not accompanied by a proportionate increase in healthy years will lead to a great increase in healthcare costs' (Knook, 2002: 21). In most industrialised countries the percentage of health-care resources[4] spent on those over 65 is already much greater than the percentage spent on the entire remaining population (Beauchamp and Childress, 2001: 260). Estimates are that by 2050 the US will spend more than a thousand billion dollars annually only on Alzheimer's disease and related dementias (Olshansky et al, 2006: 31). Shall we be able to pay for an expanded scenario along these lines? Would such costs cripple all other social and personal priorities? Besides, because wealthy people live longer, schemes like the American Medicare program (309 billion dollars in 2006) might be thought to contain an ethically dubious element. To a significant extent they are equivalent to channelling tax revenue from the population at large towards expensive care for the fairly well-off (van Wijnbergen, 2002: 37). And, as the ageing populations of developed countries require more medical attention, devouring doctors and nurses from developing countries, shortages of health-care workers in the developing world would create ever more desperate situations (Garrett, 2007: 15, 26).

Distributive justice

Ethics is not only about promoting the good and preventing the bad things in life and the real possibility of shaping it yourself, it is also about the distribution of all this. Justice is about the distribution of the (lack of) things we value (such as freedom, happiness, friendship, beautiful things and good health) and the things we do not want (a life solitary, poor, nasty, brutish, and short). At the beginning of this chapter I distinguished between all kinds of life expectancies, but I omitted one very important factor: the 'social gradient' of longevity. Life expectancies differ according to social status. Michael Marmot's recent summary starts with an illustration from the US capital:

> If you take the Metro from the southeast of downtown Washington to Montgomery County, Maryland, in the suburbs – a distance of about 14 miles – for each mile traveled life expectancy rises about a year and a half. This is the most life-enhancing journey in the world. There's a twenty-year gap between poor blacks at one end of the journey (male life expectancy fifty-seven), and rich whites at the other. (Marmot, 2005: 5)

Such inequalities in life expectancy at birth are enormous and they are universal. They exist all over the world (Mackenbach and Bakker, 2003; Marmot, 2004: 13-36). What counts as *injustice* depends on the theory of justice that is used. However, whether one refers to human rights (Buitenweg, 2007),[5] Rawls's theory of justice as fairness (Rawls, 1999a, 1999b), Dworkin's (2000) equality of welfare and resources or Nussbaum's (2001, 2006) capabilities theory, differences in average life expectancy at birth of 40 years between countries (Japan and Zimbabwe), and more than 20 years for socioeconomic groups within countries – differences that can be removed and prevented by collective social action – are hard to defend as morally acceptable.

Now imagine what would happen if in such a world substantial life extension became possible through initially very expensive biotechnology like longevity pharmaceuticals or gene therapy. The demand backed by purchasing power, certainly in the beginning, would come mainly from young adults, better educated, wealthier and higher-income individuals and those with higher initial endowments of health. Socioeconomic and health inequalities would be amplified. A small group of people with an already high life expectancy would have access to life and health span extension; many less-privileged people would not. Surely this is undesirable? 'The need-based claims of the worse off to have reasonably long lives have more moral weight than the preference-based claims of the better off to have longer lives' (Glannon, 2001: 167; see also McConnel and Turner, 2005: 61; Mauron, 2005).

But the existence of social injustice can never normally be a valid reason to object morally to any improvement in the fate of human beings who do not belong to the most underprivileged ones. As Stephen Post writes:

> If we were to insist that technological developments of all sorts wait until the world becomes perfectly just, there would be absolutely no scientific progress. Requiring equality as the prerequisite to biogerontological advance is to establish an obstacle that is virtually insurmountable, and so exceedingly high as to be implausible. Indeed

this is not a requirement imposed in any other area of scientific research
and development, from new dental treatments to organ transplantation
... Anti-aging research and, eventually, derived treatments, will emerge
in technologically advanced countries and be affordable to those who
can pay. This is the unavoidable future of all biotechnological efforts in
human enhancement. And yet scientific creativity of this sort will not
be inhibited. (Post, 2004b: 537; see also Harris 2003; Davis 2004)

Post is right in many ways. Demanding equality and perfect justice within
and between countries as a prerequisite to the development of life extension
technology is asking too much. Here, as often, 'perfection' would be the enemy of
the good. On the other hand, not being able to do everything or enough, should
be no excuse for doing nothing. Efforts like the UN Millennium Development
Goals[6] are very significant. It is important before 2015 to try to reduce by half
the proportion of people living on less than a dollar a day, to reduce by two thirds
the mortality rate among children under 5 and to try to reduce by three quarters
the maternal mortality ratio (Garrett, 2007: 32). These are challenging goals but
they are technically feasible and depend mainly on political will. In the same vein
ambitious but feasible goals could be formulated to attack the shocking disparities
in longevity between and also within countries. Within countries, Christine
Overall proposes a qualified prolongevitism that will genuinely be for all, a kind
of affirmative action in the field of life extension:

> ... as a general principle, support for increased longevity should not
> be limited by gender, socioeconomic class, sexual orientation, race, or
> ability. So the particular focus, at least in the short run, of measures to
> increase average life expectancy must be on members of groups that
> historically have been disadvantaged and that currently have low life
> expectancy. (Overall, 2003: 200)

This implies that increased research into conditions and diseases affecting groups
of people with low life expectancy, like people of colour and poor people, is
morally indicated. This kind of priority setting, including maintaining the global
priority for compression of morbidity between 60 and 80, might provoke strong
political opposition, but that is no reason to be silent about a considered ethical
judgement.

Furthermore, it is important to see that priorities do not have to be 'all or
nothing'. Serious, strenuous attempts to tackle the national and global social
gradient of longevity certainly do not require a complete halt for biogerontological
research into the diseases of the oldest older people and general underlying
processes of senescence. In relation to international injustice, one should not
forget that numbers of the old and oldest older people in developing countries
will also increase rapidly. Already the remaining life expectancy of a woman who
has managed to reach the age of 60 in Brazil (21 more years), India (18 years)

and Nigeria (17 years) is not so different from the number of years an average 60-year-old female inhabitant of the US can expect to add to her life (24 years). The WHO anticipates that the percentage of people above 60 living in developing countries between now and 2050 will rise from 60 to 85% of the total global number (Kalache et al, 2005: 36; see also Kirkwood, 1999: 8; Aboderin, 2006). In China and India older people will outnumber the total current population of the US by mid-century (Olshansky et al, 2006: 31).

Meanings of life[7]

So far we have seen that autonomy, beneficence and justice evoke important considerations in connection with life extension. Our task seems to be to weigh pros and cons in a situation of risk and uncertainty about the future. However, some important authors attempt a more definitive position, not wishing to wait and see. They take a principled stand against life extension now. Hans Jonas, Leon Kass, Francis Fukuyama, Daniel Callahan and Bill McKibben represent what one might call a natural-law position. Not only is this a significant stance in itself, its discussion points very clearly to the way in which issues of *meaning* recur in the discussion of life extension.

Important aspects of the natural-law position are: that ageing is the final stage in a natural life cycle that should be cultivated (Callahan, 1995a, 1995b; see also Overall, 2003, 2004), that ageing is a natural process to be accepted and not a disease to be defeated (Callahan, 1995a, 1995b; see also Izaks and Westendorp, 2003; Caplan, 2004, 2005; Moody et al, 2004; Scully, 2004; Derkx, 2006), that the goals of medicine and health care include therapy (treatment) and prevention but not enhancement (see also Juengst, 1997, 1998, 2004; Brock, 1998; Frankford, 1998), and that it is unnatural and selfish to prefer a society with many very old people and very few children over a society with fewer older people and a more natural succession of 'fresh' generations (McKibben in Stock et al, 2003; Kass, 2004: 317-18).

It seems simple to dismiss natural-law positions as an untenable deontological stance by observing that if substantial life extension starts to occur in nature it begins to be 'natural', or emphasising that humans have always changed nature (including their own natural features) in the course of civilization. Much the same goes for the religious versions of these arguments, referring to a God who has established the natural law. That humans should respect the will of God or that they should not attempt to play God encounters similar intellectual difficulties as the exhortation to respect nature, and additional difficulties too. Referring to the will of God is not a very strong argument in a pluralistic democratic society that includes atheists and agnostics.

However, it is possible to discover something important behind these arguments from nature or God, even if one rejects their absolute verbal form and is more inclined towards consequentialist ethics. Human nature is not blank, nor completely and always easily malleable. It results from millions of years of natural selection. As evolutionary products human beings are very complex organisms involving many trade-offs, referring back to environments in the past. We cannot design humans from scratch. Stressing that we ought to be wary of bad unintended consequences is not to claim that nothing should be changed. It is possible for a society to opt for a policy of less than one child per family to counteract undesirable effects of population growth due to increasing old-age survival, but will its individual citizens accept this policy and live up to it? Human nature is very flexible, but it is possible to ask too much of human beings. It seems relevant, for example, to speculate about the emotional implications of a population scenario with nine billion people in 2300 with an average life expectancy at birth of about 100 years and a high proportion of very old people (Basu, 2004: 93). And we should be talking here not only about what is possible for human beings, individually and as a group, but also about what is good for them and what makes their lives meaningful. To ask what desires and emotions are humanly 'natural' can be translated into a question about what desires and emotions are good and proper for human beings to have and that deserve the opportunity to be acted upon.

Authors criticising substantial life extension often point to loss of meaning. Thus, Hans Jonas writes: 'Perhaps a non-negotiable limit to our expected time is necessary for each of us as the incentive to number our days and make them count' (quoted in Post, 2004b: 536). Bill McKibben writes:

> Maybe with these tools [such as germline genetic engineering] we will in some way learn to live forever, but the joy of it, the meaning of it, will melt away like ice cream on an August afternoon ... [L]ife far beyond the parameters of what we know now, life that goes beyond the normal human expectations, may be very much like a trap, and the name of that trap is a very American one – the constant idea that more is better. If it is good to live 80 years, it must be better to live 180 years and far better yet to live 300 years. (Stock et al, 2003: 7)

Yet much can be said in response to these objections to substantial life extension. What does 'making our days count' mean exactly? Horrobin (2005: 14) notes that it seems odd to assert that people enjoy playing football today and experience no ennui in doing so only because they are aware that they cannot do it three centuries hence. Moreover, what are 'normal human expectations'? The normal expectations of young Western European female office workers in 2007 are very different from those of their counterparts in 1875. And is it natural or unnatural for human beings to think that more is better?

Perhaps the most fundamental criticism of the natural law position is expressed by Christine Overall (2004; see also 2003). She states that we should not argue against increasing human longevity by reference to the limited parameters set by current life expectancies. According to her, this commits the fallacy of begging the question. When contexts change and life expectancies become much longer, our judgement of life's possibilities and meanings will also change. Not only will childhood and age be redefined, but concepts like schooling, education, marriage, partnership, friendship, sexuality, gender, father, mother, parent, grandparent, family, work, job, career, retirement, nationality and citizenship will also acquire other meanings. Together these changes will constitute new moral systems. But I think Overall exaggerates. The way we think about human fulfilment now must be relevant to forming well-considered present-day judgements on prolongation of life. I would agree with her only if she argued that we ought not to evaluate substantial life extension *exclusively* by reference to the kind of life that we know now. Certainly, a comprehensive ethical judgement about future possibilities requires not just norms, values, facts and extrapolations but also moral imagination.

A concern with meaning is not the prerogative of natural-law critics of substantial life extension. Paul van Tongeren does not accept Callahan's arguments in favour of accepting a natural life cycle and a natural lifespan, but he emphasises the importance of knowing what the meaning of life is. 'If we ask to what extent we are allowed to, or even should, extend life, we have to realize that we can hardly answer that question as long as we do not know what life is all about' (van Tongeren, 1995: 36). Whether we think substantial life extension morally acceptable or desirable very much depends on what we think gives life its meaning. Here Walter Glannon advances an argument from personal identity:

> Would a significantly long span of time between earlier and later mental states weaken the relations between them and make them so different that they effectively belonged to two distinct persons? ... Psychological connectedness is necessary for what matters to us. (Glannon, 2001: 160; for counterarguments see Harris, 2003: 82-5)

More discussion about meanings of life is needed. But in individualistic secular societies people have many different ideas about meanings of life, so it will be difficult to reach consensus or even mutual understanding about the value of life extension. Part of the difficulty is that in modern western societies it is widely considered that meanings of life are a private matter, not appropriate subjects of public debate.

The variety in ideas about meanings of life will be hard to handle in a democracy, because differences can be wide and not matters of degree. Transhumanists like Max More (2004), Ray Kurzweil and Terry Grossmann (2004), Nick Bostrom (2003, 2005), James Hughes (2004), Gregory Stock (2002) and Aubrey de Grey (2003, 2005) feel that we should not accept biological ageing as inevitable. They argue that the fundamental biology of human beings should be changed in order to root out senescence and most of death. Other thinkers, not only of the natural-law variety, see this as a dangerous illusion, holding that the propagation and cultivation of ideas like this are fundamentally detrimental to the meanings of human lives. This difference in world view is an extremely important aspect of the debate on substantial extension of human life expectancy. What is involved is expressed very clearly in the words of Michael Lerner:

> [We] need to do the spiritual work as we grow older to accept the inevitability of death rather than acting as though aging and death could be avoided if only we had a better technology. The enormous emotional, spiritual, and financial cost of trying to hang on to life as long as possible (and to look as though we were not aging) is fostered by a marketplace that tries to sell us endless youth. It is also fostered by our cultural failure to honor our elders, provide them with real opportunities to share their wisdom, and combat the pervasive ageism with its willingness to discard people long before their creative juices have dried up, to stigmatize the sexuality of the elderly … and to provide little in the way of adequately funded and beautifully conceived long-term care facilities. (Lerner, 2006: 308-9; see also Baars, 2006)

The necessity of a humanistic gerontology and an important problem

The preceding pages on substantial life extension started from the presupposition that biogerontology offers many unprecedented promises, but I hope that they also made clear that an exclusively biological gerontology would create problems while it tried to solve others. A technological fix for existential problems will not work and might make matters worse. Like all other fields of crucial human concern, ageing must be studied in an interdisciplinary mood and mode. 'Ageing' can be studied from different perspectives and acquires different meanings in the process: (1) ageing in the sense of (increasing numbers of persons with) increasing chronological age with all its legal and social implications, (2) ageing in the sense of biological decline and senescence, which need not keep pace with chronological age, and (3) ageing in the sense of continuously interpreting the meanings of unique and vulnerable human lives as they unfold and are experienced in time (Baars, 2006). These different concepts of ageing are often intermingled and mixed up, with chaotic and sometimes dehumanising results. A study of ageing that is culturally dominated by the second concept of ageing and by the science of biological senescence might turn out to be cruel. Biogerontologal research needs to be embedded in a democratic dialogue on meanings, goals and values.

In such a dialogue all citizens should be involved. It should not be fostered by the natural sciences alone, but also by the social sciences and humanities. None of these can be practised without recourse to explicit or implied normative assumptions and human values. Most biogerontologists I know personally would immediately assent to this: they are humanistic scientists (and often know more of philosophy and sociology than humanities scholars know of the natural sciences), but the cultural status and prominence of much-publicised biogerontological progress often has an unintended and undesirable cultural impact:

> There is an irredeemable cultural logic – if death is a solvable problem, then old age will be a failure ... Locating the meaning of death in biochemical processes and striving for ever-longer lifespans denies the possibility of old age as a valued final part of the life course. (Vincent, 2006: 694)

Research on meanings of life, the value of old age and a just and humane society requires approaches and methods fitting the subject of investigation, and in this area research confining itself to a 'hard' laboratory approach is often inappropriate. An interdisciplinary humanistic gerontology, however, is a challenging task, with risks and dangers on all sides.

One important problem can be illustrated by a passage from Clifford Geertz on the religious perspective on suffering:

> ... the problem of suffering is paradoxically, not how to avoid suffering but how to suffer, how to make of physical pain, personal loss, worldly defeat, or the helpless contemplation of others' agony something bearable, supportable – something, as we say, sufferable. (Geertz, quoted in Cole, 2002: 37)

Suffering is and will be a part of human existence. But human suffering always has a social, cultural and historical context, which can change. These changes matter very much and transform the character of the moral and existential issues we have to deal with. For example: my mother's parents, Roman Catholics living in the Netherlands, had five young children in 1918-19. Between December 1918 and January 1920 four of them died of whooping cough, a contagious disease now preventable by vaccination. The little card commemorating these infants' short lives starts with the exhortation 'Parents, do not weep!' and ends with the lines 'Repeat now and for ever: what God does, is done well'. Indeed, one important aspect of religious and non-religious world views is that they offer ways to accept, endure and embrace human life as it is. But a dangerous trap for religious as well as non-religious meaning frames and related ethics is that they may become too conservative, trying to fixate and immobilise cultures and societies. The dynamics of biotechnology poses many challenges here. The task for humanists is to find a wise balance between accepting humanity as it is and aiming for an enhanced humanity that could be. Humanity never just is; inevitably it must be interpreted in a changing context.

Notes

[1] Women have a higher risk for Alzheimer's than men, age for age, and women reach higher ages: by age 85 women outnumber men two to one, although starting out life in approximately equal numbers. Moreover, Alzheimer's does not just affect women in greater numbers because they are more likely to get it. They

are also more likely to end up taking care of someone who has it, like a spouse, a parent, or a sibling (Legato, 2005: 212-13).

[2] Bernice Neugarten has in 1978 already pointed out that the evidence is scanty that 'it will be possible to stretch out the active part of life without increasing the period of physical disability' (Neugarten, 1996: 343).

[3] The seven categories of damage are: (1) cell death without matching replacement (especially important in the heart and the brain), (2) unwanted cells, eg visceral fat and senescent cells (important in arthrosis and diabetes), (3) nuclear (epi)mutations causing cancer, (4) mitochondrial mutations, (5) extracellular protein/protein cross-links (eg leading to high blood pressure), (6) extracellular aggregates (eg resulting in amyloid involved in Alzheimer's disease), and (7) intracellular aggregates (eg resulting in hardening of the arteries).

[4] I should note that it has not become clear to me what exactly is counted as 'health-care resources'.

[5] See also www1.umn.edu/humanrts/index.html

[6] www.un.org/millenniumgoals/#

[7] Autonomy, beneficence and justice are also very relevant for the experience of a meaningful life (see Baumeister, 1991). In this section on meaning of life I specifically refer to human needs for purpose, fulfilment and feeling one with or part of a valuable whole.

Acknowledgments

Research for this paper was supported by a grant (code: 050-32-570) from NWO (Netherlands Organisation for Scientific Research).

I should also like to thank Jan Baars, Adri Smaling, Hugo Letiche, Janneke van Mens-Verhulst (University for Humanistics, Utrecht), Dick Knook and Diana van Heemst (Leiden University Medical Center), Pearl Dykstra (Netherlands Interdisciplinary Demographic Institute, The Hague) and my colleagues in the research project 'Towards a *lingua democratica* for the public debate on genomics', especially Cor van der Weele and Harry Kunneman, for helpful remarks on this topic.

References

Aboderin, I. (2006) 'Ageing in Africa', in *Wellcome Focus 2006:Ageing: Can we stop the clock*, London: The Wellcome Trust.

Arking, R. (2004) 'Extending human longevity: a biological probability', in S.G. Post and R.H. Binstock (eds) *The fountain of youth: Cultural, scientific, and ethical perspectives on a biomedical goal*, Oxford: Oxford University Press, pp 177-200.

Austad, S.N. (1997) *Why we age: What science is discovering about the body's journey through life*, New York: John Wiley.

Baars, J. (2006) *Het nieuwe ouder worden: paradoxen en perspectieven van leven in de tijd*, Amsterdam: SWP, Humanistics University Press.

Baltes, P.B. (2003) 'Extending longevity: dignity gain - or dignity drain?', *MaxPlanckResearch*, vol 2003, no 3, pp 14-19.

Basu, A.M. (2004) 'Towards an understanding of the emotions in the population of 2300', in Department of Economic and Social Affairs United Nations, Population Division (ed) *World population to 2030*, New York: United Nations, pp 89-98.

Baumeister, R.F. (1991) *Meanings of life*, New York: Guilford Press.

Beauchamp, T.L. and Childress, J.F. (2001) *Principles of biomedical ethics* (5th edn), Oxford: Oxford University Press.

Benhabib, S. (ed) (1996) *Democracy and difference: Contesting the boundaries of the political*, Princeton, NJ: Princeton University Press.

Borgerhoff Mulder, M. (1998) 'The demographic transition: are we any closer to an evolutionary explanation?' *Tree*, vol 13, no 7, pp 266-70.

Bostrom, N. (2003) 'Human genetic enhancements: a transhumanist perspective', *Journal of Value Inquiry*, vol 37, no 4, pp 493-506.

Bostrom, N. (2005) 'Transhumanist values', in F. Adams (ed) *Ethical issues for the 21st century*, Charlottesville, VA: Philosophical Documentation Center (no page numbers available).

Brandt, R.B. (1959) *Ethical theory: The problems of normative and critical ethics*, Englewood Cliffs, NJ: Prentice-Hall.

Brock, D.W. (1998) 'Enhancements of human function: some distinctions for policymakers', in E. Parens (ed) *Enhancing human traits: Ethical and social implications*, Washington, DC: Georgetown University Press, pp 48-69.

Buitenweg, R. (2007) *Human rights, human plights in a global village*, Atlanta, GA: Clarity Press.

Callahan, D. (1995a) 'Aging and the life cycle: a moral norm?', in D. Callahan, R.H.J. ter Meulen and E. Topinková (eds) *A world growing old: The coming health care challenges*, Washington DC: Georgetown University Press, pp 20-7.

Callahan, D. (1995b) *Setting limits: Medical goals in an aging society* (expanded edn), Washington, DC: Georgetown University Press.

Caplan, A.L. (2004) 'An unnatural process: why it is not inherently wrong to seek a cure for aging', in S.G. Post and R.H. Binstock (eds) *The fountain of youth: Cultural, scientific, and ethical perspectives on a biomedical goal*, Oxford: Oxford University Press, pp 271-85.

Caplan, A.L. (2005) 'Death as an unnatural process: why is it wrong to seek a cure for ageing?', *EMBO Reports*, vol 6, July, pp 72-5.

Carens, J.H. (2000) *Culture, citizenship, and community: A contextual exploration of justice as evenhandedness*, Oxford: Oxford University Press.

Cole, T.R. (2002) 'On the possibilities of spirituality and religious humanism in gerontology or reflections of one aging American cultural historian', in L. Andersson (ed) *Cultural gerontology*, Westport, CT: Auburn House, pp 25-44.

Davis, J.K. (2004) 'Collective suttee: is it unjust to develop life extension if it will not be possible to provide it to everyone?', in A.D.N.J. de Grey (ed) *Strategies for engineered negligible senescence: Why genuine control of aging may be foreseeable*, New York: New York Academy of Sciences, pp 535-41.

de Grey, Aubrey D.N.J. (2003) 'The foreseeability of real anti-aging medicine: focusing the debate', *Experimental Gerontology*, vol 38, no 9, pp 927-34.

de Grey, Aubrey D.N.J. (2005) 'Foreseeable and more distant rejuvenation therapies', in S.I.S. Rattan (ed) *Aging interventions and therapies*, Singapore: World Scientific Publishing, pp 379-95.

de Grey, A.D.N.J., Ames, B.N., Andersen, J.K., Bartke, A., Campisi, J., Heward, C.B., McCarter, R.J.M. and Stock, G. (2002) 'Time to talk SENS: critiquing the immutability of human aging', in D. Harman (ed) *Increasing healthy life span: Conventional measures and slowing the innate aging process*, New York: New York Academy of Sciences, pp 452-62.

Derkx, P. (2006) 'Ouder worden: te aanvaarden natuurlijk proces of te bestrijden ziekte?', *Tijdschrift voor Humanistiek – Journal for Humanistics*, vol 7, no 28, pp 82-90.

Dworkin, R. (2000) *Sovereign virtue: The theory and practice of equality*, Cambridge, MA: Harvard University Press.

Dykstra, P.A. (2002) 'Ageing in the Netherlands in a macro and micro perspective', in R. de Bok (ed) *Ageing in Europe: The social demographic and financial consequences of Europe's ageing population*, Breda: PlantijnCasparie, pp 6-17.

Estep, P.W.III, Kaeberlein, M., Kapahi, P., Kennedy, B.K., Lithgow, G.J., Martin, G.M., Melov, S., Powers, R.W. and Tissenbaum, H.A. (2006) *Life extension pseudoscience and the SENS plan*, Technology Review (MIT), www.technologyreview.com/sens/index.aspx

Frankford, D.M. (1998) 'The treatment/enhancement distinction as an armament in the policy wars', in E. Parens (ed) *Enhancing human traits: Ethical and social implications*, Washington, DC: Georgetown University Press, pp 70-94.

Fries, J.F. (1980) 'Aging, natural death, and the compression of morbidity', *The New England Journal of Medicine*, vol 303, 17 July, pp 130-5.

Garrett, L. (2007) 'The challenge of global health', *Foreign Affairs*, vol 86, no 1, pp 14-38.

Glannon, W. (2001) *Genes and future people: Philosophical issues in human genetics*. Boulder, CO: Westview Press.

Habermas, J. (1998) *Between facts and norms: Contributions to a discourse theory of law and democracy*, Cambridge, MA: MIT Press.

Harris, J. (2003) 'Intimations of immortality: the ethics and justice of life extending therapies', in M.D.A. Freeman (ed) *Current legal problems 2002*, Oxford: Oxford University Press, pp 65-95.

Hayflick, L. (1994) *How and why we age*, New York: Ballantine Books.

Holliday, R. (1995) *Understanding ageing*, Cambridge: Cambridge University Press.

Holliday, R. (2006) 'Aging is no longer an unsolved problem in biology', in S.I.S. Rattan, P. Kristensen and B.F.C. Clark (eds) *Understanding and modulating aging*, Boston, MA: Blackwell, pp 1-9.

Holm, S. (2004) 'I want to live forever – a review of [Christine Overall's] *Aging, death and human longevity: A philosophical inquiry*', *Medicine, Health Care and Philosophy*, vol 7, no 1, pp 105-07.

Horrobin, S. (2005) 'The ethics of aging intervention and life-extension', in S.I.S. Rattan (ed) *Aging interventions and therapies*, Singapore: World Scientific Publishing, pp 1-27.

Horrobin, S. (2006) 'The value of life and the value of life extension', in S.I.S. Rattan, P. Kristensen and B.F.C. Clark (eds) *Understanding and modulating aging*, Boston, MA: Blackwell, pp 94-105.

Hrdy, S.B. (1999) *Mother nature: A history of mothers, infants, and natural selection*, New York: Random House (Pantheon Books).

Hughes, J. (2004) *Citizen cyborg: Why democratic societies must respond to the redesigned human of the future*, Boulder, CO: Westview Press.

Izaks, G.J. and Westendorp, R.G.J. (2003) 'Ill or just old? Towards a conceptual framework of the relation between ageing and disease', *BMC Geriatrics*, vol 3, no 7 (no page numbers available).

Juengst, E.T. (1997) 'Can enhancement be distinguished from prevention in genetic medicine?', *The Journal of Medicine and Philosophy*, vol 22, no 2, pp 125-42.

Juengst, E.T. (1998) 'What does enhancement mean?', in E. Parens (ed) *Enhancing human traits: Ethical and social implications*, Washington, DC: Georgetown University Press, pp 29-47.

Juengst, E.T. (2004) 'Anti-aging research and the limits of medicine', in S.G. Post and R.H. Binstock (eds) *The fountain of youth: Cultural, scientific, and ethical perspectives on a biomedical goal*, Oxford: Oxford University Press, pp 321-39.

Juengst, E.T., Binstock, R.H., Melhman, M., Post, S.G. and Whitehouse, P. (2003) 'Biogerontology, "anti-aging medicine", and the challenge of human enhancement', *Hastings Center Report*, vol 33, no 4, pp 21-30.

Kalache, A., Aboderin, I. and Hoskins, I. (2002) 'Compression of morbidity and active ageing: key priorities for public health policy in the 21st century', *Bulletin of the World Health Organization*, vol 80, no 3, pp 243-44.

Kalache, A., Barreto, S.M. and Keller, I. (2005) 'Global ageing: the demographic revolution in all cultures and societies', in M.L. Johnson, V.L. Bengtson, P.G. Coleman and T.B.L. Kirkwood (eds) *The Cambridge handbook of age and ageing*, Cambridge: Cambridge University Press, pp 30-46.

Kass, L.R. (2004) 'L'chaim and its limits: why not immortality?', in S.G. Post and R.H. Binstock (eds) *The fountain of youth: Cultural, scientific, and ethical perspectives on a biomedical goal*, Oxford: Oxford University Press, pp 304-20.

Kirkwood, T.B.L. (1999) *Time of our lives: The science of human aging*, Oxford: Oxford University Press.

Kirkwood, T.B.L. (2005) 'Understanding the odd science of aging', *Cell*, vol 120, pp 437-47.

Knook, D.L. (2002) 'Europe's ageing population and consequences for health care', in R. de Bok (ed) *Ageing in Europe: The social, demographic and financial consequences of Europe's ageing population*, Breda: PlantijnCasparie, pp 18-26.

Köhler, W. (2004) '"Ouderdom is groeiende chaos", interview met Rudi Westendorp', *M: het maandblad van NRC Handelsblad*, August, pp 34-9.

Korten, D.C. (2000) *The post-corporate world: Life after capitalism*, West Hartford, CT/San Francisco, CA: Kumarian Press/Berrett-Koehler Publishers.

Kurzweil, R. and Grossmann, T. (2004) *Fantastic voyage: Live long enough to live forever*, Emmaus, PA: Rodale.

Legato, M.J. (2005) *Why men never remember and women never forget*, Emmaus, PA: Rodale, pp 199-221.

Lerner, M. (2006) *The left hand of God: Taking back our country from the religious Right*, New York: HarperCollins, HarperSanFrancisco.

Mackenbach, J.P. and Bakker, M.J. (2003) 'Tackling socioeconomic inequalities in health: analysis of European experiences', *The Lancet*, vol 362, 25 October, pp 1409-14.

Marmot, M. (2004) *The status syndrome: How social standing affects our health and longevity*, New York: Henry Holt, Times Books.

Marmot, M. (2005) *Social determinants of longevity and mortality*, SAGE Crossroads, 28 June, www.SageCrossroads.net

Marres, N.S. (2005) 'No issue, no public: democratic deficits after the displacement of politics', Universiteit van Amsterdam, http://dare.uva.nl/document/17061

Mauron, A. (2005) 'The choosy reaper: from the myth of eternal youth to the reality of unequal death', *EMBO Reports*, vol 6, July, pp 67-71.

McConnel, C. and Turner, L. (2005) 'Medicine, ageing, and human longevity: the economics and ethics of anti-ageing interventions', *EMBO Reports*, vol 6, July, pp 59-62.

Miller, R.A. (2004) 'Extending life: scientific prospects and political obstacles', in S.G. Post and R.H. Binstock (eds) *The fountain of youth: Cultural, scientific, and ethical perspectives on a biomedical goal*, Oxford: Oxford University Press, pp 228-48.

Moody, H.R. (1995) 'The meaning of old age: scenarios for the future', in D. Callahan, R.H.J. ter Meulen, and E. Topinková (eds) *A world growing old: The coming health care challenges*, Washington DC: Georgetown University Press, pp 9-19.

Moody, H.R., Caplan, A. and Kondracke, M. (2004) *Is aging a disease?*, SAGE Crossroads, 22 January, www.SageCrossroads.net

More, M. (2004) 'Superlongevity without overpopulation', in Immortality Institute and S. Sethe (eds) *The scientific conquest of death: Essays on infinite lifespans*, Buenos Aires: LibrosEnRed, pp 169-85.

Mykytyn, C.E. (2006) 'Contentious terminology and complicated cartography of anti-aging medicine', *Biogerontology*, vol 7, no 4, pp 279-85.

Neugarten, B.L. (1996) 'Social implications of life extension [1978]', in D.A. Neugarten (ed) *The meanings of age: Selected papers of Bernice L. Neugarten*, Chicago: The University of Chicago Press, pp 339-45.

Nussbaum, M.C. (2001) *Women and human development: The capabilities approach*, Cambridge: Cambridge University Press.

Nussbaum, M.C. (2006) *Frontiers of justice: Disability, nationality, species membership*, Cambridge, MA: Harvard University Press, Belknap Press.

Olshansky, S.J., Perry, D., Miller, R.A. and Butler, R.N. (2006) 'In pursuit of the longevity dividend: what should we be doing to prepare for the unprecedented aging of humanity?', *The Scientist*, vol 20, no 3, pp 28-36.

Overall, C. (2003) *Aging, death, and human longevity: A philosophical inquiry*, Berkeley, CA: University of California Press.

Overall, C. (2004) 'Longevity, identity, and moral character: a feminist approach', in S.G. Post and R.H. Binstock (eds) *The fountain of youth: Cultural, scientific, and ethical perspectives on a biomedical goal*, Oxford: Oxford University Press, pp 286-303.

Post, S.G. (2004a) 'Decelerated aging: should I drink from a fountain of youth?', in S.G. Post and R.H. Binstock (eds) *The fountain of youth: Cultural, scientific, and ethical perspectives on a biomedical goal*, Oxford: Oxford University Press, pp 72-93.

Post, S.G. (2004b) 'Establishing an appropriate ethical framework: the moral conversation around the goal of prolongevity', *Journal of Gerontology: Biological Sciences*, vol 59, no 6, pp 534-9.

President's Council on Bioethics (2003) *Beyond therapy: biotechnology and the pursuit of happiness*, New York: HarperCollins, Regan Books.

Rawls, J. (1999a) *The law of peoples, with 'the idea of public reason revisited'*, Cambridge, MA: Harvard University Press.

Rawls, J. (1999b) *A theory of justice: Revised edition*, Cambridge, MA: Belknap Press of Harvard University Press.

Scully, J.L. (2004) 'What is a disease? Disease, disability and their definitions', *EMBO Reports*, vol 5, no 7, pp 650-3.

Stock, G. (2002) *Redesigning humans: Our inevitable genetic future*, Boston, MA: Houghton Mifflin.

Stock, G., McKibben, B. and Kondracke, M. (2003) *Do we want science to reinvent human aging?*, SAGE Crossroads, 27 March, www.SageCrossroads.net

Turner, L. (2004) 'Life extension research: health, illness, and death', *Health Care Analysis*, vol 12, no 2, pp 117-29.

van Tongeren, P. (1995) 'Life extension and the meaning of life', in D. Callahan, R.H.J. ter Meulen and E. Topinková (eds) *A world growing old: The coming health care challenges*, Washington, DC: Georgetown University Press, pp 28-38.

van Wijnbergen, S.J.G. (2002) 'Economic aspects of an ageing population', in R. de Bok (ed) *Ageing in Europe: The social, demographic and financial consequences of Europe's ageing population*, Breda: PlantijnCasparie, pp 28-39.

Vincent, J.A. (2006) 'Ageing contested: anti–ageing science and the cultural construction of old age', *Sociology*, vol 40, no 4, pp 681-98.

Warner, H. et al (2005) 'Science fact and the SENS agenda: what can we reasonably expect from ageing research', *EMBO Reports*, vol 6, no 11, pp 1006-8.

Part Three

Ageing and wisdom?
Conflicts and contested developments

ELEVEN

Wisdom: a humanist approach to valuing older people

Ricca Edmondson

The Lord created me at the beginning of his work,
the first of his acts of old ...
and I was daily his delight,
dancing before him always. (Proverbs 8:22, 30)

From the beginning of recorded history, throughout some five millennia until recent times, the idea of the life course was given shape and content by ideas concerning wisdom. Wisdom was generally expected to accumulate during a person's lifetime, though it was not automatically assumed that older people are wiser than those younger ('Better is a poor but wise youth than an old and foolish king who will no longer take advice': Ecclesiastes 4:13). But the idea that it is *possible* to become wiser today than yesterday could offer meaning and purpose to personal survival, to the presence in society of older people in general and to the practice of respecting them. This is not to suggest that wisdom was ever politically dominant in golden ages in the past. But, at least in principle, the notion of wisdom could help to make sense of life after individuals had ceased formal work; it had the capacity to play an important personal and social role in society, reconciling individuals with their own advancing life courses, guiding them in continuous attempts to develop and learn, and providing a rationale for offering the fruits of their insights and deliberations to others. Potential like this makes wisdom just as relevant today. Placing career activities alone at the centre of existence would make it hard to see what significant personal developments or public roles could be expected to remain to people after retirement age.

Exploring the topic of wisdom thus has highly practical implications. Thinking about ageing – our own or other people's – invites us to consider a range of possibilities influenced not only by personal experiences but also by the cultures in which we live. Different cultural surroundings extend varying palettes of expectation to their inhabitants, helping to make particular images of ageing seem plausible or implausible, and bringing it about that those images are easier or harder to adopt. Does growing older hold out prospects of unrelieved decline, or has it benefits to offer? Are older people on the whole to be regarded negatively, as occasionally amiable burdens to their friends and society, or can there be a real point in having them around? If older people can offer wise inspiration to others, to what extent are they supported in doing so? Cultures that do not entertain strong ideas of wisdom are cultures in which expectations of older people, from themselves and from others, are inevitably curtailed.

The way people think about older people and ageing, therefore, has an undeniable influence on policy and behaviour. Expectations about what is normal and likely influence what seems reasonable to put in place in a society (Andersson, 2002; Borup et al, 2006). It impacts on what is done by those who make policy or, like advocacy organisations, try to influence it; by those, like social workers or nursing home staff, who carry it out, as well as by individuals themselves as they grow older. As Nowotny et al argue in relation to science: 'Visions, images and beliefs cannot sharply be demarcated from knowledge ... It is important to recognize how visions and images interact' (Nowotny et al, 2001: 232). As far as ageing is concerned, the 'visions and images' most prominent in the cultural settings common to most contemporary western societies share a curious feature. The palette they offer tends to omit or play down an item central to thoughts about ageing and the life course throughout human history: wisdom. Wisdom is rarely mentioned in work on ageing and seldom discussed, even where it might be expected to figure prominently – in courses on philosophy (the name of this discipline refers explicitly to the love of wisdom). Yet both historical and ethnographic material on wisdom suggests that it is worth taking very seriously.

But we cannot simply take over the idea of wisdom, since it is not yet sufficiently clear to us what the term means, whether it means one thing or several, or what the family resemblances between different understandings of wisdom really are. This is famously illustrated by the quotation above. The image of wisdom as the Creator's precious child, whose play gives him joy, demonstrates how hard to interpret uses of the word 'wisdom' in the past can be today. Many versions of this idea are not connected with religion, but this does not necessarily make them more transparent.

To the extent that wisdom is discussed in contemporary western societies, it is frequently expected to refer to wise *individuals*. In the following section, an ethnographic example, taken from the semi-traditional society of the West of Ireland as it existed some three or four decades ago, reflects several features that have been ascribed to wise people since the earliest discussions of the topic and makes clear how they are important. This case seems at first sight, too, to be beguilingly person-centred. But in fact it also allows us to explore some limitations of an individual-focused understanding of the term. Semi-traditional life in this part of the world was intensely social, a rich source for exploring the more strongly social aspects of wisdom that are featured in succeeding sections of this chapter. Examining them can cast cases of wisdom in more urban societies in a new light. It enables us to contrast sociality-centred approaches to wisdom with images of person-centred wisdom, which downplay their social or interactive aspects, in effect forming *decontextualised* versions of what wisdom is taken to be. These can be argued to demand from prospective bearers a level of attainment that would amount almost to perfection. Accounts of wisdom stressing sociality, by contrast, possess the humanistically relevant feature of adapting more easily to the limitations and fallibility of normal human beings.

Wisdom and the wise person

An extremely appealing and multi-layered example of wisdom concerns a gentleman who lived on the tiny island of Inis Oirr off the West coast of Ireland, a man who died some two or three decades ago.[1] The following account was given by someone who knew him as he was growing up:

> Edward, my neighbour, was such a wise guy. It was almost innate in him. His house was here and my house was there … And the way he'd sit out at night, reading the stars. He'd name the stars to me … And he had a great mind, even though he had no education.

This image of the wise person as in tune with the natural as well as the human universe is one that has been potent for an extremely long time. In the past, from the oldest records of wisdom literature, this was not seen as a private interest on the wise man's part. The ancient Sumerians and Egyptians associated wisdom with understanding, and participating in, the rising and setting of the sun and the advance of the seasons; they also connected comprehending this natural order with the maintenance of social justice, in which we are all implicated (Assman, 1991). For them, justice was not just the province of the unusually wise person; it was everyone's responsibility. The Greek pre-Socratic writers in the sixth century BC saw wise people as possessing insights into the structure of the physical universe, out as far as the heavens; but they were also authorities on the conduct of everyday and political life (Edmondson and Woerner, forthcoming). These cultural connotations are not identical in this instance, of course, but the extraordinary breadth and depth of Edward's knowledge lends a degree of wonder, even magic, to his description. He stands out as able to do things that could not be expected of a normal person.

 This brings us to a complex set of issues that help explain some of the fascination 'wisdom' may have for people who are both formed by, and suffer from, life in societies more individualistic than that on the island. Edward seems to have been unusually independent of his surroundings, again to a degree that cannot be expected of most people. He seemed free from a superficial need for others' approval for his own self-worth. He did what he did in his own way, and enjoyed it, while preserving an unerring sense of values and knowledge of other people's worth. The speaker goes on:

> I would have grown up on Inis Oirr and my image of home would be that it was lovely and it was great. But I know I grew up with low self-esteem. The body language was, keep your mouth shut, others are better. Edward hadn't that. He valued other people, he valued me

> … He was at home with himself in a way others weren't. He'd enjoy what he was doing, building a garden, setting potatoes, and he'd go at his own pace. But he had an eye for what was important.

Edward's independence of mind did not, therefore, make him a hermit; this is not an example of romantic detachment from other people. Indeed, his kindness and curiosity were ignited even for those he did not know. 'He'd say, "I wonder what the people in Clare are doing and what they are like."' Edward's independence of mind was clearly far from a self-centred rebellion against social norms. He was not so much independent of society as independent of undue anxiety about it. It is not that he did not need other people at all, far from it. His life was lived among others and he constantly engaged with them. It was his use of this sociality that meant that he could see more deeply into human needs than could people around him. Hence the speaker is grateful for the fact that Edward realised that people need to be valued. He could see what others needed in terms of personal support and could give it to them.

This returns us to the issue of the contentment of the wise person, 'being at home with oneself'. Our closer inspection suggests that Edward's personal happiness (despite the fact that he and his wife were childless, a situation that might not have been easy for them to face) involves *both* individuality and sociality. The speaker's account presents Edward's attitude to his own life in the same breath as describing his interaction with others.

> It's not even about words. It's about people. He was a mighty man to sit happy in his place and be reflective on it. He wasn't dogmatic or arrogant. He'd start a story that would bring you into it – the golden road that would open up on the sea and bring you along it … He could call you into the mystery of looking at the sky and the horizon of the round island that was about you … When you reached the horizon it would open up another one.

This excerpt also attributes to Edward several capacities recurrently associated with wisdom in the history of the topic. It does so in a manner that casts light on the core of humanistic accounts of wisdom. These capacities are mutually interwoven on the basis of the person who carries them, not methodologically stripped down and independent of each other. Thus, Edward's strong sense of human priorities, which clearly involve ethical and political dimensions, is described as *part of* his capacity to enjoy simple things in life. Furthermore, he was humble, a feature associated with wisdom throughout history (Edmondson, 2008; Edmondson and Woerner, forthcoming). Socrates himself is famed for knowing that he did not know. These features are mentioned in direct connection with the fact that Edward was a storyteller and could bestow the storyteller's magical sense of escape from the quotidian world. This was not merely a matter of entertainment, for, at the same time, such stories offered hope and freed listeners to regard their own predicaments in a new light. The capacity to put other people into a different perceptual 'place' is important in wisdom (Edmondson et al, 2009) and we shall return to it below.

A characteristic not always prominent in later accounts of wisdom was Edward's personal courage, as well as a more familiar feature: his calm in the face of crisis:

> Another thing – on Inis Oirr you'd have to be strong and to be able to fight. Two guys would start something. A guy would throw out his hand and say, 'There's a spit on that.' They'd wrestle together without any spite in it.

> Edward was a small, blocky man. He had no fear, he was able to win most of these. He wouldn't allow any fear to enter into him. He wasn't a guy who'd be afraid of the dark, of the fight, of any angry situation. He had the situation worked out.

Edward is described here not as thinking about acting bravely but actually doing so. He does not merely take abstract decisions involving courageous actions; he is courageous.

Lastly, Edward was important in his community. 'He was valued because of the gift he had. People would ask him his advice, his wisdom was valued.' What made him valued, clearly, was not any status or power he might have possessed, but the convincing quality of what he said and did: the 'ethos' he communicated in his actions.

The idea that ageing might bring even a modicum of Edward's qualities is a highly enviable one and would certainly bestow purpose on becoming older. But this seems a great deal to expect for many of us. Fortunately, there are links between Edward's behaviour and examples from similar social settings that cast light on broader, more attainable notions of what wisdom might be. In contrast to the romantic image of stripped-down, individualistic wisdom, the wise person independent of humankind, not even Edward was required to develop his capacities entirely alone.

Wisdom and sociality

Ideas about wisdom have, historically, tended to centre on the capacity to respond to human problems which cannot be tackled purely in everyday terms, nor by taking refuge in experts' recommendations (Edmondson, 2005; Edmondson and Woerner, forthcoming). These problems may concern individuals themselves or other people; they may involve political or philosophical questions about how life should be lived. They demand meaningful responses to daily experience and arise from human predicaments that characteristically combine social, political, ethical and practical elements. Such predicaments consequently demand responses that combine human capacities and insights, as we can see from the example already given. It is partly the fact that these problems do require responses in combined fields that makes them difficult to account for in terms of the methodologically separate strategies of modern academic disciplines.

Studying wisdom in order to restore it as a possibility for contemporary societies demands more humanistic approaches that centre on the question how people can flourish as human beings (rather than flourishing as experts in specific fields of knowledge or professional skill) and what flourishing like this entails. We shall return to this in the chapter's concluding sections.

Here we shall first review examples that show in more detail how wisdom can be centred on social interactions and can build on, as well as evoke, responses in other people. In many such cases, these responses may be triggered by individuals who are regarded as especially wise, but the triggers form part of wise processes that do not depend on these individuals alone. Second, we shall examine examples of wise practices, which may be carried out between people who, individually, may not be particularly wise at all. In this way we can both make sense of some ancient historical material and go on to understand in more detail how everyday wisdom might become a realistic aspiration.

The first case is that of Sean Murphy, who also lived in a remote area of the West of Ireland and who died in 1996 (Edmondson, 2005). He was a 'persuasive' and 'jolly' man, known for his wit, humour and charm, and his capacity to defuse situations of conflict. Like Edward, he was not independent of his culture, but so deeply imbued with it that he could use it to optimum effect. He was a 'gifted poet and storyteller', 'a problem solver', able to 'talk things through' with people in a way that made them want to listen to him. An 'excellent judge of character', he was fond of children and treated them with affection and respect. He had 'great mercy for animals', surprising acquaintances with his capacity to train sheepdogs by looking at tasks from the dog's point of view. 'If you try to train dogs to do impossible things they are not fit to do, they are defeated straight away and will never advance at all.' Most importantly from our point of view, he was able to bring other people to solve their own problems by looking at them in new ways. One of his neighbours became distraught when he detected his son in deceit. Sean simply asked him, 'Did you make your son tell you a lie?' The neighbour did not dismiss this question, though he did not understand it. He puzzled over it for many months until at last he realised that his own excessive strictness had contributed to his son's fault.

The case of Tim O'Flaherty of Spiddal in Connemara is in many ways similar. Also convivial and a well-known conversationalist, as well as trusted in making matches between young people, he was famous for his skill in using proverbs. Proverbs, which have been part of the armoury of wisdom for millennia, are not to be dismissed as invariably flaccid clichés. They can act as the spurs that cause hearers actively to re-evaluate their own predicaments (Edmondson, 2005). His son-in-law said of Tim:

It was a way of diagnosing a situation and finding just the saying to describe it. The proverb would lay things out for you in a way that made you think about them, think what you would do in the future.

Being able to do this depended on the speaker's high order of skill in recognising *both* the key features of other people's predicaments *and* the communicative responses to them that would provoke appropriate remedies; but doing this was not entirely an independent achievement, nor presented as a case of personal expertise. It drew on a store of insights common to the speaker and his hearers. Listeners could be brought to activate their own capacities for insight by witty references to prescriptions already available in the cultural world they lived in. This form of communication is neither literal (dissecting the other person's error in direct, ponderous detail) nor 'expert'. The wise speaker's lightness of touch – a cultural prerequisite in this part of the world – is part of what makes him or her able to spark a shared and effective reaction in which the hearer's part is crucial. Like Edward, both Sean and Tim are able to activate characteristics making up their own ethos, and which convince other people in the course of communication.

These are cases in which wise people can use cultural resources to help others behave more wisely. But there are also social customs that themselves evoke wise conduct, even when used by people with no particular individual pretensions to wisdom. Cases include the small-scale habits of mutual help and support among older people which create the 'enclaves of sociality' enhancing the qualities of daily life – which Carmel Gallagher details (2008 and in this volume) – or social customs in the West of Ireland which prescribe responses to sickness and death.

A priest described in a sermon how a colleague had longed for promotion within the clerical hierarchy (author's field notes, 2005). This man had a deep prejudice against the people of County Clare, whom for undisclosed reasons he regarded as grasping and untrustworthy. At last he was granted his own parish – but it was located in County Clare. Here the social customs his parishioners followed soon revealed them as wiser than their pastor. Not long afterwards he fell ill with cancer and was brought to the university clinic many miles distant. His new flock took turns in visiting him every day and on his release from hospital they lit bonfires along his route 'home'. In this case, too, practices can be identified as wise through the insights or behaviour they provoke in those they affect.

This claim that wisdom can reside in social customs, institutions or cultural achievements, as well as in individuals, resonates with ancient traditions of wisdom literature. The Mesopotamian story of Gilgamesh, for example, one of the world's earliest anti-heroes, recounts the adventures of a rapacious and unpopular monarch who desires to acquire for his kingdom the secret of immortality (see George, 1999). After a series of adventures in which he has this secret within his grasp but loses it, Gilgamesh returns home defeated. As he trudges back towards his city, his eyes fall on the great walls that surround it. He realises that the true secrets of wisdom and immortality reside in the common achievements of civilised human beings.

Cases like this, then, suggest that wisdom need not lie within a single person only but can result from the interaction between people and their common ethos. Nor are these instances confined to the pre-industrial world; mutual 'support groups' are clear instances in which people in contemporary societies hope to offer each other wise support through talking together (Edmondson et al, 2009). The next section will examine in more detail what interaction between people without personal claims to wisdom can offer. It shows that wisdom can be a joint product among interacting, fallible human beings rather than necessarily the achievement of an outstanding individual.

'Til kingdom come: a quotidian conception of advancing wisdom

'Til kingdom come is a play written by a young woman, Angela Ryan (21 at the time of first writing), which was premiered by Selkie Theatre in Galway in 2008 in conjunction with Age Action Ireland. The play is based partly on observations the playwright made of her father in his last years; its actual story is unrelated to him, but the way he drifts between different mental worlds is acutely and credibly observed. This remarkable play is strikingly humane in its acceptance of human beings' limitations as well as their capacities for mutual support. As a text for interpretation in this context, its importance lies partly in its capacity to condense into a single script details that might take years to observe in ethnographic fieldwork, as well as its guidance in what can be learned from them. The action presents its characters as influenced by and entangled in the circumstances that lead them to see their lives as they do, but the ways in which they encounter and conflict with each other enable them to struggle against the effects of the experiences oppressing them. Their slow movement towards a more hopeful position derives from the interaction between their faults and narrowness as well as from such virtues and vision as they are able to attain. This is an important point; progress in wisdom that depends on social interaction can develop among people who start out as definitely *un*wise.

Like the conversation of Edward, Sean and Tim, this play is witty and engaging. Yet its setting is unpropitious: 'A geriatric ward in an obsolete hospital in a rural area of North Kerry'. This is 'A state-funded institution which caters for medical-card holders awaiting permanent beds in nursing homes. It is a place of transience where patients' comings and goings are determined by bureaucracy.' The play centres on an old man in his hospital bed, Jack, preoccupied by past worlds and unable to retain a consistent grasp of his unfamiliar environment. He says to the carer on the ward:

> Hello ... hello there ... who's this now? Let me see till I have a look at you. Well I declare to God but aren't you a fine girl; would you be a breed of the McGraths by any possible chance? No? Jaysus, I thought you'd the gimp of John Mac there for a minute.

He takes her for a moment to be his daughter and to have asked the neighbours in for a house Mass:

> No white-washin' done … Well glory be but she hasn't an iota of consideration. Tsk … showin' me up to be a man who can't even keep the moss from his eaves. Well, what has a man to do to get a bit of peace and quiet in his own house?

Margaret, the carer, is 'good-natured, but utterly tactless', 'brazen' but insecure, 'slipping into an affected tone of voice … when she is trying to assert her authority'.[2] She addresses her patient in a patronising manner suggesting limitations in her training: 'Now, din-dins'll be here shortly. Are ya lookin' forward to that?' She is baffled by Jack's intermittent confusion:

> I dunno is it away with the fairies he is or what. Might be just after the attention. 'Where's me daughter?' says he. Ah, I'd say he's a cute auld whore. Out to fool me up to me eyeballs. And his daughter by his side only two hours ago. Nothin' wrong with his memory then, was there?

But Jack is often panicked and perplexed when he realises he is not at home. He interprets the carer as making unwelcome advances to him when she tells him to return to bed. The small details of this interaction convey a condensed summary of the main protagonists' lives, and those of Jack's son and daughter, in a way that enables watchers to reconstruct information they are not given – guessing that there are problems in Jack's past relationships, especially with his children.

The turning point in the play comes when Margaret is phoned at work by her own son's headmaster. The boy left home that morning to take his Leaving Certificate examinations but has not appeared at school. Desperately she contacts him on his mobile phone.

> Hello? … Simon, is that you? You'd better listen carefully to me young man … I don't care what you have to say, or who you're with or how feckin 'cool' any of this might seem to you. You get your arse down to that school right away and start explainin' yerself fairly lively. Of all the stupid things I've heard this one really takes the biscuit. Have you any idea of the sacrifices I've made to school you and *this* is how you repay me, you ungrateful little pup! How could you do su … Simon? … Simon? The little fecker's after hangin' up on me.

It is listening to her shrieking at her son that makes an impact on Jack.

> Margaret: My son … my eldest son my … my pride and joy …has done an awful thing.

Jack:	And you'd like to kick the little fucker into the middle of next week.
Margaret:	Yes!! Now that you mention it, that's *exactly* what I'd like to do.
Jack:	An' I s'pose he'll be sorry then, for what he did like. Nothin' like a few pucks in the head to knock a bit a' sense into a boy.
Margaret:	Just what are you suggesting? I'm warnin' ya now. I'm in no mood for insults. Isn't it bad enough that the whole parish will be laughin' behind me back besides havin dotin' old men insinuatin' that I'm a bad mother!

She does not wish to listen, intending to rush out in search of her son. Jack says:

> And do what … roar at him again? Tell him he's useless? That you're ashamed of him? Sit down there for yerself now my girl, and listen to an old man. D'ya know there's a lot to be said for gettin' old sometimes. Sure, the longer yer here the more ya see. And I'm sorry to say, that if ya barge out that door today yer takin' the first step down a long and lonely road.

This is the 'long and lonely road' he has taken himself, as the play later makes clear. Margaret's outburst may be unprofessional, but for Jack it brings vividly to mind that he has caused his own son to break off relations with him. This enables him to offer advice to her that he has never been able to take for himself and to listen sympathetically to her account of her feelings for her child.

Margaret:	You haven't much to say for yerself today.
Jack:	Sure, aren't you sayin' it all for me?
Margaret:	What?
Jack:	Yerra, sometimes you learn more from listenin' than talkin'. If I'd cottoned on to that many moons ago, I wouldn't be where I am now. Do ya still want to knock him into the middle of next week?
Margaret:	[Laughing] Maybe just as far as Sunday.

The family relations of both are in chaos, for reasons which, the play makes clear, they are themselves responsible – even if, given human fallibility and the pressures of their circumstances, we can understand how they made the errors they did.

Thus the play's moral position is clear. The faults of each are their own faults, but we can see how they came to have them. Jack was utterly committed to his land and the duty of caring for it, particularly compelling given the particular course of Irish history. He could not imagine how, to his son, the backbreaking toil of farming in the West seemed a thankless task. Margaret, as a single mother, is determined to give her son the education she has missed. Both are forcing on their children gifts they do not want and are unsuited to receive. It is the very ordinariness of these misapprehensions that adds force to the play; the protagonists are making mistakes that any of us can make. By reacting to each other's clumsiness and pain, they can achieve the changes of perspective they need, eventually forming a friendship that allows them to move forward somewhat.

This play is not sentimental enough to imply that the characters transform each other's lives entirely, but it does show some movement for them. Jack is able to release his daughter from giving up her ambitions as a dancer to look after him; perhaps there will be a degree of reconciliation with his own son. Thus older age is shown to be a time capable of generating insight and progress – progress that may depend crucially on interaction with other people. Jack and Margaret gain in the present by their friendship, and they develop some hope and the ability to regard the future more constructively. This is a more quotidian conception of advancing wisdom. Convincing as is the case for admiring, cherishing and learning from people like Edward, Seamus and Tim, Jack and Margaret may be closer to the way in which everyday wisdom evolves in social action.

Wisdom, humanism and older people

'Til kingdom come shows particularly clearly, therefore, how wise advice from the ultra-competent need not be a feature of wisdom. Wisdom may be found in social processes that help unwise people to propel each other into positions in which their perceptions are illuminated. This has been important for the democratic tradition; it casts light on Aristotle's observation that sometimes people who are individually less than wise can, through their interaction, reach conclusions that tend to the common good (*The politics* III 1281a: 39ff). It also confronts sociological problems of structure and agency, showing how people need each other in order to confront and resist the weight of circumstances. In the cases of wisdom we have examined here, wise individuals or interactions are remarkable for their success in moving others to positions in which they can see, feel or act in new ways.

So wisdom, in these cases at least, entails processes and results that cannot easily be segmented into separate categories. They involve forms of deliberation that have emotional, ethical and experiential facets rather than involving cognitive achievements alone. This has implications for the theory of communication needed to analyse wise interaction and for what we can learn about the impacts of wise interactions on the social settings in which they take place.

Accounts of wise interaction and communication can draw on analyses of 'rhetorical' communication that have themselves played important roles in the humanist tradition. For the most part, rhetoric in this context means communication (usually social, public communication) in circumstances of uncertainty, when information is fluctuating and incomplete, but where wise decisions still need to be made, and to conduce as far as possible to the individual as well as the public good. Aristotle's *Rhetoric*, for instance, offers a classical paradigm that meticulously analyses how the speaker's qualities ('ethos'), as shown in the argument he or she makes, act on and unite with the hearer's reactions (summarised under the term 'pathos'). This makes it possible to reach the best possible conclusion in the circumstances (Woerner, 1990). It is possible to develop basic features of this account to show how wise communication is constituted and takes effect (Edmondson et al, 2009). It is, strikingly, an account that allows us to explore how people move and develop their own and others' positions in the course of engaging with each other.

This idea of rhetorical communication, which is outstandingly sensitive to the social, ethical and political qualities shown by speaker and hearers, was adopted by Cicero and Quintilan, themselves among the founding fathers of the humanist tradition. Their communicative account of wisdom is humanistic – among other respects – in its awareness of people's dependence on each other in their pursuits of an educational ideal that potentially involves lifelong learning and development. It aims at forming a 'whole man' (in Cicero's terms) who is a 'good' person, who has accurate views of the world and who is capable of taking adequate decisions about it; this person is capable of giving advice in private or in public. The type of communication involved in this form of life is both personal and interpersonal. It aims at the truth and the common good, but its perception is inevitably influenced by what the speaker (or writer) and the audience believe to be the case, what they find valuable and how it affects them. Here the idea of movement and interaction is highlighted again. According to Petrarch, Aristotle could help you work out what you ought to do, but Cicero could make you want to do it (Grant, 1971: 27).[3]

Thus, taking account of human fallibility does not suggest that we should be unconcerned whether people are virtuous or not. The fact that attitudes, arguments and behaviour are so deeply affected by 'the whole man' implies that, for societies to function well, it is important to encourage people to be wise – encouraging and supporting people like Edward, Sean and Tim in their impacts on others. This highlights the relevance of 18th-century debates in which Adam Smith ([1790] 1976) among others drew on the views of Aristotle and other Greek writers to underline the vast influence of people's habitual practices on the decisions they take. Smith emphasised how industrial societies, though on the whole protecting vulnerable sections of the population more effectively than agrarian ones, necessarily encouraged illusions – for instance, that possessions and success conduce to more happiness than they really can. These illusions could lead to radical errors on the parts both of individuals and of societies. Counteracting such flaws presupposed promoting habits of character and judgement oriented more effectively to the common good.

This in its turn does not mean (nor was it taken by Smith to mean) that the effects of political economies on people's lives do not matter. When wise or unwise people assist each other to increased wisdom, it is a cause for celebration, but it cannot be expected to reverse all the effects of oppressive social structures. Jack and Margaret struggle to create their histories under conditions not of their making. Celebrating their resistance does not entail ignoring their circumstances. It remains crucial to take action in relation to political and economic circumstances that affect not only the resources available to older people but also what ageing in particular societies actually means (Phillipson, 1998). Humanistic approaches try to encompass and respond to these different aspects of human action, concentrating not on isolated segments but on human action in its entirety, within its social and political settings.

Lastly, they seek to do this in a way that allows for the particularity of wise interactions. The examples given of wise communication here are not compatible with blanket recipes based on moral or cultural expertise; exhortations from a standpoint of super-competence have oppressive effects. Fairhurst and Baines (2008) warn against the excessive demands implicit in a decontextualised stress on the marvels attained by some older people, which seem to oblige others to comparable accomplishments. In this volume, Jolanki deplores pressures on older people to defend their adult status by constant demonstrations of their health and hard work. The instances of wise interaction we have examined do not impose obligations of this kind. On the contrary, the interviewee who talked about Edward also mentioned Leo, another man striking for his wisdom:

> He wanted me to look at areas I'd closed my mind on. He actually cared about me as a human being. Then the fear went out of me, that I had to be as good as him.

The Ciceronian tradition stresses human beings' mutual dependence in a context of equality – 'There is no single thing so like another, so closely corresponding to it, as are all of us to one another' (*On duties* III: 5, 21). This approach involves a freedom and relaxation that helps to move recipients of wisdom to new perceptions; hence the surprising playfulness, even the mischief and danger, which formed part of ancient notions of wisdom (see Denning-Bolle, 1992). These qualities may cast some light on the quotation that opens this chapter, perhaps too on the affection for 'purple' ageing among older people explored in other chapters in this book. Wise people and processes are not only significant resources to individuals and society. They can also be astonishing, creative and fun.

Acknowledgements
Many thanks to members of the writer's classes on Ageing and Wisdom, taken by both Irish and North American students at NUI, Galway between 2003 and 2008 – in particular to Elaine McCaffrey. Many thanks also to those who provided

interview material about Edward, Sean and Tim, and to Angela Ryan for kind permission to quote from *'Til kingdom come.* Thanks too to Markus Woerner and Jane Pearce of the Galway Wisdom Project.

Notes

[1] The ethnographic examples in this chapter (except for the material on Sean Murphy, for which I thank Elaine McCaffrey) are taken from the author's observations and interviews in Conamara between 1998 and 2008. This particular interview took place in September 2004.

[2] The author of the play highlights the fact that carers working on wards like this are people 'with no nursing training' but who 'serve meals, assist in the cleaning of patients/their surroundings' and in general deal with 'people in this very vulnerable state' (personal correspondence).

[3] In Renaissance political debates, humanist writers such as Petrarch and Erasmus rightly emphasised the role of virtue in government. Just as importantly, Machiavelli tried to work out political systems that could function even in the absence of virtue, emphasising in the *Discourses* that conflict too can be crucial to decision making. Exploring Jack and Margaret's clashes can augment our understanding of how this might work. They propel each other out of some of their misapprehensions and free each other for more constructive behaviour.

References

Andersson, L. (ed) (2002) *Cultural gerontology*, Westport CT: Greenwood Press.

Aristotle (1945) *Rhetorica*, Oxford: Clarendon Press.

Aristotle (1981) *The politics*, London: Penguin.

Assmann, J. (1991) 'Weisheit, Schrift und Literatur im alten Aegypten', in A. Assmann (ed) *Weisheit*, Munich: Wilhelm Fink Verlag, pp 475-500.

Borup, M., Brown, N., Konrad, K. and van Lente, H. (2006) 'The sociology of expectations in science and technology', *Technology Analysis & Strategic Management*, vol 18, nos 3/4, pp 285-98.

Cicero, M.T. (1991) *On duties*, Cambridge: Cambridge University Press.

Denning-Bolle, S. (1992) *Wisdom in akkadian literature: Expression, instruction, dialogue*, Leiden: Ex Oriente Lux.

George, A. (1999) *The epic of Gilgamesh*, London: Penguin.

Grant, M. (1971) 'Introduction', in M.T. Cicero *Selected works*, London: Penguin, pp 7-32.

Edmondson, R. (2005) 'Wisdom in later life: ethnographic approaches', *Ageing in Society*, vol 25, no 3, pp 339-56.

Edmondson, R. (2008) 'Wisdom and older people in Ireland', *Senior People Education Studies*, vol 2, no 36, pp 73-6.

Edmondson, R. and Woerner, M.H. (forthcoming) *Wisdom: crises and resources*.

Edmondson, R., Pearce, J. and Woerner, M.H. (2009) 'Wisdom in clinical reasoning and medical practice', *Theoretical Medicine and Bioethics*, vol 30, in press.

Fairhurst, E. and Baines, S. (2008) 'Health and well-being of older individuals: a case study of a Positive Image of Ageing campaign and the production of a calendar', presentation at the 6th International Symposium on Cultural Gerontology, Lleida, Spain, October.

Gallagher, C. (2008) *The community life of older people in Ireland*, Oxford: Peter Lang.

Grant, M. (1971) 'Introduction' to M.T. Cicero, *Selected works*, London: Penguin, pp 7–32.

Machiavelli, N. (2003) *The discourses*, London: Penguin.

Nowotny, H., Scott, P. and Gibbons, M. (2001) *Re-thinking science – knowledge and the public in an age of uncertainty*, Cambridge: Polity Press.

Phillipson, C. (1998) *Reconstructing old age: New agendas in social theory and practice*, London: Sage Publications.

Smith, A. (1976) *The theory of moral sentiments*, Oxford: Oxford University Press.

Woerner, M.H. (1990) *Das Ethische in der Rhetorik des Aristoteles*, Freiburg: Alber Verlag.

TWELVE

Social practices, moral frameworks and religious values in the lives of older people

Carmel Gallagher

Introduction

This chapter aims to explore aspects of social norms and values in the everyday lives of older people in Ireland. It examines social practices and community participation among older people in one urban and one rural location,[1] focusing on people's leisure interests, their involvement in clubs, their religious practices, voluntary work undertaken by them, their relationships with kin, friends and neighbours, help given and help received, their use of social services and their informal interactions. Thus it seeks to throw light on how older people live from day to day in neighbourhoods and communities: how they interact, what their social activities are, and to what extent these activities contribute to the meaningfulness and satisfaction in their lives. Many theoretical and empirical approaches in sociology depict older people's experiences in very individualistic terms. This study showed, in contrast, that *communal* interactions are highly significant to the older people concerned and that social values are crucial to how they live their lives. These values are often embedded in religious beliefs, but we shall emphasise here the ways in which these give rise to forms of friendship that are central to sustaining older people's lives.

The chapter begins by exploring the religious practices and helping activities of older people in their localities, both through formal groups and informally. It emphasises the moral frameworks, explicit and implicit, in their lives. We then examine the links between religious belief/practice and social connectedness, highlighting the significance of religion for personal meaning and the importance of social ties embodied in religious communities. While connectedness itself is not examined in depth here (see Gallagher, 2008), we shall refer to many aspects of community, social capital and friendship. The key arguments are that friendship and community are central to the creation of a more habitable social world and that older people contribute significantly to the lives of others through what they do and how they interact. To this extent older people live according to wise social practices and these practices enhance both personal and communal well-being.

This study was based in two locations. Rathmore, the primary research site, is a suburban area of Dublin, and the secondary research site, Rathbeg, is a rural area in Donegal, in the North West of Ireland. A multi-method approach was used to seek insights into older people's lives in these locations. We carried out an interview-based survey of 165 older adults in Rathmore; and ethnographic observations were conducted extensively in many settings and centres in both localities. The range of social and communal settings involved included sport and social clubs, day centres, churches, voluntary groups, pubs, special interest groups and community events. Both quantitative and qualitative data were gathered in both locations so as to examine patterns and contexts of participation across a range of arenas.[2] What did they show us about social practices around religion, volunteering and informal helping?

Religious practices and beliefs in Rathmore and Rathbeg

Religious practice was strong and significant in the lives of the older people in Rathmore and Rathbeg. Not surprisingly, though, different approaches and emphases were evident in relation to religion and spirituality (note that religion and spirituality were not expressly distinguished here). Despite the limitations of survey data in eliciting the personal meaning of religion, respondents nonetheless provided insights into their beliefs and the importance of their religion in coping with life and as a source of ultimate meaning. Furthermore, ethnographic observations revealed the practices and contexts of public religious activities. Moral frameworks were strongly shaped by membership of Christian churches. However, participation in other groups was also associated with positive values. Indeed, it appeared that a plurality of groups – voluntary, leisure and community development as well as religious – enhanced people's experience of connectedness. Thus, social worlds of meaning were created through interactions in an array of groups, of which religious groupings formed part.

Churchgoing

Reflecting the religious composition of the population in Ireland,[3] the overwhelming majority of the sample in Rathmore were members of the Catholic Church, a handful were members of the Church of Ireland and a small percentage were not members of any church or were agnostic. Religious practice was clearly important to the vast majority. Levels of regular church attendance were very high; almost one third of respondents attended Mass daily while about 40% attended at least two or three times a week. A further 40% attended Mass or religious service weekly, making a cumulative total of almost 80% who attended Mass or religious service at least once every week. It is clear that this contrasts with overall trends of decline in religious practice in Ireland. According to surveys showing trends in weekly Mass attendance, there was a decline from 87% of Catholics to around 65% of Catholics who attend weekly Mass from 1981 to 1998 (Fahey, 2002). This pattern has accelerated, with a 2002 IMS survey showing weekly Mass attendance at 48% by September 2002 (*Irish Times*, 20 September, 2002). In terms of variation by age and geographical location, the earlier surveys found that Mass attendance varied from 94% of older people in one diocese outside Dublin to 50% of all Dubliners to 41% among all 18–24 year olds in the country (Fahey, 2002).

As in Rathmore, the majority religion in Rathbeg is Catholicism. There are two other active churches – Church of Ireland and Presbyterian.[4] There is a strong adherence to institutional religious practice among both the Catholic and Protestant communities. Many older people are daily Mass-goers. Respondents who could no longer attend Mass because of disability or infirmity said they missed going but, if they attended a day centre, Mass would often be included in the programme. In addition many parishes have parish radio, relaying Mass to people who are sick or housebound.

How important was religious belief?

In the Dublin survey, participants were asked whether religion or spirituality was important to them and any additional comments they made were also recorded. Almost 70% said they felt religion or spirituality was very important to them, 17.6% said that it was fairly important, while just less than 10% said it was not very important. It was clear that people had different approaches to religion and spirituality, some devotional and pious and others taking more questioning, reflective stances, and in some cases a critical and disenchanted attitude towards the Catholic Church. However, prayer seemed important to many, regular personal prayer, prayer in coping with difficulties and prayer through Mass-going and church attendance. Many older people say set prayers including the Rosary and prayers they learned as children, and they include in these prayers all their family and people they know who are ill or who have difficult personal predicaments. While high levels of Mass-going and prayer indicate strong belief among the older age group, it is also clear that these religious practices were developed from childhood. They were supported by rhythms of communal life and institutional forms of authority that do not prevail to the same extent in Irish society today.

At the same time current trends towards more private spirituality and secularism can be contrasted with the continuing popularity of forms of prayer such as Novenas. Novenas remain popular and have been incorporated into liturgies that attract high levels of 'voluntary' church attendance. For example, a Novena of Grace held in a church in Rathmore every March attracts a packed congregation on eight consecutive evenings.[5] While public religious ritual is much less in evidence in contemporary Ireland than it was in the early decades of the state from the 1920s on, a significant religious ritual that appears to be gaining in popularity is the annual graveyard Mass taking place in many towns and villages in Ireland. Family members gather at the graves of their deceased relatives while an open-air Mass is celebrated. In Rathbeg this event is attended by most villagers whether or not they are regular churchgoers. Relatives travel from other localities including a diaspora living in other parts of Ireland and abroad who often plan their holidays to coincide with the graveyard Mass. Family members and other relatives make a special effort to be there, showing that such rituals are important in acknowledging the life of a deceased person and their place within the family and community.

Religion and sociality

The importance of social ties embodied in religious communities is evident in the lives of older people in Rathmore and Rathbeg. For many people who went to Mass daily or a few times a week, Mass was built into the structure of their day and had a social aspect to it. One man who attended Mass two or three times a week said: 'It gets you on an early start and you meet people.' Another respondent who attended daily Mass said:

> I get up at 7.00 every morning. I know the people who live around [name of area]. After Mass every morning we have a chat. I meet fellas, hear the news, what's going on … they're well up to date on everything. One man I speak to – I don't know his name – I chat about Gaelic football with a neighbour on the 'X' Road and I don't know his name. (Interview, July 2002)

It might be argued that membership of a common moral community, in this case membership of the Catholic Church, makes intrusion in the form of greeting and chatting after Mass 'legitimate'. But there were many interactions such as these in other settings, which can be interpreted through a particular understanding of friendship. It will be argued here that such place-based friendships help to create enclaves that encourage tolerance and other-regarding behaviour.

Older people are particularly active in parish work. Indeed many of the respondents said that it was older people who do the bulk of work in parishes, and the researcher found much evidence of this. Church groups were the most common group in which respondents were involved, with 15.2% of the Rathmore sample helping in their church in some capacity. The types of work that the older adults did in their parishes included membership of parish councils, serving as Ministers of the Word (reading the scriptures at Mass) or Ministers of the Eucharist (giving out the Eucharist at Mass), cleaning the church, helping to prepare the Liturgy, helping with the church collection, singing in the church choir, helping with fund raising and so on.

In the study, involvement in a club or a formal social group was selected as one of five indicators of connectedness and many of the most connected respondents proved to be active in church groups. The social capital literature recognises the importance of both organisational and diffuse social ties for building up trust, generalised reciprocity and democratic practices. However, social capital theorists disagree on the exact nature of associational life that is said to be conducive to different forms of social capital. A very striking aspect of involvement in church-based groups among the older people in this study was how differentiated it was by social class. There was a strong statistical correlation between involvement in church-based groups and belonging to a white-collar background. Within the social capital literature, Hall (1999) has drawn attention to a widening difference between the levels of social capital available to the working classes and the middle classes, arguing that 'the forms of civic involvement available to the least privileged are more fragile in the face of secular trends' (Hall, 1999: 458). Such class differences in community participation might therefore be fruitful areas of attention in future research.

Religion, spirituality and well-being

While much work has been conducted on religion and health in the US, it is only recently that the social-gerontological and policy literature in the UK has begun to recognise the centrality of spirituality and religion to well-being in older people and to debate and reflect on the implications of this for care of older people[6] (see, for example, Jewell, 2004). In Scotland, for example, Harriet Mowat (2004) has explored the links between successful ageing and the idea of the spiritual journey. A longitudinal study in the UK, the Southampton Ageing Project, found evidence of decline in older people's allegiance to the Christian religion (Coleman et al, 2004). However, the fact that they ceased to be members of the Christian churches did not necessarily mean that they had lost their beliefs or that they lacked spiritual needs (Coleman et al, 2004: 186). Indeed, the authors argued that the churches should not take their older members' faith for granted and should not pass lightly over their obligations to their older members (Coleman et al, 2004: 185).

While spirituality has emerged as a separate subject of investigation from religion and is often contrasted positively with religion, especially in the UK literature, the two concepts are closely interrelated. Commentators such as Coleman have questioned the growing polarity between religion and spirituality, while Dillon and Wink's (2007) longitudinal study of older people in California has demonstrated that both church-centred religiousness and spiritual seeking enhance social and personal functioning for older adults. Coleman has suggested that, for older people in particular, talk of the spiritual is intimately associated with religion: 'Even getting them to speak about spiritual beliefs outside of the context of religious beliefs is not easy, although not impossible' (Coleman, 2006, quoted in Burke, 2007: 54).

In the Californian study the authors examined the consequences of being religious and being spiritual. Dillon and Wink's (2007) study suggests that religion, which was defined by belief in God, prayer and attendance at communal worship, is closely related to connectedness with other people and sense of community. The authors found that spirituality, which was defined by non-tradition-centred beliefs, sense of connectedness with a sacred other and involvement in practices such as meditation, was closely related to personal development and inner awareness. They also found that religion was positively associated with several dimensions of everyday functioning, with concern for others and a commitment to the social good, with life satisfaction, and with cushioning against some of the adversity and loss associated with old age (Dillon and Wink, 2007: 215-16). Those who were religious showed higher levels of life satisfaction than did their non-religious or spirituality-seeking peers. Furthermore, being religious provided a strong buffer against depression. However, both religious individuals and spiritual seekers preserved their sense of control in the face of adversity (Dillon and Wink, 2007: 204). Dillon and Wink found that both religious and spiritual individuals participated in a greater range of social activities and personal hobbies, and more frequently, than those who were neither religious nor spiritual. Furthermore, the positive association between religiousness or spiritual seeking and everyday purposeful activities was independent of good physical and mental health (Dillon and Wink, 2007: 214-15).

The significance of religion in the lives of older people

For many older people in Irish society, religion is interwoven into their lives and can be observed in their public religious practices, their private prayer, their use of language and their understanding of religion as a resource to cope with adversity. In an interview in Rathbeg an older resident spoke about deceased members of the community known to both him and the researcher. After each deceased person's name he invariably added: 'God be good to him and all those belonging to him' in a natural way that suggested that faith and religion were not compartmentalised in his life. Inglis (1998) has commented on the embeddedness of religion in everyday life in Irish society in the past. He conceptualises the declining position of the Catholic Church as a dilution of the moral influence of the Church, which symbolically dominated Irish life in a pervasive way (Inglis, 1998: 18). However, Cassidy (2002) has reviewed the impact of modernity on religious beliefs and practices in Ireland based on survey data related to the period 1980 to 2000. He finds evidence of significant decline in three areas, namely, the belief in the moral authority of the Catholic Church, attendance at religious services and confidence in the Catholic Church in Ireland. However, he also finds little evidence of the growth of secularisation of Irish society leading to a loss of a sense of the spiritual, or to a decline in either the belief in traditional core Christian doctrines or the sense of the importance of God, religion or prayer in the lives of Irish people (Cassidy, 2002: 40-1).

Religious practice is no longer enforced in the same way in a pluralistic urbanised Ireland by the norms of small communities or by the rhythms of communal life. However, it retains both social and personal significance for the majority of older people and for significant numbers of the general population in Ireland. It seemed clear in this study that people who attend Mass regularly see it as giving consistent meaning to their lives. Moreover, the fact that older people who cannot attend Church in their locality will participate through televised or radio Mass, or seek opportunities to attend Mass at a day-care centre, clearly suggests that such religious practices are deeply meaningful to our respondents. However, it is clear from the UK experience and from trends in religious decline in Irish society that older people's adherence to religion and the cultural resource that religion represents should not be taken for granted. To explore this cultural resource in more detail, we shall now turn to the interconnections between religion and how older people engaged with others.

Religious values and altruism

As we have already indicated, churches have been seen in the social capital literature as strong repositories of positive communal values (see, for example, Gill, 1999; Davie, 2000; Herbert, 2003). Putnam (2000: 66-7) argues that, in the US, religiosity rivals education as a powerful correlate of most forms of civic engagement. Research in Britain by Gill (1999) finds a statistically significant correlation between participation in voluntary service groups and churchgoing. Furthermore, in Gill's work the forms of voluntary activity most closely related to membership of a religious group are services, residents'/tenants' associations, women's groups, political party, pensioners and trade union groups. In contrast, sports and social club membership are least closely related to religious group membership.

Volunteering and churchgoing

Approximately 30% of older people in the study of Rathmore and Rathbeg did some form of voluntary work, mainly charitable, church or community development. This is somewhat higher than the rates suggested in other studies; for example, a report on volunteering in Ireland suggested a rate of 25% for this age group (National Committee on Volunteering in Ireland, 2002: 16-17). In the present study, while there was a statistically significant correlation between churchgoing and volunteering, it was not as strong or as clear-cut as in Gill's (1999). Older people who went to church two or three times a week were the group most likely to volunteer while those who went on a daily basis or once a week were equally likely to volunteer. Those who were irregular or non-churchgoers were less likely to volunteer.

It appears that the same values and dispositions are often involved in religious practice and volunteering. This may be more pronounced in Britain where churchgoing is a minority activity,[7] and belonging to and practising one's religion is perhaps more intentional. In the present study older people who go to church a couple of times a week may be displaying a more purposive approach to how they choose to spend their time than either daily or weekly churchgoers. Perhaps it suggests an effect of being a person who, while very committed to church, is measured in their religiosity, neither formulistic nor pious in their religious practice. While the value base of Christianity strongly urges practical social concern for others, undertaking voluntary work is a conscious action that involves making room for it among one's other concerns.

Helping and positive neighbouring

Apart from formal voluntary work, the extent to which older people in the study helped others informally was very striking. Positive neighbouring was strongly evident in both Rathmore and Rathbeg. Older people both gave each other and received considerable amounts of practical help, and helping activities contributed to satisfaction with life both for givers and receivers. Forty per cent of the sample said they helped someone outside their own household while 14.5% said they received informal help with daily tasks from someone outside their household. Neighbours were the most frequent recipients of the respondents' help, followed by their own children or grandchildren. Help that the study participants gave to their neighbours ranged from providing companionship and giving lifts to personal care and house-maintenance tasks.[8] Many people spoke about the practical help and support they received from neighbours in their day-to-day lives. A female interviewee who lived alone said:

> They [neighbours] call into me ... I can't go out. One phones me every night. They're very good to me. (Interview, June 2002)

A recurring theme in the interviews in Rathmore and Rathbeg was how helpful, considerate, dependable and friendly people's neighbours were. One-to-one relationships with neighbours and friends involving support and practical help were vital for those experiencing incapacity and those living alone. However, it was clear that positive relationships with neighbours enhanced life both for those with and those without significant kin or friendship networks.

In addition to overt forms of helping, there were many examples of older people giving encouragement to each other in unobtrusive ways that demonstrated kindness and understanding. This was more than general valuing of good neighbours or feelings of general goodwill towards those in one's locality. In one neighbourhood, a group of women looked after their neighbour who was developing symptoms of dementia by supporting her in continuing normal social interaction. They did this by unobtrusively monitoring her movements in the neighbourhood and inviting her to accompany them on short trips to the shops and to social events. They encouraged her to continue to host a small prayer service in her home and then helped her to provide hospitality at it.

Explicit and implicit Christian values

The moral basis of neighbourliness can be understood as an expression of reciprocity (Bulmer, 1986: 10) and/or as an expression of the Christian injunction to 'Love your neighbour'. The relationship between altruism, reciprocities and neighbouring has been explored in depth by Bulmer and Abrams in their work on neighbouring (Bulmer, 1986). In his empirical work on Good Neighbouring schemes, Abrams argues that altruism is closely associated with reciprocities and entails benefits to the giver as well as the receiver. In a slightly nuanced explanation that introduces the idea of generosity, Bulmer suggests that there is an 'inexpressible' reciprocity involved; while his Good Neighbours got as much as they gave they found it very difficult to give an account of what exactly it was that they received:

> Belief in the altruistic nature of the action and attachment to a norm
> of beneficence as distinct from a norm of reciprocity appeared to be
> crucial conditions upon which the acts of giving and helping depended.
> (Bulmer, 1986: 108)

In the Christian tradition, the concepts of charity and love call for a dimension of 'gratuity' in the Christian person's relations with others (Martin, 2006). The Christian ideal of gratuitous love is close to the 'norm of beneficence' that Bulmer identifies.

Reciprocities are not a simple question of 'give and take' involving calculated exchanges. Both Abrams and Bulmer demonstrate how both specific and generalised reciprocities can be understood in terms of a series of reciprocal relationships where the person receiving care actively responds and stores up basic experiences and ethical obligations, which may emerge later on in altruistic behaviour on their part or be given expression in other sets of reciprocal relationships. Bulmer makes the further suggestion that generalised reciprocity among neighbours might develop into commitment and friendship. In Rathmore and Rathbeg, there were many examples of informal helping that involved a considerable commitment to non-immediate relatives, neighbours and friends. The helping activities of the respondents went well beyond the everyday sociability and civilities of communal life. It was evident that helpers had a strong sense of affinity with others and a strong sense of obligation consistent with the Christian injunction to 'Love your neighbour'. It was also evident that helpers got satisfaction from their work and from the friendships that were created.

A resident of Rathbeg, who was a committed practising Catholic and retired nurse, described her motives for nursing a sick cousin over several years in strong altruistic terms:

> I looked after [person's name] when she was ill, a cousin of mine. I
> looked after her for years – she had several small strokes … I took it as
> my duty I suppose, maybe because she didn't have anyone else. I was
> full-time able to do it and I did it … No, I didn't even think about it
> … I mean I just did it and that was all – no second thoughts about it.
> (Interview, March 2001)

Many volunteers displayed social concern in Christian terms, although this was not the only factor associated with volunteering. For some interviewees their Christianity was explicit in the terms in which they spoke about their work. One man in Rathmore, who made a significant contribution in his locality by organising social events and by improving the environment through cultivating plants and flowers, appeared motivated by a strong sense of Christian duty. He spoke about how he had coped with considerable personal difficulties and the degree to which he was motivated by a strong sense of God in his life. The religious minister in the parish described the man's work in religious/vocational terms as follows: 'God bless [name of man's] Ministry at [name of area]'. Other residents cited the man's work as an example of positive involvement in the community and made comments such as:

> There's one man in the complex and there's not enough hours in the day for all he does.

For others, it did not become clear to what extent they were motivated by their religious beliefs, but their Christian or humanistic ethos was implicit in how attuned they were to the lives of other people in their locality and in their willingness to undertake practical work to help them. One of the main organisers of a public/voluntary initiative to develop sheltered housing and day-care facilities for older people in the environs of Rathbeg spoke about his reasons for taking on the task:

> I saw lovely older people who felt in the way in their own homes …
> Rejection is the worst thing that can happen to anyone … I wanted
> to make sure people felt wanted again and never feel a nuisance. They
> feel they are important now – instead of a nursing home they got a
> new life and made new friends. (Interview, August 2003)

It is not possible to say to what extent this man was religious or what his personal belief-system involved.[9] However, his practical concern for his 'neighbour' was strongly evident in the terms in which he spoke about his work, and his interactions and friendship with the day-centre users were clearly a source of great personal satisfaction to him. His concern and commitment were of major social benefit in a scattered rural community, particularly for the older people who attended the day centre or lived in the sheltered accommodation. Previously such individuals would have remained somewhat isolated in their homes, without peer companionship, or would have had to go to residential care in a place some distance from their own locality. In the study we observed many examples of impressive day-care and residential facilities that resulted at least in part from the vision, commitment and energy of volunteers in Rathbeg.[10]

Friendship in Rathmore and Rathbeg

The concept of friendship emerged as a central idea in interpreting the nature of connectedness among older people in Rathmore and Rathbeg. All the different types of friendship documented, including long-standing one-to-one friendships, friendships among club members and more generalised friendship among neighbours, appeared to involve the development of shared moral understandings. As well as fun and sociability, which were key processes observed in many groups, participants in senior citizens' clubs, active retirement associations, church groups and community groups displayed kindness and a sense of obligation towards others. For example, the Secretary of an active retirement association (ARA) in Rathmore spoke about how she encouraged quieter people to participate at whatever level they were comfortable with. She praised members who, she said, were always supportive and protective of each other and added that they gave particular attention to anyone who was demonstrating signs of early dementia.

A form of generalised friendship was evident in many daily interactions in Rathmore and Rathbeg. Edmondson (2001) has previously described a form of 'distributed intimacy' in her ethnographic work in the West of Ireland. She suggests that communicative forms associated with traditional societies mean that emotional satisfaction may be derived from daily contacts spread throughout the locality in which one lives and does not necessarily rest only on intimate and personal relationships (Edmondson, 2001: 68). The Rathmore and Rathbeg study did emphasise the significance of cultural practices involving greeting and conversing with others in one's locality whom one does not know intimately, though we would interpret it somewhat differently.

These findings also suggest a contrasting understanding of friendship to that advanced by some writers, including Pahl (2000), for example, who views friendship as 'a relationship built upon the whole person that aims at a psychological intimacy' and that has 'connotations of freedom, choice, individuality and, crucially, subversion.' (Pahl, 2000: 163, 166). The elements of friendship identified in this study appear closer to the traditional idea of friendship as developed by Aristotle and Cicero and understood in the Christian concept of 'personhood', involving an essential moral component (Bellah et al, 1996: 115). On the basis of the present study, it is suggested that friendship among older people is best seen as a relational and multidimensional concept involving a number of processes such as fun, sociability, solidarity, obligation, respect and acknowledgement.

Moral values and connectedness

The study found that interactions within localities through helping activities, religious/voluntary groups, leisure activities and informal interactions help to create social and moral worlds where people experience a sense of involvement, belonging and fulfilment. Through dense reciprocal relationships involving kin, neighbours and friends, as well as through the work of intermediate groups such as voluntary groups, clubs and church-based groups, enclaves of sociality are co-created where older people experience a sense of worth and purpose. It can be argued that, for life to be satisfying, people must be connected within enclaves of sociality that provide opportunities for sociability and friendship, for learning and personal development and for giving as well as receiving (Gallagher, 2008: 319).

Activities such as volunteering and informal helping involve communicating an agreed set of expectations about appropriate standards of behaviour and thus help to create a more habitable social world. Some older people stand out as 'creators of community' in both their everyday interactions and their broader social concern for others in the wider community. The idea of 'good example' was suggested by the lives of many individuals who were exemplars of positive neighbouring, and many people explicitly and spontaneously acknowledged the work of such individuals in their localities. Putnam, in his work on declining social capital in the US, has emphasised the interactive effects between friendship, reciprocities and good example in his discussion of the ripple effects of 'doing good' (Putnam, 2000: 121-2). Furthermore, he suggests that, while doing good *for* other people may be laudable, it is not part of the definition of social capital. It is, he suggests, when we do things *with* others that we reinforce bonds within the community (Putnam, 2000: 116-17).

Charles Taylor (1994) has argued that a sense of what is good needs to be articulated and given expression so that people can have possibilities for making moral choices (Taylor, 1994). A vision of what was good is certainly articulated in many of the groups in Rathmore and Rathbeg, in particular social clubs, voluntary/community groups and church groups. Positive moral orientations were also expressed through common cultural practices such as greeting others, social practices at funerals, helping at times of difficulty and so on. Such practices can be regarded as representing collective wisdom – a cultural resource that entails both personal and communal benefits. From a public policy point of view it can be argued that a good life in old age must be understood in terms of community – that older people, regardless of any limitations of physical or mental capacity, must have the opportunity to remain involved with others and engaged in meaningful activity (Gallagher, 2006: 70).

Summary: a culture of friendship

In the course of compiling rich details of the lives of older people in two geographic localities in Ireland, we have found evidence of strong moral and religious values in the lives of older people. These are embedded in social practices that arguably are the foundations of connectedness. Contrary to suggestions that Ireland is now a secular, post-Christian society, we have highlighted the influence of religion as a source of ultimate meaning, as well as the importance of social ties generated through common membership of Christian churches. Christian values, either explicit or implicit, were evident in the lives of those who helped others.

What constituted a good life for older people in the study were social interactions and helping activities involving family, neighbours and friends. Being connected with others in one's locality or community through informal helping, voluntary activities or communal leisure was associated with satisfaction with life and sense of purpose. Informal and formal helping were key aspects of connectedness that contributed to satisfaction and enjoyment of life for givers and recipients alike.

Older people in the study were strongly other-regarding. The contribution made by individual older people was very significant; they sometimes even provided key inputs to public policy initiatives. While some stood out in terms of their voluntary and community work, it was not essential to be a social activist to influence the lives of others positively. Small meaningful interactions enhanced the lives of older people involved in such reciprocities. The moral and sociable aspects of friendship were highlighted in the types of friendship observed in Rathmore and Rathbeg. People valued the kindness and helpfulness of neighbours that was demonstrated through many helping tasks, visiting and support at times of particular difficulties. In many cases neighbours were friends. Friendships in socio-spatial settings involved obligations that appeared to arise out of sharing life space, habitual interactions and knowing and understanding one another's situation.

Cultural practices such as greeting and chatting and meeting for communal religious or social celebrations represent a form of collective wisdom: they engender behaviour that is important to living good lives, both for the actors concerned and for those affected by what they do. Here locally based groups provide important contexts for positive sociality. Friendship creates enclaves of sociality where individuals experience a sense of belonging and purpose. We might therefore argue that friendship and community are key to the achievement of a good life and that older people through their wise interactions and social practices are a vital resource in our society.

Notes
[1] 'The participation of older people in their communities', PhD study, National University of Ireland, Galway, 2005, based on explorations carried out between 2000 and 2005.

[2] The data was integrated to develop typologies of the main ways in which older adults in Rathmore and Rathbeg are connected within their communities and an index of connectedness was developed. The chapter will not present data on these overall measures, but detailed findings are available in Gallagher (2008). Note that, here, the quantitative data is derived from the Rathmore survey while the qualitative data is derived from both study areas.

[3] The 2002 Census classified the population of Ireland by religious denomination as follows. Catholic: 88.4%, Protestant denominations (Church of Ireland being the

largest): 3.8%, Christian (unspecified): 0.6%, other religions: 1.6%, no religion/not stated: 5.6% (2002 Census of Population, CSO).

[4] While membership of these Protestant churches is proportionately small, both churches have regular church services and members are active in church-related work. The Protestant church is strong in Donegal compared with its overall numerical strength in the Republic of Ireland, making up 10.8% of the population of the county (Derry and Raphoe Action, 2001: 2).

[5] A Novena is a sequence of nine days' prayer, usually involving Mass each day, with a themed reflection and set of readings running through the period. Novenas of Grace are associated with the life of St Francis Xavier. In rural Ireland, Novenas are fairly large-scale social events.

[6] Within the Christian churches in the UK, initiatives have been undertaken by the Christian Council on Ageing and the Methodist Homes for the Aged Care Group (Jewell, 2004: 13-14). The non-denominational organisation, Age Concern, England has also developed initiatives to respond to the spiritual needs of older people in a secular society (Burke, 2007).

[7] In the 1950s about 50% of the population of England attended some form of religious service every week in contrast with about 10% today, and this includes all faith communities (Burke, 2007: 4).

[8] Visiting was the most frequently mentioned helping activity – for example, visiting a neighbour who had reduced mobility or visiting a neighbour in hospital. Tasks done for neighbours ranged from instrumental help to more general 'watch and ward' activities. Instrumental help given to neighbours included doing household chores, running errands such as collecting medical prescriptions, carrying household refuse bins in and out, giving lifts, looking after a pet, shopping, providing a meal, and doing maintenance jobs such as gardening or repair work. Many spoke about helping if a neighbour was ill.

[9] This informant was not a survey participant and was not questioned about his religious beliefs or practices.

[10] Social care services for older people in Ireland are delivered through a mixed economy of welfare model. Many day-care services are provided through a partnership between public bodies and voluntary bodies. A fuller description of such centres can be found in Gallagher (2008).

References

Bellah, R., Madsen, R., Sullivan, W., Swidler, A. and Tipton, S. (1996) *Habits of the heart: Individualism and commitment in American life*, Berkeley, CA: University of California Press.

Bulmer, M. (1986) *Neighbours: The work of Philip Abrams*, Cambridge: Cambridge University Press.

Burke, G. (2007) *Spirituality: Roots and routes*, London: Age Concern.

Cassidy, E. (2002) 'Modernity and religion in Ireland: 1980-2000', in E. Cassidy (ed) *Measuring Ireland: Discerning values and beliefs*, Dublin: Veritas, pp17-45.

Coleman, P.G. (2006) 'Spirituality, health and ageing', David Hobman Memorial Lecture, Age Concern England and King's College London, 30 January.

Coleman, P.G., Ivani-Chalian, C. and Robinson, M. (2004) 'Religious attitudes among British older people: stability and change in a 20-year longitudinal study', *Ageing and Society*, vol 24, no 2, pp 167-88.

Davie, G. (2000) *Religion in modern Europe*, Oxford: OUP.

Derry and Raphoe Action (2001) *Protestants in community life – findings from a Co. Donegal survey*, Raphoe: Derry and Raphoe Action.

Dillon, M. and Wink, P. (2007) *In the course of a lifetime: Tracing religious belief, practice and change*, Berkeley, CA: University of California Press.

Edmondson, R. (2001) 'Studying civic culture ethnographically and what it tells us about social capital', in P. Dekker and E.M. Uslaner (eds) *Social capital and participation in everyday life*, London and New York: Routledge, pp 59-72.

Fahey, T. (2002) 'Is atheism increasing? Ireland and Europe compared', in E. Cassidy (ed) *Measuring Ireland: Discerning values and beliefs*, Dublin: Veritas, pp 46-66.

Gallagher, C. (2006) 'Social policy and a good life in old age', in E. O'Dell (ed) *Older people in modern Ireland: Essays on law and policy*, Dublin: First Law, pp 48-71.

Gallagher, C. (2008) *The community life of older people in Ireland*, Oxford: Peter Lang.

Gill, R. (1999) *Churchgoing and christian ethics*, Cambridge: Cambridge University Press.

Hall, P. (1999) 'Social capital in Britain', *British Journal of Political Science*, vol 29, no 3, pp 417-61.

Herbert, D. (2003) *Religion and civil society – rethinking public religion in the contemporary world*, London: Ashgate.

Inglis, T. (1998) *Moral monopoly – the rise and fall of the Catholic Church in modern Ireland*, Dublin: Gill and Macmillan.

Jewell, A. (2004) 'Nourishing the inner being – a spirituality model', in A. Jewel (ed) *Ageing, spirituality and well-being*, London: Jessica Kingsley, pp 11-26.

Martin, Rev D. (2006) 'In a changing Ireland has social care practice left religious and spiritual values behind?', address to seminar, 3 April, Centre for Social and Educational Research, Dublin Institute of Technology.

Mowat, H. (2004) 'Successful ageing and the spiritual journey', in A. Jewel (ed) *Ageing, spirituality and well-being*, London: Jessica Kingsley, pp 42-57.

National Committee on Volunteering in Ireland (2002) *Tipping the balance – report and recommendations to Government on supporting and developing volunteering in Ireland*, Dublin: National Committee on Volunteering in Ireland.

Pahl, R. (2000) *On friendship*, Cambridge: Polity.

Putnam, R. (2000) *Bowling alone: The collapse and revival of American community*, New York: Simon and Schuster.

Taylor, C. (1994) *Sources of the self – the making of the modern identity*, New York: University of Cambridge.

THIRTEEN

'Woo-hoo, what a ride!' Older people, life stories and active ageing

Lorna Warren and Amanda Clarke

Introduction

A popular email is currently being widely circulated:

> Life should NOT be a journey to the grave with the intention of arriving safely in an attractive and well preserved body, but rather to skid in sideways, chocolate in one hand, wine in the other, body thoroughly used up, totally worn out and screaming 'WOO-HOO what a ride!'

What is appealing about this message is its explicit lay challenge to exhortations towards active and healthy ageing: looking after yourself is all fine and good, but what is more important is to indulge and have fun. Of course, few of us live our later lives in terms of this either/or choice. Most of us would like to think that we work at both. Neither is our journey to the grave unaccompanied, but is influenced by those we travel with or meet along the way. Nevertheless, policy echoes both the individualistic focus and the implied dichotomy (Kemp and Denton, 2003), only this time without the fun. The opposite of 'active' and 'healthy' ageing in later life is seen as a negative dependency.

This chapter develops further our exploration of the notion of active ageing, questioning the limited understanding of this central concept in current policy and research on ageing (ESRC, no date: 2). Elsewhere (Clarke and Warren, 2007), we argue that older people experience active ageing in a diversity of ways, both shared and unique, that are not necessarily captured in existing research, showing how active ageing is important to looking ahead beyond retirement, as well as being understood in terms of people's pasts. This chapter focuses on understanding active ageing as a relational experience. It is based on Clarke's series of biographical interviews with older people, central to which is the belief that to understand ageing we have to examine older people's experiences in the much broader context of their lives (Clarke, 2001). Here we demonstrate that, whether we go for 'attractive and well preserved' or 'worn out and screaming', choices we make about activity in later life are influenced, and sometimes constrained, by a sense of freedom. But they also place value on participation in wider society.

Background

'Active ageing' took off as a policy slogan in the 1990s, against a backdrop of population ageing and labour market change (Walker, 2006). The desire to limit the social protection costs associated with the trend towards early exit from the labour force in most developed countries started to intensify as the post-war baby boom generation headed towards retirement. At the same time, businesses began to recognise the need to adjust to workforce ageing, not least to maximise recruitment potential, while legislation set out to tackle the endemic ageism in labour markets. However, although emphasis by the Organisation for Economic Co-operation and Development (OECD, 1999) on the economic aspects of active ageing has tended to dominate policy, other governmental and policy organisations have offered more comprehensive definitions, usefully summarised by Davey (2002). Alongside working longer and retiring later, the European Union (1999a, 1999b) has included being active after retirement, engaging in health-sustaining activities, and being as self-reliant and involved as possible as key elements of active ageing for individuals. The global focus of the World Health Organization (WHO) has looked beyond physical well-being and independence to social justice and citizenship (WHO, 1999). Similarly, the UK Better Government for Older People (BGOP) programme linked lifelong learning, community involvement and volunteering to 'active ageing' in addition to employment (Hayden and Boaz, 2000). These findings were reflected in the government document *Opportunity Age* (DWP, 2005), where involvement in local decision making, learning and volunteering are identified as important for older people. In other words, 'active ageing' is not construed simply in terms of productivity and health in these policy ideas, but incorporates the concepts of self-reliance, mutual obligation and social responsibility (Walters, 1997).

Nevertheless, government approaches to active ageing still tend to be concerned predominantly with 'productive ageing' and workforce participation (Clarke and Warren, 2007). Moreover, with the exception of the BGOP programme – albeit itself largely a consultative exercise (Warren and Maltby, 2000) – the involvement of older people in defining expectations for active healthy ageing are typically limited (Howarth, 1998; Reed et al, 2003). Policy's focus on individuals preparing for and acting as 'retirees' (Rudman, 2006) means that older people's concern with 'achieving ordinary things in life' (Joseph Rowntree Foundation, 2004: 39) is typically overlooked.

This chapter explores the fit between discourses of active ageing in policy and older people's views of possibilities for being and acting. It shows that, rather than promoting a promised personal 'freedom', albeit contingent on relentless projects of self-reflection and improvement (Rudman, 2006: 181), active ageing as it is thought about by our interviewees actually depends on a perceived sense of freedom that older people may subsequently choose to use in helping others. The rich heterogeneity and subtle nuances of older people's responses regarding active ageing have important implications for policy rationale, devised as it is within dominant frameworks of productivity, income and health.

Processes in 'ordinary' later life

Our evidence is derived from a previously documented in-depth, life-story study of 23 informally recruited older people (13 women and ten men) living in South Yorkshire, UK from 1997-99 (Clarke, 2001; Clarke and Warren, 2007). Using biographical approaches to capture the life stories of 'ordinary' older people (Hazan, 1994; Midwinter, 1991), we can understand more fully the ways in which diverse experiences and attitudes *throughout life* may affect individual circumstances and colour perceptions in older age (Bernard and Meade, 1993). Biographical approaches allow for the possibility that the later decades need not be a period of sickness and decline, but neither are they necessarily characterised by health, liberation and 'refurbishment' (Blaikie, 1999). Instead, viewing later life as a process opens up diverse possibilities for ongoing development and engagement or, conversely, withdrawal and disengagement from society (Slater, 1995). Rather than guiding individuals along set paths (Chambers, 1994), biographical methods provide people with the opportunity to talk about what is important to them. This allowed the themes we comment on below to emerge from participants' own life stories.

Ideas and contradictions

This chapter is organised under the main headings of 'freedoms' and 'helping others', chosen because they were two of the strongest themes to emerge from interviews. Participants clearly were very much engaged in the present, talking of the freedoms they enjoyed in later life compared to their younger years. Ironically, in light of the current emphasis on active ageing and paid/productive employment, freedom was engendered not only by a sense of contentment but also by decreasing familial and occupational commitments, which allowed them to pursue old as well as new activities and roles. Although some still were very much engaged in caring roles (as parents, grandparents or spouses), men and women discussed how much they enjoyed life since external demands and social pressures had lessened (see Thompson et al, 1990; Bamford, 1994; Coleman et al, 1998).

However, participants also referred to some of the more negative experiences of later life, mainly due to a decline in physical capabilities and financial constraints. Yet these did not always impact on individuals' everyday lives in anticipated ways. Rather than fostering passivity, as structural approaches to ageing emphasise, participants showed great resilience and determination in living their lives *despite* such constraints. Further, they spoke overwhelmingly of their participation in society – through the numerous activities in which they were engaged and the help that they offered to others.

Freedoms

Freedom from caring for others

Those who had cared substantially for others in the past appeared to value the freedom from caring later life had brought. Reginald Green (78) explained that his wife had suffered from mental health issues for the majority of their married life. He had been the main carer for their two children, as well as holding down a full-time job as a travelling salesman. As a result, Reginald felt that he had changed: 'I became very introverted.' After his retirement, his wife left him and he now lived alone. However:

> One morning, when I was walking past a little second-hand shop, the owner said, 'There's Reginald, he's whistling.' I had reverted. Since my wife left me it's as though a load has been lifted off me. Whilst I still see her regularly, I couldn't live with her again. I am back in personality to what I was when I was younger.

This freedom was despite the fact that his lack of finances was a worry to him and he was due to go into hospital for cancer surgery. He could now express himself and 'please [his] damn self' (see Thompson et al, 1990), leaving the kitchen looking like a bombsite and choosing instead to read, which cost him little since he 'raided' second-hand bookshops, and to sit as a model for a sculptor. Despite severe breathing problems, he also continued to work in his son's shop every morning and went to the pub every night for a pint.

Freedom from occupational constraints

While Reginald chose to staff the shop phone for his son, other participants talked a great deal about the freedom later life brought in terms of being released from occupational constraints (see Thompson et al, 1990) and subsequent regular demands on their time (see Bamford, 1994) – or living life to a clock, as Peter White (72) described it. Even those who led very active lives said that this was very different from the busyness of their working lives. George and Anne Daley (aged 78 and 79 respectively), who always found it hard to find time to be interviewed, said:

> When we were working, slogging away at school and that sort of thing, we hadn't the time to devote to some of the things that we have done since, our personal interests and so on.

Tom Howarth (77) recalled:

> When I was selling insurance, the life rather lived me in those days and perhaps now I'm living life a bit more, now that there's nothing I have to do in the future.

Freedom to enjoy activities and to learn

After Gladys Peters (93) had retired in her 70s, she and her husband were able to take a holiday together for the first time in their married lives. However, participants' interests and activities did not always necessarily require a great deal of energy or expense. The wide range of activities mentioned included gardening, reading, going to the gym, painting, attending church or other religious activities, walking in the countryside, drinking in the pub, attending classes at college, sitting as a sculptor's model (see Thompson et al, 1990; Carnegie Inquiry, 1993).

Enjoyment also came from spending time with family and friends (see Matthews, 1986; Jerrome, 1989) or from simply observing life (see Carnegie Inquiry, 1993; Coleman et al, 1998). William Buxton (79) spent most days at African-Caribbean centres for older people. He said, 'We just play dominoes, laugh and talk. It's all homely like, you know.' Participants also talked about enjoying contact with younger people. Maureen Williams said that she mixed 'mainly with younger women' at her church and Reginald Green said he preferred to talk with the students at his local pub because they were 'more interesting' than his peers.

Peter White (72) said that he now appreciated the 'simple things' in life more. 'You don't appreciate nature as much when you're younger. You haven't got time. Whereas now, I've got interested in wild flowers and walking in the countryside.' Some participants enjoyed gardening, particularly Tom Howarth who lived in the country and the Daleys who gardened together, as a couple. Even participants without a garden, such as Maureen Williams who lived in a flat, said that they enjoyed planting their window boxes and tubs. Women participants also enjoyed knitting and sewing. Gladys Peters (93) had learned to crochet at the age of 70 and spent her time crocheting for charity and making gifts for friends. She described a typical day:

> I'm busy all the time. I get up and get myself ready. I wash the pots and then get down and have a couple of hours in the morning on my sewing work, two hours lay down in the afternoon and then start again, work on my crocheting until I go to bed.

Similarly, Betty Lomas (90) had taught herself to paint watching *Painting with Ashley* on television:

> I was getting on for 70 when I took up painting. Everybody has got something they can do. I didn't know I could paint. I've always said

it, 'If you've got a talent, if there's anything you do, and you know it's there, and you can do it, you must do it.' And I did.

Due to mobility problems, Betty could not leave her flat on her own, so she spent some of her time indoors painting and drawing – something that she had always wanted to do but had never had the time in the past. Betty also enjoyed watching people from her window:

> It's lovely here, I see people I recognise. There's a man and a woman
> ... he's got a Scottie dog and she holds the dog while he goes to the
> paper shop and that little dog never misses looking where he is going
> to and coming from. And there is a girl who goes past in the morning
> ... I can see her because she peroxides her hair. And I see the children
> walking to school.

Participants also talked about discovering new or neglected activities and spoke of returning to learning – for example, Dipti Sur (70): 'I go to English classes, sewing classes and exercise classes. I enjoy going there, it's not something I've done before.' George Daley said: 'Life's still an open book. As a young child looks at the world with starry eyes, we're still to some extent like that, we've a lot to learn.' Despite the fact that Anne Daley was suffering from a terminal illness and could catch infections very easily, George and his wife participated in numerous activities in retirement, pursuing their long-standing interest in social and political issues. These included caring for injured badgers, rambling, attending classical music concerts, philosophy classes and campaigning for Amnesty International and Greenpeace.

Likewise, Josephine Buxton (61) described herself as 'playing at catch-up now because I have the thirst for learning ...Life is a learning process. Experience is the University of life.' Josephine, who was forced to take retirement from her work as a nursing assistant because of a back injury, said that this gave her more time to do other things: 'I have the freedom to do the things that I want to do and I value that very much.' Despite spending a great deal of her time caring for her grandchildren, she described varied activities: 'I go to college, I read, I go to Church. Monday, I go to sugar craft. Tuesday, I go swimming and Wednesday, I go to polish my English up and Friday, I go for maths.'

Replacing activities and downsizing

Although some participants had disengaged from former activities, mainly because of ill health, they had found alternative activities and roles (see Bury and Holme, 1991). Bill Carter (80) had been the champion onion grower in his village, but could no longer garden due to a stroke. However, he looked forward to visits from his daughter and friends, and visited his wife in a nursing home on a daily basis. Bill said that he could not walk down to the village any more but was taken by car once a week to the luncheon club; he particularly enjoyed the outings they arranged. Daisy Lovett (91) said that, since she was unsteady on her feet, she no longer went dancing, although this was also to do with the fact that her husband had died and she did not have a dancing partner. However, she still participated in keep-fit classes and had a busy social life, which revolved round the church and meeting her friends either at their homes or hers. Muriel Brown and the Graysons said that they had been upset when illness had prevented them from taking holidays abroad, but had since enjoyed coach holidays in Britain.

Jim Caldwell (84) had given up fishing regularly because he had no one to take him, but said that he found plenty of other things to do: 'I always go out at about 12 o'clock, have a walk down town. Sometimes I walk down street and call in pub and have a pint of beer. Then back about 4 o'clock.' Listening to Jim, it was apparent that going to the pub had always been part of his social life; as a soldier and a miner he said it had always been important to him to have lots of friends. Jim had just been diagnosed with pneumoconiosis, a legacy of his years spent as a miner. When he was asked what he would change about his present life, he answered: 'If I had a bit of money spare, I would go and get some sun on my back.' Indeed, some participants acknowledged that they would not feel so positive about later life if they were struggling financially.

The Graysons said that they were 'more comfortably off' than they had ever been, but in this instance it was their health that had prevented Lillian and Ernest (both aged 83) from doing all the things they had planned to do in retirement. They rarely left their rented upstairs flat. They shopped once a week together and Lillian occasionally went to the local luncheon club and Ernest to 'socials' at the Blind Institute. Lillian said: 'We thought when we retired, we would have a lovely time, holidays and everything, but...' Her husband (unusually – since Lillian did most of the talking during interviews) interrupted: 'I expect everyone thinks that.' Lillian continued: 'We've been too poorly, on and off.'

Initially Lillian Grayson, like Betty Lomas and Reginald Green, had taken on part-time work after she had 'officially' retired. For Lillian and Reginald, this was partly from financial necessity and but also because they enjoyed 'being busy'. Indeed, for some people, activities seemed to replace paid work in part. When Bill Carter (84) first retired, he left home early each morning to work on his allotment – just as he had done when he was a factory worker. Tom Howarth (77) admitted that one of the reasons he had devoted so much time to volunteer activities was to make the transition from paid work to retirement easier. His interviews took place in his study, surrounded by files, folders, books and an electric typewriter. Betty Lomas (90) said that retirement from her job as an insurance collector had meant that she was free to take on other, more interesting work – first, as an usher in the Crown Court and after that working behind the bar at the Greyhound Stadium. She then ran the local 'Over Sixties Club', only stopping when she had a knee replacement.

Helping others

Betty and Tom Howarth were not the only examples of how participants became involved in social and community issues.[1] A number of other respondents, freed from paid work and familial responsibilities, actively chose to use their abilities and skills to help other people – whether this was through formal (working with a voluntary organisation) or informal volunteering. Those who helped others in some way said that it helped them too, connecting them to social issues and concerns (see Bury and Holme, 1991; Bamford, 1994). Dorothy Twigg (83) began to work as a volunteer for a local charity after she was widowed. 'I knew I was going to crack up, I was crying to everybody … but someone in the family said, "Why don't you try a voluntary job?"' Dorothy began work in an Oxfam shop, then for a local charity on the reception desk. She enjoyed this; it reminded her of when she had worked in her mother's sweetshop as a child. She now worked as a 'visitor', talking and listening to other older people.

Following the death of her best friend, and despite suffering from cancer herself, Janice Roberts (64) commenced work for two voluntary organisations – one that offered other older people emotional and practical support and the other offering advice on a health helpline. She said:

> I think for an older person not to be wanted and not to be needed is absolutely terrible. It's the best thing when somebody says, 'Oh I'm glad to see you. Oh you have helped me.'

Janice's use of the word 'needed' suggested giving practical help, while her use of the word 'wanted' implied reciprocal acts of friendship and love, both of which she said that she gained through voluntary work (see Bury and Holme, 1991; Bamford, 1994).

Most participants helped others in an informal way, for instance visiting an older or sick person, doing shopping for someone, giving advice, transporting and escorting or, as in Josephine Buxton's case, 'cheering up' her neighbour when she was anxious. Peter White (72) helped his neighbours with jobs around the house and garden, and taking them out for car rides in the country. He also visited nursing home residents, explaining that his desire to help other people resulted from his own experiences of caring for his terminally ill wife (see Bamford, 1994).

Jim Caldwell (74) lived in a sheltered housing complex and described reciprocal exchanges between himself and his neighbours:

> I'll do errands for them if they like. One across here, we get on well together. If I give her something then she gives me something.

Those who helped other people in some way indicated that this was part of their lifelong beliefs. George Daley said:

> If people would only realise that the greatest happiness that people can get is when they are actually doing something for someone else. That's when you get real satisfaction.

Daisy Lovett (91) articulated the feelings of other participants when she said that she felt that you 'reap what you sow' in life. When she commented to her daughter that people were 'so kind' to her, her daughter replied: 'Well, mother, a lot depends on you and you've always helped other people and you've always been friendly'. Daisy nursed her husband – who had Alzheimer's disease – at home until his death and now washed up at the coffee bar at her church and fetched library books for a disabled, younger neighbour.

Generativity

These interviews revealed the prevalence of reciprocal exchanges between older people and their families, friends and others (see Matthews, 1993; Matthews and Campbell, 1995). Even among those who experienced ill health, one way in which reciprocity was maintained was by passing on experiences to others. As we have noted previously (Clarke and Warren 2007), all participants who were asked said that they enjoyed telling their life stories as part of the study and some said that they enjoyed telling stories and passing on their experience to others in everyday life. Life stories, then, are one way in which an older person may pass on knowledge and values to the younger generation.[2]

Following her first meeting with Amanda Clarke, Daisy Lovett (91) requested a copy of her interview tapes and subsequently got in touch to say how much she had enjoyed playing them back. She was delighted to receive a copy of the transcript; it gave her the opportunity to 'pass on something' to her family so they could 'remember me when I'm gone'.

Peter White (72) regularly recounted stories from his past to younger people and to children, taking great pleasure from this activity:

> When I start telling them stories, I feel that I've got their attention. I think this is because you're ancient [laughs]. I mean, little stories, if you haven't gathered them together at our age, there's something wrong with you.

He hoped that his stories would have 'some worth':

> The only way we're going to learn for the future is through our experience, in my opinion, in the past.

Similarly, Doreen Thomas (96) said that she enjoyed sharing stories from her life and passing on advice to the family (see Moloney, 1995). Not all participants felt the same way, despite agreeing to take part in biographical interviews. Margaret

Wallace (74) felt that she had little to pass on to the next generation and thought that older people should 'give way' to younger people: 'We're the ones that are dying off and we should realise that and give way.' However, Margaret was the exception; most participants believed the sharing of their stories to have some value for others. William Buxton (79) felt that he could pass on his wisdom to his family:

> When you're young, you just don't think about what's happening next. As you get older, you weigh up, because you have experienced things along the way so you know that you shouldn't walk that road. I'm here to guide my family.

William believed in the importance of sharing the lessons learnt from his past mistakes with his family and was actively engaged in generativity.

Interpreting the interviews

In 1997, the nation's favourite poem was Jenny Joseph's 'Warning; when I am an old woman I shall wear purple' (Martz, 1991). Here Jenny Joseph looks forward to older age as a time of irresponsibility and belated self-expression. In later life, she would be free to do the things that she had longed to do but had never had the courage, hampered by the responsibilities of being a parent, employee or homeowner. This notion of freedom was indeed reflected in participants' accounts of their everyday lives. Men and women indicated that freedom from work and family commitments afforded them more time to take part in interests and activities of their choosing, and to meet with family and friends (see Thompson et al, 1990; Bamford, 1994; Coleman et al, 1998).

Supporting Howarth's (1998) research, findings suggest that, when older people are released from occupational concerns or familial commitments, they may 're-engage' with the present. But this engagement may take very different forms from the goal-oriented engagement of youth or middle age: Gladys's crotcheting, William Buxton's domino playing, Betty Lomas's window gazing and Peter White's storytelling. This is less radical than some of Jenny Joseph's promised pavement-spitting, railing-rattling activities; it has led some 'activity-driven middle-aged researchers' to feel that older people have *dis*engaged from society (Howarth, 1998: 675-6). Erikson et al (1986), for instance, are unsure if they can describe their participants as having 'vital' involvement in society because their activities and relationships – albeit varied – are not identical to those with which participants engaged when younger (Erikson et al, 1986: 324-5).

Cumming and Henry (1961) suggested that as people grew older they disengaged internally from society, apparently concentrating on themselves and their memories, as well as disengaging socially and culturally. Investing in other people or in the environment was, they claimed, substantially reduced. However, our participants in their accounts gave the overriding impression of involvement and participation in society rather than disengaging themselves from the outside world, decreasing their social roles and activities, and detaching themselves from employment, community, family and friends. This reflects the findings of other studies (Thompson et al, 1990; Bamford, 1994; Howarth, 1998) and seems to support a modulated version of 'continuity' rather than 'activity' theory:

> Continuity theory is *evolutionary*. It assumes that the patterns of ideas and skills, which people use to adapt and act, develop and persist over time; that a course of developmental direction can usually be identified; and that the individual's orientation is not to remain personally unchanged but rather consistent with the individual's past. (Atchley, 1993: 5-6, emphasis in original)

Activity theory (Havighurst, 1963) suggests that 'successful ageing' is linked to activity in later life, providing new social roles. Leisure or hobbies, for instance, can fill voids left by retirement from paid work. Caring for grandchildren or others can replace caring for a spouse. In the present study, although helping others built on participants' past roles and skills, it still differed from their caring roles in the past – as children, spouses and parents. In these roles, they said, often they felt *obliged* to help (see Lewis and Meredith, 1988). The Carnegie Inquiry (1993) reports that there is no evidence that people choose to volunteer as a replacement activity for work and family responsibilities. Rather, it is argued that volunteering in older age is a matter of continuity; few older people help others unless they did so when they were younger (Carnegie Inquiry, 1993: 83), as in the case of Daisy Lovett and George Daley. Others, like Peter White and Janice Roberts, were directly motivated to help others by the experience of caring for people close to them in their terminal illness and, in Janice's case, when she herself had cancer.

Erikson et al (1986) contend that it is important to consider the role of generative experience in the individual's overall philosophy of life – that is, to recognise the extent to which his or her world view incorporates a broad sense of integral concern for the well-being of the world and other human beings (Erikson et al, 1986: 101). This was most obviously illustrated through the social and political concerns of some participants. We have seen that some of them took voluntary jobs, others used their past experiences and skills to help others and some took paid work. This demonstrates how 'work' and/or busyness, some of it remunerated financially, can continue post-retirement but most often through voluntary activities. This challenges the emphasis of political-economy perspectives on the dependent social position of older people (Walker, 1980; Townsend, 1981; Phillipson, 1982).

As illustrated by the various activities they took part in, participants in our study did all they could to enjoy their lives, despite physical and financial problems (see Phillipson, 1982; Thompson et al, 1990). Their sense of contentment and outright happiness was more in evidence than some of their physical and material situations might lead one to expect. Winifred Blinkhorn and Reginald Green, for example, seemed active and happy despite their physical and financial limitations. The Carnegie Inquiry (1993) started from the premise that leisure defines the third age for many and is a major element in it for all. Research suggests that participation in leisure, and gaining pleasure and a sense of achievement from it, are important factors in life satisfaction (Carnegie Inquiry, 1993; Walker and Hennessey, 2004).

Our participants' experiences and views also to some extent supported the study by Bury and Holme (1991) of people aged over 90, which found that, although good health and material circumstances were important to older people, they did not always appear essential for high levels of activity inside or outside the home. As at any point in life, older age is characterised by diversity as well as commonality, whether in the way such factors impinge on people's lives or in their attitudes towards their circumstances (see Jerrome, 1989). The impact of individual agency in the face of physical and/or financial need must not be neglected. A biographical approach emphasises individual agency and difference, in contrast to structured dependency approaches, which tend, paradoxically, to reinforce the negative images of later life that they set out to challenge (Bury, 1995).

Freedom, constraint and connection

We have argued elsewhere that a common strategy in older age is to take 'a day at a time' (Clarke and Warren, 2007). This does not preclude planning ahead or reviewing the past. But neither does it suggest that we typically live our lives in constant vigilance against ageing *or* as a debauched 'woo-hoo' rush to our graves. What it does mean is that our activities are set against a backdrop of constantly appraised opportunities – or freedoms – alongside our desire to connect with others. Such is the progressing of 'ordinary' lives of people who have lived long and survived many experiences (Bytheway, 1995: 128).

The fact that both men and women in the study talked about their participation in society – whether this was a continuation of what they had always done or undertaken in new and challenging ways – supports the idea that development and change in later life is possible; that experiences in later life can be rewarding and positive and therefore should be encouraged. Through their involvement in activities outside and inside the home, and their relationships with other people, family and friends, participants showed that, for the most part, they can transcend the constraints that later life brings into focus. However, for some older people, later life is an ongoing struggle. The stories here describe how lives have been lived, are lived and might be lived.

In attempting to counterbalance the ubiquitous images of later life as worn-out, used-up decline into dependency (albeit dependency sometimes caused by fun at earlier stages), it is important not to 'create new dualisms of super-ageing in which story-lines of physically fit, creative, active, adventurous ageing become the new unachievable oppressions' (Feldman, 2001: 276; see also Bytheway, 1995). Rather, we need to pay closer attention to what older people themselves say about their lives; to the wide range of experiences and circumstances that accompany growing older and the meanings individuals attributed to later life (Minkler, 1996). In other words, we should incorporate into our research, policies and practices not just how older people are socially constructed – both culturally and in terms of the political economy of ageing – but also how they socially construct themselves (Reed and Clarke, 1999: 213).

Above all, participants' stories revealed the need to recognise the various ways in which older men and women live their lives – focusing more on their abilities, what they can (and feel free to) offer, as well as receive from, society. As Jewell (1999) points out:

> In a society that tends to be ageist, marginalising older people and making them feel a burden upon others, the need is great for the affirmation of their continuing value as unique and socially connected human beings and of their wisdom as a resource for others. (Jewell, 1999: 11)

Notes

[1] Involvement in social and community issues may, of course, have been a reflection of the research group (Clarke, 2001); as volunteers, they were by nature people who were concerned to be active in society in one way or another.

[2] Generativity may have been a reflection not only of the research group – see note (1) – but also the methods used: that is, arguably biographical approaches inevitably place value on the passing on of stories. As researchers using such methods, we embody the idea that what people have to say will be of interest/use to others.

References

Atchley, R. (1993) 'Continuity theory and the evolution of activity in later adulthood', in J. Kelly (ed) *Activity and aging: Staying involved in later life*, London: Sage Publications, pp 5-16.

Bamford, C. (1994) *Grandparents' lives: Men and women in later life*, Edinburgh: Age Concern Scotland.

Bernard, M. and Meade, K. (1993) (eds) *Women come of age*, London: Edward Arnold.

Blaikie, A. (1999) *Ageing and popular culture*, Cambridge, Cambridge University Press.

Bury, M. (1995) 'Ageing, gender and sociological theory', in S. Arber and J. Ginn (eds) *Connecting gender and ageing: A sociological approach*, Buckingham: Open University Press, pp 15-20.

Bury, M. and Holme, A. (1991) *Life after ninety*, London: Routledge.

Bytheway, B. (1995) *Ageism*, Buckingham: Open University.

Carnegie Inquiry (1993) *Life, work and livelihood in the third age*, Fife: Carnegie UK Trust.

Chambers, P. (1994) 'A biographical approach to widowhood', *Generations Review*, vol 4, no 3, pp 6-8.

Clarke, A. (2001) 'Looking back and moving forward: a biographical approach to ageing', PhD thesis, Department of Sociological Studies, University of Sheffield.

Clarke, A. and Warren, L. (2007) 'Hopes, fears and expectations about the future. what do older people's stories tell us about active ageing?', *Ageing and Society*, vol 27, no 4, pp 465-88.

Coleman, P.G., Ivani-Chalina, C. and Robinson, M. (1998) 'The story continues: persistence of life themes in old age', *Ageing and Society*, vol 18, no 4, pp 389-419.

Cumming, E. and Henry, W. (1961) *Growing old: The process of disengagement*, New York: Basic Books.

Davey, J. (2002) 'Active ageing and education in mid and later life', *Ageing and Society*, vol 22, no 1, pp 95-113.

DWP (Department of Work and Pensions) (2005) *Opportunity age: Opportunity and security throughout life*, www.dwp.gov.uk/opportunity_age/

Erikson, E., Erikson, J. and Kivnick, H. (1986) *Vital involvement in old age: The experience of old age in our time*, New York: W.W. Norton.

ESRC (Economic and Social Research Council) (no date) *The new dynamics of ageing – an interdisciplinary research programme*, www.esrcsocietytoday.ac.uk/ESRCInfoCentre/Images/NDA%20Full%20Programme%20Specification_tcm6-15545.pdf

European Union (1999a) *Towards a Europe of all ages*, Brussels: European Commission.

European Union (1999b) *Active ageing: Pivot of policies for older people in the new millennium*, Brussels: European Commission.

Feldman, S. (2001) 'Please don't call me "dear": older women's narratives of health care', *Nursing Inquiry*, vol 6, no 4, pp 269-76.

Havighurst, R. (1963) 'Successful ageing', in R.H. Williams, C. Tibbits and W. Donahue (eds) *Processes of ageing (vol 1)*, Chicago: University of Chicago Press, pp 299-320.

Hayden, C. and Boaz, A. (2000) *Making a difference: Better Government for Older People evaluation report*, Coventry: Local Government Centre, University of Warwick.

Hazan, H. (1994) *Old age constructions and deconstructions*, Cambridge: Cambridge University Press.

Howarth, G. (1998) '"Just live for today": living, caring, ageing and dying', *Ageing and Society*, vol 18, no 6, pp 673-89.

Jerrome, D. (1989) 'Virtue and vicissitude: the role of old people's clubs', in M. Jefferys (ed) *Growing old in the twentieth century*, London: Routledge, pp 151-15.

Jewell, A. (1999) *Spirituality and ageing*, London: Jessica Kingsley.

Joseph Rowntree Foundation (2004) *Older people shaping policy and practice*, York: Older People's Steering Group, Joseph Rowntree Foundation.

Kemp, C.L. and Denton, M. (2003) 'The allocation of responsibility for later life: Canadian reflections on the roles of individuals, government, employers and families', *Ageing and Society*, vol 23, pp 737-60.

Lewis, J. and Meredith, B. (1988) *Daughters who care: Daughters caring for mothers at home*, London: Routledge.

Martz, S.H. (ed) (1991) *Grow old along with me the best is yet to be*, Watsonville, CA: Papier-Mache Press.

Matthews, A. and Campbell, L. (1995) 'Gender roles, employment and informal care', in S. Arber and J. Ginn (eds) *Connecting gender and ageing: A sociological approach*, Buckingham: Open University, pp 129-43.

Matthews, M. (1993) 'Issues in the examination of the care giving relationship', in S.H. Zarit, L.I. Pearlin and K.W. Schaie (eds) *Caregving systems: Informal and formal helpers*, Hillsdale, NJ: Lawrence Erlbaum Associates, pp 107-18.

Matthews, S.H. (1986) *Friendships through the life course: Oral biographies in old age*, London: Sage Publications.

Midwinter, E. (1991) 'Ten years before the mast of old age', *Generations Review*, vol 1, no 1, pp 4-6.

Minkler, M. (1996) 'Critical perspectives on ageing: new challenges for gerontology', *Ageing and Society*, vol 16, no 4, pp 467-87.

Moloney, M. (1995) 'A Heideggerian hermeneutical analysis of older women's stories of being strong', *Image – the Journal of Nursing Scholarship*, vol 72, no 2, pp 104-9.

OECD (Organisation for Economic Cooperation and Development) (1999) *Maintaining prosperity in an ageing society: Policy brief*, www.oecd.org/dataoecd/21/10/2430300.pdf

Phillipson, C. (1982) *Capitalism and the construction of old age*, London: MacMillan.

Reed, J. and Clarke, C. (1999) 'Nursing older people: constructing need and care', *Nursing Inquiry*, vol 6, no 3, pp 208-15.

Reed, J., Cook, G., Childs, S. and Hall, A. (2003) *Getting old is not for cowards: Comfortable, healthy ageing*, York: Joseph Rowntree Foundation.

Rudman, D.L. (2006) 'Shaping the active, autonomous and responsible modern retiree: an analysis of discursive technologies and their links with neo-liberal policy rationality', *Ageing and Society*, vol 26, no 2, pp 181-202.

Slater, R. (1995) *The psychology of growing old: Looking forward*, Buckingham: Open University Press.

Thompson, P., Itzin, C. and Abendstern, M. (1990) *I don't feel old: The experience of later life*, Oxford: Oxford University Press.

Townsend, P. (1981) 'The structured dependency of the elderly: the creation of social policy in the twentieth century', *Ageing and Society*, vol 1, no 1, pp 5-28.

Walker, A. (1980) 'The social creation of poverty and dependency in old age', *Journal of Social Policy*, vol 9, no 1, pp 45-75.

Walker, A. (2006) 'Active ageing in employment: its meaning and potential', *Asia-Pacific Review*, vol 13, no 1, pp 78-93.

Walker, A. and Hennessey, C. (eds) (2004) *Growing older: Quality of life in old age*, Buckingham: Open University Press.

Walters, D. (1997) 'The "active society": new designs for social policy', *Policy & Politics*, vol 25, no 3, pp 221-34.

Warren, L. and Maltby, T. (2000) 'Averil Osborn and participatory research: involving older people in change', in T. Warnes, L. Warren and M. Nolan (eds) *Care services for later life: Transformations and critiques*, London: Jessica Kingsley, pp 291-310.

WHO (World Health Organization) (1999) *The global embrace 1999*, www.who.int/docstore/globalmovement/embrace1999/index.htm

FOURTEEN

Does eldership mean anything in the contemporary West?

James Nichol

This chapter explores the idea of 'eldership' in contrasting cultural contexts. It begins with accounts of traditional eldership as practised in Guatemala, New Zealand and Samoa, going on to compare them with understandings within European populations in New Zealand and Great Britain. In the first group of settings, we can witness the continuing strengths of eldership as a formal public and family role within indigenous communities, as well as a willingness to value a more individualised understanding of eldership within sections of the European community in New Zealand. Consideration of the British experience introduces a participative inquiry involving people born between 1940 and 1956 with a declared belief in 'creative' ageing (Nichol, 2007). People who took part in this study rejected eldership as an identification, while affirming a belief in later-life development and contribution. This they explored under the thematic headings of 'slowing down to find it', 'purple' eldership and 'guardianship'. The process of carrying out the inquiry uncovered doubts and uncertainties about the recognition of older people; but it also led the participants to affirm a conception of 'mature' peership and of mature peer groups as potential spaces for mutual recognition, reflection and a sense of shared experience.

Eldership in Guatemala

A Guatemalan story illustrates the traditional role of elders. The Goddess of Water has been dismembered and her heart captured by the Lords and Ladies of Death. Her (non-divine) partner collects her bones together and descends into the infernal realm to recover her heart. He succeeds at a price, returning to the earth's surface with only a toe bone and a tooth to go with the recovered heart of the Goddess, himself so badly wounded that he dies.

Four elders – Grandmother Growth, the Father of the Mountain, the Old Woman and the Old Man – now intervene. Covering the body of the man and the toe bone, tooth and heart of the Goddess with a blanket, they sing their wisdom. 'The world wept and whimpered in the ground while the two gods and two old humans sang the ancient life-giving songs' (Pretchel, 2002: 99) After the old ones have nearly exhausted their repertoire of 200 songs, the blanket is lifted. Man and Goddess (now a mortal woman) have revived and are whole. The elders comment, 'It's the same every year' (Pretchel, 2002: 99).

This story contrasts the distinctive roles of the younger and older generations. For the former the action presents a vivid and dramatic trial. The old ones participate through their knowledge of the 'ancient life-giving songs' and with the relative detachment of those who have seen it all before. They have not 'retired', but they have progressed to a different and more reflective way of making an impact on their world, using their resources as culture bearers.

In recording this tale, Pretchel is not a detached observer. Rather, he describes himself as someone who has spent his life 'married to the meaning' of such stories. The Guatemalan highlands are the place:

> ... where I could be trained into something useful ... There with my good friend and zany father, the old man Chiviliu, and several hundred other old Mayan men and women, like a friar I became another of their wool-blanket-wearing order, dedicated to remembering back to life She who had been dismembered and therefore do what we could to keep Holy Nature dancing. (Pretchel, 2002: 141)

The context is the defence of indigenous people and their land in the exceptionally difficult circumstances of the 1980s. The storying activities of the elders are not simply forms of reminiscence. They have an active role in maintaining cultural identity in times of political stress.

The New Zealand experience: Maori, Samoan and European perspectives

Political circumstances in New Zealand are less harsh, yet the same principles apply. Maori, the indigenous people, have a formal system of eldership now deployed in a contemporary reaffirmation of their culture. The elders (*kaumatua*) have the role of passing on custom and tradition (*tikanga*), partly through the institution of the *Marae*, a traditional meetinghouse with its surrounding land (www.maori.org.nz). Ideally everyone should have access to a *Marae* that they can call their own. Durie (1994) shows how traditional Maori concepts have influenced contemporary moves towards distinctive public health strategies for Maori, articulated in new and revised forms from the early 1980s onwards and significantly influential in public policy making. Membership of a *Marae* is now recognised as a determinant of public health for Maori. *Kaumatua* are the guardians of the Marae system and the protocols and conventions through which it operates. The elders are a step closer than other people to the past and the ancestors. Their influence is paramount in questions involving cultural integrity – if not necessarily in day-to-day political leadership.

But much of the flavour of Maori eldership is less public and formal. Batten (2000) quotes an interview in which Rangi Mataamua talks affectionately of his grandfather, who had:

... got no degrees but was probably the wisest person I know ... When I was about five we first started going eeling, and we'd wade out into the middle of the lake and we'd set our nets, and we sleep out there by the lake, and he talked to me ... he taught me where I came from, and who I am, and I suppose that's the most important thing that I've ever learned. (Batten, 2000: 203)

In Maori and Polynesian families more generally, it is common for grandparents – especially grandmothers – to be the primary caregivers for young children. Lupe (2007), from a New Zealand based Samoan perspective, suggests that such arrangements, among other factors, have had a significant impact on cultural perceptions of older women specifically, compared with attitudes long held in Europe. Recalling the formal role of some older women as storytellers in Samoan culture, she makes her point through comparing the traditional *fagogo* (folktale) 'Loa and Sine' with the European fairytale 'Rapunzel'.

The two stories contain similar themes. Rapunzel is an adolescent girl kept prisoner in a tower by a witch, her guardian and stepmother. A wandering prince hears her singing and is enchanted. Observing how the witch uses Rapunzel's hair as a ladder he learns to climb it too. They fall in love. Discovering this, the witch cuts off Rapunzel's hair and leaves her in the desert, subsequently using the hair to trick the prince. When he discovers his error he jumps out of the tower and is blinded. Both broken-hearted, Rapunzel and the prince are eventually reunited after years in the wilderness. The witch plays no further role.

In 'Loa and Sina' another mother and daughter live in isolation from the world. Loa is part human and part ogress with cannibal tendencies. Sina is a prisoner to her mother and kept away from other people. One day a young male, Fitilo'ilo'i, ventures onto Loa's land and meets Sina. They fall in love. Soon enough Loa suspects a male visitor. She tricks both Sina and the young man, and, with Sina out of sight, swallows him whole. Sina, who has been calling Fitilo'ilo'i for most of the day, becomes very weak. It is apparent to Loa that Sina is close to death. Feeling pity for Sina, Loa vomits up the young man, who is still alive and intact. At the end of the story they all three live together.

Lupe's analysis suggests among other things that Pacific culture, for a complex range of reasons, supports a structure of feeling that is friendly to the older woman and provides a place for her under the same roof as the young couple in a way not easily paralleled in contemporary Europe.

Batten (2000: 5) asks, 'What is it that distinguishes an elder from one who is merely old?' She herself is a New Zealander of European descent and, for her as for many others, the English word 'elder' has taken on a flavour from the Maori word *kaumatua*, since Maori use 'elder' as their preferred translation for it when speaking English. 'Elder' therefore has a resonance for at least some people in the wider New Zealand society created by this bicultural context. However, Batten's approach to eldership differs from the Maori one. Whereas Maori *kaumatua* are given a formal leadership role by their communities and take public responsibility for being culture bearers, Batten internalises eldership. For her it is connected to a midlife shift into what she calls 'soul work', a shift that is likely to involve a response to specific challenges from outside (divorce, illness, redundancy) or from within (loss of satisfaction or meaning). The fruits of this work can be found in 'resilience ... spaciousness and serenity'. She approvingly cites Betty Freidan (1993), who talks of integrating previously unrealised parts of oneself and moving towards wholeness of spirit even in the face of physical decline.

In this both Batten and Freidan are influenced by Jungian understandings of 'midlife crisis' as a crisis of meaning (Biggs, 1993, 1999), one linked to a developmental process described as 'individuation' (von Franz, 1978). Individuation means that people experience a need to become more fully themselves, 'whole, indivisible and distinct from other people and collective psychology (though also in relation to these)' (Samuels et al, 1986). This process is seen as being supported by the practice of 'active imagination' (Hannah, 1981; Samuels et al, 1986), whether or not guided by a professional therapist. Batten's (2000) account is individualistic, assumes an autonomous, bounded self and places importance on what McLeod (1997: 3) calls 'dignity'. Her narrative of eldership is Romantic in a nineteenth-century sense (Taylor, 1989). It features the ordinary person as hero of his or her own moral journey and the qualities that this brings.

Participatory inquiry into eldership: the process

My own research was built around a study of people born between 1940 and 1956 with a belief in the creative possibilities of ageing. I had been alerted to the idea of 'eldership' while resident in New Zealand and was interested to know what, if anything, it might inspire among people in Britain at the point of entering later life. I used a methodology in the broad tradition of cooperative inquiry (Heron, 1996; Heron and Reason, 2001; Reason, 2003) in which those of us involved would all have both participant and researcher roles. From the perspective of humanistic gerontology, this approach allowed the study to address participants' subjectivity and include moral and existential themes (Heywood et al, 2002; Crossley, 2005). It provided the space for 'an expanded image of aging' (Moody, 1988) where personal stories could generate meaning (McAdams, 1993, 1996; Polkinghorne, 1996; Frank, 2004b) and creative potential could be celebrated (Cohen 2000, 2005; Cole and Sierpina, 2007) in the service of 'human flourishing' (Lincoln and Guba, 2000).

The process began with an interview for all 16 participants (including me) followed by enrolment in one of two groups. Each inquiry group then met for a full weekend organised around a story/dialogue process (Labonte and Feather, 1996), which was followed by a six-month period allowing space for personal action inquiries. The research ended with a follow-up weekend with each group. As containers of narrative, the inquiry groups were part of what McLeod (1997: 24) considers to be 'a revival of oral tradition' under postmodern conditions. Participants knew that the stories presented were necessarily fragmentary glimpses into people's lives and that they were being told in the context of negotiation and relationship building. The inquiries did not attempt to achieve narrative unity; they did not arrive at consensual agreements or conclusions.

Each inquiry group agreed a formal group purpose when it first met. Both groups avoided the term 'eldership' or indeed any specific reference to age. In one case the purpose was 'to open a space for the common exploration of being the age that we are'. The other was 'to use a process of personal and group inquiry to nurture richness in our lives now and in the future'. One co-inquirer said that 'for me this is all about what it means to be 50-plus' and she did not want to use expressions about 'being old and wise and all that stuff'. Another picked up a sense of 'if you can't be cool, be quaint!' in my choice of eldership as a suggested topic. Indeed, both inquiry groups' purposes emphasised lived experience at a point in time and did not assume that age itself was necessarily their foreground preoccupation. This fits in with accounts (Biggs, 1999; Gilleard and Higgs, 2000) suggesting that we are witnessing cultural moves away from a staged sense of the life course and towards the extension of an indeterminate midlife into what were once considered to be the later years.

Threads of eldership

At the same time, there are indications throughout the research that, without using the language of eldership, people did have views about qualities linked to potential contributions specific to older people. These seem to me to be three: 'slowing down to find it'; 'purple' eldership; and 'guardianship'. I shall therefore briefly examine each of these in turn.

'Slowing down to find it'

A participant, Kate, noted a degree of slowing down and greater contentment in her life. She spoke of a 'denser and richer' quality of experience, frequently sitting by her pond, 'watching the frogs and the newts and just *loving* the beauty of the world'. At the same time she made it clear that she was not 'slowing down and losing it' but rather 'slowing down and finding it'. As an artist, she was creating new and different forms of work because 'my resources have not grown less'. She named as a role model a ceramicist who moved into a new way of working at the age of 82, describing his capacity to do that as 'one of my navigational points'. Similarly, another participant talked of seeing her life 'through a developmental prism if you like' but no longer in an 'I must develop myself!' way. Now development was something natural, 'something that just naturally happens, because we're here and we're at this point in our lives, basically – rather than something I have to do about it. And that's a bit different.'

There was a willingness on the part of many inquirers to express such changes in languages of spiritual development, though not generally in confessional terms as aspects of a devotional religion. One co-inquirer discussed '*intimations*' of spiritual development that would not necessarily follow the lines of past practice. Another spoke of Divinity as bigger than the specific path. Anton brought in the latter years of Goethe's (redeemed) Faust as a potent image: '[He] just spends years interminably reclaiming land from the sea ... that business of bringing into consciousness what is not conscious at present.' Anton talked of this as a process that could be 'either joyful or disturbing' and mused that it was little recognised culturally, except when 'given a brand name like psychotherapy'. Something similar was more tentatively suggested by Charlotte's choice of vocabulary when she apprehended '*numinous* possibilities' in dream-like images, which appeared to be guiding her development.

'Purple' eldership

To some extent the participants above were using a form of individuation narrative (von Franz, 1978) to express their current understanding of personal change and development, though, in line with the findings of other researchers (Cohen, 2005), without any dramatic sense of crisis. Other co-inquirers were more iconoclastic. At the time of their primary interview, several mentioned Jenny Joseph's poem 'Warning' (quoted in Ram Dass, 2000: 120-1; see also Warren and Clarke in this volume). It begins:

> When I am an old woman, I shall wear purple
> With a red hat, which doesn't go.

For a number of inquirers the problem with the word 'eldership' lay in its patriarchal overtones and an apparently unbalanced emphasis on the serious side of life. Sarah recalled how

> a woman at a dance camp I went to last year formally became a crone. There was this croneship ceremony and it was gloriously celebratory of the fact that she is – yes, she is old and she can be wild and creative and have fun and all those things. Um, so, yeah – you can be wise in the sense of having experience ... but that doesn't mean you sit seriously in your rocking chair [laughs] clutching your walking stick.

Paula made a similar point. 'You know there's a lot of fun like – I don't know, drumming, which years ago my mother's generation wouldn't have had the opportunity to do.' Sam said: 'There's something about wanting to be a model of eldership and not a tired, complacent ... boring model of eldership'. He wanted to be riding his bike at 70. Kate was drawn to 'all these images of outrageous old people' and hoped to be playing in a rock band at 75. Mark took 'purple' eldership closer to the core of identity when he said:

I see myself as being more iconoclastic and, um, cutting across things, and, um worrying less about what people think of me ... a sort of inner version of 'when I am old I shall wear purple'. When I am old I shall think purple.

He talked about becoming a 'purple fogey'. 'Purple' eldership seems therefore to be a kind of anti-eldership in the traditional sense, resisting limitation and marginality with counter-cultural panache.

Guardianship

Towards the end of their meeting cycles, the two inquiry groups looked at possible futures. One discussed the idea of a 'guardian' role. This idea does correspond to traditional views of eldership (Pretchel, 2002; Dunn, 2004) and can also be seen in terms of generativity as put forward by Erikson (1994, 1997) and somewhat reframed by McAdams (1993, 1996). The idea was for individual members of an ongoing group to use the support of the group to intervene in social and political issues that affect the legacy that our generation will leave.

For example, Frances wanted planning permission to put a wind turbine on her roof. She said she was unlikely to get it because she lived in a listed building within an urban conservation area where it would be seen as 'a blot on the landscape'. But without changes in the patterns of energy production and consumption the city would one day be 'awash ... We are arguing that there are new circumstances, which should revise our whole way of thinking'.

Frances as guardian was asking people, through a micro-example, to understand chains of cause and effect over a long period of time, to imagine their consequences and to take responsibility for the welfare of future generations – to think in terms of a legacy. The key characteristics of her action were the ability to define an issue in a clear and comprehensive way and a willingness to defend the future and those who will live there, rather than being in the thrall of a continuous present.

Recognition

But identity is not simply a question of what people think, or imagine or do. It depends also on how others respond. Arthur Frank (2004a) analyses the wounding caused when physicians *misrecognise* patients in clinical settings, citing (Taylor, 1994): 'a person or group of people can suffer real damage ... if people or the society around them mirror back ... a confining picture of themselves'. Paula explored this point when she said:

What's occurring to me is that when I am being the person, the best person, the best version of the person that I know I am, quite a lot flows. If I don't get that fed back to me in some way – which is where the supportive friends, community, whatever, activities, comes in I – it gradually falls away. And I become what other people expect me to be. And, and I put *myself* in this little box, and I behave like the version of a 60-plus would behave and I potter to the shops and I go to the library and I come home and I – well I don't usually watch the telly, but, you know, do those kinds of activities.

An environment like the inquiry group allows Paula to 'reconnect' with herself and the issue is about holding that reconnection in the everyday world.

When Kate caught sight of 'lizardy skin' on her forearm, she linked this to the thought, 'Oh my God I'm suddenly not visible to you because I'm an older woman.' As part of a group of older women artists, she had recently met with a much younger arts administrator and felt patronised and dismissed. 'She was making assumptions about our levels of professionalism and our levels of nous about the contemporary world, because she *saw* us as a group of older women.' Wrinkles are experienced less as a physical blemish than as a badge of public disempowerment.

Sam said that he lived with a sense of being judged all the time, as one of perhaps two single men living in a long street mostly inhabited by couples and families. He worries that people think:

> I'm some pervy old guy who lives on his own and rides a bicycle, doesn't have a car … So there is something there about my identity in the community that I don't like and I really, really, really feel dreadfully uncomfortable about it … for me, certainly there's a whole sense of 'My God it's scary being a single bloke our age in Bristol'.

Frances reported the most ease with an eldership role and this may be in part because, at just under 65, she was the oldest member of the inquiry and felt different from the baby boomers who formed its cultural centre of gravity. However, her ability to wear the mantle was also facilitated by her grounding in a Quaker community where she was in fact a formally recognised elder. She was used to giving what she had to offer in a context where it was likely to be received in the same spirit. There was a cultural match between 'elder' and 'community', allowing the fundamental unity of narrative and social identity suggested by Jenkins (2004: 16) when he contended that: 'the theorisation of identification must … accommodate the individual and collective in equal measure'.

But Frances's experience was not typical of participants in the eldership inquiry. Co-inquirers were more likely to struggle with a degree of mismatch between who they believed they were and what they had to give and what was – or seemed to be – reflected back by the wider community. Eldership, to be vital and effective, requires an invitation as well as the will. Without these, people cannot step into this role and it is perhaps what they experienced as a lack of invitation that led many participants to shy away from the concept as well as the identification.

Mature peership

Under these circumstances, even the role beginning to be developed by people of European descent in New Zealand becomes problematic. Instead, inquirers articulate a sense of *mature peership* – prefigured by what many had said in preliminary interviews when they talked about their hopes and potential contributions for the inquiry process. Asked about what they would value from the inquiry groups, interviewees placed a strong emphasis on engagement with people. They talked about contact with people, companionship and being open to new networks and connections. One wanted 'to listen to other people' and liked the idea of 'being in a group where there's a similar age range'. Another talked of 'working with a bunch of people who were all going through … a similar stage of life' and also referred to 'journeying companions'. Charlotte was 'really curious about how other people are handling ageing', while Paula wanted to meet 'like-minded people' who were 'exploring the same issues, rather than spending money buying lots of things'. Sarah wanted to 'listen to other people' and to hear their thoughts in a way that would help her also 'to think some of that through myself'. If participants experienced a lack of recognition in the outside world, then the inquiry itself might offer a place for mutual recognition.

The relational dynamics of inquiry were also seen as important to its work as a space for *reflection* (Biggs, 1999). Anton saw the quality of relationship it involved as the key to inquiry success. 'The telling of stories deepens … the trust in a group and enables them to get to know each other and respect each other at a deeper level.' What mattered about the stories was the 'awareness' that the teller could bring, and the capacity to express 'something of their uniqueness' – and not the 'menu of – of things'. Anton hoped that the inquiry would provide a 'container' that could 'maximise the potential that exists in that space'. There was a sense of the wealth to be gained by listening to others. Mark was interested in people's 'non-material adventure' and wanted to contribute 'feelings and thoughts' about 'their purpose, identity, way of being'. For Kate the inquiry might enable depth and 'healing' as the groups developed in trust and it became possible to share the dark side, 'some of the fear and frustrations as well'.

This significant linking of the inquiry community itself with the flourishing of a later-life identity, or at least sensibility, was confirmed at the end of the process. In her group's final dialogue, Paula talked about what happens for her when she hears other people's stories, rather than her own. She said that she takes in hitherto unknown possibilities and can go away with a 'seed'. The group is 'a place where possibilities happen', not one for working through an agenda. Anton talked of a quality of magic 'that can't be legislated for. It either happens or it doesn't happen.' The value placed by participants on the inquiry space recognised that identity, as lived, is dependent on available forms of connection and belonging. Inner resources and personal will are not sufficient for us to become the people we want to be. Creating forms of collectivity in which to flourish was therefore seen as a necessary task for our own developmental well-being. In a similar context

Becker (1997: 202-3) draws attention to the small group setting, whether or not allied to a broader social movement, as providing opportunities for people to develop their own personal and collective narratives and 'amend normalising ideologies to reflect their particular views'. Through buffering themselves against 'more generalised ideologies of normalcy' they can 'facilitate agency'. As they talk together, people's narratives develop and change and their views of normality, of what to expect from life, are reshaped. A form of resistance and empowerment becomes possible through practices of 'multivocality', developing sites where alternative voices can flourish.

Conclusion: vulnerability, reflection and experience

This inquiry had two agendas. The first was that it would be a fruitful and catalytic experience for the inquirers. The second was to find out how a group of people with a declared interest in creative ageing responded to the idea of 'eldership'. When developing the inquiry, I adopted eldership as an aspirational rather than purely descriptive term, potentially standing for distinctive forms of later-life creativity and contribution in contemporary British conditions. My hope was that the inquiry would identify and say something about those forms from the standpoint of the inquirers.

Participant evaluations six months after the inquiry suggested that the first agenda was successful (Nichol, 2007). On the second, most participants shied away from 'eldership' and took the process in a different direction. But their manner of doing so shows elements of paradox and contradiction. Unable to see themselves in the roles that older people have had in the past and retain in some other cultures, and unwilling to identify with the concept of eldership as presented by me, inquirers nonetheless believed in continuing development in later life and that they had something distinctive to offer. The inquiry process, instead of delineating new models of eldership, powerfully revealed participants' vulnerability and confusion about ageing when the question became more fully present for them. Within the crucible of inquiry, this was as true of me in my participant role as it was of my co-inquirers. As we worked through our responses to the challenge we had given ourselves, we found ourselves placing a high value on the setting of a mature peer group offering space for reflection and a sense of shared experience within the group. In the summer of 2008 (three years after completion of the original inquiry), a group of inquiry veterans re-constellated to develop a workshop and support group initiatives for the wider public.

References

Batten, J. (2000) *Growing into wisdom: Change and transformation at midlife*, Auckland: Tandem.

Becker, G. (1997) *Disrupted lives: How people create meaning in a chaotic world*, Berkeley, CA: University of California Press.

Biggs, S. (1993) *Understanding ageing: Images, attitudes and professional practice*, Buckingham: Open University Press.

Biggs, S. (1999) *Mature imagination: Dynamics of identity in midlife and beyond*, Buckingham: Open University Press.

Cohen, G. (2000) *The creative age*, New York: Avon Books.

Cohen, G. (2005) *The Mature mind: The positive power of the aging brain*, New York: Basic Books.

Cole, T.R. and Sierpina, M. (2007) 'Humanistic gerontology and the meanings of aging', in J.M. Wilmoth and K.F. Ferraro (eds) *Gerontology: Perspectives and issues* (3rd edn), New York: Springer, pp 245-64.

Crossley, N. (2005) *Key concepts in critical social theory*, London: Sage Publications.

Dunn, M. (2004) 'Why do so few become elders?', in J. Hepple and S. Sutton (eds) *Cognitive analytic therapy in later life*, Hove: Brunner-Routledge, pp 67-82.

Durie, M. (1994) *Whaiora: Maori health development*, Auckland: Oxford University Press.

Erikson, E. (1994) *Identity and the life cycle*, New York: W.W. Norton.

Erikson, E. (1997) *The life cycle completed*, New York: W.W. Norton.

Frank, A. (2004a) *The renewal of generosity: Illness, medicine and how to live*, Chicago, IL: The University Press.

Frank, A. (2004b) 'Thinking with stories', unpublished notes from Arthur W. Frank master class, University of Bournemouth, Institute of Health and Community Studies, Centre for Qualitative Research, 19-20 April.

Freidan, B. (1993) *The fountain of age*, London: Vintage.

Gilleard, C. and Higgs, P. (2000) *Cultures of ageing: Self, citizen and the body*, London: Prentice-Hall.

Hannah, B. (1981) *Encounters with the soul: Active imagination*, Boston, MA: Sigo Press.

Heron, J. (1996) *Co-operative inquiry: Research into the human condition*, London: Sage Publications.

Heron, J. and Reason, P. (2001) 'The practice of co-operative inquiry: research "with" rather than "on" people', in P. Reason and H. Bradbury (eds) *Handbook of action research: Participative inquiry and practice*, London: Sage Publications, pp 179-88.

Heywood, F., Oldman, C. and Means, R. (2002) *Housing and home in later life*, Buckingham: Open University Press.

Jenkins, R. (2004) *Social identity* (2nd edn), London: Routledge.

Labonte, R. and Feather, J. (1996) *Handbook on using stories in health promotion practice*, Ottawa: Minister of Supply and Services.

Lincoln, Y.S. and Guba, E.G. (2000) 'Paradigmatic controversies, contradictions, and emerging confluences', in N.K. Denzin and Y.S. Lincoln (eds) *Handbook of qualitative research* (2nd edn), London: Sage Publications, pp 163-88.

Lupe, K. (2007) 'An ocean with many shores: indigenous consciousness and the thinking heart', in P. Culbertson, M. Agee and C. Makasiale (eds) *Penina uliuli: Contemporary challenges in mental health for Pacific peoples*, Honolulu, HI: University of Hawai'i Press, pp 122-35.

McAdams, D.P. (1993) *The stories we live by: Personal myths and the making of the self*, New York and London: The Guilford Press.

McAdams, D.P. (1996) 'Narrating the self in adulthood', in J.E. Birren, G.M. Kenyon, J.-E. Ruth, J.J.F Schroots and T. Svenson (eds) *Aging and biography: Explorations in adult development*, New York: Springer, pp 131-48.

McLeod, J. (1997) *Narrative and psychotherapy*, London: Sage Publications.

Moody, H. (1988) 'Towards a critical gerontology: the contribution of the humanities to theories of aging', in J.E. Birren and V. Bengston (eds) *Emergent theories of aging*, New York: Springer, pp 19-40.

Nichol, J. (2007) 'Social spaces for mature imaginations: reflections on a participative inquiry', unpublished PhD thesis, School of Health and Social Care, University of the West of England.

Polkinghorne, D.E. (1996) 'Narrative knowing and the study of lives', in J.E. Birren, G.M. Kenyon, J.-E. Ruth, J.J.F Schroots and T. Svenson (eds) *Aging and biography: Explorations in adult development*, New York: Springer, pp 77-99.

Pretchel, M. (2002) *The toe bone and the tooth*, London: Thorsons.

Ram Dass (2000) *Still here*, London: Hodder & Stoughton.

Reason, P. (2003) 'Co-operative inquiry', in J.A. Smith (ed) *Qualitative psychology: A practical guide to research methods*, London: Sage Publications, pp 205-31.

Samuels, A., Shorter, B. and Plaut, F. (1986) *A critical dictionary of Jungian analysis* London: RKP.

Taylor, C. (1989) *Sources of the self: The making of the modern identity*, Cambridge: Cambridge University Press.

Taylor, C. (1994) *Multiculturalism*, Princeton, NJ: Princeton University Press.

von Franz, M.-L. (1978) 'The process of individuation', in C.G. Jung (ed) *Man and his symbols*, London: Picador, pp 157-254.

FIFTEEN

Talk about old age, health and morality

Outi Jolanki

Introduction

How do older people approach fundamental issues involved in the process of growing older? What exactly does ageing mean to them – what changes does it bring to the ways they see themselves and their relations to the rest of society? This investigation tries to approach questions like these by responding to the ways in which people converse and interact in their daily lives. They do so not only directly but indirectly too, and the implications of their talk may be particularly eloquent and rich. The investigation gives special weight to conversation relating to health, a central preoccupation in contemporary notions of ageing. Indeed, questions connected to health contribute largely to the meanings bestowed on ageing itself. Here we see that approaches to health can themselves encapsulate and display profounder social attitudes, attitudes touching on what is desirable or undesirable for human beings, on what should be done and how we should relate to it – in a word, moral attitudes relating to ageing.[1]

This chapter presents some findings of a discourse-analytical study of meanings conferred on old age and health in the talk of older people themselves. In contrast to commoner ways of studying norms and values, focusing directly on moral ideas, this chapter concentrates on the talk and the practical interaction in which moral arguments are used. This approach involves exploring whether and how notions of health and old age are constructed as moral matters, and what kinds of arguments can be interpreted as moral when they are used in real-life settings (Jayuusi, 1991; Bergmann, 1998; Nikander, 2002).

The account given here is based on biographical interviews with people who are 90 years of age or older. The arguments presented develop earlier approaches to these questions – for a fuller description of the analytical approach and data sets used, see Jolanki et al (2000); Jolanki (2004). The original 250 interviews that were taped (of which 184 were with women, 66 with men) were made in the region of Tampere, in southern Finland, in the years 1995-96, as part of a project called Vitality 90+ (Jylhä and Hervonen, 1999). The interviewees were approached because of their exceptionally high ages; most respondents participating in these biographical interviews were exceptional even within their own age group, since most still lived alone in their own homes and were relatively independent. Some in the overall project lived in sheltered housing or in nursing homes. The interviewees whose talk is quoted in this chapter all fell into the first group of people living by themselves at home, though they received some help from relatives or home help services. Three of them were widows and one was a single woman. All but one came from poor farming families, were born and raised in the rural surroundings of Tampere and had moved to town in early adulthood to work. All had received basic education, but relatively briefly, and they had no formal professional training. They had mostly been employed in manual work. Tampere is the second largest town in Finland and a major trade centre, situated in a landscape composed mainly of woods and lakes. During the first decades of the 20th century, when the interviewees moved to the town, it was a rapidly developing industrial setting characterised by large paper mills and textile factories.

Discursive and rhetorical approaches

The research here represents small-scale qualitative research, and draws on the ideas of social constructionism and the methods of discourse and rhetorical analysis.

Discursive psychology offers tools for exploring the different, sometimes conflicting meanings attached to health and old age, and how these meanings are brought forward, substantiated or refuted (Potter and Wetherell, 1987; Wetherell and Potter, 1992; Potter, 1996). The key idea of the discursive approach is to see language not as a transparent medium that merely describes reality, but as a central tool that constructs different versions of speakers' social worlds. The idea of multiple versions of the world and the possibility of choosing between them (even if the choice is more imaginary than a real option) is one that directs our attention to the argumentative and rhetorical context of talk (Billig, 1996). Students of rhetoric emphasise that talk is often functional; it is designed to be persuasive, to win hearts and minds. (Wetherell et al, 2001: 17; cf Edmondson, 2007). Talk about one's own experiences of ageing, or defining oneself as old or not old, is linked to self-definitions and the process of positioning oneself as a certain kind of person. To take a position in talk, though, is not necessarily a piece of conscious activity, nor does it necessarily stem from free choice. Certain positions are often considered more proper, believable or realistic than others. Positions, in their turn, entail ideas about how one should act or behave. That is, positions taken in talk also have normative and moral dimensions (Edley and Wetherell, 1997; Wetherell and Edley, 1999).

Health and old age as discursive and rhetorical constructions

When the participants in this project were asked about their views of old age and how they saw their own ageing, their responses could be seen as 'balancing' between two contrasting positions. Their talk moved along an axis between distancing themselves from the identity of 'old', claiming to be physically and socially active and in good health, and adopting the identity of 'old' in a way that served to *legitimate* ill health and inactivity. It became evident that, in talking in this way, the participants were not only giving factual reports of their health, but also 'performing' their identities as worthy members of society and defining themselves as virtuous actors. Definitions of health and old age entailed both moral evaluations and definitions of the participants' social identities.

Activity as a preferable option

Physical and social activity and the ability to do things were constructed in the interviews as constitutive of good health and as an outward indication of it. This kind of 'activity talk' concerned not only keeping oneself busy by doing home chores, engaging in leisure activities, meeting other people and participating in social activities outside the home, but also, in general, showing an active and positive stance towards life. The content of the participants' accounts and their use of rhetorical tools exhibited their feeling that being active in all imaginable ways was clearly the preferable option.

The names in the extracts that follow have been replaced with fictional ones and the letter 'I' refers to the interviewer. The numbers refer to the code of the interview, 'W' to the gender and the last number to the age of the interviewee. The interviewee below, Saima Tuominen, is a woman who moved from the countryside to the town at the age of 21 and worked most of her life as a self-employed masseuse. At the time of the interview she was a widow who had been married twice and had had five children. She depicted herself as someone in exceptionally good health. In the following excerpt, the important element is the implicit contrast between the talk of the interviewer and that of the interviewee:

I:	What about this ageing, how have you experienced your ageing? Have you noticed anything?
Saima:	No, I haven't noticed anything, that I'm getting older.
I:	There haven't been any adverse effects?
Saima:	None whatsoever. Everything is fine. It was not long ago that we went over to the war veterans' club, they were playing the accordion or I'm not quite sure what it was, we were doing this ring dance. I've always been one for a dance, I have.
I:	What about the mental side, do you feel that there have been changes in that respect, for instance in your memory?
Saima:	Well yes, I suppose there have been some small changes memory-wise, but nothing really. I still go racing around.
I:	And what about your hearing and your eyesight?
Saima:	My eyesight's pretty good, very good. I don't need glasses at all, the doctor said, try to wear your glasses it keeps your eyesight nice and sharp. But I do see extremely well. My

hearing, my ears tend to get blocked. Sometimes I hear a bit too well! My age is beginning to weigh on these, they're all slack. That's been a major factor that I've always had a draught in here, the window open in the bathroom and the door open to the balcony. But I think that's fresh air, because I don't really dare go outside a lot, I do still go out.

I: Do you go out every day?

Saima: Yes, I do go out every day, I take the lift down and then I take the stairs back up, that's good exercise. But I don't dare walk the stairs down, you might miss your step and fall down the stairs, I don't want any accidents happening. That's why I take the lift down and walk up. They're all quite amazed. It makes you feel super, this walking. It's not a few who say, you can't be 90 yet. And I say I am, I'm a bit over 90!

Research interviews are of course also interaction situations. In this extract a particularly interesting issue is the interaction between the interviewer and the interviewee. The interviewer's questions imply that the experience of old age can be expected to equal physical decline. This is visible in the way she specifies the question about old age to mean 'any adverse effects' when the interviewee denies having noticed that she is getting older. The interviewer's questions imply that Saima might not be as able or active as she presents herself and accordingly old age is repeatedly constructed in terms of bodily deterioration. Saima clearly questions this formulation and constructs various alternative interpretations of old age and of her identity. With talk about dancing and going 'racing around', she produces herself as an independent, self-reliant agent who has an active social life. Following Radley and Billig (1996: 228), we may say that this excerpt shows how 'old' serves here as a 'restrictive definition'. We can see that the interviewee, in order to evade this kind of restrictive definition, associates herself with activities that are generally connected with young people.

In her account of her senses and physical abilities, Saima balances between conceding problems with her health and qualifying their effects on her everyday life, and constructing herself as 'still active and able'. Here she uses the voices of the other people she speaks to ('They're all amazed', 'You can't be 90 yet'), adding to them accounts of her activities to implicitly distance herself from the stereotypical idea of the 'frail old' person. Using this notion of being 'good for one's age' allows the interviewee to claim credit against normative expectations of frailness (Coupland et al, 1989). It is obvious that the 'experience' of old age is constructed here as a health matter alone, and that the 'changes' associated with old age (mental or physical) refer only to the alleged worsening of cognitive and physical abilities.

The following extract comes from the interview with Liisa Mattila, a woman aged 92. In her early adulthood she worked in the country as a housemaid in the big house owned by a local wealthy family, before moving to Tampere to work in a factory. She returned to the countryside to look after her aged mother but moved back to the town after her mother's death. She remained unmarried and had no children, but kept up close relations with her siblings and their children. From the very beginning she depicted herself as someone who had always been healthy and strong:

Liisa: I've been healthy and it's a great gift isn't it? [Talks about her work life] I've had the strength to work. And Taina, my brother's daughter, she can testify to this, I do all the cleaning here, I even take the rugs out to be aired and the linen and everything. I wash my own clothes so I mean even now I have strength. Taina can testify that I'm not lying one bit here, it's all true. What else can I add, I don't know really. Except that I have this cholesterol and blood pressure, but even they don't bother me. [Omitted talk]

I: So what about nowadays, do you go out at all?

Liisa: Well not really, I do sometimes go to these clubs, once a week I go to town when Taina comes along, she's afraid that I may fall over so she carries my shopping bag. I haven't gone out, I like to be out here and do what I do here and stay healthy. What with my legs I can't really move around all that much any more, but I can still keep my home nice and tidy. Every day I go around and do things, I sit down only for a short while, I never sleep during the daytime, I sit down only for a short while and then I think of something again and then I'm off again.

In this extract Liisa positions herself as a fundamentally healthy person, who has in fact always been healthy and strong. She concedes some problems with her health (her cholesterol level and blood pressure, 'my legs'), but qualifies her difficulties in many ways. The rhetorical effect of Liisa's talk is that she is still healthy, still active and is managing on her own. Being 'healthy' is reformulated as having the strength to work and still having enough strength to do the chores at home. The latter part of the excerpt illustrates how the question about social activities is interpreted as a health issue, which is a recurrent phenomenon in the conversation. Here Liisa is forced to give a negative answer to the question about going out, which could undermine everything she has said previously about herself. She does concede having some difficulties. But, in the end, talk about her activities at home serves to reformulate the central issue of the questions: the reason why she has retained her health is precisely that she stays at home. This kind of talk serves as corrective face work, and enables her to reconstruct her identity as active and healthy.

Liisa uses several rhetorical devices to support her claims of activity, such as outside witness ('Taina can testify that I'm not lying'), various extreme formulations (she 'never sleeps during the daytime') and a detailed account of her daily schedule. These rhetorical devices indicate that she knows that her arguments can be questioned. The small temporal modifiers – 'even now' and 'still' - mark her talk as age-relevant, and at the same time characterise her as different from ordinary older people. If we take into account that talk is always used to undermine contrasting (implicit or explicit) views as well as to argue *for* something (Billig, 1996), then Liisa's detailed depiction of her daily activities at the same time conveys, by contrast, a picture of what she considers a normal day for ordinary older people. Liisa herself becomes constructed as someone who is able to cope on her own and whose everyday life is filled with a variety of different activities. Her body is indeed a 'busy body' (Katz, 2000).

Old age as a legitimate cause for ill-health and inactivity

The notion of old age as its own explanation for health ailments is often found in the talk not only of older people themselves (Coupland et al, 1989, 1991; Coupland and Coupland, 1994), but also of younger people (Nikander, 2002). When the respondents in this project conceded that they had trouble with their health and that they were less able (to do home chores or 'jobs') and active (which affected going out and social activities), their disclosures of old age served as self-evident explanations, as 'common-places' (Billig, 1996), which required no further argument. For example, one participant said, 'Old age doesn't come all by itself, you do always get these [illnesses]' (Jolanki et al, 2000: 363); here the notion of old age is crystallised in a common phrase. Another participant said: 'You won't be getting the sort of answers that are perhaps expected of me. I'm well aware of that but there's nothing I can do about it. I'm old so I'm old' (Jolanki et al, 2000: 363). Old age is produced here as a time of unavoidably declining physical and mental capacity, which justifies participants' inability to fulfil social expectations. In both of the excerpts, age is used as a category-based, stable and uncontrollable attribution (Coupland et al, 1991).

So, in this kind of talk, old age is described as a common fate for everyone. However, it seems that adopting the social position of 'old' did not necessarily free the participants from their feelings of responsibility to try to resist the adverse effects of old age and to try to be active. Talk about old age was often followed with detailed talk about difficulties in daily life and health problems. It seems that the task of this kind of talk was to manage moral blame, which was done in several ways. Detailed accounts of difficulties and ailments served to prove that health troubles were real and severe. This kind of talk seemed intended to show that the speaker was not complaining 'for nothing', but was definitely forced to be 'inactive'. Extreme formulations and detailed accounts were also used in respondents' talk to back up their claims that they were trying to keep on the move and socially active, in spite of their difficulties. In the next extract the interviewee, Anna Nieminen, is a woman aged 91 who had been born into a large farming family. She lived all her life in a small village near Tampere, but she and her husband both worked in different manual labour occupations in the town. She explicitly aligns herself with the category of the old when, at the start of this extract, she talks about the day hospital she visits once a week:

Anna: But what I've been doing there is a rhythm that I've been sleeping there, because they've got these rooms there, I've slept in the daytime maybe an hour or something. I'm beginning to get old, I need my rest. And I'm not, like I said, I'm in no trouble. It was just over 12 months ago that I had this small blood clot. But it passed, although I almost lost this leg and really most of the right side is pretty bad [talks about hospital visit]. But I can walk all right, I don't necessarily need my cane, but of course it tires more easily, I don't have the energy and I can't walk long distances anyway. But this hand it's a bit sort of, it can't cope with all these jobs, and it begins to hurt up here and then [unclear] but nevertheless it does move … My eyesight, that's slowly going now. [Omitted talk] Oh, I mean, this life has been quite a complex thing, but I suppose it's getting towards the end of it. I'll be 91 in November, if I live that long.

Keeping oneself occupied, being an active and outgoing person, was often contrasted in these interviews with being idle, sitting around or sleeping during the daytime. This contrast was also often used in talk to define old age, and to give grounds for defining oneself as old or not old. In Anna's talk we see how illnesses and the gradual loss of the senses are depicted as external facts that just happen, for no other reason than advancing age. Anna's statement 'I'm beginning to get old' and the disclosure of chronological age constructs her age as an important feature (Nikander, 2002, 75-85) in relation to her health. She aligns herself with the group of older people whose life is coming to an end, which provides a self-evident reason for her need for rest and her health problems. Thus sleeping during the daytime is constructed as a normal and *necessary* part of the day of older people – that is, it is justified, in sharp contrast to the talk in the earlier extracts. The reference to old age overrides all possibilities of choosing one's behaviour or actions and thus removes any moral blame.

Nonetheless the claim that Anna makes when she says, 'I'm in no trouble' qualifies the seriousness of her health problems and serves as corrective face work. It is followed by an argumentation chain in which she moves back and forth, conceding that her health has deteriorated and qualifying its effects on her life. On the other hand, the rhetorical effect of Anna's talk is that *she* is in no trouble, even though her body suffers from ailments. Respondents often rhetorically externalised the 'failing' body parts as Anna did here ('this leg', 'this hand ... it can't cope with all these jobs') and, in this way, they were able to distance themselves from their 'failing' bodies, which served to minimise the threat to their identities as able and independent (Jolanki, 2004).

Once Anna had told the interviewer about her family life and her husband's health situation and his death, the interviewer proceeded to ask more about her own health:

I: So what about your own health at the moment, then?
Anna: Well, it's pretty good. I have to say I'm reasonably happy, nothing really. I mean they do have to keep me steady when we're out and about, I tend to be a bit unsteady when I'm out. But I mean I think I've managed pretty well really.
I: Well, how have you looked after this health of yours?
Anna: Well, nothing special really. I've just tried to do the odd job, just to keep myself occupied and then kept in touch with people as much as possible. If it continues too long, I tend to get down, I mean I've always been the kind of nature that's happy and mobile. When I was younger I could never stay still for very long and I was always coming and going whenever possible. You have to. I'm not saying that, but you have to. [Anna goes on to talk about injuring her knee.]

Anna's response that her health is 'pretty good', and especially the extreme-case formulation 'nothing really', might be contested as unrealistic on the basis of all that has been said before. Even though she concedes having some problems with her health she also mitigates health problems ('I *tend* to be *a bit* unsteady') and limits them to certain situations ('when I'm out'). Also, rhetorically, Anna's talk creates the effect that 'health' is an issue that has to do with more than just bodily state, and the standard of health is the inner mental state of being *happy* with one's life, and *managing well*. So, in this respect, Anna's talk also broadens out the narrow concept of health.

The interviewer's second question included the assumption that Anna has looked after her health in some way. It was very rarely in these interviews that the worth of self-care was openly denied, even though the interviewees did sometimes evade the question or they postponed their answers, as Anna did here. In the subsequent utterance, Anna redefined the question as asking whether she has kept herself occupied and whether she has taken part in social activities. Anna's confession that 'she tends to get down' implied trouble with her mental well-being. Mental health issues were rarely mentioned in these interviews and, when they were, it was usually in a veiled and vague manner, and qualified in many ways. Anna constructed herself as having been 'happy and mobile' and physically and socially active *as a younger person*, and her current state in terms of enforced staying still ('you have to'). This kind of talk serves to undermine any implicit doubt that she may not have kept herself occupied enough, nor been sufficiently socially active, which might have caused her to get 'down'. Thus an implicit moral argument is present here. It is preferable to be 'happy, mobile and socially active', since this is conducive to good health and might even provide protection against depression.

Anna's 'message' needs to be interpreted in the context of her concession. She has conceded that she has lost control of her body, at least to the extent that she needs other people to keep her steady. In the previous extract she spoke of her memory troubles. As Featherstone and Hepworth (1995) have contended, being able to control oneself cognitively, bodily and emotionally is required to achieve the status of adult; conversely, losing bodily control and cognitive skills produces the danger of social unacceptability and losing that status. As a result of the latter, older people might not be the objects of moral reprehension, but they might well be assigned a childlike, patronised status. In all the extracts shown here, the participants were balancing between conceding some changes in their health status and mitigating the threat to their adult status, and at the same time advancing their claims to a positive self-image. The term 'positive self-image' does not refer here to an objectively existing entity, but to a socially constructed moral category that reflects prevailing social preferences (Hepworth, 1995: 177). In the light of this data to be independent and active serves as a basis for a 'positive' image.

Can old age be seen as mental and spiritual development?

One way to picture old age has been to see it as a time of mental and spiritual development enabled by, and born as a result of, long life experience. Talk that could be called 'wisdom discourse' was present in these conversations, but I regard it as a 'weak discourse' here for several reasons. First, as the earlier extracts indicated, 'mental issues' were often interpreted as health issues. This kind of talk concerned problems with memory or feelings of depression. Or, alternatively, the participants talked about 'mental activities' as a means to manage their own health and prevent cognitive impairment. Second, talk about 'mental factors' in a more positive light – for example, talk about the value of long life experiences – was rather rare. Third, when the participants talked about old age as a time of mental development and increased understanding of life, these episodes were long, detailed descriptions replete with different rhetorical tools. This tells us that the arguments clearly seemed to require a lot of rhetorical backup to support them against doubts.

However, the participants occasionally did argue for the value of long life experience as a way to acquire a deeper understanding and a broader perspective on life, as in the following extract. The interviewee, Maria Laakso, is a woman aged 92, who is one of the few interviewees to come from a middle-class family (her father was a journalist and her mother a housewife). She herself went to commercial school after elementary school and married an engineer. The family settled to live near Tampere on a farm. Her husband worked elsewhere and she took care of the farm with the help of paid workers. Her views on older people's lifelong experience and depth of understanding were rare in their eloquent style and clearly articulated message, but the content of what she says and its sentiments were expressed in other interviews too:

> I: Do you think you have changed during your lifetime?
>
> Maria: Yes, I suppose I have become less constrained. I remember that I used to be terribly shy and hardly dared to say anything. Even when I got married I was terribly like, I couldn't [unclear] talk with people. But now I can ... [unclear] it's many years now since I've been less constrained in the sense that I can speak my mind and even answer back if there is something I don't like. But at that time, I do not understand why at first I was so awfully shy and of course it was because I did not, really a child, like, doesn't know anything really ... This is a fact. Common sense says it's like that. There's no two ways about it. That could comfort younger people who notice that they don't yet know anything. But that's how it is, you don't know anything when you're young. You haven't been able to pick up the experience; all you know is some things quite superficially. And what you've seen around, but that's entirely different from being there, being involved. To live it.

Maria constructed old age as a time of positive change from 'constrained' youth to emancipated old age and thus implicitly argued against the cultural common-sense interpretation of old age, which tends rather to equate old age with senility. She might have given the impression of praising herself if she had said straight out that older people are wiser than younger people. Instead, Maria's talk constructed this as an obvious external fact by using contrasting category entitlement (young–old), which she backed up with naturalisation ('common sense', 'This is a fact,' 'That's how it is,' 'of course', 'There's no two ways about it'). It is not an easy task for the interviewee to try to undermine the taken-for-granted view of older people as senile, which is perceptible in her talk and in the way she uses various argumentative devices to legitimise her claim. One way to create a factual version is through detailed description and narrative (Potter, 1996). Maria constructed her present 'wisdom' through a development narrative from childhood through marriage and to old age, which has brought her life experience. The use of extensive argumentation (different rhetorical tools, a variety of arguments) indicates that she was conscious that her own position is disputable and requires a lot of 'argumentation work' to become believable and be taken seriously.

Conclusion

The issues that come to the surface in this analysis seem to echo broader cultural discourses in contemporary thinking on old age. Cultural discourses are theoretical abstractions, which do not determine but rather offer resources for thinking (Holstein and Gubrium, 2000). Yet, they furnish us with ideas about the possible ways to define 'old', and the identities and positions that are seen as possible and proper for older people in a given society. The detailed analysis of older people's own talk given here shows how they use different discourses of old age to construct identities and to give shape and meaning to their own experiences of old age. But the analysis also shows that the identities offered within these discourses can be constraining and restrictive.

Modern gerontological research has questioned the notion that there is an inevitable link between old age and ill health. It rejects the notion that physical and mental deterioration, losses and dependency in old age are inevitable and take place as law-like processes about which an individual can do very little. One such attempt to challenge 'fate discourse' is research that advocates active and positive old age (Featherstone and Hepworth, 1995; Blaikie, 1999; Katz, 2005). This 'activity discourse' stresses the meaning of individual action contributed by the way one grows old; it underlines the need to see older people as agents and as a heterogeneous group. To improve the health of older people and to promote their agency is certainly an important goal not only for a society, but also for individual people themselves. For an individual, this discourse opens up the possibility of influencing their own ageing or even 'keeping old age at bay' with their own actions. There are also obvious socio-political interests in promoting the health of older people and increasing their levels of activity. In public language, old age is constructed mainly as a health issue and a matter of public expenditure (Cole, 1992; Blaikie, 1999).

However, there are dangers involved in emphasising individual activity and presenting the active body as the ultimate ideal of the ageing body (Katz, 2000). It may lead to imposing all moral responsibility on the individual, whose life choices are then seen as determining whether or not they are 'active' and ageing in a 'positive way' (Cole, 1992; Featherstone and Hepworth, 1995; Hepworth, 1995). This seriously underestimates the extent to which human beings are social and political agents, presenting them as unrealistically isolated masters of their own destinies. Also, this focus on health has meant reducing older people's lives and identities to a 'health concern', and leaving other possible aspects of human life in old age outside serious consideration (Cole, 1992: 238-9; Katz, 2005: 194-5).

As the analysis here indicates, definitions of old age in these conversations do tend to revolve around health issues. But this is not as straightforward as might be assumed. It brings with it exigent moral 'work' in which older people struggle within available discourses of justification in order to retain their human standing. Discourses of old age comprise ambivalent ideas of what is expected of older people and what is age-appropriate behaviour and, as was evident in the data extracts, positioning oneself as old or not old was indeed an ambiguous task. Both the content and the rhetorical organisation of participants' talk showed that, to be active, to be independent and to manage on one's own was the preferable option. To concede the opposite called for explanation and justification. However, it seems that the traditional discourse of old age as decline is still strong. Extensive and detailed evidence is required if the speaker wishes to argue otherwise, particularly if they have reached extreme old age themselves. If one 'fails' to be 'active', aligning oneself to the category of old serves as a self-evident cause and explanation for one's situation. So, the idea of a collective fate that all people face at a certain age still helps to ward off individual responsibility for ill health and 'inactivity', and, according to my interpretation, it can allow respondents to retain their social worth and continue to depict themselves as morally virtuous persons.

Talk about wisdom and life experience was present in this data, but wisdom discourse was 'weak discourse' among these respondents. To argue for the value and meaning of long life experience seemed to require extensive argumentation. On the basis of these conversations, reasons for this can only be suggested. It may be that the majority of the people interviewed simply did not perceive old age in these terms. At the same time, the research setting itself did not direct discussion specifically into existential or developmental issues. But the idea that old age could be seen as a time of wisdom and experience might not be the 'lived reality' current in contemporary societies. These explanations, at individual and social level, of course do not exclude one another. As a precaution it needs to be noted that we could not take as a self-evident starting-point the *assumption* that old age is related to wisdom, since that might mean imposing yet another compelling stereotype on older people and adding another 'task' to the list of how to be successfully aged. Yet, from this perspective, 'activity'-based or 'successful' ageing might receive other, collective meanings and broader interpretations than those dealing with individual health and bodily functions (Savishinsky, 2004; Edmondson, 2005). To study the ways older people themselves address the idea of wisdom and life experience in their everyday lives could illuminate different meanings of wisdom, both as an individual quality and in terms of its social ramifications (Edmondson, 2005, expanded and developed in this volume). There are some signs that the representations of old age and older people's positions in society may be broadening (Cole, 1992; Blaikie, 1999; Tulle, 2004; Thane, 2005), but there still seems little room in public discourse for seeing old age as something else, and something more, than an individual 'body project' to keep fit and healthy. This stress on fitness, with the considerable constraints it imposes, seems still to be reflected in individual thinking about old age.

Note

[1] The author wishes to thank two copyright holders for permission to re-use portions of previously published articles:

'Old age as a choice and as a necessity: two interpretative repertoires', Jolanki, O., et al (2000) © Elsevier.

'Moral argumentation about health and old age', Jolanki, O. (2004) © Sage Publications.

References

Bergmann, J. (1998) 'Introduction: morality in discourse', *Research on Language and Social Interaction*, vol 31, nos 3/4, pp 279-94.

Billig, M. (1996) *Arguing and thinking: A rhetorical approach to social psychology*, Cambridge: Cambridge University Press.

Blaikie, A. (1999) *Ageing and popular culture*, Cambridge: Cambridge University Press.

Cole, T. (1992) *The journey of life. A cultural history of aging in America*, Cambridge: Cambridge University Press.

Coupland, N. and Coupland, J. (1994) '"Old age doesn't come alone": discursive representations of health-in-ageing in geriatric medicine', *International Journal of Aging and Human Development*, vol 39, no 1, pp 81-95.

Coupland, N., Coupland, J. and Giles, H. (1989) 'Telling age in later life: identity and face implications', *Text*, vol 9, no 2, pp 129-51.

Coupland, N., Coupland, J. and Giles, H. (1991) *Language, society and the elderly*, Oxford: Basil Blackwell.

Edley, N. and Wetherell, M. (1997) 'Jockeying for position: the construction of masculine identities', *Discourse and Society*, vol 8, no 2, pp 203-17.

Edmondson, R. (2005) 'Wisdom in later life: ethnographic approaches', *Ageing & Society*, vol 25, no 3, pp 339-56.

Edmondson, R. (2007) 'Rhetorics of social science: sociality in writing and inquiry', in W. Outhwaite and S. Turner (eds) *The SAGE handbook of social science methodology*, London: Sage Publications, pp 479-98.

Featherstone, M. and Hepworth, M. (1995) 'Images of positive aging: a case study of *Retirement Choice* magazine', in M. Featherstone and A. Wernick (eds) *Images of aging: Cultural representations of later life*, London and New York: Routledge, pp 29-47.

Hepworth, M. (1995) 'Positive ageing: what is the message?', in R. Bunton, S. Nettleton and R. Burrows (eds) *The sociology of health promotion. Critical analyses of consumption, lifestyle and risk*, London and New York: Routledge, pp 176-90.

Holstein, J.A. and Gubrium, J.F. (2000) *The self we live by. A narrative identity in a postmodern world*, New York and Oxford: Oxford University Press.

Jayuusi, L. (1991) 'Value and moral judgement: communicative praxis as moral order', in G. Button (ed) *Ethnomethodology and the human sciences*, Cambridge: Cambridge University Press, pp 227-51.

Jolanki, O. (2004) 'Moral argumentation in talk about health and old age', *Health: An Interdisciplinary Journal for the Social Study of Health, Illness and Medicine*, vol 8, no 4, pp 483-503.

Jolanki, O., Jylhä, M. and Hervonen, A. (2000) 'Old age as a choice and as a necessity: two interpretative repertoires', *Journal of Aging Studies*, vol 14, no 4, pp 359-72.

Jylhä, M. and Hervonen, A. (1999) 'Functional status and need of help among people aged 90 or over: a mailed survey with a total home-dwelling population', *Scandinavian Journal of Public Health*, vol 2, pp 106-11.

Katz, S. (2000) 'Busy bodies: activity, ageing and management of everyday life', *Journal of Ageing Studies*, vol 14, no 2, pp 135-52.

Katz, S. (2005) *Cultural aging: Life course, lifestyle, and senior worlds*, Peterborough: Broadview Press.

Nikander, P. (2002) *Age in action: Membership work and stage of life categories in talk*, Helsinki: Academia Scientiarum Fennica 321.

Potter, J. (1996) *Representing reality: Discourse, rhetoric and social construction*, London: Sage Publications.

Potter, J. and Wetherell, M. (1987) *Discourse and social psychology: Beyond attitudes and behaviour*, London: Sage Publications.

Radley, A. and Billig, M. (1996) 'Accounts of health and illness: dilemmas and representations', *Sociology of Health and Illness,* vol 18, no 2, pp 220-40.

Savishinsky, J. (2004) 'The volunteer and the *Sannyasin*: archetypes of retirement in America and India', *International Journal of Aging and Human Development*, vol 59, no 1, pp 25-41.

Thane, P. (2005) 'The 20th century', in P. Thane (ed) *History of old age*, Los Angeles, CA: Paul J. Getty Museum, pp 263-300.

Tulle, E. (2004) 'Rethinking agency in later life', in E. Tulle (ed) *Old age and agency*, New York: Nova Science Publishers, pp 175-89.

Wetherell, M. and Edley, N. (1999) 'Negotiating hegemonic masculinity: imaginary positions and psycho-discursive practices', *Feminism and Psychology*, vol 9, pp 335-56.

Wetherell, M. and Potter, J. (1992) *Mapping the language of racism. Discourse and the legitimation of exploitation*, New York: Columbia University Press.

Wetherell, M., Taylor, S. and Yates, S.J. (eds) (2001) *Discourse theory and practice*. London: Sage Publications.

Afterwords

SIXTEEN

Exploring positive images of ageing: the production of calendars

Eileen Fairhurst and Sue Baines

Introduction

This volume deals with a variety of ways in which ageing can be understood and older people responded to. We have seen that a humanistic approach to gerontology embraces a genuine multidisciplinarity that combines contributions from a variety of standpoints and disciplines – and attempts to deal with some of the real questions as well as the richness that this variety represents.

In this connection there is a growing interest in, and an accumulating corpus of knowledge on, visual representations of ageing, which reflect precisely this two-sidedness with which gerontology must deal. Visual images are extraordinarily powerful, but also extraordinarily ambiguous, and interpreting them underlines the need for gerontology to confront profound ethical and political questions. We can take as an example here images of ageing in photography. For instance, Blaikie (1994, 1995) has examined photographs as a means of exploring how they represent memory through a focus on generational relationships. Featherstone and Hepworth's (1995) focus on photographic images in retirement magazines resulted in their identification of midlife as a new stage of the life course. Similarly, Blaikie and Hepworth (1997) showed how contemporary photographs convey meanings of ageing. Clearly, some of these imputed meanings may require criticism, not only celebration. Different kinds of care relationships depicted in photographs have been the concern of Johnson and Bytheway (1997). At the same time there has been an emphasis, especially by policy makers, on positive ageing. Images abound of examples of older people 'doing' positive ageing – however questionable some notions of positive ageing may be. An alternative view is offered by those who examine images to allow the 'deconstruction of the image of old age as a necessary phase of bodily decline' (Featherstone and Wernick, 1995: 6). This contribution, too, concentrates on images of positive ageing but, unlike previous studies, examines photographs in calendars that were explicitly produced as part of a 'positive images of ageing' campaign. Photographic images presented here, then, were not retrieved from a picture library, nor were they derived from photographic exhibitions or previously published books of photographs. Images offered here were designed to support older people, as part of a campaign, which, like this book, was called Valuing Older People.[1]

Supporting 'positive ageing' does not comprise just one set of attitudes. The rest of this Afterword explores some of the different interpretations of positive ageing which the makers of the calendar conveyed and shows how the reader's political and moral views also influence how he or she reads the pages they see. It outlines the purposes of the campaign, considers how photographs culturally construct valued images (Johnson and Bytheway, 1997), points to how a calendar's layout offers a 'prompt' for interpretation and finally poses some matters for further exploration.

The Valuing Older People programme and Positive Images of Ageing campaign

The Valuing Older People programme is a multi-agency activity, begun in the city of Manchester in 2003, 'to improve services and opportunities for the city's older population. It challenges Manchester's public agencies, businesses and communities to place older people at the centre of the extensive plans for the regeneration and reshaping of the city'.[2] The Positive Images of Ageing campaign is one part of this overall programme. It aims 'To promote a positive and healthy attitude towards ageing, to promote healthy lifestyle choices that reduce the impact of ageing, to challenge negative stereotypes of older people, to challenge the public to re-evaluate their attitudes towards older people, to challenge local agencies to revisit the way they deal with/deliver services to older people.'[3] In other words, this campaign is a deliberate intervention into an ongoing public debate about the meaning of ageing itself, an intervention that seeks to steer the debate into particular directions.

As part of this campaign, four calendars have been produced and the calendar for 2009 is in production. The intent is to depict 'positive and challenging images of older people'. Calendar production is steered by the Positive Images task group, to which a number of older people belong. The Positive Images campaign, then, has been clearly located within a social and political context.

At the same time, these calendars can be seen as a part of a humanistic project. The older people pictured in these calendars have volunteered themselves as opposed to being supplied by, or hired from, a modelling agency. Older people, through their membership of the Positive Images task group, have been involved in the production process of calendars. It could reasonably be argued that the calendars have been a co-production between older people and professionals.

Calendars and the 'cultural transmission of valued images'

The four calendars produced so far have each had a unifying theme that is manifest in the images that are shown for each month. These themes are printed on the front cover of the calendars – namely, 'Challenging older people in Manchester' for 2005; 'Growing older with attitude in Manchester' for 2006; 'Older and bolder in Manchester' for 2007 and 'Manchester – a city for all ages' for 2008. Following the aims of the wider Positive Images of Ageing campaign, the images under the umbrella of the specific calendar theme are supposed to be interpreted along social/political/ethical lines. 'Challenging', 'attitude', 'bolder' and 'all ages' are descriptions that typically are not linked to the category 'older'. It is in this way that the images can only be interpreted along the lines suggested. All photographs are commissioned and possibly 'documentary' (see Johnson and Bytheway 1997). As Zalot's (2001) analysis of wall calendars has shown, photographs have a range of meanings but those meanings are bounded in a number of ways. The thematic nature of the calendars serves as one instance of 'bounding'.

Calendars and layout

The layout of calendars can also be seen in this way. Among other things, quotes, contextualisation of the scene/image depicted and the naming of individuals shown are all matters that feature on the calendar's layout. The four calendars here, however, use these in different combinations.

The 2005 calendar with the theme of 'Challenging older people in Manchester' accompanies each image with a quote from a 'famous' person, often an older famous person, for instance Nelson Mandela. Every photograph has a non-personalised caption and participants are listed at the end of the calendar. Participants are not named individually but primarily are assigned to a category: seven photographs refer to individuals as being members of different kinds of clubs.

The 2006 calendar with its theme of 'Growing older with attitude' dispensed with quotes from the 'famous'. Rather, it concentrated on shaping and unpacking the 'attitude' part of the theme through visual imagery, especially 'sexuality'. Three of the photographs showed hetero- or same-sex relationships. A declaratory statement accompanied each photograph. For instance, a picture of a man on a swing in a children's play park had beneath it, the statement: 'the youngest swinger in town'. Unlike the 2005 calendar, named participants were attributed to each month and listed at the end.

Quotes were part of the page layout of the 2007 calendar with its theme of 'Older and bolder in Manchester'. In this calendar, though, their use changed. Quotes from individuals who were named were found on each picture. In addition, at the end of the calendar, named participants, together with contextualisation of/commentary on the picture were attributed to each month. A feature of this contextualisation was an emphasis on images describing new activities taken up after retirement.

The 2008 calendar with its theme of 'Manchester– a city for all ages' returned to the use of quotes from 'famous' people to accompany the picture for each month. Added to these are verbal contextualisations of the pictures and indications of the nature of the relationship depicted, as well as the names of the participants.

Now, by using some photographs (available from www.manchester.gov.uk/), I want to show how captions may steer our interpretations of images.

The caption for the first image reads '90 and still captain of the team'. Given that this image is part of the calendar with the theme of 'Challenging older people in Manchester' we are invited to see this as an untypical activity for a man aged 90.

This is because we do not expect 90-year-old men to be so physically able and active as to be 'fit enough' to play a 'tough' game like rugby. It is precisely the untypicality of the image that points to its 'challenge'. The 'unexpectedness' of such an image may lead also to an interpretation of this photograph as 'how marvellous' the man is. 'Marvelling', with all its social ambiguity, is something to which these calendars consistently invite us.

Source: 'Challenging older people in Manchester' 2005 calendar

The second image was the front cover of the 2006 calendar with its theme of 'Growing older with attitude in Manchester'. As noted previously, this calendar used the images to unpack the category of 'attitude'. Here, by showing an older person 'playing' on a child's toy, the category of 'acting your age' is made contestable. We have cultural ideas about what kinds of actions are appropriate at certain ages; these attitudes are used in order to challenge them. Perhaps we are expected to 'marvel' again at the freedom from convention this individual has achieved.

Since this image also comes from the same calendar as the previous one, it leads us to consider how 'attitude' is being presented. The caption for the third image is 'out and about in the city'. The background of this image is Manchester's Gay Village, which is associated with

Source: 'Growing older with attitude in Manchester' 2006 calendar

younger rather than older gay men. Not only does this image question our assumptions about sexuality and chronological age but also it unsettles our taken-for-granted expectation that particular spatial areas may be associated with specific age-related activities.

The fourth image comes from the 'Older and bolder' calendar. Underneath the image is a quote from the woman: 'I'm busier now than when I was working.' She is described as a voluntary researcher carrying out research on the needs of minority ethnic elders in Manchester. Both the quote and the caption encourage the interpretation of this image as offering the possibility of an active life after retirement as opposed to 'languishing' in inactivity and decline. In addition the use of the word 'voluntary' suggests that older people are able to 'contribute' to society rather than simply acting as recipients of benefits.

Source: 'Growing older with attitude in Manchester' 2006 calendar

Summary/issues for further exploration

My comments have suggested that images are not just images. All images are intended to be interpreted along social/political/ethical lines. They embody specific agendas; whether or not these agendas are taken up as the image maker anticipates depends, in turn, on the social, political and ethical

Source: 'Older and bolder in Manchester' 2007 calendar

position of readers. The images commented on here reflect Edmondson and von Kondratowitz's call in their introduction to this volume for a gerontology 'concentrated on the social complexity of the human condition'. Older people are literally and metaphorically the central focus of each image. The fact that not a single image in any of the four calendars depicts older people as 'objects of need' (see Edmondson and von Kondtratowitz's introduction) might be seen as addressing one of the deficiencies of current gerontology. Nevertheless, the decision made against the use of 'object of need' images is undoubtedly a moral/ethical one.

Gerontology itself involves interpretations from a number of sides, namely older individuals themselves and different generational members, as well as policy makers. Thus we cannot take politics and philosophy out of our reading of images. Visual images are all around us – as well as other metaphors embedded in our attitudes to ageing and human development. The growing research interest in relations between generations bodes well for a humanistic gerontology. Exploring and mapping out the varieties of such interactions is situated in recognising that individuals of different ages participate 'in their own and others' developing life courses' (Edmondson and von Kondratowitz's introduction). A humanistic gerontology could embrace the myriad of these contemporary images and acknowledge there are many ways of valuing older people – but that doing so inescapably involves complex dimensions of engagement and critique.

Notes

[1] The study reported here was part of an inter-university project, Older People, Urban Regeneration and Health and Well-being, which was funded by the Higher Education Funding Council for England (HEFCE), Urban Regeneration: Making a Difference.

[2] www.manchester.gov.uk/site/scripts/documents_info.php?documentID=3428

[3] www.manchester.gov.uk/site/scripts/documents_info.php?categoryID=500099

References

Blaikie, A. (1994) 'Photographic memory, ageing and the life course', *Ageing and Society*, vol 14, no 4, pp 479-97.

Blaikie, A. (1995) 'Photographic images of age and generation', *Education and Ageing*, vol 10, no 1, pp 5-15.

Blaikie, A. and Hepworth, M. (1997) 'Representations of old age in painting and photography', in A. Jamieson, S. Harper and C. Victor (eds) *Critical approaches to ageing and later life*, Buckingham: Open University Presss, pp 102-17.

Featherstone, M. and Hepworth, M. (1995) 'Images of positive ageing', in M. Featherstone and A. Wernick (eds) *Images of ageing: Cultural representations of later life*, London/New York: Routledge, pp 29-47.

Featherstone, M. and Wernick, A. (1995) 'Introduction' in M. Featherstone and A. Wernick (eds) *Images of ageing: Cultural representation of later life*, London/New York, Routledge, pp 1-15.

Johnson, J. and Bytheway, B. (1997) 'Illustrating care: images of care relationships with older people', in A. Jamieson, S. Harper and C. Victor (eds) *Critical approaches to ageing and later life*, Buckingham: Open University Press, pp 132-42.

Zalot, M. (2001) 'Wall calendars: structured time, mundane memories and disposable images', *Journal of Mundane Behavior*, vol 2, no 3, www.mundanebehavior.org/issues/v2n3/zalot.htm

SEVENTEEN

Gateways to humanistic gerontology

Ronald J. Manheimer

The contributors to this fine volume on humanistic gerontology come from a broad array of fields and quite a number of countries and languages of origin. For most, the study of ageing was not the focus of their formal education. Something must have lured them into the realm of the ageing – a favourite grandparent, an opportune moment for a dissertation topic, grant money to research one of the 'challenges' faced by older adults, or possibly an intriguing aged character in a novel, such as the 'ancient clerk' Mr Chuffy in Dickens's *Martin Chuzzlewit*.

Whichever gate they have traversed, once humanistic scholars enter the land of older people they are bound to encounter familiar faces – their own. That's when the fun begins. For here is a hermeneutic circle or set of concentric circles through which, by virtue of the scholar's own ageing process, he or she moves ever closer towards the centre. As the scholar attempts a deeper understanding of what it means to grow old, he or she must struggle with the problem of finding a suitable framework – one that includes the student of ageing as well as the subjects.

My first gateway beckoned to me in the autumn of 1976 as I planned to offer a course on philosophers' autobiographies at a senior centre in Olympia, Washington. I was just then teaching at a highly innovative undergraduate college nearby and had my students reading John Stuart Mill's (and likely his co-author in shadows, Harriet Taylor's) famous essay on *The subjection of women* (Mill, 1869). In this fiery critique of 'The legal subordination of one sex to the other', Mill says of women's character, 'we do not yet know who they are'. Given the social conditions of inequality with respect to suffrage, divorce and property law (not to mention access to independent careers), women's development had been severely restricted to the degree that their true merit and contributive powers were as yet unknown. Mill was not a great believer in arguments 'from nature' as he was also an ardent critic of arguments from religious revelation or church authority in general. Yes, he was a man of reason, though he tipped his hat to the life of feelings.

My first reaction to my small and educationally and socioeconomically eclectic senior centre group was right out of the Mill/Taylor essay. Of older people, I thought to myself, given the pervasive stereotypes (my own included), social messages encouraging older people to disengage from both work and social life, and beliefs about ageing as a disease, *we do not know who they are*. I was convinced that, by bringing to my group some of my favorite philosophers – albeit through their personal narratives rather than abstract essays – I would help to liberate these students from the shackles of inequity. Works of the humanities, I then believed, provided a mirror to the soul and a window into the lives of others. And so off we went, reading about Mill's psychological depression in his early 20s and about how he fell in love with Mrs Taylor. We eavesdropped on Simone de Beauvoir's account of her youthful affair with Jean-Paul Sartre. And we gazed into the seemingly empty swimming pool in the metaphysically minded T.S. Eliot's personally reflective poem 'Burnt Norton'.

A mystical lotus ascends from Eliot's watery mirage, Jean-Paul jilts Simone and John Stuart comes to the realisation that the faults in his own upbringing reflect wider inadequacies of his society. The lotus led us into a discussion about supreme powers, revealing the traditional believers and the doubters among us. The antics of the French existentialists threw open the door to discussion about love, sex and marriage, past, present and future. And Mill's turning the microscope of self-examination into a telescope of social criticism launched us into an examination of whether the experience-based knowledge and cultural heritage we brought with us from the past still meant something in the present.

'Old men should be explorers,' the less than liberated Mr Eliot told us. Given my initial framework, I was sure Eliot was talking about the life of the mind, the kind of thing that philosophers like to do – reflect. Wasn't that exactly what my group was doing by relating important ideas drawn from famous thinkers to their own experiences and beliefs? Ageing, I thought, was a philosophical time of life. Echoing Schopenhauer, if the first half of life is the front side of a quilt, the second half reveals how the quilt was made. Just look at that incredible needlework! But, oh, there do seem to be a few loose threads.

Engaged in life review, our little group, gathered around pushed-together bridge tables, was showing how we had played our cards in life. Some had a full house while others felt they had been dealt from the bottom of the deck. Does your life add up to something that feels complete or do you feel you've missed out on opportunities or made some bad choices over which you are still brooding? As if we had lifted a chapter out of Erik Erikson's (1980) discourse on the eight epigenetic stages of life, there we were negotiating 'integrity versus despair', the dialectic of old age, with the looming goal just ahead of us: wisdom. It was right around the time that wisdom popped up that my group took an unexpected turn and knocked over my framework.

'We want to know whether our views are still relevant to a younger generation,' said one member. 'Why don't you invite some of your students from the college to join our group?' suggested another. 'Should we be doing something more with the great stories people have been telling? Maybe write them down?' asked another.

So there I was, caught in the transition from the disengagement theory to the activity theory of ageing, without the benefit of knowing anything about either. The group members were not satisfied with contemplation. Mirrors and windows were fine, but they wanted action. Prompted (or rather, prodded), I organised us into a planning group and soon we had an intergenerational class, a public lecture series entitled 'What should be the future of our heritages?' (funded by the Washington Commission for the Humanities), and all kinds of classes on writing memoirs, poetry and doing living theatre. I was now in the empowerment business. And the 'deserving elderly' were taking their cues from the likes of Gray Panthers provocateur Maggie Kuhn. 'Deserving, hell!' they shouted.

Over 30 years later, I preside over the North Carolina Center for Creative Retirement (NCCCR) in the mountain town of Asheville, NC. NCCCR is part of the University of North Carolina at Asheville. Like most lifelong learning institutes (LLIs) in the US, the Center is member-led and thrives on peer learning and teaching. With 1,800 annual members, several nationally acclaimed weekend workshops, an environmental education programme, community leadership seminars and an applied research arm, the Center is like a small college within the larger campus setting. We even have our own building.

Across the interval of these decades, I have seen and tried out several other frameworks for understanding ageing and the enterprise of lifelong learning: productive ageing, spiritual ageing, gender liberated ageing, transformational ageing and even, I hate to admit it, 'silver industries' ageing (the Center is two thirds funded through revenues). While critical gerontology was busy revealing the dark side of the science of ageing (the hidden ideological agendas, the dependency-making social policies, the evils of instrumental reason and their practitioners who want to cure us of ageing by manipulating our telomeres), others were pointing out that the whole enterprise of the study of ageing was something of a hypostatised sham. 'There is no such thing as ageing or the elderly,' announced Gilleard and Higgs (2000) in their insightful *Cultures of Ageing*. 'We've made it up.' Moreover, especially with the coming of age of the boomers, the very people whom we identify as 'the elderly' shun the label. There are, in fact, multitudes of ways that we age and identify with our chosen peers but these are so diverse (ethnicity, geography, gender, sexual orientation, social class, educational background, religious orientation, work status) as to resist easy classification.

What happens then to a centre for 'creative retirement' if our prospective clientele claim at age 70 that they're still 'too young' or too busy still working to sign up? If age and retirement status are no longer the attributes on which affinities are based for our 'learning community' then what is the social glue that both attracts and keeps people involved in helping to plan curricula and teach courses, monitor budgets and render marketing campaigns, conduct research and disseminate findings? As age and retirement status become irrelevant, we move toward a new paradigm – age neutral. Many organisations are making this shift – senior centres become enrichment centres, a College for Seniors becomes the Evergreen Society, a developer's Senior Living division becomes Heritage Habitations. The organisation that was known formerly as the American Association of Retired Persons has legally changed its name to just AARP (hoping, as was the case with IBM, that gradually no one will know what the acronym used to stand for). Ageing is out; age neutral is in.

Does this amount to a paradigm collapse? More likely it's that there are multiple both overlapping and mutually contradictory paradigms coexisting in our various disciplinary domains and cultural milieus. Likewise, there are mixed and contrary messages coming from the media of popular culture that range from articles on how to stay youthful by using anti-ageing potents, to tips for reinventing yourself in retirement (how to morph from being a high school algebra teacher to a stand-up comic), or advice on how to age gracefully and become a wise elder (in part by attending special workshops). There is no cultural consensus about the one right way to grow old. If ageing and later life is a matter of social construction but there are no certified architects, then it's each person for themselves.

And what does this mean about the role of the academic humanist who has stepped through the gateway to ageing? Do we have privileged knowledge that would guide the masses of midlife and older adults toward an ideal of maturity? Or, through our various critiques and subtle interpretations, are we contributing to the blurring of later life as a distinct stage with unique qualities and characteristics and only adding to the increasing ambiguity of what it means to grow old? Academic humanists have a penchant for the subversive. That's part of our training – to notice what others have overlooked, to question what others take for granted, to find the exception to the rule, to work from the parts to the whole and back again to the parts. Perhaps the role of the academic humanist in stalking the elusive older person is precisely to loosen the bounds of prejudice and two-dimensional thinking. The humanist, in the postmodern era, lauds the multiple meanings, values and pathways of the neo-elderly. And if age-neutral is the talisman of liberation, so be it.

But wait. There is one other paradigm that seems to be making a comeback – 'positive ageing'. Floated as a potentially viable term in the early 1980s, positive ageing addressed the strengths of mature adults while acknowledging the inevitable weaknesses and losses. Somehow, the campaign for positive ageing failed to elect a slate of leaders. But the term has been resurrected recently, perhaps revivified by the popularity of the 'happiness school' of psychology, 'positive psychology'. This has given the field of ageing new research possibilities for understanding – for example, how an attitude such as optimism might be correlated with vitality and longevity. Positive psychology claims Aristotle as its godfather, citing the Schoolman's discussion of *eudaimonia* in the *Ethics*, where Aristotle makes happiness ('activity in accordance with virtue') the goal of development.

The jury is still out on positive ageing, though one of its strengths is precisely the ambiguity of the term, since it can serve as a rallying cry for a multitude of age-liberation endeavours, as well as an umbrella for the emerging 'life coach' industry that is hoping to guide (for a small fee) the bewildered baby-boom generation to Elysian fields of the ageless body and timeless mind (Chopra, 1993).

This volume opened with the editors' assertion that 'the problem of meaning' is the 'essential core of humanistically oriented gerontology'. Meaning, in turn, implies 'norms and values', which, in turn, 'makes people's experiences into *life courses* rather than simple concatenations of events'. The goal then of this volume is to demonstrate how humanists and the humanities can unite what has been rendered asunder by the fragmenting influence of highly specialised, compartmentalising scientific enterprises with their unique nomenclatures and guild-approved methodologies. What we are searching for is an embracing discourse of discourses that nevertheless makes no claim to produce the 'master narrative' that would eclipse all other narratives. One thinks of E.O. Wilson's (1998) term 'consilience', the attempt to discover the intrinsic order of the universe through rational means. Wilson hoped to build a bridge between the natural sciences and the humanities, domains that would be united through a common quest.

Whether the study of ageing will eventually disclose an underlying intelligibility that is not the result of a projected ideology (reductive explanation, methodological dictum, religious epiphany) remains to be seen. For now, let us celebrate the multiple meanings of ageing and ask Mr Chuffy to please serve the tea.

References

Chopra, D. (1993) *Ageless body, timeless mind: The quantum alternative to growing old*, New York: Harmony Books.

Erikson, E.H. (1980) *Identity and the life cycle*, New York: W.W. Norton.

Gilleard, C.J. and Higgs, P. (2000) *Cultures of ageing: Self, citizen, and the body*, New York: Prentice Hall.

Mill, J.S. (1869) *The subjection of women*, www.constitution.org/jsm/women.htm

Wilson, E.O. (1998) *Consilience: The unity of knowledge*, New York: Vintage.

Index

Page references for notes are followed by n

Critical Perspectives on Ageing Societies
Edited by Miriam Bernard and Thomas Scharf

This important book brings together some of the best known international scholars working within a critical gerontology perspective to review and update our understanding of how the field has developed over the last twenty-five years and provide a challenging assessment of the complex practical and ethical issues facing older people, and those who conduct research on ageing, in the 21st century.

PB £24.99 US$39.95 **ISBN** 978 1 86134 890 6
HB £65.00 US$99.00 **ISBN** 978 1 86134 891 3
240 x 172mm 200 pages May 2007

Rural Ageing
A good place to grow old?
Edited by Norah Keating

This important book addresses a growing international interest in 'age-friendly' communities, examining the conflicting stereotypes of rural communities as either idyllic and supportive or isolated and bereft of services.

PB £24.99 US$39.95 **ISBN** 978 1 86134 901 9
HB £65.00 US$99.00 **ISBN** 978 1 86134 902 6
240 x 172mm 168 pages May 2008

Ageing in a Consumer Society
From passive to active consumption in Britain
Ian Rees Jones, Martin Hyde, Christina R Victor, Richard D Wiggins, Chris Gilleard and Paul Higgs

This book provides a unique critical perspective on the changing nature of later life by examining the engagement of older people with consumer society in Britain since the 1960s. People retiring now are those who participated in the creation of the post-war consumer culture. These consumers have grown older but have not stopped consuming; their choices and behaviour are products of the collective histories of both cohort and generation.

PB £24.99 US$39.95 **ISBN** 978 1 86134 882 1
HB £65.00 US$99.00 **ISBN** 978 1 86134 883 8
240 x 172mm 160 pages Sept 2008

Community and Ageing
Maintaining quality of life in housing with care settings
Simon Evans

This important book investigates changing concepts and experiences of community across the lifecourse and into older age and how they play out in housing with care settings. An overview of how the housing with care sector has developed, both in the UK and internationally, is provided. The book emphasises the central importance of a sense of community for older people's quality of life and explores the impact of a range of factors including social networks, inclusive activities, diversity and the built environment.

PB £24.99 US$39.95 **ISBN** 978 1 84742 070 1
HB £65.00 US$85.00 **ISBN** 978 1 84742 071 8
240 x 172mm 224 pages tbc Sept 2009

Ageing in Urban Neighbourhoods
Place attachment and social exclusion
Allison E. Smith

This unique book addresses the shortfall in knowledge regarding older people's attachment to deprived neighbourhoods and offers a re-conceptualisation of environmental gerontology. The author examines new cross-national research and challenges the common view that ageing 'in place' is optimal, particularly within areas that present multiple risks to the individual.

PB £25.99 US$41.95 **ISBN** 978 1 84742 270 5
HB £65.00 US$89.95 **ISBN** 978 1 84742 271 2
240 x 172mm 248 pages tbc Sept 2009

Family Practices in Later Life
Pat Chambers, Graham Allan, Chris Phillipson and Mo Ray

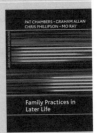

Family Practices in Later Life challenges many common stereotypes about the nature of family involvement as people age. The book explores diversity and change in the family relationships older people maintain, looking at how family relationships are constructed and organised in later life.

PB £24.99 US$39.95 **ISBN** 978 1 84742 052 7
HB £65.00 US$85.00 **ISBN** 978 1 84742 053 4
240 x 172mm 144 pages tbc Sept 2009

To order copies of this publication or any other Policy Press titles please visit **www.policypress.org.uk** or contact:

In the UK and Europe:
Marston Book Services, PO Box 269, Abingdon, Oxon, OX14 4YN, UK
Tel: +44 (0)1235 465500
Fax: +44 (0)1235 465556
Email: direct.orders@marston.co.uk

In the USA and Canada:
ISBS, 920 NE 58th Street, Suite 300, Portland, OR 97213-3786, USA
Tel: +1 800 944 6190
(toll free)
Fax: +1 503 280 8832
Email: info@isbs.com

In Australia and New Zealand:
DA Information Services,
648 Whitehorse Road Mitcham,
Victoria 3132, Australia
Tel: +61 (3) 9210 7777
Fax: +61 (3) 9210 7788
E-mail: service@dadirect.com.au